THE REHNQUIST COURT

THE REHNQUIST COURT

A Retrospective

EDITED BY MARTIN H. BELSKY

OXFORD
UNIVERSITY PRESS

2002

OXFORD
UNIVERSITY PRESS

Oxford   New York

Auckland   Bangkok   Buenos Aires   Cape Town   Chennai
Dar es Salaam   Delhi   Hong Kong   Istanbul   Karachi   Kolkata
Kuala Lumpur   Madrid   Melbourne   Mexico City   Mumbai   Nairobi
São Paulo   Shanghai   Singapore   Taipei   Tokyo   Toronto

and an associated company in Berlin

Published by Oxford University Press, Inc.
198 Madison Avenue, New York, New York 10016

www.oup.com

Oxford is a registered trademark of Oxford University Press

Library of Congress Cataloging-in-Publication Data
The Rehnquist court : a retrospective / edited by Martin H. Belsky.
p.   cm.
Includes bibliographical references.
ISBN 0-19-514839-8
1. United States. Supreme Court.   2. Rehnquist, William H., 1924–
3. Conservatism—United States.   4. Law and politics.   I. Belsky, Martin H.
KF8748.R44   2001
347.73′26—dc21   2001021444

1 3 5 7 9 8 6 4 2

Printed in the United States of America
on acid-free paper

For the Belsky-Waits Family:
Kate, Allen, Marcia

PREFACE

The articles in this book note the trends, countertrends, and surprises revealed in the decisions of the Supreme Court under the leadership of Chief Justice William Rehnquist. This is the third volume in a series, all based on conferences held at the University of Tulsa College of Law. The first two books, edited by the late Chapman Distinguished Professor Bernard Schwartz, looked at the impact and legacy of the Warren and Burger Courts.

This book highlights the fact that the "old order" established by the Justices of the Warren Court is gone, perhaps never to be resurrected.

Of course, unlike the context of the previous books, the total legacy of the Rehnquist Court is still not written. In fact, the articles are based on papers presented in September of 1998 and edited before the Court's controversial December 2000 decision in *Bush v. Gore* and the tragedies of September 11, 2001.

Changes in the mood of this country, the practice of law, the impact of politics on selection of Justices, and a more visible and easily accessible judicial review process are some of the factors leading to this perhaps permanent change. As indicated in a recent addendum to my introductory article, these trends were reaffirmed in the *Bush v. Gore per curium* decision. There may, however, be some impact on the Court's federalism and individual rights jurisprudence as a result of the new national government and national security focus resulting from the events of September 2001.

I would like to thank my two student research assistants, Anthony P. Condurso, Class of 2000 and Tamar Willis, Class of 2001.

CONTENTS

Contributors   xi

1. The Rehnquist Court: A Review at the End of the Millennium   3
    Martin H. Belsky

I. THE CONSTITUTIONAL CORPUS

2. Free Expression and the Rehnquist Court   15
    Burt Neuborne
3. The First Amendment in Cyberspace   34
    Bruce J. Ennis
4. The Rehnquist Court and the Search for Equal Justice   44
    J. Harvie Wilkinson III
5. The First Freedom and the Rehnquist Court   69
    John T. Noonan, Jr.
6. Confessions, Search and Seizure, and the Rehnquist Court   80
    Yale Kamisar
7. The Rehnquist Court and Economic Rights   116
    Lino A. Graglia

II. A BROADER PERSPECTIVE

8. The Rehnquist Court: Some More or Less Historical Comments   143
    Lawrence M. Friedman
9. A Journalist's Perspective   159
    David Savage

10. The Rehnquist Court and the Legal Profession   167
    Jerome J. Shestack

11. The Constitutional Jurisprudence of the Rehnquist Court   195
    Erwin Chemerinsky

12. The Rehnquist Court and State Constitutional Law   217
    Marie L. Garibaldi

13. The Importance of Dialogue: Globalization, the Rehnquist Court, and Human Rights   234
    Claire L'Heureux-Dubé

14. Liberalism, the Constitution, and the Supreme Court   253
    Robert H. Henry and Arthur G. LeFrancois

15. William H. Rehnquist in the Mirror of Justices   274
    David J. Garrow

CONTRIBUTORS

Martin H. Belsky, Dean and Professor of Law, University of Tulsa College of Law

Erwin Chemerinsky, Sydney M. Irmas Professor of Law and Political Science, University of Southern California

Bruce J. Ennis, Esquire, Jenner & Block

Lawrence M. Friedman, Marion Rice Kirkwood Professor, Stanford Law School

Marie L. Garibaldi, Justice, Supreme Court of New Jersey

David J. Garrow, Presidential Distinguished Professor, Emory University Law School

Lino A. Graglia, Dalton Cross Professor of Law, University of Texas School of Law

Robert H. Henry, Judge, Tenth Circuit United States Court of Appeals

Yale Kamisar, Clarence Darrow Distinguished Professor, University of Michigan Law School

Arthur G. LeFrancois, Professor of Law, Oklahoma City University School of Law

Claire L'Heureux-Dubé, Justice, Supreme Court of Canada

Burt Neuborne, John Norton Pomeroy Professor, New York University Law School

John T. Noonan, Jr., Judge, Ninth Circuit, United States Court of Appeals

David Savage, *Los Angeles Times*

Jerome J. Shestack, Wolf, Block, Schorr & Solis-Cohen, Past President, American Bar Association

J. Harvie Wilkinson III, Chief Judge, Fourth Circuit, United States Court of Appeals

THE REHNQUIST COURT

THE REHNQUIST COURT
A Review at the End of the Millennium

MARTIN H. BELSKY

An unexpected consequence of the impeachment trial of President Clinton has been the public recognition of William H. Rehnquist. Sitting as the presiding judge for more than a month[1] at the trial of the President,[2] he gave the desired appearance of solemnity and seriousness.[3] News stories in all the media gave background stories on the Chief Justice. Informed citizens and even law students suddenly had an interest in this dignified personage.[4]

The longer-term legacy of the Chief Justice, however, will be his leadership of the Supreme Court. During his tenure, because of changes in personnel on the Court,[5] Chief Justice Rehnquist has been able to witness and even shape a dramatic change in constitutional jurisprudence[6] in issues ranging from criminal procedure[7] to the scope of federal power[8] to federal court authority over state government actions.[9]

This book is intended to give an overview of the present status of development of the Rehnquist legacy and some suggestions as to its future direction. The idea for this volume came from Chapman Distinguished Professor Bernard Schwartz. In 1993, Professor Schwartz developed a decade long strategy of holding major conferences on the Supreme Court at the University of Tulsa College of Law. The papers presented at these conferences would be then included in bound volumes for future readers. The first conference would review the Warren Court and would be "a retrospective" from a distance of more than twenty-five years.[10]

The second would review the Burger Court and would explore whether the decisions rendered by that Court indicated a "counter-revolution or confirmation" of the principles set in place by the Warren Court.[11] The intent was to put the Burger Court into the context of then present jurisprudence of the Rehnquist Court.[12]

There were to be two more conferences to be organized by Professor Schwartz—one on the Rehnquist Court and one on the Supreme Court in the twenty-first century.[13] Professor Schwartz, in fact, did begin the planning work on the Rehnquist Court Conference, which was held in the fall of 1998. Bernard Schwartz, however, suffered a tragic death in December 1997. I and others have described what a loss his death was for the profession, legal education, and constitutional and particularly Supreme Court scholarship.[14]

To honor him, the University of Tulsa College of Law decided to proceed with the Rehnquist Court Conference, and this volume based on that conference is in his memory.

When Professor Schwartz selected the title for this conference and book, he used an interrogative at the end of his statement—"The Rehnquist Court: Farewell to the Old Order in the Court?" However, he had strong feelings that the old order had in fact changed. He was convinced that, perhaps with a few exceptions, the liberal jurisprudence of the Warren Court was gone. Even the so-called centrist bloc of the Rehnquist Court was "still composed of Justices more conservative than their predecessors."[15] He did, however, suggest that there were a few exceptions to the rightward trend of constitutional law by the Rehnquist Court. Professor Burt Neuborne describes one of these exceptions, the surprising continuity in the free speech jurisprudence of the Court. He notes that this was in spite of and not because of the Chief Justice, who was not able to persuade his colleagues to turn back some of the major Warren Court precedents. This "resilience" was due, Neuborne argues, not just to the attitudes of the new members of the Court—the "accident of personnel"—but also to "the intellectual power of a true free market in ideas."

Bernard Schwartz was not a computer guru. In fact, he didn't use a computer but, rather, wrote his talks and articles and books in long-hand—to be typed by a secretary and then edited by him. He, however, was concerned about the impact of new technology and our constitutional corpus. Attorney Bruce Ennis responds to this concern in his piece on the first amendment in cyberspace. Ennis looks at *Reno v. ACLU/ALA*,[16] the "Court's first exposure to cyberspace," and concludes that the Court will look at internet speech on an *ad hoc balancing* basis rather than by applying traditional categorical rules.

In contrast, equal protection jurisprudence is an area, says Judge J. Harvie Wilkinson, III, in which a clear doctrine has been aggressively established by the Rehnquist Court. The guiding principle, Judge Wilkinson argues, has been "racial justice" or a nondiscrimination principle, although this nondiscrimination principle was not limited to racial classifications but also applied to classifications based on gender or sexual orientation.

Wilkinson traces the evolution from race-based remedies to a condemnation of any race-based discrimination, even so-called benign classifications. It is an appropriate method of constitutional analysis in light of the "New America," which is increasingly diverse, and where application of any racial classifications takes us into an impossible multicultural "thicket."

Judge John T. Noonan, Jr.'s opening comments mirror Judge Wilkinson's concern about traditional classifications. His topic was "church and state,"[17] but there is no single church in the United States, The old rubric is an obsolete one based on old European concepts. Moreover, attempts by the law to categorize or classify relationships by people to an "invisible, impalpable Being" are, at best, intrusive. Judge Noonan reviews the small number of cases on this topic. He notes the impact of the equal access speech doctrine and the new establishment clause jurisprudence[18] and concludes that religion has not fared badly in the Rehnquist Court. He then concentrates on the application of the free exercise clause and indicates that different currents reinforce each other—the setting of clear law based on a secular premise and an orderly society and a disinclination to enlarge benefits given to religion, even to perhaps threatened nonmainstream minority religions.

Professor Yale Kamisar takes a look at criminal justice and particularly the Rehnquist Court changes in the standards to assess police interrogations and search and seizure. As to search and seizure law, the Rehnquist Court dramatically reversed the trend of the Warren Court. First it expanded a cost-benefit analysis developed during the Burger Court to narrow the scope of the Fourth Amendment exclusionary rule. Then, the Court, in applying the Fourth Amendment, also give more leeway to the police.

As to confessions, Professor Kamisar reviews the attempts by Congress to legislatively overrule the decision in the 1968 Omnibus Crime Control Act and the challenges and restrictions to *Miranda v. Arizona*[19] that began in the Burger Court.[20] Kamisar, through his review of the cases, indicates that the Rehnquist Court has narrowed the restrictions on confessions and has allowed concededly bad ones to be used at trials but believes, somewhat hopefully, that the core of the *Miranda* decision will survive. He does note the Fourth Circuit decision in *United States v. Dickerson*,[21] which thirty-one years after passage applied the 1968 statute to indicate that the pre-*Miranda* standards of voluntariness had been established by federal statute. That case, of course, was recently decided by the Rehnquist Court and the Chief Justice in a seven–two decision, reaffirmed the validity of *Miranda* and the invalidity of congressional attempts to "overrule" that decision.[22] Professor Kamisar indicates that this and other cases in the future may mean that a complete evaluation on the Rehnquist Court and criminal justice may need to await a quarter-century perspective.

The last commentator on the constitutional corpus of the Rehnquist Court is Professor Lino A. Graglia. He gives a skeptical review of the concept of judicial review. Many of the concepts (e.g., applying the Bill of Rights to the states) are unsupportable. Like the Burger Court before it, the Rehnquist Court did not change this trend of decision making, despite the elevation of Rehnquist to Chief Justice and the appointment of five Justices by Republican Presidents Reagan and Bush. The fact that this Court is considered "conservative" is only because it "enacts liberal policy preferences less frequently or reliably." There are only two exceptions—affirmative action and application of the Takings Clause.

In a series of decisions, the Court changed the nature of judicial review of government actions affecting property—especially as it relates to regulations restricting property use. Graglia would prefer that the incorporation doctrine be totally rejected, but until it is, what is wrong with a conservative agenda as to property rights being put into place? Still, because of changes in the Court's composition in the last two years and potentially in the future, he suggests that the doctrines established by these cases will not be extended, and may in fact be limited.[23]

Perhaps the most significant change in constitutional law made by the Rehnquist Court has been in the area of federalism. As Professor David Garrow stresses, this dramatic revolution in thinking about the balance of power between the federal government and the states is Rehnquist's most important legacy. First, the Court has ended the over sixty-year-old[24] presumption that the federal government has almost total power under the Commerce Clause.[25] Until *Lopez v. United States* in 1995, congressional action was upheld as long as there was a rational basis to conclude that the activity to be regulated had an impact, however small, on interstate commerce.[26]

The motive and purpose of a law or implementing federal regulation was just not relevant as congressional power under the Commerce Clause was plenary.[27] *Lopez* changed the calculus. The Commerce Clause is not without limits and the basic presumption is now changed. The Tenth Amendment[28] limits the power given to the federal government. Commerce Clause authority is limited to three areas: (1) the channels of interstate commerce, (2) the instrumentalities of interstate commerce, and (3) activities having a *substantial relation* to interstate commerce or that *substantially affect* interstate commerce.[29] Thus it cannot usurp local law by making a federal crime out of activities in a state that "neither regulates commercial activity" nor shows a substantial connection of that activity to interstate commerce.[30]

Even if Congress details with substantial findings the potential impact of a problem, such as domestic violence, on interstate commerce, there are things that are truly local in nature, such as intrastate violence and family law. In those areas and others, Congress, under the Commerce Clause, may not regulate.[31] Finally, because of the strong federalism concerns expressed in the Tenth Amendment, Congress does not have power under the Fourteenth Amendment either.[32]

Even if there is authority for Congress to act under the Commerce Clause or another constitutional provision, the Court will monitor how the power is carried out—in light of the independent sovereign authority of the states. The federal government cannot, for example, commandeer state police to carry out a federally enacted regulatory scheme.[33]

The Court has also reestablished the power of the Eleventh Amendment to bar federal lawsuits against states or state officials, except in special cases, even when Congress has authorized such suits.[34]

Justice Marie L. Garibaldi of New Jersey indicates that the Court has also been supportive of the power of state supreme courts to apply their own constitutions, even if such application provides broader rights than those granted by a more conservative United States Supreme Court.

Justice Garibaldi indicated that this deference, however, has not been total. State courts must be careful to make it clear that its decisions are applying state constitutional principles and not merely interpreting federal constitutional doctrines. Both agree that this new "judicial federalism" provides "a healthy diversity in judicial policy."[35]

Eight other commentators sought to put the Rehnquist Court jurisprudence into a broader perspective. Professor Lawrence M. Friedman discusses the continuing political role of the Court—in its historical sense of impacting society by its highly visible actions. Institutionally, the Court has changed—taking fewer cases but with more opinions. This is due, in part, to the new reality that it is less of a collegial body and that it is more difficult to forge coalitions or obtain consensus. He rejects the complaints about the Supreme Court and the need for constraint. Only opponents of the decisions complain about an "activist Court," he urges. Although some Justices worry about the issue of legitimacy, Friedman stresses that the public does not focus on debates on "original intent" or use of legislative history and generally respects it. Finally, he suggests that the labels of "conservative" and "liberal" are relative ones. Sharing Professor Graglia conclusions, he states that compared to the 1890s, the Rehnquist Court is contemporary—even liberal.

David Savage gives us a journalist's perspective on the Rehnquist Court. In an earlier book,[36] Savage had concluded that the Court would not make radical changes. He still agrees with that conclusion. Some decisions are "conservative" and others "liberal," but there is no warring of ideological factions.

Jerome Shestack's broader perspective comes from his position as the former President of the American Bar Association. He notes the role of the Chief Justice as the spokesman for the Court and perhaps the whole judiciary. Chief Justice Rehnquist, he argues, has been able to implement a large portion of his agenda. Shestack then looks at the impact of the Court on the legal profession, reviewing its decisions on the attorney–client privilege, use of the Interest on Lawyers Trust Accounts (IOLTA), and the Paula Jones case. He is concerned that the Court has a "lack of familiarity with a lawyer's day to day practice." Shestack then takes a look at the Chief Justice's role in the administration of justice and internal court administration. He concludes with mini-portraits of each of the present Justices' relationships with the organized bar.

Professor Erwin Chemerinsky develops a framework to analyze the decisions of the Rehnquist Court. He urges that the Court is motivated by conservative political values and strongly relies on history—particularly historical practices at the time of ratification of a constitutional provision—to justify its interpretations. Criminal defendants almost always lose, recognizing the clear conservative bent. State laws banning physician assisted suicide will not receive privacy or equal protection stringent review as there is no clear tradition or historical support for such analysis. States would not be required to participate in a federal regulatory scheme as early congresses did not attempt to exercise such authority and therefore it probably was felt not to exist. Professor Chemerinsky strongly challenges this method of constitutional jurisprudence, especially because some of the historical record is often manipulated.

In contrast to previous theoretical perspectives, Claire L'Heureaux-Dubé, Puise Justice of the Canadian Supreme Court, gives a practical review of the Rehnquist Court's international impact and a critique of its provincialness. The world and the law are becoming more global, and this affects the process of judging and lawyering. American judicial principles and even methodology have heavily influenced the judiciary of many other countries. However, the Rehnquist Court is less influential than its predecessors. The judiciary and the decisions of the courts in foreign countries have become more sophisticated, the issues more similar and international in nature, and with technology and more interaction, decisions and jurists more available. This is enhanced by the fact that there are fewer decisions resolved by the Rehnquist Court; that many of the decisions focus on originalism—which is of little help to foreign courts; and most important, the members of the Court do not seem interested in taking part in the international dialogue on common issues such as human rights.

Judge Robert Henry, of the Court of Appeals for the Tenth Circuit, together with Professor Arthur G. LeFrancois, reviews the jurisprudence of members of the Rehnquist Court with a Schwartzian[37] skepticism of the concept of "original intent" and "cost-benefit analysis." Professor Schwartz saw himself as the "conservative" seeking to preserve constitutional aspirations that he thought had been developed in the Warren Court from a new jurisprudence often formulated not by members of the Rehnquist Court but by their law clerks as a kind of "Junior Supreme Court."[38]

So what is the legacy of the Rehnquist Court? Professor David Garrow indicates that he well may be recognized as the second greatest or perhaps the greatest Chief Justice of the twentieth century. This is strongly contested by other symposium participants, particularly Jerome Shestack. Garrow notes that he (Rehnquist) has been able to effectuate an agenda, remarkably consistent from that first developed as a Supreme Court clerk, for example, in his promotion of a federalism agenda and criminal justice. He has been extremely effective and popular within the Court itself, and as indicated by Professor Bernard Schwartz in an earlier book, has been more willing than may have been recognized to compromise his positions to get a strong majority.[39]

Perhaps, however, as Professor Garrow concludes, the most dramatic legacy will be the lessening of the role of the Court in American life. This would have troubled Professor Schwartz, who hoped that the Rehnquist Court and future Courts would continue to have a major role by exercising its power to use the Constitution as a means "to meet the practical necessities of the contemporary society."[40]

Addendum

Since the original writing of this introductory article, two significant events—one legal and one horrible—have occurred which probably will impact history's assessment of the Chief Justice and the Rehnquist Court. With a few exceptions, however, the articles in this book still reflect what most believe will be the Rehnquist Court's legacy. The Court's rightward trend has been characterized by the high personal visibility of the Chief Justice, the sharp conflict between two sets of Justices, moderated by Justices Kennedy and O'Connor in the center, and the focus on a new federal-state balance.

The *Bush v. Gore*[41] decision confirmed the split among the Justices but also indicated that this split is not always logical. Justices who had been pushing a "states' rights" agenda now urged federal court intervention overturning a decision by the highest state court. Justices who had traditionally sought an increased federal court role now urged deference to the state courts. Partisanship, it was urged by some commentators, overtook jurisprudence.[42]

Still, it looks like there will not be that dramatic of an impact on the Court's credibility or philosophy as once predicted. The Court did limit its decision in this case to its facts, and recent press reports indicate that then Governor Bush would have won the election in any event. The public and the bar want the Court to have credibility and they will give it.[43] Still, it does seem that Justice Garibaldi's belief that the majority of the Supreme Court will be supportive of state supreme courts' ability to apply their own constitutions must be somewhat tempered.

It is more likely that the events of September 11, 2001 will have a more lasting impact on the Court's reputation and legacy. The response to the terrorist attacks and plane crashes in New York, Washington, D.C., and Pennsylvania has been a renewed focus on the national government, including a new "Homeland Security" office. It is hard to believe that the Rehnquist Court will continue its efforts to decrease federal power and federal court authority in dealing with criminal justice in a post-Twin Towers society.[44] In addition, how the Court handles cases challenging the new anti-terrorist legislation and Executive Orders will be a focus of future Supreme Court analyses.

Notes

1. The trial began on January 7, 1999. It concluded with an acquittal on February 12, 1999. Judge Posner has opined that, in fact, there was only one real day of trial—when both sides presented evidence. Posner, *An Affair of State* 1, n.2 (1999).

2. The only specific power given the Chief Justice in the Constitution is to preside over the trial of the President in the Senate after impeachment by the House of Representatives. U.S. Const. Art. I, § 3, cl. 6. See Fish, "Office of the Chief Justice," in *The Oxford Companion to the Supreme Court* 140 (Hall ed., 1992).

3. The Chief Justice obviously saw his role as more ceremonial than adjudicative. "He interpreted his powers narrowly. He made few rulings, none either substantive or remotely likely to affect the outcome." Posner, supra note 1, at 130.

4. But cf. Posner, supra note 1, at 130. After first describing Chief Justice Rehnquist's robe with yellow stripes, Judge Posner states: "The most solemn form of American trial was thus presided over by the highest judge in the land *dressed in a funny costume* [italics in original]. . . . [T]he appearance he presented makes it difficult to believe that the American people any longer expect their officials to be more dignified, aloof and impressive than themselves."

5. Justice Potter Stewart had left the Court in 1981 and was replaced by Justice Sandra Day O'Connor. When Justice Rehnquist was elevated to Chief Justice, replacing Chief Justice Burger in 1986, his slot was taken by Antonin Scalia. Justice Anthony Kennedy replaced Justice Lewis Powell. Justice William Brennan was replaced by Justice David Souter in 1990. Justice Thurgood Marshall was replaced by Justice Clarence Thomas in 1991. Justice Byron White was replaced by Justice Ruth Bader Ginsburg in 1993. Justice Harry Blackmun was replaced by Justice Stephen Breyer in 1994. O'Brien, "The Rehnquist Court: Holding Steady on Freedom of Speech," 22 *Nova L. Rev.* 713, 714 (1998).

Most commentators divided the Court as follows: The Chief Justice and Justices Scalia and Thomas as the more conservative; Justices Stevens, Ginsburg, and Breyer as the more liberal; and Justices Kennedy, O'Connor, and Souter as in between. The case that most point to as an illustration of this division is Planned Parenthood v. Casey, 505 U.S. 833 (1992). See Sullivan, "The Jurisprudence of the Rehnquist Court," 22 *Nova L. Rev.* 743, 749–50 (1998).

6. Professor Bernard Schwartz suggested that the Chief Justice, with a majority that can "translate his conservative views into Supreme Court jurisprudence" can create a legacy of the Rehnquist Court that will be "the reverse image of the [liberal] Warren Court." Schwartz, *A History of the Supreme Court* 373–75 (1993).

7. See, e.g., Arizona v. Evans, 514 U.S. 1 (1995) (evidence seized pursuant to an illegal arrest not inadmissible when due to mere error by input into computer and police acted in good faith).

8. See, e.g., Printz v. United States, 521 U.S. 898 (1997) (federal statute could not require state law enforcement officer to investigate whether receipt or possession of gun would be in violation of federal law).

9. See, e.g., Kimel v. Florida Board of Regents, 528 U.S. 62 (2000) (Age Discrimination in Employment Act cannot be applied to state government employers).

10. See *The Warren Court: A Retrospective* (Schwartz ed., 1996). The Conference that led to the chapters in this book was held in the fall of 1994.

11. See *The Burger Court: Counter-Revolution or Confirmation* (Schwartz ed., 1998). The Conference that resulted in the chapters in this book was held in the fall of 1996.

12. See Schwartz, "The Burger Court in Action," in *The Burger Court: Counter-Revolution or Confirmation* 261 (Schwartz ed., 1998).

13. Professor Schwartz, in fact, at the time of his death had had discussions about a series of issues that he thought the Supreme Court would have to face in the near and not so near future. Among the issues he considered including were privacy in an increasingly technological age, federal power and particularly executive power in a shrinking global environment, constitutional criminal procedure in the post-DNA investigatory process, and government and the First Amendment in a computer and conglomerate media information distribution setting.

14. See, e.g., O'Hara, "Foreword," in *The Burger Court: Counter-Revolution or Confirmation* v–vi (Schwartz ed., 1998); Mauro, "Remembering A Supreme Scholar," *Legal Times*, Jan. 5, 1998, at 8; Saxon, "Bernard Schwartz Dies at 74," *N.Y. Times*, Dec. 26, 1997. See generally "In Memoriam: Bernard Schwartz," 33 *Tulsa L.J.* 1041–96 (1998).

15. Schwartz, supra note 6, at 375–76.

16. 521 U.S. 844 (1997).

17. Judge Noonan's presentation was titled at the conference "Church and State." The article in this volume is Noonan, "The First Freedom and the Rehnquist Court," *The Rehnquist Court: Farewell to the Old Order in the Court.*

18. Judge Noonan indicates that the cases on the Establishment Clause stand for the proposition that "religion is not established when a religious organization is aided to perform a perfectly secular mission." For an analysis that suggests that the Rehnquist Course's establishment clause jurisprudence goes even farther, allowing previously forbidden government entanglement or cooperation with religion, see Belsky, "Antidisestablishmentarianism: The Religion Clauses at the End of the Millennium," 33 *Tulsa L.J.* 93 (1997).

19. 384 U.S. 436 (1966).

20. See also Belsky, "The Burger Court & Criminal Justice: A Counter-Revolution in Expectations," in *The Burger Court: Counter-Revolution or Confirmation* 131 (Schwartz ed., 1998).

21. 166 F.3d 667 (4th Cir. 1999), *cert. granted*, 120 S. Ct. 578 (1999).

22. Dickerson v. United States, 531 U.S. 876, (2000).

23. Compare Belsky, "Doing What It 'Takes': A Look at How the Courts Have Responded to Nollan, Lucas and Dolan," 2 *Environmental Outlook* 51 (Winter 1996); Belsky, "Dolan v. City of Tigard (1994): Making it 'Rougher' for Land Use Management," 3 *Footnotes* 1 (Spring 1995); Belsky, " The Public Trust Doctrine and Takings: A Post-Lucas View," 3 *Albany Law School J. Science & Technology* 17 (1994).

24. The historical story is well known. Until late 1936, the United States Supreme Court had set limits on the power of the federal government to enact legislation under the Commerce Clause. This, of course, had put a crimp on attempts by Franklin Delano Roosevelt and the New Deal to establish a new social and economic agenda. See, e.g., Schechter Poultry Corp. v. United States, 295 U.S. 495 (1935); Carter v. Carter Coal Co., 298 U.S. 238 (1936). Frustrated, Roosevelt sought to increase the number of Justices and thus

"pack the Court." The Court then indicated a broader power of the federal government under the Commerce Clause. See, e.g., National Labor Relations Board v. Jones and Laughlin Steel Corp, 301 U.S. 57 (1937); Wickard v. Filburn, 317 U.S. 111 (1942).

25. See United States v. Lopez, 514 U.S. 549 (1995).

26. See Hodel v. Virginia Surface Mining and Reclamation, 452 U.S. 264 (1981).

27. United States v. Darby, 312 U.S. 100 (1941).

28. U.S. Const., amend. X: "The powers not delegated to the United States by the Constitution, nor prohibited by it to the States, are reserved to the States respectively, or to the States."

29. United States v. Lopez, 514 U.S. 549 (1995).

30. Id. (declaring invalid a federal statute that punishes possession of a firearm in a school zone).

31. United States v. Morrison, 529 U.S. 598, 616–18 (2000).

32. Id. at 619–627.

33. Printz v. United States, 521 U.S. 898 (1997) (outlawing requirement that state or local chief local law enforcement officer investigate information received from gun registrants).

34. Seminole Tribe of Florida v. Florida, 517 U.S. 44 (1996); Kimel v. Florida Board of Regents (2000). There is an inherent immunity from federal jurisdiction, absent explicit consent. 528 U.S. 62.

35. Compare Executive Order on Federalism, Exec. Order No. 13083, 63 Fed. Reg. 27,651 (1998):

(e) Our constitutional system encourages a healthy diversity in the public policies adopted by the people of the several States according to their own conditions, needs, and desires. States and local governments are often uniquely situated to discern the sentiments of the people and to govern accordingly.

(f) Effective public policy is often achieved when there is competition among the several states in the fashioning of different approaches to public policy issues. The search for enlightened public policy is often furthered when individual States and local governments are free to experiment with a variety of approaches to public issues. Uniform, national approaches to public policy problems can inhibit the creation of effective solutions to those problems.

36. Savage, *Turning Right: The Making of the Rehnquist Supreme Court* (1992).

37. Judge Henry's presentation at the Conference was titled "The Rehnquist Court—A Critique a la Bernard Schwartz." The chapter in this volume is Henry and La Francois, "Liberalism, the Constitution, and the Supreme Court."

38. See Schwartz, supra note 6, at 369–72.

39. Schwartz, *The Unpublished Opinions of the Rehnquist Court* 8–9 (1996).

40. Schwartz, supra note 6, at 380.

41. Bush v. Gore, 531 U.S. 98 (2000).

42. See e.g., Blumstein & Sherry, *The 2000 Presidential Election: What Happens When Law and Politics Collide?*, 18–27 (2000); "9 Views on Bush v. Gore," *The Chronicle of Higher Education*, Jan. 5, 2001, at B16.

43. For a more detailed discussion of the case, its history, and its impact see Martin H. Belsky, "Bush vs. Gore, A Critique of Critiques," 37 *Tulsa L. Rev.* 45 (2001).

44. See e.g., Greenhouse, "Will the Supreme Court Reassert National Authority," *N.Y. Times*, September 20, 2001, at A-1.

THE

CONSTITUTIONAL

CORPUS

FREE EXPRESSION AND
THE REHNQUIST COURT

BURT NEUBORNE

"Continuity" is not a word ordinarily associated with William Rehnquist. For much of his judicial career, the Chief Justice has been an apostle of legal discontinuity; a vigorous critic of Supreme Court doctrine, including much of our modern free speech heritage.[1] From his appointment as an Associate Justice in 1972, Justice Rehnquist was a frequent dissenter in important First Amendment cases.[2] In the years before he was named Chief Justice in 1986, Justice Rehnquist's most influential free speech opinion for the Court was *Posadas de Puerto Rico Associates v. Tourism Co.*,[3] where he almost derailed the emerging commercial speech doctrine by persuading a narrowly divided Court that the "greater" power to ban an activity like gambling carries with it the "lesser" power to ban truthful commercial speech about its lawful availability.[4] But "continuity" is the only accurate way to describe the free speech jurisprudence of the Rehnquist Court.

In part because Chief Justice Rehnquist has been no more successful than Associate Justice Rehnquist in persuading his colleagues to limit free speech protection,[5] the free speech jurisprudence of Rehnquist Court in the first twelve terms of his Chief Justiceship has echoed and deepened the powerful First Amendment doctrine the Rehnquist Court inherited. Even with two important First Amendment setbacks,[6] the Rehnquist Court has been among the strongest free speech courts in the nation's history. Indeed, where free expression is concerned, it would probably be more accurate to call it the Brennan/Kennedy Court.

By my unscientific count, the Supreme Court has considered free expression[7] issues at least eighty-two times over the twelve terms of the Chief Justice's tenure.[8] My even less scientific assessment of the Court's opinions indicates acceptance of free speech arguments forty-nine times, rejection twenty-five times, usually in marginal settings, with eight mixed results generally tilting toward the First Amendment position. In part, the success rate of free speech arguments in the Rehnquist Court is an accident of history.

When Chief Justice Rehnquist assumed office in 1986, his colleagues were Justices Brennan, White, Marshall, Stevens, Blackmun, Powell, O'Connor, and Scalia. Justices Brennan, Marshall and Blackmun, usually but not always joined by

Justice Stevens, constituted a strong free speech bloc. Chief Justice Rehnquist, often joined by Justice White, was generally lukewarm to expansive free speech arguments. Justice Scalia was an unknown quantity but was presumed to be skeptical about expansive free speech arguments. The free speech center consisted, therefore, of Justice Powell, and an unpredictable Justice O'Connor.

Within a year, Justice Powell was gone, forced by ill health into a premature retirement that deprived the Court of its most respected centrist voice. Robert Bork was nominated to replace Justice Powell. The fierce confirmation battle over Judge Bork is now the stuff of history.[9] We are still paying for the erosion of civility and moderation that characterized that bare-nuckle brawl. But Bork's defeat, and the ultimate emergence of Anthony Kennedy to fill Lewis Powell's seat, had an enormous impact on the course of free expression jurisprudence. "Justice" Bork would almost certainly have gravitated to the Rehnquist position, leaving Justice O'Connor alone in the center, confronted with an energized and intellectually able group of conservative Justices who were downright hostile to Justice Brennan's First Amendment model. Justice Kennedy, on the other hand, unexpectedly bloomed into an extraordinary defender of free speech, reinforcing the Brennan position and profoundly altering the free speech dynamics of the emerging Rehnquist Court.

When Justices Marshall and Brennan left the Court in 1990–91, the potential for free speech revisionism was still present. But Justice Souter embraced Brennan's free speech legacy, and Justice Thomas's commitment to libertarian principles led him to support free speech arguments in many cases, especially when they are linked to the right to use one's property to advance one's beliefs. Finally, when Justices Ginsburg and Breyer replaced Justices Blackmun and White, the loss of Justice Blackmun's voice was ameliorated by the fact that both Justices Ginsburg and Breyer were likely to be stronger free speech votes than Justice White. Thus, although five members of the Court retired during the Rehnquist years, including all three great defenders of free expression, the resulting Court maintains an almost seamless continuity with the protective free speech decisions of the past thirty-five years.

But the accident of personnel does not wholly explain the resilience of free speech doctrine in the Rehnquist Court. The intellectual power of a true free market in ideas—both as an instrumental necessity for institutions of personal choice such as democracy and market capitalism and as a normative ideal reflective of human dignity—is fully capable of persuading new generations of adherents. When newly appointed Justices, freed from the tumult of politics and vested with awesome responsibility, contemplate the Court's successful development of a system of free expression, it should not surprise us that they demonstrate a strong predisposition to continue the Court's legacy of free speech protection.

At the risk of oversimplification, the system of free expression inherited by the Rehnquist Court consisted of three key components: (1) judicial acceptance of the primacy of free expression as a trumping social value, a value orientation that translates into an extremely high burden of justification for any effort at censorship;[10] (2) prophylactic refusal to permit speech regulation based on content; and (3) insistence on a set of First Amendment procedural protections that minimize the opportunity for improper censorship. Each of the three components was embraced, deepened, and enlarged by the Rehnquist Court.

The Rehnquist Court and the Primacy of
Free Expression as a Trumping Value

The fundamental difference between protection of free speech in the United States and its treatment in other liberal democracies is the degree of primacy accorded to free expression as a trumping social value in our legal system. When free expression bumps up against almost anything else in our system—whether it is privacy, anguish, equality, or patriotism—free expression usually trumps the countervailing value.

It was not always that way in our constitutional history.[11] Although the celebrated Holmes–Brandeis opinions foreshadowed the event, and several significant free speech decisions preceded it, I believe that the modern free speech era begins in 1964 with Justice Brennan's decision for the Court in *New York Times v. Sullivan*,[12] not only because the opinion set forth the crucial ground rules for libel but because it provided a general justification for robust First Amendment protection based on the primacy of free expression as a trumping value—an explanation that persuaded its generation. Fittingly, the continuity that was to mark the Rehnquist Court's free speech cases was signaled by the Chief Justice himself in his opinion for a unanimous Court in *Hustler Magazine v. Falwell*,[13] reaffirming the Court's commitment to the primacy of free expression.

It is fashionable today to understate the importance of the Chief Justice's opinion in *Hustler*. After all, the opinion was unanimous, and, in retrospect, the case could hardly have been decided otherwise. But its importance as a signal of continuity was dramatic. The lower courts, by ruling that damages for intentional infliction of emotional distress could be recovered in connection with a Hustler magazine parody accusing Rev. Jerry Fallwell of sleeping with his mother, had mapped an end run around *Times v. Sullivan*. Most significantly, the lower courts had elevated values of privacy, dignity and repose to a level roughly equivalent to free expression.

Without directly overruling the case, it would have been possible for the Supreme Court to back away from the commitment to the primacy of free expression that is at the core of *Times v. Sullivan*. A Supreme Court with a new Chief Justice who had been avowedly skeptical about much First Amendment doctrine; two new Justices of strongly conservative bent who were untested in First Amendment waters; a senior Justice whose First Amendment attachment was weak at best; and a junior Justice with no strong First Amendment tradition, could have opted for free speech revisionism. But the dog did not bark. The Chief Justice's unanimous opinion for the Court in *Hustler* not only extended the reach of *Times v. Sullivan* to the full range of tort but resoundingly reaffirmed the Court's commitment to the primacy of free expression as a trumping value that undergirds its modern First Amendment jurisprudence.[14]

Continuity also marked the Rehnquist Court's most celebrated free speech achievement—the holdings in *Texas v. Johnson*[15] and *United States v. Eichman*[16]— that burning the American flag as an act of protest is protected by the First Amendment. In two foundational cases—*Brandenburg v. Ohio*[17] and *Police Department v. Mosley*,[18]—the pre-Rehnquist Court had required government to prove an extremely close nexus between speech targeted for censorship and a perceived harm arising from it, and had virtually forbidden regulations that targeted speech on the basis of content. With those two building blocks in place, the flag-burning cases were simply logical applications of settled principles.

The fear that flag burning is so offensive that it might move onlookers to a breach of the peace ran headlong into *Brandenburg*, and the focus on protest in the Texas statute at issue in *Texas v. Johnson* made the case a sitting duck for the ban on content-based regulation. When adherents of prosecuting flag burners enacted a federal statute that attempted to eliminate the vulnerable focus on protest, the *Eichman* Court, once again, invalidated the federal statute, reinforcing the primacy of free expression, even in the absence of a facially obvious effort to target content.

As with the *Hustler* decision, it is tempting to downplay the doctrinal importance of the flag-burning opinions as inevitable applications of settled principles. But the closeness of the vote—each case was 5–4—coupled with the passion of the Chief Justice's dissent in *Texas v. Johnson* and the continued efforts to amend the Constitution to permit prosecution of flag burners, make clear that the Court could easily have backed away from the implications of prior free speech jurisprudence. That it did not is a tribute to the power of the free speech ideal, and to its attractiveness to both sides of the political spectrum.

The narrow majority in *Texas v. Johnson*, consisting of Justices Brennan, Marshall, Blackmun, Scalia, and Kennedy, reached across the political spectrum. Indeed, in my opinion, the power of the flag-burning decisions does not rest on Justice Brennan's opinions for the Court, which were not among his best, but on the fact that in a context of unmistakable clarity both ends of the political spectrum united to reaffirm our commitment to the primacy of free speech as a transcendent value. The Rehnquist Court's flag-burning opinions were a constitutional watershed that cemented the transcendence of the free speech principle as the cornerstone of a new generation's jurisprudence.[19]

In two sets of cases, however, continuity with the past led the Rehnquist Court into uncharted First Amendment waters. The pre-Rehnquist Court had recognized that privacy in one's home might be a value of constitutional dimensions that could hold its own with free expression.[20] In several cases, the Rehnquist Court sought to balance free expression rights against privacy in the home, or another constitutional right deemed to have equivalent value. Not surprisingly, the resulting mix is more complex than the straightforward cases in which free expression was deemed a trumping value.

In *Frisby v. Schultz*,[21] the Court was confronted with a broad prohibition on residential picketing. When the smoke cleared, the Court had upheld a ban on massed, targeted picketing of a residence but had invalidated a ban on neighborhood picketing in the vicinity of a residence. *Frisby* is hardly a model of precision, but its obvious thrust is an effort to protect as much free expression as possible without surrendering all vestiges of privacy in the home.

Similarly, in *Madsen v. Women's Health Center*[22] and *Schenck v. Pro Choice Network*,[23] the Court was confronted with district court injunctions limiting expression in the immediate vicinity of abortion clinics that had been the target of unlawful blockage. In *Madsen*, the Court upheld a narrow district court injunction.[24]

The *Schenck* Court upheld an injunction on picketing and chanting in the immediate vicinity of the center but struck down prophylactic provisions preventing unwanted face-to-face communication with persons approaching the center. *Schenck* and *Madsden* leave many questions unanswered, but the thrust of the two cases is clear—the Rehnquist Court is committed to preserving *both* free expression and the right of a woman to have reasonable access to a medical facility offering abortions. The fascinating question is in how many other settings, if any, will free expression mutate from a trumping value into a just another value that must coexist with others deemed equally important?

Reno v. ACLU,[25] suggests that free expression will continue to trump countervailing values, including privacy, but because of the appallingly drafted statute before the Court in *ACLU v. Reno,* the jury is still out on what the balance might be with a narrower statute.

A second area of unsettled free expression law in the Rehnquist Court involves settings in which a conflict of interest exists between or among the First Amendment players. The pre-Rehnquist Court had expanded the First Amendment universe beyond the speaker to include hearers, conduits, and targets.[26] Generally, when a single, identifiable speaker wishes to speak, and identifiable hearers wish to hear, First Amendment rights are at their apogee. Problems emerge, as in hate speech or fighting words, when the speaker wishes to speak but hearers or targets wish the speaker to remain silent. The conflicts become more complex when more than one potential speaker is involved, both of whom wish to use the same conduit, or when a judgment must be made whether to treat someone as a speaker or a conduit for the purposes of First Amendment analysis. Suffice it to say that cases emerge in which it is hard to know who is entitled to the First Amendment mantle.

Pre-Rehnquist Court cases had tended to resolve conflicts between speakers and hearers in favor of the speaker,[27] except in the narrow confines of the "fighting words" doctrine,[28] or when the hearer was part of a "captive audience."[29] The Rehnquist Court simply continued the tradition of tilting to the speaker,[30] in the absence of special circumstances.

The easiest of the "conflict" cases heard by the Rehnquist Court involved efforts to deny, on Establishment Clause grounds, "speaker" status to religious groups seeking to use public facilities to express a religious message. In *Lamb's Chapel v. Center Moriches Union Free School District,*[31] *Rosenberger v. Rector of the University of Virginia,*[32] and *Capitol Square Review Board v. Pinette,*[33] the Rehnquist Court firmly rejected efforts to deny religious speakers full free speech protection.

Other conflicts within the First Amendment universe have been more difficult to resolve. The problem of involuntary hearers remains troublesome. Pre-Rehnquist Court doctrine made it clear that merely because a message was grossly offensive to hearers, it did not lose its First Amendment protection.[34] The flag-burning cases, the hate-speech cases, the indecency cases, and *Hustler* strongly endorse the right of a speaker to say things a hearer wishes to avoid. But, in selected contexts, the Rehnquist Court was more sympathetic to involuntary hearers. *Frisby's* partial upholding of a ban on residential picketing, *Schenck's* invalidation of a ban on unwanted face-to-face speech, *McIntyre's* careful endorsement of Title VII's ban on certain offensive speech in an employment context, and *Rock Against Racism's* concern about noise are prime examples of a tilt toward the listener. Unfortunately, the Court has not attempted a systematic discussion of the relative First Amendment rights of speakers and hearers, leaving the cases to be decided on an ad hoc basis.

The most intransigent First Amendment conflict cases involved bitter disagreements over who gets to wear the free expression mantle in settings in which more than one candidate for the job is present. In *Turner Broadcasting Company v. FCC* (*Turner I*),[35] for example, when Congress required that cable broadcasters transmit the signal of all over-the-air broadcasters, cable owners, over-the-air broadcasters, and hearers all claimed to be *the* protected First Amendment party.

The *Turner I* Court recognized that cable broadcasters are classic speakers entitled to full First Amendment protection in most contexts but carved out important free expression interests for persons seeking access to cable facilities, as well as for hearers. The net result is a complex mixture of speaker, hearer, and conduit rights that have not been fully sorted out.

Similarly, in *Denver Area Educational Consortium v. FCC*,[36] cable broadcasters, leased access programmers, public access programmers, and hearers all claimed to be the true beneficiary of the First Amendment. As with *Turner I*, the Rehnquist Court (minus the Chief Justice this time) made no effort to choose definitively among the competing players. Each received a modicum of protection. Cable broadcasters were permitted to ban certain sexually explicit programming from their leased access channels, but hearers were protected against having to formally request the availability of sexually explicit programs and public access broadcasters received significant protection. Indeed, Justice Breyer's decision for the *Denver Area* Court self-consciously declined to resolve the First Amendment conflict, electing to defer the ultimate decision about whose First Amendment claims take priority until we gain a greater understanding of the technology.

Justice Thomas's separate opinion in *Denver Area*, joined by the Chief Justice and Justice Scalia, urged a return to a simpler day when the First Amendment universe was confined to speakers.[37] Independent programmers and hearers, argued Justice Thomas, do not have protectable First Amendment interests that can conflict with a cable owner's "speaker" interest in using his property to communicate as he sees fit.

In two cases, conflicts over who should be treated as the protected speaker were more clearly resolved. In *Hurley v. Irish-American Gay, Lesbian and Bi-sexual Group of Boston*,[38] the Court upheld the right of the sponsors of Boston's St. Patrick's Day Parade to bar formal participation by a gay and lesbian group, ruling that the organizer of a private parade is entitled to speaker rights over who may participate. In *Arkansas Educational Television v. Forbes*,[39] the Court ruled that a public television station, not the candidates, should be viewed as the true speaker when the station decides whom to invite to participate in an electoral debate. But the speaker's usual plenary rights were limited by the Court to ensure that the First Amendment interests of candidates and hearers would be respected by the government speaker. *Forbes* is, therefore, more doctrinally complex than it appears, because it recognizes the fact that the First Amendment universe can no longer be confined to the traditional speaker.

The Rehnquist Court and Content-Based Regulation

A second pillar of pre-Rehnquist Court First Amendment law was the ban on content-based regulation of speech.[40] The Rehnquist Court embraced the concept. A series of conventional decisions echo the concern that differential treatment of speakers is an invitation to content-based discrimination.[41] In *Leathers v. Medlock*,[42] the Court clarified its differential treatment cases, holding that differential treatment of speakers is forbidden as a means of avoiding the risk of discrimination on the basis of content. Where content-based discrimination is unlikely, therefore, the ban on differential treatment of categories of speakers may be relaxed.

In both *Turner I* and *Turner II*, however, the Court was closely divided on whether a requirement that cable broadcasters transmit the signal of over-the-air broadcasters was a content-based regulation. In each case, a narrow majority held that the ban was not content based, principally because no significant difference exists in the nature of the content of cable and over-the-air broadcast.

If *Leathers v. Medlock* signaled a relaxation of the ban on differential treatment, *RAV v. City of St. Paul*[43] constituted the most controversial application of the doctrine in the Court's history. In *RAV*, a five-person majority of the Court struck down a hate-speech ordinance because it singled out speech expressing racial intolerance for selective prohibition. The majority agreed that certain face-to-face exercises of hate speech, like cross burning, would be unprotected if they constituted an implied threat, or threatened an imminent breach of the peace under the fighting-words doctrine. Thus, suggested the majority, a general statute banning threats or fighting words could be constitutionally applied to the nighttime cross burning before the Court. Where, however, a statute singles out hate speech for punishment, the state has unconstitutionally regulated on the basis of content, invalidating the statute on its face. Four members of the Court disagreed with the effort to apply the ban on content-based regulation to wholly unprotected speech, preferring to invalidate the St. Paul ordinance on overbreadth grounds.

The Rehnquist Court was consistent with past Courts, as well, in being utterly inconsistent in its approach to the ban on discriminatory treatment based on content. Taken literally, a ban on content-based discrimination would swallow the Court's habit of treating obscenity, libel, and fighting words as separate categories subject to greater regulation than the rest of the speech universe.[44] Instead of moving in that direction, the Rehnquist Court has expanded the category of disfavored content—occasionally called "low value" speech—to include much speech about sex.[45]

The Rehnquist Court decided at least ten cases involving sexually explicit speech. Sexy speech lost six times, won once, survived two minor skirmishes, and secured one precarious tie. *Osborne v. Ohio*[46] continued the tradition of reading statutes banning speech that involves the sexual exploitation of children very generously. *Fort Wayne Books v. Indiana*[47] and *Alexander v. United States* predictably permitted authorities broad discretion in forging effective remedies for repeated violations of the obscenity laws.[48] *FW/PBS, Inc. v. City of Dallas*[49] declined to apply prophylactic First Amendment procedural rules to protect sexually oriented businesses against discretionary licensing.

Most dramatically, in *Barnes v. Glen Theater, Inc.*,[50] the Court upheld a ban on nude dancing, despite a recognition that it constituted a form of expression. The analysis in *Barnes* ushers in a sliding scale of free expression, ranging from intensely protected political speech to slightly less protected aesthetic expression to modestly protected commercial expression, to barely tolerated speech about sex. Whether such an overtly value laden approach to protecting free expression can be squared with the Court's insistence that content-based regulation is uniquely dangerous remains a riddle.

Speech about sex prevailed in *ACLU v. Reno*,[51] but only because the statue banning "indecent" speech on the Internet if it could be viewed by minors was so overbroad, and so ineptly drafted, that it could not be saved. *Denver Area Consortium*[52] was, at best, a weak tie. Viewers were relieved from having to affirmatively request sexually explicit programs, but cable operators were given the power to prevent their transmission completely, even on leased access channels.[53]

The Rehnquist Court's acceptance of a sliding scale of speech protection is exemplified as well in its approach to commercial speech. Unlike speech about sex, though, the Rehnquist Court has tended to increase the level of commercial speech protection. Commercial speech arguments carried the day seven times in the Rehnquist Court, losing three times in relatively narrow contexts.[54]

First Amendment Procedure

In addition to substantive protections, the pre-Rehnquist Court had built an elaborate set of procedural protections designed to prevent the erosion of free speech values. First Amendment procedure does not ask whether the speech before the Court is protected. Rather, it asks whether the procedures surrounding the attempt at regulation are too dangerous to be tolerated. At least five variants of the doctrine existed: the ban on prior restraints, the ban on unduly vague statutes, the ban on overbroad statutes, the ban on standardless licensing, and the ban on unilateral executive censorship.

The Rehnquist Court has enthusiastically continued the tradition of rigorous review of First Amendment process. Efforts to regulate speech were invalidated eight times, often in cases of great importance, because of defects in the process of regulation. In *Houston v. Hill*,[55] the Court invalidated a statute preventing criticism of police during the course of their duties because it vested too much discretion in the police to decide whether to tolerate criticism. In *Airport Commission v. Jews for Jesus*,[56] the Court invalidated a flat ban on all First Amendment activity in Los Angeles Airport as unconstitutionally overbroad, even though some regulations were undoubtedly valid. In *City of Lakewood v. Plain Dealer Publishing Co*,[57] the Court invalidated a standardless licensing provision governing the placement of newspaper sales racks.

In *Riley v. National Federation for the Blind*,[58] the Court invalidated rules governing charitable solicitation that were deemed unnecessarily broad. In *Sable Communications Co. v. FCC*,[59] the Court unanimously invalidated a ban on telephone communication with sexually oriented services as unnecessarily overbroad. In *Forsyth County v. Nationalist Movement*,[60] the Court invalidated a sliding-scale fee license fee system for demonstration because of its capacity for abuse. Finally, in *Reno v. ACLU*,[61] the Court invalidated a ban on "indecent" communications on the Internet capable of being seen by minors as hopelessly overbroad and unnecessarily intrusive.[62]

Negative Continuity

The Rehnquist Court's penchant for continuity in the free expression usually translates into broad First Amendment protection. In one significant area, however, continuity has resulted in a troubling capacity for government censorship. Where speech is paid for by the government, the Rehnquist Court has displayed a broad toleration for censorship. In *Hazelwood School District v. Kuhlmeier*,[63] the Court upheld broad control over student newspapers because the newspapers were paid for by the school district. The Court explicitly analogized the school principal to the owner/publisher of a private newspaper. The ensuing doctrine requires students wishing to publish a genuinely free press to attempt unsupervised, underground journals. Viewed from another perspective, *Kuhlmeier* suggests that the true speaker in a student press case is the government itself, not the student editors. In that sense, *Kuhlmeier* is the model that Justice Thomas urges the Court to return to in his separate opinion in *Denver Area*.[64] Under Justice Thomas's analysis, speech merges with property.

In *Rust v. Sullivan*,[65] Chief Justice Rehnquist, writing for a narrow five-person majority, ruled that doctors employed by the government in connection with a family planning and pre-natal health program could be forbidden from discussing abortion with their patients. The Chief Justice reasoned that because the government was paying for the program, it was entitled to define the scope of the communication. In effect, the *Rust* majority treated the government as the speaker, with the doctor serving as a conduit.

Similarly, in *United States v. Kokinda*,[66] the Court upheld a ban on First Amendment activity on a public sidewalk abutting a post office on the ground that because the government owned the sidewalk, it was entitled to control the speech taking place on it.[67] Finally, in *National Endowment for the Arts v. Finley*,[68] the Court upheld vague standards such as "decency" and "respect" in connection with subsidies to the arts, reasoning that government had more regulatory power when it was spending its own money.

Taken together, *Kuhlmeier*, *Rust*, *Kokinda*, and *Finley* paint a disturbing picture of the government's freedom to use its property to skew the free market in ideas. Ironically, the government property cases are more protective of the government's speaker rights than are the sophisticated media cases such as *Turner I* and *Denver Area* that suggest limits on the automatic link between speaker status and private property.

In *Rosenberger v. Rector of the University of Virginia*,[69] however, the Court ruled that limits existed on the ability of government to use subsidies to control speech. In *Rosenberger*, the University of Virginia offered subsidies to student publications but declined to subsidize religious publications. Justice Kennedy, writing for the Court, ruled that subsidies may not be allocated on the basis of content.

When, held Justice Kennedy, the government is the true speaker as in *Rust*, it may use its property to advance the content it wishes discussed. But, wrote Justice Kennedy for the *Rosenberger* Court, when the government is subsidizing private speakers, it may not discriminate on the basis of content.

The Court has not yet considered how to decide whether the government is functioning as a speaker or a facilator of the speech of others. Similarly, in *Arkansas Educational Television v. Forbes*,[70] the Court viewed a candidate debate sponsored by a public television station as a form of public subsidy. Under the principles of *Kulmeier* and *Rust*, that should end the analysis, with the government speaker free to use its property to advance its message, and only its message. But in the spirit of *Rosenberger* and the media cases, the Court acknowledged a second set of speakers — the candidates — and limited the televisions station's ability to discriminate on the basis of content.

Snapshots

A full picture of any Court requires an assessment of the Court's work, not only doctrinally but in specific context. Somewhat arbitrarily, I have chosen democracy and the media as contextual prisms through which to observe the Rehnquist Court's free expression decisions.

The Rehnquist Court and Democracy

By my count, the Rehnquist Court decided at least sixteen cases dealing with the constitutional implications of voting or running for office.[71] In seven cases, the First Amendment argument carried the day. First Amendment concerns were rejected on five occasions. One case was a tie, tilting toward the First Amendment. The other three did not turn on a First Amendment argument.

The striking thing about the democracy cases is the lack of a normative theory underlying the Court's democracy work. Unlike most First Amendment settings, the Rehnquist Court, like the Courts that preceded it, seems to lack a model of the democracy it wishes to protect. Voting is viewed solely as an instrumental exercise. Thus, in *Burdick v. Takushi*, the Court held that states can ban write-in voting, and in *Timmons* the Court held that states can deny voters the right to cast a ballot for a candidate on a preferred party line. Third parties are viewed as necessary nuisances. The autonomy of the major parties is scrupulously preserved,[72] as in *Tashjian* and *Eu*, but barring a genuinely arbitary law, as in *Norman v. Reed*, third parties and independents are left to the tender mercies of the two-party cartel.

The Rehnquist Court and the Mass Media

The Rehnquist Court has decided at least seventeen cases dealing with the First Amendment rights of mass media.[73] First Amendment arguments prevailed in eight cases, were rejected in five cases, with four ties. The media's most serious loss came in *Cohen v. Cowles Media*, where the Court rejected the argument that the First Amendment superseded a contractual promise to respect the anonymity of a source. In addition to *Hustler*, the media's most important win was *Florida Star v. BJF*, reasserting the autonomy of the print media. *Cohen v. Cowles* continues the Court's rejection of media exceptionalism. *Florida Star* reaffirms *Tornillo*.

The most interesting media cases were the four ties. In *Turner I,, Turner II, Denver Area*, and *Arkansas Educational Television*, the Court sought to divide the First Amendment baby among owners, users, and hearers. Not surprisingly, the process has just begun.

Conclusion

The Rehnquist Court has broken little new doctrinal ground in the area of free expression. It has, however, applied preexisting First Amendment doctrine vigorously, occasionally, as in the flag-burning cases, moving the doctrine to new levels. But the fundamental free speech issues that the Rehnquist Court inherited remain unresolved. Do effective constitutional limits exist on the government's ability to use subsidies to control public discourse? How should conflicts between speakers and hearers be resolved? When, if ever, should persons be treated as conduits, as opposed to speakers? What is the relationship between money and speech? When powerful speakers use their private property to speak, do mechanisms exist to permit weak voices to be heard? And, what is the relationship between First Amendment doctrine and laws regulating the democratic process?

Appendix

Significant First Amendment Cases: 1986–1998

October Term 1986

Ansonia Bd. of Educ. v. Philbrook, 479 U.S. 60 (1986)
Munro v. Socialist Workers Party, 479 U.S. 189 (1986)
Tashjian v. Republican Party of Connecticut. 479 U.S. 208 (1986)
FEC v. Mass Citizens for Life, 479 U.S. 238 (1986)
Hobbie v. Unemployment Appeals Comm'n, 480 U.S. 136 (1987)
Arkansas Writers' Project, Inc. v. Ragland, 480 U.S. 228 (1987)
Meese v. Keene, 481 U.S. 465 (1987)
Board of Directors of Rotary International v. Rotary Club of Duarte, 481 U.S. 532 (1987)
O'Lone v. Shabazz, 482 U.S. 342 (1987)
City of Houston v. Hill, 482 U.S. 451 (1987)
Airport Comm'n v. Jews for Jesus, 482 U.S. 569 (1987)
Edwards v. Aguillard, 482 U.S. 578 (1987)
Corporation of Presiding Bishop v. Amos, 483 U.S. 327 (1987)
Rankin v. McPherson, 483 U.S. 378 (1987)
San Francisco Arts & Athletics v. Olympic Comm., 483 U.S. 522 (1987)

October Term 1987

Virginia v. American Booksellers Ass'n, 484 U.S. 383 (1988)
Bowen v. Kendrick, 487 U.S. 589 (1988)
City of Lakewood v. Plain Dealer Publishing Co., 486 U.S. 750 (1988)

Lyng v. Northwest Indian Cemetery Prot. Ass'n, 485 U.S. 439 (1988)
New York State Club Ass'n v. City of New York, 487 U.S. 1 (1988)
Debartolo v. Florida Gulf Coast Council, 485 U.S. 568 (1988)
Communications Workers v. Beck, 487 U.S. 235 (1988)
Employment Division v. Smith, 485 U.S. 660 (1988)
Riley v. National Fed. of the Blind, 487 U.S. 781 (1988)
Frisby v. Schultz, 487 U.S. 474 (1988)
Meyer v. Grant, 486 U.S. 814 (1988)
Boos v. Barry, 485 U.S. 312 (1988)
Shapero v. Kentucky Bar Ass'n, 486 U.S. 466 (1988)
Hazelwood Sch. Dist. v. Kuhlmier, 484 U.S. 260 (1988)
Hustler Magazine v. Falwell, 485 U.S. 46 (1988)
Lyons v. International Union, 485 U.S. 360 (1988)

October Term 1988

Fort Wayne Books v. Indiana, 489 U.S. 46 (1989)
Massachusetts v. Oakes, 491 U.S. 576 (1989)
Texas Monthly, Inc. v. Bullock, 489 U.S. 1 (1989)
Board of Trustees v. Fox, 492 U.S. 469 (1989)
Ward v. Rock Against Racism, 491 U.S. 781 (1989)
Sable Communications v. FCC, 492 U.S. 115 (1989)
Eu v. San Francisco City, 489 U.S. 214 (1989)
Hernandez v. Comm'r, 490 U.S. 680 (1989)
County of Allegheny v. ACLU, 492 U.S. 573 (1989)
Frazee v. Illinois Dep't of Employment, 489 U.S. 829 (1989)
Texas v. Johnson, 491 U.S. 397 (1989)
Harte-Hank's Communication, Inc. v. Connaughton, 491 U.S. 657 (1989)
Florida Star v. B. J. F., 491 U.S. 524 (1989)
City of Dallas v. Stanglin, 490 U.S. 19 (1989)

October Term 1989

FW/PBS, Inc. v. City of Dallas, 493 U.S. 215 (1990)
United States v. Kokinda, 497 U.S. 720 (1990)
Rutan v. Republican Party, 497 U.S. 62 (1990)
University of Pennsylvania v. EEOC, 493 U.S. 182 (1990)
Employment Div. v. Smith, 494 U.S. 872 (1990)
Board of Educ. v. Mergens, 496 U.S. 226 (1990)
Jimmy Swaggert Ministries v. Board of Equalization, 493 U.S. 378 (1990)
Austin v. Michigan Chamber of Commerce, 494 U.S. 652 (1990)
United States v. Eichman, 496 U.S. 310 (1990)
Butterworth v. Smith, 494 U.S. 624 (1990)
Osborne v. Ohio, 495 U.S. 103 (1990)
Milkovich v. Lorain Journal Co., 497 U.S. 1 (1990)
Peel v. Attorney Disciplinary Comm'n of Illinois, 496 U.S. 91 (1990)

October Term 1990

Barnes v. Glen Theatre, Inc., 501 U.S. 560 (1991)
Gentile v. State Bar, 501 U.S. 1030 (1991)

Leathers v. Medlock, 499 U.S. 439 (1991)
Rust v. Sullivan, 500 U.S. 173 (1991)
Masson v. New Yorker, 501 U.S. 496 (1991)
Lehnert v. Ferris Faculty Ass'n, 500 U.S. 517 (1991)
Cohen v. Cowles Media, 501 U.S. 663 (1991)

October Term 1991

Forsyth County v, Nationalist Movement, 505 U.S. 123 (1992)
Norman v. Reed, 502 U.S. 279 (1992)
Burdick v. Takushi, 504 U.S. 428 (1992)
Lee v. Weisman, 505 U.S. 577 (1992)
RAV v. City of St Paul, 505 U.S. 377 (1992)
Simon & Schuster, Inc. v. New York State Crime Victims Bd., 502 U.S. 105 (1992)
Burson v. Freeman, 504 U.S. 191 (1992)
Lee v. International Society for Krishna Consciousness, 505 U.S. 830 (1992)
Lee v. International Society for Krishna Consciousness, 505 U.S. 632 (1992)

October Term 1992

Alexander v. United States, 509 U.S. 544 (1993)
Zobrest v. Catalina Foothills, 509 U.S. 1 (1993)
Church of the Lukumi Babalu Aye, Inc. v. Hialeah, 508 U.S. 520 (1993)
United States v. Edge Broadcasting, 509 U.S. 418 (1993)
Lamb's Chapel v. Center Moriches Sch. Dist., 508 U.S. 384 (1993)
Edenfeld v. Fane, 507 U.S. 761 (1993)
El Vocero v. Puerto Rico, U.S. 508 U.S. 147 (1993)
City of Cincinnati v. Discovery Network, 507 U.S. 410 (1993)

October Term 1993

Board of Educ. of Kiryas Joel v. Grumet, 512 U.S. 687 (1994)
Turner Broadcasting v. FCC, 512 U.S. 622 (1994)
Waters v. Churchill, 511 U.S. 661 (1994)
Madsen v. Women's Health Ctr., 512 U.S. 753 (1994)
City of Ladue v. Gilleo, 512 U.S. 43 (1994)
Ibanez v. Florida Dep't of Business, 512 U.S. 136 (1994)
CBS, Inc. v. Davis, 510 U.S. 1315 (1994)

October Term 1994

United States v. National Treasury Employees Union, 513 U.S. 454 (1995)
United States v. X-Citement Video, 513 U.S. 64 (1994)
Rosenberger v. Rector of the Univ. of Virginia, 515 U.S. 819 (1995)
Lebron v. National R.R. Passenger Corp., 513 U.S. 374 (1995)
Capitol Square Review Bd. v. Pinette, 515 U.S. 753 (1995)
Hurley v. ILGO. 515 U.S. 557 (1995)
McIntyre v. Ohio Elections Comm'n, 514 U.S. 334 (1995)
Florida Bar v. Went For It, 515 U.S. 618 (1995)
Rubin v. Coors Brewing, 514 U.S. 476 (1995)

October Term 1995

Denver Area Educ. v. FCC, 518 U.S. 727 (1996)
Board of County Comm'rs v. Umbehr, 518 U.S. 668 (1996)
44 Liquor Mart v. Rhode Island, 517 U.S. 484 (1996)
O'Hare Truck Serv. v. City of Northlake, 518 U.S. 712 (1996)
Colorado Republican Campaign Comm. v. FEC, 518 U.S. 604 (1996)

October Term 1996

Turner Broadcasting v. FCC, 520 U.S. 180 (1997)
Schenck v. Pro-Choice Network, 519 U.S. 357 (1997)
Reno v. ACLU, 521 U.S. 844 (1997)
Glickman v. Wileman Bros. & Elliott, 521 U.S. 457 (1997)
City of Boerne v. Flores, 521 U.S. 507 (1997)
Timmons v. Twin Cities Area Party, 520 U.S. 351 (1997)
Agostini v. Felton, 521 U.S. 203 (1997)

October Term 1997

National Endowment v. Finley, 524 U.S. 5696 (1998)
Arkansas Educ. Television v. Forbes, 523 U.S. 666 (1998)

Notes

This essay is dedicated to the memory of my long-time colleague, Bernard Schwartz. I have attempted to write it the way I think Bernie would have, with attention to doctrinal development and little patience for high theory.

1. O'Brien, "The Rehnquist Years: A Supreme Court Retrospective: The Rehnquist Court: Holding Steady on Freedom of Speech," 22 *Nova L. Rev.* 713 (1998).

2. Eg. *Virginia State B. of Pharmacy v. Virginia Citizens' Consumer Council*, 425 U.S. 748, 781 (1976) (Rehnquist, J., dissenting) (declining to recognize free speech protection for commercial speech); Wooley v. Maynard, 430 U.S. 705, 719–22 (1977) (Rehnquist, J., dissenting) (declining to recognize First Amendment right to refuse to display "Live Free or Die" motto on license plate); Richmond Newspapers, Inc. v. Virginia, 448 U.S. 555, 604 (1980) (Rehnquist, J., dissenting) (declining to recognize First Amendment right of press to be present at criminal trial); Minneapolis Star v. Minnesota Comm'r of Revenue, 460 U.S. 575, 593 (1983) (Rehnquist, J., dissenting) (declining to invalidate discriminatory tax provisions treating publications differently). Although he concurred in the result of NAACP v. Claiborne Hardware Co. 458 U.S. 886, 907 (1982) (upholding First Amendment protection for economic boycotts), Justice Rehnquist declined to join the Court's opinion. In Buckley v. Valeo, 424 U.S. 1 (1976), Justice Rehnquist voted to abolish expenditure caps, and to invalidate public financing, but upheld limits on campaign contributions.

3. 478 U.S. 328 (1986).

4. *Posadas* was limited, and perhaps overruled, in 44 Liquormart v. Rhode Island, 517 U.S. 484 (1996).

5. I count at least twenty occasions in which the Chief Justice dissented from important opinions of the Court accepting a free speech argument. The dissents are noted in the appendix. Chief Justice Rehnquist's best known free speech dissent was his passionate *cri de coeur* in Texas v. Johnson, 491 U.S. 397, 421–39 (1989), arguing that burning the American flag as an act of protest is not protected by the First Amendment. The Chief Justice's free

speech dissents appear to have been less frequent in recent years. McIntyre v. Ohio, 514 U.S. 334, (1994), upholding the right to anonymous political speech, is the most recent case in which the Chief Justice disagreed with the Court in an important case granting expansive free speech protection. In fact, on several occasions in recent years, the Chief Justice has surprised observers by concurring in expansive free speech opinions in areas where he had once dissented. See Board of Comm'rs v. Umbehr, 518 U.S. 668 (1996) (extending *Elrod v. Burns* to independent contractors); O'Hare Truck Serv. v. City of Northlake, 518 U.S. 712, 116 (1996) (same); 44 Liquormart, Inc. v. Rhode Island, 517 U.S. 484 (1996) (invalidating advertising ban as unnecessarily broad); Rubin v. Coors Brewing Co., 514 U.S. 476, 1585 (1995) (invalidating advertising ban as inadequately justified); Capitol Square Review Bd. v. Pinette, 515 U.S. 753 (1995) (upholding right to display political symbol in public park).

6. I will discuss two major setbacks to free speech during Chief Justice Rehnquist's tenure: the decimation of the student press in Hazelwood Sch. Dist. v. Kuhlmeier, 484 U.S. 260 (1988) and the enunciation of appalling rules governing subsidized speech in Rust v. Sullivan, 500 U.S. 173 (1991). The common thread that unites *Hazelwood School District* and *Rust* is the Court's tendency to view speech as something that is bought with property. In *Buckley*, that idea translates into a First Amendment ban on limiting campaign spending. In *Hazelwood School District* and *Rust*, it translates into the power to censor speech paid for by the government. In fairness, the Rehnquist Court did not invent the problem, and its opinions are merely continuations of earlier themes.

7. I have excluded the Religion Clause cases unless they also present free speech issues. Thus, I have included such cases as Lamb's Chapel v. Center Moriches Union Free Sch. Dist. 508 U.S. 384 (1993), and Rosenberger v. Rector of the Univ. of Virginia, 515 U.S. 819 (1995), but have excluded such cases as Zobrest v. Catalura Foothills Sch. Dist. 509 U.S. 1 (1993), and Employment Div. v. Smith, 494 U.S. 872 (1990). If the touchstone is continuity, the Religion Clause cases decided by the Rehnquist Court display less continuity than the free expression cases.

I have included ballot access cases because they pose free speech issues, even though the Court often ignores them. Thus, I have included such cases as Munro v. Socialist Workers Party, 479 U.S. 198 (1986), Tashjian v. Republican Party of Connecticut, 479 U.S. 208 (1986), Eu v. San Francisco City Democratic Party, 489 U.S. 214 (1989), and Timmons v. Twin Cities Area New Party, 520 U.S. 351 1364 (1997). I have, somewhat arbitrarily, excluded the racial reapportionment cases such as Shaw v. Reno 509 U.S. 630 (1993), primarily because they are not traditionally viewed as free expression cases. Although this is not the place, I believe that we should reconceptualize cases dealing with participation in the democratic process as quintessential free expression cases.

8. I have listed the Rehnquist Court's free expression cases in an appendix.

9. Bronner, *Battle for Justice: How the Bork Nomination Shook America* (1989).

10. The high burden of justification in free expression cases is generally phrased in two ways. Efforts to censor must be shown as "necessary" to advance a "compelling" governmental interest by the "least drastic means." Alternatively, efforts to censor must be shown as necessary to deal with a "clear and present" danger of extremely serious harm that cannot be avoided by less drastic means. The two tests often overlap completely. See generally Ginsberg v. New York, 390 U.S. 629 (1968); Illinois Bd. of Elections v. Socialist Workers Party, 440 U.S. 173 (1979).

11. Schwartz, *A History of the Supreme* Court 221–23 (1993).

12. 376 U.S. 254 (1964).

13. 485 U.S. 46 (1988).

14. The Rehnquist Court revisited *New York Times v. Sullivan* on at least three other occasions. Hartke-Hanks Communications, Inc. v. Connaughton, 491 U.S. 657 (1989); Masson

v. New Yorker Magazine, 501 U.S. 496 (1991); Milkovich v. Lorrain Journal, 497 U.S. 1 (1990). On each occasion, I believe the Court was true to the spirit of *New York Times v. Sullivan*. In *Hartke-Hanks*, the Court declined to impose a duty of reasonable investigation on newspapers but did provide for liability for "purposeful avoidance of the truth.' In *Masson*, the Court rejected the notion that improperly placing quotation marks around a paraphrase was per se malice. Instead, the Court remanded to determine whether falsely attributing a quote materially harmed the alleged source. Conversely, in *Milkovich*, the Court rejected the notion that couching a statement as an opinion resulted in a *per se* exemption from libel. Instead, the Court remanded to determine whether the statement was an implied assertion of fact. The Chief Justice voted with the majority in *Hartke-Hanks* and *Masson*, and wrote for the Court in *Milkovich*.

15. 491 U.S. 397 (1989).

16. 496 U.S. 310 (1990).

17. 395 U.S. 444 (1969).

18. 408 U.S. 92 (1972).

19. For similar examples, in somewhat less dramatic settings, of the Rehnquist Court's use of free expression as a trumping value, see, e.g., Rankin v. McPherson, 483 U.S. 378 (1987) (overturning conviction for hyperbolic language threatening President); FEC v. Massachusetts Citizens for Life, 479 U.S. 238 (1986) (overturning limit on political spending by grassroots groups); Boos v. Barry, 485 U.S. 312 (1988) (striking down ban on protests within 500 feet of foreign embassy); Florida Star v. BJF, 491 U.S. 524 (1988) (striking down ban on publication of name of rape victim); Rutan v. Republican Party, 497 U.S. 62 (1990) (extending *Elrod v. Burns* to promotions); Butterworth v. Smith, 494 U.S. 624 (1990) (invalidating ban on disclosure by witness of grand jury testimony); Lee v. International Society for Krishna Consciousness, 505 U.S. 830 (1991) (invalidating flat ban on leafletting in airports); City of Ladue v. Gilleo, 512 U.S. 43 (1994) (invalidating local ban on all signs on esthetic grounds); United States v. National Treasury Employees Union, 513 U.S. 454 (1995) (invalidating ban on honoraria to lower level gov't employees); City of Cincinnati v. Discovery Network, 507 U.S. 410 (1993) (invalidating ban on sidewalk newsracks containing commercial material); 44 Liquormart v. Rhode Island, 517 U.S. 392 (1996) (invalidating ban on liquor price advertising); McIntyre v. Ohio, 514 U.S. 334 (1995) (invalidating ban on anonymous electoral speech). For rare cases in which the Rehnquist Court found adequate justification for preventing protected expression, see Burson v. Freeman, 504 U.S. 191 (1991) (upholding ban on electioneering within 100 feet of poles), and Austin v. Michigan Chamber of Commerce, 494 U.S. 652 (1990) (upholding Michigan ban on independent expenditures by corporations in support of candidates).

Finally in the two *Krishna Consciousness* cases, Lee v. International Society for Krishna Consciousness, 505 U.S. 632 and 505 U.S. 830 (1991), the Court drew an impossibly fine line between leafleting in an airport, which was deemed protected by the First Amendment, and soliciting funds for charitable or political causes in an airport, which was deemed unprotected. Although it may be an act of hubris to attempt to reconcile the two cases, my take is that Justice O'Connor, who was the swing vote, simply did not view soliciting money as a transcendent, trumping value on a level with free expression.

20. See Rowan v. Post Office Dep't, 397 U.S. 728 (1970).

21. 487 U.S. 474 (1988).

22. 512 U.S. 753 (1994).

23. 519 U.S. 357 (1997).

24. See Madsden v. Florida Women's Ctr., 512 U.S. 753 (1994), (upholding injunction limiting picketing and chanting in immediate vicinity of abortion center).

25. 521 U.S. 844 (1997). This case concerned a challenge to the Communications Decency Act's provision to protect minors from harmful materials on the Internet. Jus-

tice Stevens found this provision facially overreaching, and thus in violation of the First Amendment.

26. The free speech universe was initially confined to speakers, with hearers entering the picture in an occasionally rhetorical flourish. The independent interests of hearers were recognized in such cases as Lamont v. Postmaster Gen., 381 U.S. 301 (1965), and First Nat'l Bank of Boston v. Bellotti, 435 U.S. 765 (1978). Conduits enter the picture with Red Lion Broadcasting Co. v. FCC, 395 U.S. 367 (1969). Targets are explored in *New York Times v. Sullivan* and its progeny.

27. See Cohen v. California, 403 U.S. 15 (1971); Collin v. Smith, 578 F.2d 1197 (7th Cir.), *cert. denied*, 439 U.S. 916 (1978); Skokie v. National Socialist Party, 69 Ill. 2d 605, 14 Ill. Dec. 890, 373 N.E.2d 21 (1978).

28. See Chaplinsky v. New Hampshire, 315 U.S. 568 (1942).

29. Lehman v. Shaker Heights, 418 U.S. 298 (1974).

30. R. A. V. v. City of St. Paul, 505 U.S. 377 (1992); Texas v. Johnson, supra note 15.

31. 508 U.S. 384 (1993).

32. 515 U.S. 819 (1995).

33. 515 U.S. 753 (1995).

34. Cohen v. California, 430 U.S. 15 (1971).

35. 512 U.S. 622 (1994) (Turner I). See also Turner Broadcasting v. FCC, 520 U.S. 180 (1997) (Turner II).

36. 524 U.S. 727 (1996).

37. Id. at 812–838.

38. 515 U.S. 557 (1995).

39 . 523 U.S. 666 (1998).

40. Police Dep't v. Mosely, 408 U.S. 92 (1972); Minneapolis Star v. Minnesota Comm'r of Revenue, 460 U.S. 575 (1983).

41. E.g., Arkansas Writers' Project v. Ragland, 480 U.S. 228 (1987) (invalidating differential tax scheme on publications); Texas Monthly, Inc. v. Bullock, 489 U.S. 1 (1989) (invalidating exemption of religious journals from sales tax); Simon & Schuster v. New York State Crime Victims Bd., 502 U.S. 105 (1991) (invalidating differential treatment of earnings from publication).

42. 499 U.S. 439 (1991). The case held that Arkansas' imposition of a sales tax on cable television services while not taxing print media services, was not a violation of the First Amendment.

43. 505 U.S. 377 (1992). The Chief Justice joined the majority opinion in *RAV*. He had filed a lone dissent in *Minneapolis Star*, and had dissented in *Arkansas Writers Project* and *Texas Monthly*. He joined the Court's opinion in *Simon & Schuster*.

44. It would be possible to abandon the categorical approach and require each effort a censorship to meet the same standard. The results in most fighting-words and libel cases would not change. Obscenity might be more difficult, because it would be necessary to articulate the precise evil it is believed to cause and to demonstrate its close causal nexus to the evil.

45. The process could be described as a refusal to view certain categories of speech as worthy of primacy in the hierarchy of social values.

46. 495 U.S. 103 (1990).

47. 489 U.S. 46 (1989).

48. Fort Wayne Books 489 U.S. 46 (1989), upheld the use of state RICO laws to impose extremely serious penalties on what had been relatively minor offenses. Alexander v. United States, 509 U.S. 544 (1993) upheld broad forfeiture provisions resulting in the forfeiture of both protected and unprotected material.

49. 493 U.S. 215 (1989).

50. 501 U.S. 560 (1991).

51. 521 U.S. 884 (1997).

52. Denver Area Educ. Consortium v. FCC, 524 U.S. 727 (1996).

53. The two other sex speech cases in which free speech arguments prevailed were United States v. X-Citement Video, 513 U.S. 64 (1994), and Sable Communications Co. v. FCC, 492 U.S. 115 (1989). *Sable Communications* dealt with an absurdly overbroad ban on telephoning sexually explicit services that was allegedly designed to protect children, but was unnecessarily destructive of the rights of an adult. *X-Citement Video* reasserted the requirement that obscenity statues contain a scienter element, but did so in a case in which the scienter requirement was read into the statute to save a conviction.

54. The Rehnquist Court's successful commercial speech cases include Shapero v. Kentucky Bar Ass'n, 486 U.S. 466 (1988) (upholding right to solicit clients by mail); Peel v. Attorney Disciplinary Comm., 496 U.S. 91 (1990) (upholding truthful attorney advertising); Edenfield v. Fane, 507 U.S. 761 (1993) (upholding right to face-to-face client solicitation by accountants); City of Cincinnati v. Discovery Network, 507 U.S. 410 (1993) (invalidating ban on sidewalk newsracks containing commercial material); Ibanez v. Florida Dep't of Business, 512 U.S. 136 (1994) (upholding truthful advertising); Rubin v. Coors Brewing Co., 514 U.S. 476 (1995) (invalidating ban on advertising alcohol content of beer); 44 Liquormart v. Rhode Island, 517 U.S. 484 (1996) (invalidating ban on liquor price advertising). Commercial speech argument were rejected in Board of Trustees v. Fox, 492 U.S. 469 (1988) (declining to require admission of commercial vendors into college dormitories); Florida Bar v. Went For it, 515 U.S. 618 (1995) (upholding thirty-day delay on soliciting victims of accidents); Glickman v. Wileman Bros & Eliot, 521 U.S. 457 (1997) (upholding New Deal statute requiring growers to pay for generic advertising campaigns approved by majority of growers).

55. 482 U.S. 451 (1987).

56. 482 U.S. 569 (1987).

57. 486 U.S. 750 (1988).

58. 487 U.S. 781 (1988).

59. 492 U.S. 115 (1989).

60. 505 U.S. 123 (1992).

61. 521 U.S. 844 (1997).

62. The Court narrowed the injunction in *Schenck* because it was too broad. Unlike the application of the overbreadth doctrine to statutes, however, the Court merely narrowed the overbroad injunction instead of declaring it facially void. Why doesn't the Court always follow that practice when confronted with an overbroad federal statute?

Process-based arguments were rejected by the Rehnquist Court in FW/PBS, Inc v. Dallas, 493 U.S. 215 (1989) (licensing scheme for sexually oriented businesses); Osborne v. Ohio, 495 U.S. 103 (1990) (rejecting vagueness and overbreadth challenge to child pornography statute); and National Endowment for the Arts v. Finley, 524 U.S. 569 (1998) (rejecting challenge to vagueness of terms "indecent" and "disrespectful" in context of subsidy plan, where terms were merely precatory).

63. 484 U.S. 260 (1987).

64. *Denver Area Consortium, v.* FCC, 524 U.S. at 812–38.

65. 500 U.S. 173 (1991).

66 . 497 U.S. 720 (1990).

67. In Waters v. Churchill, 511 U.S. 661 (1994), the Court adopted procedures for resolving disputes over the dismissal of public employees for job site speech that tilts dramatically toward the employer. Under *Waters*, a public employer's reasonable perception arrived at after a fair investigation that speech adversely affecting the job site occurred is determinative.

68. 524 U.S. 569 (1998).

69. 515 U.S. 819 (1995).

70. 523 U.S. 666 (1998).

71. The successful First Amendment/democracy cases were, e.g., FEC v. Massachusetts Citizens for Life, 479 U.S. 238 (1986) (invalidating ban on expenditures by grass roots political entities); Tashjian v. Connecticut, 479 U.S. 208 (1986) (invalidating ban on open primary); Eu v. San Francisco City Democratic Party, 489 U.S. 14 (1989) (invalidating a party endorsement in primary); Rutan v. Republican Party, 497 U.S. 62 (1990) (invalidating patronage promotions); Norman v. Reed, 502 U.S. 279 (1991) (invalidating arbitrary limits on third parties); McIntyre v. Ohio Elections Comm'n, 514 U.S. 334 (1995) (upholding right of anonymous political speech but reaffirming validity of campaign disclosure laws); Colorado Republican Campaign Comm. v. FEC, 518 U.S. 604 (1996). First Amendment arguments were rejected in Munro v. Socialist Workers Party, 479 U.S. 189 (1986) (upholding ballot access petition requirement of 1%); Austin v. Michigan Chamber of Commerce, 494 U.S. 652 (1990) (upholding ban on corporate expenditures in support of candidate) Burdick v. Takushi, 504 U.S. 428 (1992) (denying right to cast write in vote); Burson v. Freeman, 504 U.S. 191 (1992) (upholding ban on electioneering within 100 feet of polls); Timmons v. Twin Cities Area New Party, 520 U.S. 351 (1997). Arkansas Educ. Television Network, 523 U.S. 666 (1997), granting broad but not unlimited discretion to select candidates for a public television sponsored debate was, in my opinion, a First Amendment tie. Three cases did not explicitly turn on First Amendment concerns, although they obviously implicate them. Morse v. Republican Party of Virginia, 517 U.S. 186 (1996) (Section 5 of Voting Rights Act applies to changes in nominating rules of political parties operating in covered subdivisions); U.S. Terms Limits v. Thornton, 514 U.S. 779 (1995) (term limits for members of Congress violates the Constitution); Romer v. Evans, 517 U.S. 620 (1996) (ban on enactment of civil rights law protecting gays violates Equal Protection clause).

72. See also Colorado Republican Campaign Comm. v. FEC, 518 U.S. 604 (1996) (invalidating ban on party expenditures prior to selection of candidate). For a case cutting against major party autonomy, see Morse v. Republican Party of Virginia, 517 U.S. 186 (1996) (requiring parties in subdivisions covered by Section 5 of the Voting Rights Act to pre-clear changes in candidate nominating procedures).

73. First Amendment arguments triumphed in the following media cases: Arkansas Writers Project v. Ragland, 476 U.S. 1113 (1986); City of Lakewood v. Plain Dealer, 486 U.S. 750 (1988); Hustler Magazine v. Falwell, 485 U.S. 46 (1988); Texas Monthly v. Bullock, 489 U.S. 1 (1989); Florida Star v. BJF, 491 U.S. 524 (1989); Harke-Hanks v. Connaughton, 491 U.S. 657 (1989); Masson v. New Yorker, 501 U.S. 496 (1991); Simon & Schuster v. Crime Victims Bd., 502 U.S. 105 (1991); and El Vocero v. Puerto Rico, 508 U.S. 147 (1993). Media assertion of First Amendment rights were rejected in Hazelwood v. Kuhlmeier, 484 U.S. 260 (1988); Milkovich v. Lorrain Journal, 497 U.S. 1 (1990); Leathers v. Medlock, 499 U.S. 439 (1991); Cohen v. Cowles Media, 501 U.S. 663 (1991); and United States v. Edge Broadcasting Co., 509 U.S. 418 (1993). Ties were recorded in Turner I, 512 U.S. 622 (1994); Turner II, 520 U.S. 180 (1997), Denver Area, 518 U.S. 727 (1996), and Arkansas Educational Television, 523 U.S. 666 (1997).

3

THE FIRST AMENDMENT IN CYBERSPACE

BRUCE J. ENNIS

It is far too early to know how the Rehnquist Court, or future Courts, will apply the First Amendment to the many novel questions that will arise in cyberspace, but the Court's holdings in *Reno v. ACLU/ALA*[1] answer several important questions. The Court's mode of analysis in that and related decisions suggests that the Court will rely more heavily on ad hoc balancing, and less heavily on categorical analysis, in deciding future First Amendment questions arising in cyberspace, and even in other "new" modes of communication such as cable TV and direct broadcast satellite.[2]

The Broad Holding of *Reno*

The *Reno* case was extremely important because it was the Court's first exposure to cyberspace and no one knew before the decision whether the Court would apply the strict scrutiny traditionally used to review content regulation of the print medium, the more deferential scrutiny used to review content regulation of broadcast radio and TV, as the Solicitor General's Office was urging, or the unspecified but less than strict scrutiny the Court had applied the previous term in reviewing content regulation of cable TV in the *Denver Area* case.[3] Although *Reno* involved regulation of "indecent" or "patently offensive" speech, it seemed likely that the *standard* of review the Court applied to judge the constitutionality of regulating that type of speech would later be applied to judge the future regulation of political speech, libel, and other types of speech in cyberspace.

One of the most interesting things about the *Reno* decision is that the Court did not specify the standard of review it was applying. *Reno* involved a law that regulated nonbroadcast speech on the basis of its content—making it illegal to "display" "indecent" or "patently offensive" communications on the Internet if those communications would be "available" to minors. The Courts did say that the law's regulation of Internet speech had to satisfy "the most stringent review of its provisions," but the Court did not expressly apply or even mention the strict scrutiny test. Instead, without explicitly acknowledging what it was doing, the Court *balanced* the government's interest in shielding minors from indecent (but not obscene) speech, against the First Amendment interest of adult speakers to communicate, and adult listeners to receive, indecent speech, and decided that the balance tipped decidedly in favor of protecting speech between adults. The basic holding of the Court was that government cannot constitutionally reduce the adult population to reading and viewing only what is appropriate for children. The fact that all nine Justices concurred in that holding, including both the "categorical" Justices and the "balancing" Justices, suggests that the opinion's ambiguity regarding the precise standard of review the Court was applying may have been intentional.

The important point for the future, however, is that the Court squarely rejected the government's argument that government regulation of Internet speech should receive the same relaxed scrutiny as government regulation of broadcast speech. The Court expressly held that because there is no problem of spectrum scarcity on the Internet, and because Internet speech is not as intrusive as broadcast speech — as Internet users must affirmatively request the speech that shows up on their computer screens — there was no justification for relaxing the standard of scrutiny.[4]

The Supreme Court's decision in *Reno* effectively forecloses any attempt to regulate indecent speech on the Internet that remotely resembles the Communications Decency Act (CDA)[5] provisions struck down in that decision. If that law had been struck down only on vagueness grounds, Congress could have responded with a more narrowly drawn law regulating a more precise category of speech (e.g., regulating speech that is "harmful to minors," or "obscene for minors," rather than regulating speech that is "indecent" or "patently offensive" for minors).[6] But the Court's decision rests on a much broader rationale. As noted, all nine Justices espoused that view that *any* law that unduly interferes with adult access to material that is constitutionally protected for adults would violate the First Amendment. Thus, even if Congress narrowed the sweep of a future law to prohibit *only* speech that would be "obscene for minors," and thus not constitutionally protected for minors, because that speech would still be constitutionally protected for adults, even that narrower law would violate the First Amendment if it unduly interfered with adult access to that speech.

And as the Court found, because of the way the Internet works, it is generally impossible for a speaker to ensure that his or her speech is accessible only by adults. Accordingly, a prohibition on "obscene for minors" speech would unconstitutionally force speakers to refrain from engaging in that speech even though it was intended for adults, and was lawful for adults, because minors would also be able to gain access to that speech.

In short, in view of the Court's rationale and the technological inability of *speakers* to prevent minors from gaining access to speech communicated through most of the diverse ways of communicating in cyberspace (including newsgroups, listservs, chatrooms, and websites that do not have CGI script capability), most (but not all) *speaker-based* restrictions on Internet speech are likely to be found unconstitutional.[7]

Post- *Reno* Possibilities

At present, the only way it is technologically possible, in most forms of communication in cyberspace, to permit speech for adults but prohibit that same speech from reaching minors is to block or filter that speech at the *user* end of the communication. Because blocking or filtering at the user end *is* technologically possible for most if not all forms of communication in cyberspace, Congress might try to *require* blocking or filtering at the user end. That is unlikely, however, because it would be politically difficult for Congress to make it a crime for a parent to fail or refuse to install or use blocking software, and passages in *Reno* suggest that parents may have a constitutional right to expose their own children even to obscene speech, or to speech that would otherwise *not* be constitutionally protected for minors. Moreover, it would be virtually impossible for government to enforce such a law.

But Congress might find it politically expedient to take steps to assist parents who voluntarily choose to use blocking or filtering software. It could, for example, require speakers to label or rate their own speech in a way that could be recognized by user-based software. However, that requirement would raise constitutional problems that would be even more substantial than the already substantial problems that would be raised by requiring broadcast speakers to rate their own speech.[8] Accordingly, Congress may decide to limit any federal labeling requirements to requiring that all browsers and all Internet access providers offer end users the capacity to block or screen for age. That requirement would probably be found constitutional.

Because the CDA regulated noncommercial speech, it was not necessary for the Court to decide the extent to which Congress may constitutionally regulate Internet speech that does no more than propose a commercial transaction. However, because of the value the Court placed on this new and "unique" means of communication, it is likely that speech that falls in the gray area between commercial speech and noncommercial speech will be analyzed as a restriction on noncommercial speech, and it seems certain that commercial speech on the Internet will receive at least as much protection as commercial speech in other media. Indeed, as others have noted, it is arguable that the *Reno* Court's rejection of three cases that are often invoked to support restrictions on commercial speech (*Ginsberg v. New York, FCC v. Pacifica,* and *Renton v. Playtime Theatres*), and its reliance on three cases that are often invoked to oppose restrictions on commercial speech (*Bolger v. Young's Drug Products, Carey v. Population Services International,* and *Sable Communications v. FCC*), may signal increased protection for commercial speech in *all* media.[9]

In addition, it may turn out that the Commerce Clause rationale of the 1997 decision in *American Library Association v. Pataki,*[10] from the federal court in New York's Southern District, will provide even greater protection for commercial speech on the Internet than the First Amendment provides. In *Pataki,* the court relied on the Commerce Clause to strike down New York's attempt to regulate Internet speech that would be "harmful to minors," finding that New York's regulation unconstitutionally projected New York law into conduct that occurs wholly outside New York, unduly burdened interstate commerce, and subjected Internet speech to the risk of inconsistent state legislation. Of course, the Commerce Clause would not limit *federal* attempts to regulate commercial speech, but most regulation of commercial speech is by states, so *Pataki* may prove to be a significant barrier to *state* efforts to regulate commercial speech in cyberspace.

The *Reno* Balancing Test

As I noted earlier, it is my belief that the decision in *Reno* reflects the majority's balancing of the rights of adults against the rights of minors rather than application of the Court's more traditional "categorical" rules. It is also my view that *Reno* was not the first decision to reflect a shift from categorical analysis to balancing analysis, and as I explain later, I think it is no accident that the principal decisions reflecting that shift before *Reno* were also decisions involving a relatively new mode of communication—cable TV. Before discussing those decisions—the *Denver Area* case and *Turner Broadcasting System, Inc. v. FCC*,[11] it might be well to review the major differences between a "balancing" approach and a "categorical" approach to resolving First Amendment issues.

Under a categorical approach, the Justices decide which predetermined category is most appropriate for the speech at issue in the case under review and then apply the legal rules that have already been established for judging speech within that category. Once the appropriate category has been determined, application of the legal rules established for that category is a relatively straightforward and inflexible process. Accordingly, selection of the appropriate category largely determines whether the speech regulation at issue will be upheld or struck down.

In sharp contrast, under a "balancing" approach, there are no fixed categories, and no inflexible rules. In each case, the Justices decide which particular facts and legal interests are relevant to the speech issue before the Court. They then give those facts and legal interests such weight as they deem appropriate in the circumstances of that case, balance the competing facts and interests, and reach a decision. Clearly, under a "balancing" approach, it is more difficult to predict the likely outcome in any given case because it is impossible to know how much weight each Justice will deem appropriate for the particular facts and interests that Justice deems most relevant in that case.

For these reasons, it is widely believed—and I generally share that view—that categorical rules are more likely to be protective of offensive or highly controversial speech than are balancing rules, because under a categorical approach, the identity or odious nature of the speech or speaker is largely irrelevant.[12]

Until recently, categorical rules have been the accepted rules for evaluating all speech claims. Actually, there are several categorical rules, and the distinctions between them have begun to blur, but for present purposes, the four most important categorical rules are strict scrutiny, *O'Brien* scrutiny, the commercial speech test, and the broadcast speech test.

STRICT SCRUTINY   This is the hardest test for the government to meet. If a case is evaluated using strict scrutiny, the government almost always loses. The government must show that it has a compelling interest to regulate speech and that the means it has chosen to further that interest are the least restrictive means that could be used to achieve that interest. This is the test used to evaluate almost any content-based regulation of the *print* medium, which is why content regulation of books, magazines, and newspapers almost always fails.

But the strict scrutiny test applies more broadly than to the print medium. It applies to any *content-based* regulation of political speech, or of any other type of noncommercial speech.[13]

O'BRIEN SCRUTINY[14] This is an intermediate scrutiny test. It is fairly difficult for the government to meet but much easier to meet than the strict scrutiny test. Under *O'Brien* intermediate scrutiny the government need not show a compelling interest, but it must show it has a substantial and important interest. It need not show the means it has chosen are the least restrictive, but it must show the means are reasonably tailored to serve the government's interest, without unduly burdening speech.

This test applies to regulation of *conduct* that has an *incidental* impact on speech, as in *O'Brien*,[15] itself and also to regulation of the speech activities of speech entities, as long as the regulation is *content neutral*.[16]

COMMERCIAL SPEECH The test for commercial speech (i.e., for speech that does no more than propose a commercial transaction, such as an advertisement) is also an intermediate scrutiny test, but it is slightly different from the *O'Brien* test. Under the commercial speech test, as under the *O'Brien* test, the government must show that it has a substantial interest. But, it must also show that the regulation directly and materially advances that interest. And in addition to showing that the regulation is reasonably tailored, it must also show that the regulation reaches no further than is necessary to achieve that interest.[17]

Despite the similarities between the *O'Brien* test and the commercial speech test, there is serious tension between the two tests because the *O'Brien* test applies only to content-*neutral* regulations, whereas all regulation of commercial speech is content *based*.[18]

However, because of the similarities between these two tests, in recent years the Supreme Court has blurred the distinction between the two, citing commercial speech cases as precedent in *O'Brien* cases and vice versa,[19] with the result that the test for content-neutral regulation of noncommercial speech is now nearly indistinguishable from the test for content-based regulation of commercial speech. The unification of these two categorical rules may itself be an early, if nonexplicit, indication of the growing dissatisfaction with categorical rules felt by several members of the Court.

BROADCAST SPEECH The test for evaluating regulations of broadcast speech (i.e., radio or TV speech that is broadcast through the airwaves pursuant to a government license) is *far* less strict than strict scrutiny, and much easier for the government to meet, but the Supreme Court has never articulated precisely what the test is. The important point is that until the *Denver Area* decision, this test has been the only test that allowed content-based regulation of noncommercial speech without requiring the government to show a compelling interest achieved in the least restrictive way.[20]

Although the precise limits on the government's power to regulate the content of broadcast speech have never been clear, it is clear that under the test for broadcast speech, the government has some power to regulate the content of broadcast speech directly, not just incidentally, and can do so in circumstances in which the government would surely fail to satisfy the strict scrutiny test.

The principal justification for this relaxed standard of review has been that broadcast is unlike other media because of spectrum scarcity. The theory is that because not everyone who wants to be a broadcast speaker can do so (because only one speaker can speak on each broadcast frequency), and since the government must of necessity decide who can have a broadcast license to use each frequency, the government should have greater leeway in regulating broadcast speech than other speech.[21]

Until recently, nearly every regulation of speech was judged by selecting and then applying one of these categorical rules, with reasonably predictable results. But that is changing. and the main reason it is changing is the perception shared by many members of the Supreme Court that these relatively rigid categorical rules do not work well when applied to new mediums of communication, such as cable and the Internet. Instead of trying to decide which categorical rules to apply to cable and the Internet, those Justices apparently believe it would be better to abandon the categorical approach and to engage in a balancing approach, in which the new characteristics of cable and the Internet can figure appropriately in the balance. But this tension between the "categorical" Justices and the "balancing" Justices has not been resolved, and the same Justices may engage in a balancing approach in one case and a categorical approach in the next. Accordingly, applying the First Amendment in the information age is an uncertain and tricky business.

The Approach in *Denver Area*

The growing tension between the categorical approach and the balancing approach erupted in the *Denver Area* case, and it is not a mere coincidence that that case involved content regulation of cable speech. In that decision, Justices Kennedy and Ginsburg bitterly criticized Justices Breyer, Stevens, O'Connor, and Souter for applying a balancing test, rather than the categorical strict scrutiny test, to a regulation of the content of noncommercial cable speech.[22] The important point is not the three holdings of the Court. There were badly fractured opinions, and no holding received five votes on the same rationale. What is significant is that four Justices refused to apply the categorical strict scrutiny rule to a content-based regulation of noncommercial cable speech. And they made clear that they were refusing to apply categorical rules precisely because they were unclear about the extent to which traditional First Amendment rules should or should not apply to cable, the Internet, and other new information technologies.[23]

The Approach in *Turner II*

The growing importance of the balancing approach was also critical to the decision in *Turner*, the case in which the Court, by a five to four vote, upheld the constitutionality of the "must carry" provisions of the 1992 Cable Act.[24] The main difference between the majority and the dissent was that the majority thought that the must-carry provisions were not content based, whereas the dissent thought they were. Because of that difference of opinion, the majority purported to apply the *O'Brien* intermediate scrutiny test and upheld the law, whereas the dissent would have applied strict scrutiny and would have struck the law down. But even though the majority ostensibly applied the *O'Brien* test, it actually applied a more stringent version of the traditional *O'Brien* test, borrowed from commercial speech precedents, and required the government to show that the government's interest was real, not just speculative, and also required the government to show that the must-carry provisions would further that interest in a direct and material way. But the test the majority applied cannot simply be described as *O'Brien* with a vengeance, because in other ways, the majority applied a less demanding test than the traditional commercial speech test, by requiring *deference* to the predictive judgments of Congress.

Moreover, although both the majority and the dissent purported to apply various versions of the traditional categorical tests, in reality, balancing played a truly critical role in the majority's decision. Although Justice Kennedy, the Court's most emphatic proponent of the categorical approach, wrote the majority opinion, his views carried the day only because he was joined by the Court's principal proponents of balancing, Justices Breyer, Souter, and Stevens (and, interestingly, by Chief Justice Rehnquist). And it is clear that careful balancing of the competing rights and interests of broadcasters, cable operators, cable programmers, cable viewers, and non–cable viewers, was critical to the majority's decision. In fact, it is clear that the interest that was accorded the most weight in the majority's opinion was the interest of non–cable households in having access to a multiplicity of diverse broadcast sources.

Essentially, the First Amendment interest of non–cable viewers in having access to broadcast speakers was balanced against, and found to be worthy of greater protection, than the First Amendment interest of cable operators in deciding which speakers to carry on their cable systems.[25]

The Present Approach

The striking difference between the way the majority viewed the First Amendment interests at issue in *Turner II* and the way Justice Thomas viewed those interests in dissent in *Denver Area* may help to explain why several Justices are shifting from a categorical approach to a balancing approach, and why that shift is being reflected in cases involving "new" speech technologies and modes of communication. For Justice Thomas, the *only* interest entitled to First Amendment protection was the essentially property interest of the cable operators who owned the physical transmission components of the cable system. For the *Turner II* majority, the interests of cable programmers, broadcasters, and cable subscribers and over-the-air broadcast viewers were also entitled to First Amendment protection.

In situations involving only one interest protected by the First Amendment (e.g., the paradigmatic situation of a police officer attempting to silence a soap box orator), it has been relatively simple to develop and apply categorical rules. But when resolution of the case has an impact on more than one interest protected by the First Amendment, it has proved increasingly difficult to develop and apply categorical rules because in order to decide which categorical rule to apply, it is often necessary to decide which of the interests arguably protected by the First Amendment is entitled to recognition, or at least to the highest priority.

In effect, in cases involving multiple interests protected by the First Amendment, the Court is compelled to engage in a balancing of the interests on the First Amendment side of the equation, and it is therefore natural that the Court, having begun a balancing process, would then balance those interests against the interests favoring restriction of First Amendment rights. Precisely because of their speech-enhancing capabilities, the "new" modes of communication, such as cable TV and the Internet, generally involve multiple interests that are arguably protected by the First Amendment. Accordingly, there will be more pressure on the Court to balance the competing interests in these multi-interest cases than there has been in cases involving fewer interests protected by the First Amendment. Whether balancing will prove to be more or less speech enhancing, in the context of these new modes of communication, than categorical analysis remains to be seen.

Notes

1. 521 U.S. 844 (1997). I refer to the respondents as ACLU/ALA because the case was a consolidation of two separate challenges, one filed by a group of plaintiffs led by the ACLU and one by a group of plaintiffs led by the American Library Association. I represented the ALA challengers throughout, and represented the ACLU challengers, as well, for purposes of argument in the Supreme Court.

2. Many of the thoughts in this chapter have been developed in conversations with my colleagues in the Washington, DC, office of Jenner & Block, principally Paul Smith, Don Verrilli, Ann Kappler, Nory Miller, and John Morris. In addition, portions of this chapter are elaborations of ideas presented during the 1996 and 1997 Communications Law Symposiums of the Practicing Law Institute. An excellent law review article published in the summer of 1998 by Professor Jerome A. Barron reaches similar conclusions. See Barron, "The Electronic Media and The Flight from First Amendment Doctrine: Justice Breyer's New Balancing Approach," 31 *U. Mich. J.L. Ref.* 817 (1998).

3. Denver Area Educ. Telecommunications Consortium, Inc. v. FCC, 518 U.S. 727 (1996).

4. Although it is still true that, in general, Internet users must affirmatively request the speech that shows up on their computer screens, two developments since *Reno* was decided qualify that fact somewhat. First, mass marketers are beginning to send unsolicited e-mail messages to computer screens, and some of those messages could be regarded as indecent (or even obscene). Because the computer users have not in any way manifested a desire to receive those messages, or any unsolicited messages, it cannot be said that they have affirmatively requested that information. Dealing with this situation is a complex issue that is beyond the scope of this chapter, but it may lie in the fact that virtually all these unsolicited e-mail messages (or at least of the sexually oriented ones) are messages which propose a commercial transaction and thus could be regulated as "commercial speech."

Second, "push" technology is beginning to send content that has not specifically been requested to computer users who subscribe to that particular push service. For example, persons who indicate an interest in receiving information about new developments in microbiology will receive periodic bulletins on their computer screens alerting them to new developments in that field and providing Internet links to additional information.

Although the users do not affirmatively request the specific bulletins or information that pops up on their computer screens, they have affirmatively expressed an interest in receiving that type of information (and generally have paid a subscription fee for that service), so it can fairly be said that they have affirmatively requested that information. However, unlike most of the unsolicited e-mail messages described previously, the content of the information conveyed by push technology should not be regarded as "commercial speech," even though the subscriber pays for the push service; the fact that a subscriber pays for *The New York Times* does not make the content of the information in each issue commercial speech, because that content is not itself proposing a commercial transaction. Thus, although further refinements of "push" technology may create closer analogies to broadcast TV or radio, in their present form most push technologies seem to fit comfortably within *Reno's* observation that the Internet is different from broadcast because Internet users must affirmatively request the information that appears on their screens.

5. See Mcguire, "The Sword of Damocles Is Not Narrow Tailoring: The First Amendment's Victory in *Reno v. ACLU*," 48 *Case W. Res. L. Rev.* 413, 415–17.

6. The Court did not decide whether the CDA is too vague under the Due Process Clause, but it did decide that the CDA is too vague to satisfy the specificity requirements of the First Amendment.

7. If speaker-based restrictions do not "unduly" interfere with the ability of adults to communicate and receive information that is constitutionally protected for adults, they will be upheld unless they unduly interfere with the rights of *minors* to send or receive that information. In *Reno*, Justice O'Connor, joined by Chief Justice Rehnquist, concurring in part and dissenting in part, agreed with the majority's conclusion that the CDA's "display" provision was unconstitutional because it unduly interfered with communications between adults, but she would have upheld the law as applied in one very narrow set of circumstances: communications in which the *only* recipients are known to be minors *and* the speech at issue is not constitutionally protected *for minors*. Justice O'Connor, again joined by Chief Justice Rehnquist, then made clear her view that "patently offensive" speech *is* constitutionally protected, even for minors, if it "has some redeeming value for minors or does not appeal to their prurient interest."

In effect, Justices O'Connor and Rehnquist believed Congress could not constitutionally limit even minors' access to Internet speech unless the speech could be found "obscene as to minors." However, because they believed a substantial amount of the speech regulated by the CDA would meet that standard, they thought a facial challenge to the statute, as applied to minors, would be inappropriate. The narrowness of this dissent, joined by only two Justices, suggests that the Court will look skeptically at any regulation of Internet speech that is not, at a minimum, obscene as to minors.

8. Parents can more easily control their children's access to Internet speech than to broadcast speech. In addition the Internet does not share with broadcast the supposed spectrum scarcity that has traditionally been thought to justify more intrusive regulation of broadcast than of other forms of communication. Finally a speaker rating requirement imposed on the Internet would apply to literally millions of average citizens, often speaking spontaneously and without the benefit of legal advice, rather than to a relatively few broadcast speakers. All these facts would make an Internet rating requirement even more constitutionally suspect than a broadcast rating requirement. The emergence of new technology that can block all speech except speech that has been rated appropriate for children by a third-party rating bureau whose values the parent shares, further undercuts the need for, and thus the justification for, any governmentally imposed Internet rating system.

9. DeVore, "*Reno v. ACLU*: A Commercial Speech Authority," *LDRC Libelletter*, July 1997, n.4.; See Sable Communications v. FCC, 492 U.S. 115 (1989); Renton v. Playtime Theatres, 475 U.S. 41 (1986); Bolger v. Young's Drug Prod., 463 U.S. 60 (1983); FCC v Pacifica, 438 U.S. 726 (1978); Carey v. Population Serv. Int'l, 431 U.S. 678 (1977); Ginsberg v. New York, 390 U.S. 629 (1968).

10. 969 F. Supp. 160 (S.D.N.Y. 1997).

11. 520 U.S. 180 (1997) (*Turner II*).

12. See generally Sullivan, "Post-Liberal Judging: The Roles of Categorization and Balancing," 63 *U. Colo. L. Rev.* 293 (1992). The author defines categorization and balancing and their application to cases.

13. In the *Denver Area* case, discussed infra, the Court did *not* apply strict scrutiny to a content-based regulation of cable speech. However, that is because a majority of the Court did not apply categorical rules at all, and instead applied a balancing test.

14. United States v. O'Brien, 391 U.S. 367 (1968).

15. Id. at 382.

16. Seid, "A Requiem for *O'Brien*: On the Nature of Symbolic Speech," 23 *Cumb. L. Rev.* 563, 603, 606 (1992–93).

17. Central Hudson Gas & Elec. Corp. v. Public Serv. Comm'n, 447 U.S. 557, 566 (1980).

18. Nutt, "Trends in First Amendment Protection of Commercial Speech," 41 *Vand. L. Rev.* 173, 178 (1988).

19. "The Supreme Court, 1992 Term-Leading Cases," 107 *Harv. L. Rev.* 224, 225 (1993).

20. Henshaw, "*Denver Area Educational Telecommunications Consortium, Inc. v. FCC*: Reconciling Traditional First Amendment Media Jurisprudence With Emerging Communications Technologies," 41 *St. Louis U. L.J.* 1015, 1019–22 (1997).

21. Murphy, "Can the Budweiser Frogs Be Forced to Sing a New Tune?: Compelled Commercial Counter-Speech and the First Amendment," 84 *Va. L. Rev.* 1195, 1216 (1998).

22. Denver Area Educ. Telecommunications Consortium, Inc. v. FCC, 518 U.S. 727 (1996). The Court held that Congress could constitutionally permit cable operators to censor indecent speech on leased access cable channels but held that Congress could not constitutionally permit cable operators to censor indecent speech on public access channels and could not constitutionally require cable operators to segregate and block indecent speech unless the cable subscriber affirmatively requested access to that speech.

23. Tobenkin, "The Supreme Court's Non-Decision and the Need for a New Media Speaker Paradigm," 7 *S. Cal. Interdisc. L.J.* 205, 206 (1998).

24. See also Turner Broadcasting System, Inc. v. FCC, 512 U.S. 622 (1994).

25. The weight the majority gave to the First Amendment interests of viewers, even compared with the First Amendment interests of cable operators, suggests that a careful balancing of the rights of both the press and would-be listeners, may outweigh many of the interests states have relied on to restrict news gathering activity.

4

THE REHNQUIST COURT AND THE SEARCH FOR EQUAL JUSTICE

J. HARVIE WILKINSON III

The Supreme Court's struggles with racial division in the United States are subject to a special form of judgment. The verdict on the Court's work in the area of race will not be pronounced by an academic circle of court watchers, or by the legal profession at large, or even by the broader audience of public opinion. The Court in the area of race will almost assuredly be judged by history. Future generations of Americans will want to know whether the Rehnquist Court got the big questions right.

Was the Rehnquist Court right on race or was it wrong? It seems on the surface an oversimplified question, much too crude for the subtle and sophisticated dissection we generally give the Court's work. And yet the Justices themselves must be acutely aware that race has played so large and so tragic a role in American history that the efforts of each generation of jurists to deal with it will in the end warrant the broadest and most sober measure of historical judgment.

Most of us today are not interested in the doctrinal progressions of *Dred Scott v. Sandford*[1] or *Plessy v. Ferguson*.[2] We only know at this point in time that the Supreme Court got those two cases terribly wrong and that *Brown v. Board of Education*[3] was supremely right.

Before passing judgment, however, we must first ask exactly what the Rehnquist Court has done in the area of race relations. The first part of this chapter describes the guiding principle of racial justice that has emerged from the Rehnquist Court. I then proceed to ask why that time-honored principle has proved so controversial in present-day debates. Finally, I address whether the Rehnquist Court's chapter in the story of race relations in the United States is likely to prove a lasting one. Will it continue to hold sway on the Court? Will it—should it—stand the test of time?

Evolution of the Nondiscrimination Principle

The guiding principle of the Rehnquist Court's race cases has been the nondiscrimination principle. All racial classifications, no matter which race is burdened or benefited, are presumptively unconstitutional. All must be subject to the most searching scrutiny. This principle emerged only during the Rehnquist Court. Previously, the Court drew distinctions among race-based remedies, approving some as "benign," "remedial," or even "necessary," while striking down others. Although the Burger Court set in motion a tentative retreat from the excesses of past race-based policies, it is the Rehnquist Court that will be remembered for first developing a unitary nondiscrimination principle, applicable to all governmental racial classifications.

The Court's modern race jurisprudence can be traced through three phases. The first stretches roughly from the 1968 decision of *Green v. County School Board*[4] decision to the 1980 decision of *Fullilove v. Klutznick*.[5] The Court's impatience with southern school desegregation efforts during the decade of the 1960s led it to approve race-based remedies. In these decisions, the Court measured progress toward racial equality through the use of numerical racial benchmarks.[6]

The second phase was marked by cases such as *Firefighters Local Union No. 1784 v. Stotts* (1984)[7] and *Wygant v. Jackson Board of Education* (1986).[8] With these decisions, the Court began a qualified retreat from its past approval of race-based remedies. It limited the use of racial preferences by insisting on findings of identified discrimination practiced by the specific governmental unit utilizing racial classifications.

The third phase, which began in 1989 with the decision in *City of Richmond v. J.A. Croson Co.*,[9] marked the full emergence of the Rehnquist Court's nondiscrimination principle. During this current period, the Court has condemned all use of race, equating benign racial classifications with all other forms of discrimination.[10]

During the first phase of the Court's modern race jurisprudence, the approval of explicit race-based remedies was commonplace.[11] Frustrated by more than a decade of delay in the implementation of the *Brown II* mandate that school desegregation proceed with "all deliberate speed,"[12] the Court itself began to review desegregation remedies in southern states.[13] Race-neutral policies were marked by an absence of results and thus precipitated judicial orders for race-based remedies. In *Green v. County School Board* (1968),[14] the Court considered just such a race-neutral "freedom of choice" plan.[15]

New Kent County, Virginia permitted any student in the county to choose which of the county's two schools to attend.[16] The Court rejected that remedy, paying close attention to the numbers.[17] It observed that under New Kent's plan, 85 percent of the county's black children and no white children attended the previously all-black school.[18] The statistics emboldened the Court to hold that affirmative, race-conscious action was necessary to achieve any meaningful amount of integration.[19]

Following the lead established by the *Green* decision, the Court actively endorsed the remedial use of race. In *North Carolina State Board of Education v. Swann* (1971),[20] the Court again faced a statute constructed in a race-neutral fashion: no student could be assigned to a school because of that student's race.[21] The Court rejected the statute and called for a specific race-based response:

> [T]he statute exploits an apparently neutral form to control school assignment plans by directing that they be "color blind"; that requirement, against the back-

ground of segregation, would render illusory the promise of *Brown v. Board of Education*. Just as the race of students must be considered in determining whether a constitutional violation has occurred, so also must race be considered in formulating a remedy.[22]

In fact, the Court in this period approved trial court desegregation remedies which relied heavily on racial numbers. For example, in *Swann v. Charlotte-Mecklenburg Board of Education* (1971),[23] the district court judge required the defendant school board to undertake efforts to achieve a seventy-one to twenty-nine ratio of white-to-black children in the individual schools, a ratio reflective of the white and black student populations.[24] The Court held the use of "mathematical ratios" to be a "useful starting point in shaping a remedy to correct past constitutional violations."[25]

Although the modern movement toward affirmative action programs arose from this impatience with school desegregation in the South, the Court extended its attachment to numbers beyond that limited context. In *Griggs v. Duke Power Co.* (1971),[26] the Court found that testing devices used by private employers would most often be declared unlawful when they resulted in a numerical disparity among the races.[27] Only those tests that bore a demonstrable relationship to job performance would pass muster under Title VII of the 1964 Civil Rights Act.[28]

Race by numbers appeared in the Court's voting rights decisions too. In *United Jewish Organizations of Williamsburgh, Inc. v. Carey* (1977),[29] in separate opinions, the Court upheld the use of racial criteria in a New York legislative redistricting scheme.[30] Justice White explained in his plurality opinion that the use of "specific numerical quotas in establishing a certain number of black majority districts" did not violate the Equal Protection Clause.[31] "[T]he creation of substantial nonwhite majorities in approximately 30% of the senate and assembly districts in Kings County was reasonably related to the constitutionally valid statutory mandate of maintaining nonwhite voting strength."[32]

In the next term, in a decision that shaped the future of higher education in this country, the Court countenanced the use of race as a criterion for admissions decisions. In *Regents of the University of California v. Bakke* (1978),[33] the Court— again in a series of separate opinions—found unlawful a racial quota system. Yet the *Bakke* decision is perhaps best remembered for its holding, as expressed in Justice Powell's decisive opinion, that race could be considered a plus factor by a university seeking to achieve diversity within its student body.[34]

Justice Brennan, writing for four of the five Justices who comprised the majority on this second aspect of the Court's holding, wrote:

> [T]his should not and must not mask the central meaning of today's opinions: Government may take race into account when it acts not to demean or insult any racial group, but to remedy disadvantages cast on minorities by past racial prejudice, at least when appropriate findings have been made by judicial, legislative, or administrative bodies with competence to act in this area.[35]

The separate opinions of the fractured Court in *Bakke* raised questions about the legality of numerical set-aside programs outside the realm of education. The Court's next decisions, regarding both private employment and public contracting, put such doubts to rest. In *United Steelworkers of America v. Weber* (1979),[36] the Court once again approved a numerically race-based remedy.[37] Specifically, the Court rejected a white steelworker's Title VII challenge to an employer's affirmative action plan which reserved 50 percent of the places in an in-plant craft-training program for blacks until such time as the percentage of black craft workers in the plant approximated the percentage of blacks in the local labor force.[38]

And the very next term, in *Fullilove v. Klutznick* (1980),[39] the Court approved a federal minority business enterprise (MBE) program requiring at least 10 percent of all federal funds for local public works to be used by grantees to procure goods or services from MBEs.[40] In a plurality opinion stressing the deference owed by the Court to Congress as a remedial actor, Chief Justice Burger wrote: "[W]e reject the contention that in the remedial context the Congress must act in a wholly 'color-blind' fashion."[41]

This early race-based jurisprudence was of course premised on the existence of a biracial society. The solutions approved in these cases were viewed as attempts to rectify centuries of injustices perpetrated against African Americans by white society. For example, in commenting on Title VII in the *Weber* decision, the Court noted:

> It would be ironic indeed if a law triggered by a Nation's concern over centuries of racial injustice and intended to improve the lot of those who had "been excluded from the American dream for so long," constituted the first legislative prohibition of all voluntary, private, race-conscious efforts to abolish traditional patterns of racial segregation and hierarchy.[42]

As such, the race-based actions of governments and private employers were seen as responses to the discrimination which manifested itself in each area of American society, whether it was the children's schools or the adult workplace. But as the Burger Court wound down, and perhaps because America faced a multiracial—rather than biracial—future, the Court began to rein in the excesses of the race-based solutions it had previously endorsed.

A common theme in the Court's second phase of modern race decisions was an insistence on proof of specific discrimination by the government institution involved as a prerequisite to any remedy drawn in racial terms.

For example, this principle surfaced in *Firefighters Local Union No. 1784 v. Stotts* (1984).[43] There, a consent decree had been entered in a class action Title VII suit that required the Memphis Fire Department to fill 50 percent of job vacancies with qualified black candidates.[44] No findings of actual discrimination on the part of the department or the city were made by the district court.[45] When city budget deficits forced the fire department to reduce staff through its neutral "last hired, first fired" policy, the district court enjoined layoffs because of their discriminatory effects.[46]

The Supreme Court, however, found the injunction to be an inappropriate exercise of the district court's power because the most recently hired black employees, protected from dismissal by the court's order, had never been proven to be victims of discrimination.[47] "[M]ere membership in the disadvantaged class is insufficient to warrant a seniority award; each individual must prove that the discriminatory practice had an impact on him."[48]

The Court in *Stotts*, however, grounded its decision in the limits on a district court's power to modify a consent decree.[49] It did not consider whether the voluntary adoption of a plan for race-based layoffs would be constitutional.[50]

The Court faced that question two years later in *Wygant v. Jackson Board of Education* (1986).[51] There, a Court majority, writing in separate opinions, held the race-based layoff policy unconstitutional.[52] The school board alleged that it had a legitimate interest in employing minority teachers to serve as role models for minority students.[53] Because this interest rested on societal discrimination, the plurality—in an opinion authored by Justice Powell—rejected it:

> No one doubts that there has been serious racial discrimination in this country. But as the basis for imposing discriminatory legal remedies that work against innocent people, societal discrimination is insufficient and over expansive. In the absence of particularized findings, a court could uphold remedies that are ageless in their reach into the past, and timeless in their ability to affect the future.[54]

Although the Court did not demand strict color-blindness in the laws, the nondiscrimination principle was beginning to take shape.[55]

This slowly developing principle, so often articulated in individual and plurality opinions, finally emerged with the blessing of a Court majority during Chief Justice Rehnquist's third term as the leader of the Court.[56]

The third phase of the Court's modern race jurisprudence began with *City of Richmond v. J.A. Croson Co.* (1989).[57] As in *Fullilove*, the Court again considered a minority set-aside public contracting program, but this time enacted by a city government.[58] The Court struck down the Richmond set-aside, and articulated several important elements of the nondiscrimination principle.[59]

First, all racial classifications must be examined under strict scrutiny, regardless of the race of the persons benefited or burdened by the program.[60]

Second, only particularized findings of identified discrimination can support a race-based, governmental remedy: "Like the 'role model' theory employed in *Wygant*, a generalized assertion that there has been past discrimination in an entire industry provides no guidance for a legislative body to determine the precise scope of the injury it seeks to remedy. It 'has no logical stopping point.'"[61]

Third, even when findings of identified discrimination provide a compelling remedial interest, government's "outright racial balancing" through a "rigid numerical quota" system cannot be deemed narrowly tailored to that interest.[62]

Despite the certainty with which the nondiscrimination principle was announced in *Croson*, it was immediately dealt a setback in the very next term. In *Metro Broadcasting, Inc. v. FCC* (1990),[63] the Court upheld two FCC minority preference policies. The Court reasoned that *Croson* could not control in this case because it involved a city program, not one approved by Congress.[64] Free from *Croson*'s constraints, the Court announced a demonstrably less rigorous standard of review:

> We hold that benign race-conscious measures mandated by Congress—even if those measures are not "remedial" in the sense of being designed to compensate victims of past governmental or societal discrimination—are constitutionally permissible to the extent that they serve important governmental objectives within

the power of Congress and are substantially related to achievement of those objectives.[65]

The Court also declared the correction of minority underrepresentation in broadcasting and the achievement of programming diversity to be important governmental objectives.[66] Understandably, the coexistence of *Croson* and *Metro Broadcasting* resulted in profound uncertainty for lower courts considering the constitutionality of race-based affirmative action programs.

Such doubt was finally dispelled, and the nondiscrimination principle announced in its clearest and strongest form, six years later in *Adarand Constructors, Inc. v. Pena* (1995).[67] There, the Court considered race-based presumptions in federal contract awards. The Court reiterated that the most searching standard of review would be applied to laws creating "benign"[68] as well as invidious distinctions.[69] It further held that the equal protection component of the Fifth Amendment—as applied to the federal government—requires nothing less than does the Equal Protection Clause of the Fourteenth Amendment—as applied to the states.[70] The Court then announced that all racial classifications employed by any level of government are suspect: "[W]e hold today that *all* racial classifications, imposed by *whatever* federal, state, or local governmental actor, must be analyzed by a reviewing court under strict scrutiny."[71]

To the extent that *Metro Broadcasting* was inconsistent with such a holding, and to the extent *Fullilove* required that federal racial classifications be reviewed more indulgently, they were both overruled.[72]

Though the emergence of the nondiscrimination principle can best be discerned in the public contracting cases, the Rehnquist Court rejected racial classifications just as strongly in the voting rights context. The Court's decision in *Shaw v. Reno* (1993)[73] illustrates this point. There the Court considered a redrawn majority–minority congressional district of "dramatically irregular shape."[74] The three-judge district court in North Carolina had rejected petitioners' equal protection claim, holding that "majority–minority districts have an impermissibly discriminatory effect only when they unfairly dilute or cancel out white voting strength."[75]

The Supreme Court rejected that cramped reading of its precedent, holding that one may state a claim under the Equal Protection Clause by alleging that a reapportionment scheme is "so irrational on its face that it can be understood only as an effort to segregate voters into separate voting districts because of their race, and that the separation lacks sufficient justification."[76]

Moreover, the Court held that such racial gerrymanders must be subject to strict scrutiny, even when the district lines were drawn to favor the minority.[77] The *Shaw* Court thus advanced the nondiscrimination principle by recognizing that racial segregation of voters is a pernicious act in itself, independent of any diluting effects the practice might have.

Since *Shaw*, the Rehnquist Court has only strengthened its resolve in the face of obvious racial gerrymandering. In *Miller v. Johnson* (1995),[78] the Court rejected as unconstitutional a Georgia congressional district that was redrawn with race as the predominant motivating factor.[79] The Court reaffirmed that the assignment of voters on the basis of race must be subject to strict scrutiny and to the extent *United*

Jewish Organizations v. Carey dictated otherwise, it was no longer deemed control-ling.[80] One term later, the Court handed down *Shaw v. Hunt* (1996)[81] and *Bush v. Vera* (1996)[82] on the same day.

In *Shaw v. Hunt*, the Court considered the same serpentine North Carolina district that had been at the center of the earlier *Shaw v. Reno* decision.[83] It found the racially contrived district did not satisfy the requirements of strict scrutiny.[84] The Court, with Chief Justice Rehnquist writing, reminded state legislatures that there must be a specific finding of "identified discrimination" in order to show a compelling interest for a race-conscious remedy:

> A generalized assertion of past discrimination in a particular industry or region is not adequate because it "provides no guidance for a legislative body to determine the precise scope of the injury it seeks to remedy." Accordingly, an effort to allevi-ate the effects of societal discrimination is not a compelling interest.[85]

In *Bush v. Vera*, the Court, in a series of separate opinions, found several oddly shaped Texas voting districts to have been drawn with race as the predominant mo-tivating factor.[86]

Applying strict scrutiny, the Court once again struck down the racial gerryman-der as unconstitutional. In her plurality opinion, Justice O'Connor pointedly re-jected a view of American voters as "mere racial statistics."[87]

Bush v. Vera underscores problems the Rehnquist Court might have envi-sioned with race-based remedies in a multicultural society. The challenged Texas districts reflected racial gerrymandering in extreme detail. Each racial subgroup sought a voice for itself and refused to accept the challenge of coalition building outside its own group. Indeed the state's own Voting Rights Act proposal had noted that the black community felt it "was necessary to assure its ability to elect its own Congressional representative *without having to form coalitions with other minority groups*."[88]

In two of the other three districts at issue, the Court observed that the highly ir-regular district lines were drawn so as to separate "Hispanic voters from African-American voters on a block-by-block basis[.]"[89] Apparently, party leaders had agreed to create a safe Hispanic seat while at the same time preserving an adjacent safe African-American seat.[90] Undoubtedly, the Court feared the effects of such racial division in our nation's multicultural politics: "Our Fourteenth Amendment jurisprudence evinces a commitment to eliminate unnecessary and excessive gov-ernmental use and reinforcement of racial stereotypes. We decline to retreat from that commitment today."[91]

Yet another area in which the Rehnquist Court forcefully applied the nondis-crimination principle involved the exercise of peremptory challenges of jurors. *Bat-son v. Kentucky* (1986),[92] decided in the last term of the Burger Court, held that a criminal defendant could lodge an equal protection challenge to the prosecution's use of peremptory challenges to dismiss potential jurors on the basis of their race.[93] In three decisions, the Rehnquist Court expanded the equal protection principle.

First, in *Powers v. Ohio* (1991),[94] the Court held that a criminal defendant may object to the race-based exclusion of jurors regardless of whether he or she is a member of the same race as the excluded jurors.[95] Then, also in 1991 in *Edmon-*

son v. *Leesville Concrete Co.*,[96] the Court extended *Batson* beyond the criminal context.[97]

Edmondson held that the Equal Protection Clause also forbids private litigants in civil cases from using peremptory challenges to exclude jurors on account of race.[98] And finally, in *Georgia v. McCollum* (1992),[99] the Court held that the Equal Protection Clause precludes not only the state but also a criminal defendant from exercising peremptory challenges on the basis of race.[100]

In these cases, the party defending its peremptory juror strikes often argued that the challenges were necessary in order to purge racial animus from the jury pool. The Court's response to this argument in *Edmonson* was typical:

> [I]f race stereotypes are the price for acceptance of a jury panel as fair, the price is too high to meet the standard of the Constitution. Other means exist for litigants to satisfy themselves of a jury's impartiality without using skin color as a test. If our society is to continue to progress as a multiracial democracy, it must recognize that the automatic invocation of race stereotypes retards that progress and causes continued hurt and injury.[101]

By expanding the *Batson* principle beyond the criminal context and beyond those cases in which the defendant shares the same race as the excluded jurors, the Court recognized the universal harm of racial discrimination in the jury selection process and condemned all forms equally.[102]

As the Rehnquist Court applied the nondiscrimination principle in the juror selection context to expand *Batson's* reach, it was willing to read Title VII of the 1964 Civil Rights Act aggressively so as to expand its coverage. In the 1970s, with the decisions in *Griggs* and *Weber*, the Burger Court had interpreted Title VII forcefully to encourage race by the numbers. But the Rehnquist Court occasionally read Title VII to allow more plaintiffs to vindicate their interests in the nondiscrimination principle.[103]

Before *Robinson v. Shell Oil Co.* (1997),[104] it was anything but clear that a former employee would be covered by Title VII. However, in *Robinson* the Rehnquist Court held exactly that, thereby expanding to former employees the reach of the nondiscrimination principle embodied in Title VII's language.[105]

The Rehnquist Court's embrace of the nondiscrimination principle was not limited to race. First, in *Romer v. Evans* (1996),[106] the Court invalidated an amendment to the Colorado Constitution, achieved via a statewide referendum, that "prohibit[ed] all legislative, executive or judicial action at any level of state or local government designed to protect homosexual persons."[107] The nondiscrimination principle existed to prevent singling out "homosexuals, but no others,"[108] from the protection of the laws.[109]

Invoking Justice Harlan's admonition from his *Plessy* dissent that the Constitution "neither knows nor tolerates classes among citizens,"[110] the Court found the Colorado amendment unsupported by any rational basis.[111] The amendment was, in the words of Justice Kennedy, "inexplicable by anything but animus toward the class that it affects."[112]

The strength of the nondiscrimination principle outside the race context was again evident in *United States v. Virginia* (1996).[113] There, the Court required the venerable Virginia Military Institute (VMI) to admit women to its ranks.[114] It was the purpose of the nondiscrimination principle to sweep away stereotypical class assumptions, in this case that women were unfit for the rigors of military education.[115]

The Court was unpersuaded by Virginia's arguments in favor of the single-sex institution, especially the belief that admission of women would compromise the "adversative" training method practiced at VMI for years. Justice Ginsburg wrote: "Surely that goal [of producing citizen-soldiers] is great enough to accommodate women, who today count as citizens in our American democracy equal in stature to men."[116] In both *Romer* and *Virginia*, the Court addressed the distinctions as simple forms of discrimination indefensible under the Constitution's equal protection mandate.[117]

As this history shows, the emergence of the nondiscrimination principle in the Court's race jurisprudence was anything but certain. Initially a majority approved of—and now a strong and tenacious minority holds out for—the use of race-based preferences to remedy our nation's shameful history of discrimination. But the lesson the Rehnquist Court took from this history was clear: Race must have no place in public life. And if government does use race, it must have a powerful reason to do so in order to satisfy the requirements of our Constitution.

This principle developed only through the most closely divided decisions. It occupies, therefore, a potentially transitory position in American law. It is yet uncertain whether the Rehnquist Court's triumph will be of a permanent nature or only an interlude between Courts allowing for a race-based United States.

Democracy and the Nondiscrimination Principle

Why did the nondiscrimination principle prove so controversial? It was, after all, a standard that Congress had fashioned in the Civil Rights Act of 1964,[118] and one that appeared to have won broad acceptance in American life. And yet, as we have seen, the attempts to invoke it provided some of the most divisive battles on the Rehnquist Court. Interestingly, Justices of all persuasions took issue with it. In the contract set-aside and voting rights cases, it was the more liberal Justices who protested the application of the nondiscrimination principle.[119] And in the decisions on peremptory jury strikes and those on women's and gay rights, it was the conservative Justices who raised their voices in dissent.

I believe the controversy over the nondiscrimination principle can be traced to one overriding concern. When a Rehnquist Court majority invoked the principle, it did so in an activist fashion. The principle of race neutrality (or of sexual equality) was generally summoned to strike down the enactments of the democratic branches of government. Whether it was a city council ordinance as in *J.A. Croson Co.*[120] or a legislative redistricting plan as in *Miller v. Johnson*,[121] or a statewide referendum as in *Romer v. Evans*,[122] the Court served notice that the exercise of popular sovereignty would not protect discriminatory acts.

The dissenters on the Rehnquist Court thus donned the mantle of judicial self-restraint. The dissenters in *Romer* protested that the Court majority was choosing sides in the culture wars of politics, that it was invalidating even the "modest attempt by seemingly tolerant Coloradans to preserve traditional sexual mores"[123] by enacting an amendment to their state's constitution.[124]

Dissenters in the voting rights cases complained of the Court majority's intrusion into the intensely political exercise of legislative redistricting. "I am certain only," wrote Justice Stevens in *Bush v. Vera,* "that bodies of elected federal and state officials are in a far better position than anyone on this Court to assess whether the Nation's long history of discrimination has been overcome. . . ."[125] Also, the dissenters in *Croson* complained that the Court would not even allow elected bodies the leeway to redress America's history of racial injustice.[126] "The majority's unnecessary pronouncements," Justice Marshall lamented, "will inevitably discourage or prevent governmental entities, particularly [s]tates and localities, from acting to rectify the scourge of past discrimination."[127]

The Rehnquist Court thus invoked the powerful constitutional principle of nondiscrimination to override the normal dictates of federalism and of judicial self-restraint. The question that its record on race poses is a stark one: Should the states and the democratic branches of the federal government be allowed to experiment with race-based (or sex-based) solutions to social problems?

The Rehnquist Court majority rather regularly answered this question: "No." This supposedly conservative Court turned suddenly activist when the popular branches of government sought to draw invidious distinctions. Sometimes the discrimination was alleged to be benign, as with race-based affirmative action programs.[128] Sometimes it was said to be justified by federal statutes such as the Voting Rights Act.[129] Sometimes the discrimination was alleged to be blessed by tradition, as with VMI's long history of all-male military training.[130] And sometimes it was said to represent the voice of the people themselves, as in Colorado's statewide referendum on gay rights.[131] None of this mattered to the Rehnquist Court. Discrimination was discrimination, and even popular majorities had no right to practice it.

The Rehnquist Court's judicial activism in support of the nondiscrimination principle stands in contrast to the Burger Court's more passive stance. On occasion, as in *United Steelworkers of America v. Weber,*[132] the Burger Court exercised restraint with respect to racial goals set by the private sector. The Burger Court also practiced restraint, however, with respect to racial preferences adopted by the democratic branches of government. Its decision in *Fullilove v. Klutznick*[133] represented, perhaps, the apogee of judicial restraint in the face of race-based government action. In his plurality opinion, Chief Justice Burger continually returned to a theme of "appropriate deference"[134] to Congress: "It is fundamental that in no organ of government, state or federal, does there repose a more comprehensive remedial power than in the Congress, expressly charged by the Constitution with competence and authority to enforce equal protection guarantees."[135]

Although the pattern is not altogether clear-cut,[136] the Burger Court was more apt than the Rehnquist Court to invoke traditional maxims of judicial restraint to uphold the exercise of race-based action.

The question is whether the Rehnquist Court's activism on behalf of the nondiscrimination principle was justifiable. On the one hand, it will be argued that racial justice is the most combustible issue in all of American politics and that its very volatility suggests that the Court should leave it alone. Democracy is generally better suited to handling hot potatoes than the courts because it allows the fullest array of citizens and viewpoints to be heard and because it is more adept at acts of compromise.

Thus, the argument runs, the profound differences on race in the United States should be resolved in the political arena. Whether race-based remedies are necessary to redress the tragic errors of American history or whether they represent only the newest form of an old iniquity is said to be the essential political question.

Was it even necessary for the Rehnquist Court to intervene on behalf of color-blindness? There was no shortage of political proposals to curb affirmative action. In 1995, sponsors in the House and Senate introduced the Equal Opportunity Act,[137] a bill which prohibited the intentional discrimination or granting of preferences on the basis of race, color, national origin, or sex with respect to federal contracting, employment, or other programs.[138] This legislation was reintroduced in virtually the same form as the Civil Rights Act of 1997.[139]

The most celebrated effort to curtail racial preferences—the California Civil Rights Initiative of 1996 (CCRI)[140]—won 54 percent of the statewide vote. Shortly after that vote, federal district judge Thelton Henderson (N.D. Cal.) invalidated the referendum on the grounds that the CCRI violated both the Equal Protection Clause's guarantee of equal access to the political process and the Supremacy Clause because the CCRI was preempted by Title VII of the Civil Rights Act of 1964.[141] The decision, later reversed on appeal,[142] was widely decried as judicial activism at the time: "A system which permits one judge to block with the stroke of a pen what 4,736,180 state residents voted to enact as law tests the integrity of our constitutional democracy."[143]

A troubling question remains, however: If Judge Henderson's efforts to preserve affirmative action from the political sword were judicial activism, then what of the Rehnquist Court's efforts to end it?

There is a strong argument that the Rehnquist Court should have stayed its hand and allowed the political process to play itself out. History has not been kind to conservative interventionism as the assessments of the Court's *Lochner* and anti-New Deal eras amply attest. In intervening on behalf of the nondiscrimination principle, the Rehnquist Court majority took an enormous historical risk. Future historians might conclude that in restricting racial preferences the Court blocked yet again the efforts of African Americans and other minorities to enter not only the ranks of the learned professions but also the mainstream of American life.

Such fears recurred when the Fifth Circuit, acting in the case of *Hopwood v. Texas*,[144] pushed the Supreme Court's color-blind principle to its limits and helped precipitate a dramatic drop in minority enrollments in several of the nation's most prestigious law schools.[145] At the University of Texas School of Law, only ten black students were admitted for the 1997–98 academic year, compared to sixty-five in the year before.[146] Similar drops occurred in the University of California law schools, where a Board of Regents resolution ending racial and gender preferences took effect.[147] Admissions of black students dropped from 104 to twenty-one at the UCLA School of Law and from seventy-five to fourteen at UC Berkeley.[148] One Berkeley law professor was quoted as saying, "It's so stunning it's almost unbelievable. . . . What do we think? The leading public university in the most diverse state and the most diverse educational system is going to just withdraw behind some siege wall and be a white institution? It's preposterous."[149]

It is not clear, however, that the judgment on the Rehnquist Court should rest on the short-term movement of racial statistics. Notwithstanding the force of the argument against judicial activism on affirmative action, I believe the Rehnquist Court was correct and courageous to pursue the course it did. The case for intervention cannot be clinched in terms of the framers' original intent or in the intimative language of the Fifth and Fourteenth Amendments. Rather, the legitimacy of the Rehnquist Court's course rests on the Court's own precedent, the *Brown* decision itself.

Brown stood for something so simple and so luminous that it will shine forever—namely, the principle that public bodies may not draw distinctions based on race. If we are human beings in the sight of God and American citizens in the eyes of the law, then lines drawn on race should have no place. It was just such lines, of course, that *Brown* condemned. That decision is not just another "precedent." Rather, like *Marbury v. Madison*,[150] it has become a constitutional principle in itself, as basic to American life as amber waves of grain.

It may be forlorn to hope that race can be purged from a society whose psyche it has permeated for so long. In myriad informal ways, public decision makers will, with the best and worst of intentions, take race into account. But should the law sanction and encourage such a course? Of course not. Without the law as a rein on race-based decisions, the use of race will proceed at a gallop. And without law as a break, citizens will resort to race-based rhetoric with alacrity, plunging public discourse into a toxic state. The fact that race may be a natural venom is not an argument for preferences. Rather, it is all the more reason for courts to stand vigilant against the use of it.

The Rehnquist Court thus rightly sensed that the ecumenical standard of citizenship must remain the ideal. The fact that the ideal of race neutrality may remain imperfectly achieved hardly means that the United States abandons the quest. To its credit, the Rehnquist Court did not retire while the country organized its political life, its educational institutions, its public entitlements, and its employment practices along racial lines.

A course of constitutional inaction would have done much to ensure that race remained embedded as the foundation of American life. With *Brown*, the Warren Court took the lead in dismantling discrimination. Whether Congress would have summoned the courage to act without the Court's example remains a matter of much doubt. Similarly, with such cases as *Croson* and *Adarand*, the Rehnquist Court emboldened those who sought to embody the nondiscrimination principle through referendum or in legislation. Without the Court's constitutional example, the political process might once again have lost heart.

It is useful at this point to examine the character of the civil rights litigation reaching the Rehnquist Court. It is a matter of no small moment that *Brown* was a southern case. For the South had a more intimate acquaintance with a society organized along racial lines than any other region. Those segregated street cars, schools, and water fountains defied the American dream in every sense.

More than three decades after the *Brown* decision, many of the civil rights cases reaching the Rehnquist Court continued to come from the South.[151] In part, this was attributable to the fact that Section 5 of the Voting Rights Act[152] covers primarily southern states and their political subdivisions. Thus, major cases pertaining to congressional and state legislative redistricting came from Florida,[153] Georgia,[154] North Carolina,[155] and Texas.[156] In these cases, plaintiffs often claimed that districts were unconstitutionally drawn on the basis of race while the governmental entities defending them protested that the Department of Justice refused to approve anything but plans which created racially safe seats.[157] The voting rights cases were not the only ones to emerge from the South. Other decisions, such as *Croson*, reflected the region's continuing efforts to come to terms with its history of racial discrimination, while still others, such as *United States v. Virginia*, reflected the region's more traditional outlook on sexual mores.

By the time of the Rehnquist Court, the South's struggle with issues of race was hardly unique. Yet how one sees the southern experience is important in how one views the Rehnquist Court and race. One lesson people draw from those bleak days of southern segregation is that we must spend our national life atoning for the wrongs of the past and remediating its effects.

Under this view, as Justice Marshall argued, the debt to the oppressionist past remains an unpaid one:

> [R]acial classifications drawn for the purpose of remedying the effects of discrimination that itself was race based have a highly pertinent basis: the tragic and indelible fact that discrimination against blacks and other racial minorities in this Nation has pervaded our Nation's history and continues to scar our society.[158]

One can respect this view, but it is assuredly not the view the Rehnquist Court took of the southern experience. Its view drew more on the inherent evils of race as an organizing legal principle. The tragedy of southern life was that race demeaned everyone—those who took advantage of segregated arrangements as well as those who were the victims of them. Racial segregation threatened to suffocate all the better angels of our nature—our need for personal freedom, individual opportunity, and a communal life based on mutual regard and respect.

The movement to race-based preferences threatened to recreate this whole dismal state of affairs. It promised to resurrect the worst instincts of the Old South. The Rehnquist Court moved to prevent the United States from coming full circle, from returning to race as its organizing principle. It understood better than most that race as an element of public life would bring great rancor and little respite: "The dangers of such [racial] classifications are clear," wrote Justice O'Connor. "They endorse race-based reasoning and the conception of a Nation divided into racial blocs, thus contributing to an escalation of racial hostility and conflict."[159] The evils of the race-based regime—the injustices to those rejected, the stigmatization of those preferred, and the dehumanization of both the favored and the scorned—would not be permitted to recur.

The Rehnquist Court thus declined to permit this historic instrument of demagoguery and division to chart a course for twenty-first-century America. For the Rehnquist Court, the southern past did not speak principally of guilt and reparation. Rather, it laid bare the dangers of a race-based regime.

Many of the race cases that came before to the Rehnquist Court not only bore a southern stamp. They tended, more often than not, to arise in the familiar context of black–white relations. To be sure, the occasional case would evidence emerging friction between African Americans and other racial or ethnic minorities. For example, in *Johnson v. DeGrandy*,[160] the Court considered the competing efforts of black and Hispanic voters to maximize the electoral districts each group controlled in Dade County, Florida.

Similarly, the voting districts at issue in *Bush v. Vera* were drawn specifically to avoid competition between, and thereby guarantee safe seats for, black and Hispanic candidates. But by and large, the Rehnquist Court plaintiffs were African Americans alleging employment discrimination,[161] contesting the adequacy of school desegregation remedies,[162] and seeking representation in Congress and state legislatures, or on civil juries.

Or, as in *Taxman v. Board of Education*[163] and *Shaw v. Reno*,[164] the plaintiffs were whites challenging remedial employment preferences or majority–minority districts created for blacks. Either way, the battleground tended to feature the traditional combatants of the biracial United States. If one were to look only at the Supreme Court cases, one would be led to believe that racial tension in the United States remained predominantly a matter of black and white. That impression, however, ignores the dazzling demographic changes taking place in the United States during the time of the Rehnquist Court.

The Nondiscrimination Principle and New America

New America is emerging as we speak. According to the Census Bureau, the foreign-born population—most recently estimated at 9.3 percent of the total population—is at its highest level since the 1930s.[165] More than one-quarter of this segment hails from one country—Mexico—whereas another quarter comes to the United States from Asia.[166]

In addition to Mexico, members of foreign-born populations most often claim the Philippines, China, Cuba, and India as their birthplace.[167] Surging immigration helps explain this phenomenon. The Immigration and Naturalization Service reports that legal immigration to the United States increased by 27 percent from 1995 to 1996, with most new immigrants being Latin American or Asian arrivals.[168] "We've never had this kind of diversity before, and neither has anybody else," comments Loyola University sociologist Philip Nyden.[169]

New America will only become more diverse. The Census Bureau projects that the non-Hispanic white population will be only a bare majority in 2050, and that the United States will have no racial or ethnic majority sometime thereafter.[170] Already, Hawaii and New Mexico do not have either a racial or ethnic majority, and California should follow suit by the year 2000.[171] By 2010, the Hispanic population, projected to be 13.8 percent of the total population, is expected to outnumber the black population, which is projected to be 13.5 percent.[172]

New America's diversity is recognizable outside the statistics too. Former President Clinton noted that five school districts in the United States each serves more than 100 racial and ethnic groups.[173] Detroit holds an annual Latino film festival and Seattle enjoys a Latino literary scene.[174] Houston, which has experienced substantial growth in its Asian-American population, is experiencing "a profusion of mini-Chinatowns."[175] In addition to its two older Chinatowns, the Texas city now has a "booming" Vietnam town, a Korean town, and a growing Cambodian community.[176]

The diversity in the United States is not restricted to the major metropolises. The Hispanic population of Durham, North Carolina, has grown from a few thousand to approximately 12,000 persons in the past year.[177] There is a significant Hispanic work force in Omaha, Nebraska; Garden City, Kansas; and Arkansas.[178] America's multicultural status is visible from sea to shining sea.

The question, of course, is what direction this new multicultural country will take. Immigration adds vitality and variety to the United States, as it always has. It is possible that New America will become a land of unprecedented economic power and cultural diversity, a mighty universal nation that the world has not heretofore seen. But there is another scenario. One-third of the new immigrants lack a high school diploma, many do not speak English, and many reject the idea of assimilation as a call for "Anglo conformity."[179]

Thus, writes William Booth in the *Washington Post*, "the neighborhoods where Americans live, the politicians and propositions they vote for, the cultures they immerse themselves in, the friends and spouses they have, the churches and schools they attend, and the way they view themselves are defined by ethnicity."[180] If diversity could make this a true land of destiny, we could also be witnessing what one scholar terms the "twilight of common dreams."[181]

There is a curious disconnect between the rapid changes in the country and the docket of the Rehnquist Court. The odd thing is that the cases themselves often did not deal much with this emerging New America. The settings were quite frequently traditional, both in their regional flavor and in their bipolar racial perspectives. The debates on the Court itself seldom ventured onto the multicultural terrain or discussed the problems posed by unprecedented racial and ethnic diversity in New America. It is fair at least to ask whether the Court was caught in a sort of time warp, where civil rights issues remained frozen in the tableau of that greatest of civil rights eras, the decade of the 1960s.

Herein lies the irony. It matters not that the Rehnquist Court failed to explore multiculturalism extensively in its decisions. It is not even critical that the Court declined to ask how the emergence of a New America should affect the law of civil rights. Without ever really plumbing these questions, the Rehnquist Court embraced the proper principle to guide a multiracial nation.

If the United States was a changed nation, the principle itself was changeless— as timeless as Justice John Marshall Harlan's reminder that "Our Constitution is color-blind, and neither knows nor tolerates classes among citizens."[182] That exhortation becomes more pertinent with the passage of time and the march of demographics. Indeed, it is inconceivable that a multiracial society could be constructed on anything other than transracial legal standards.

It is, in fact, the advent of American multiculturalism that will justify the course of the Rehnquist Court in the eyes of history. A race-based legal regime has even less to commend it in a multiracial nation than in a biracial society.

According to the 1990 census, roughly one-half of native-born twenty-five to thirty-four-year-old Asian Americans and two-fifths of Hispanics married spouses of a different racial or ethnic group.[183] To have government benefits or electoral districts or school admissions or employment practices all turn on someone's race will therefore present decision makers with a formidable classification problem.

To devote prodigious efforts to devising the correct racial categorizations of American citizens is about as divisive an enterprise as it is possible to imagine. The new specialty of racial science would have many an odious historical pedigree. Whether an American citizen is two-fifths this or three-fourths that ought to be in the eyes of law a matter of supreme irrelevance. The more diverse the United States becomes, the more compelling the color-blind ideal remains.

The problems multiculturalism poses for race-based regimes do not end there. The Voting Rights Act has been read by the Department of Justice to require "[s]tates to create majority–minority districts wherever possible"[184] (a majority–minority district being one in which there is at least a majority of minority voters). In a biracial political order, determining what constitutes a majority–minority district poses no special difficulty. In a multicultural society, the task can become quite complex. For example, must the minority voters in a majority–minority district all be of one minority? Or may we combine compatible minority interests for that purpose? How then do we determine which minority interests are compatible (and subject to combination) and which are antithetical?

And just how broad is the definition of a minority interest supposed to be? May we lump all Hispanic Americans together as a single minority interest or must we recognize the different characteristics of the Mexican American, Cuban American, and Puerto Rican American communities? State legislatures can hardly be expected to know the answers to all these questions, and when courts try to provide them, no end of racial animosity will result.

Having the politics of New America run by such legal requirements of race guarantees our country a future of racial fragmentation. Surely the Rehnquist Court was correct to criticize the insistence of the Department of Justice on majority–minority voting districts and to reject the use of race as a predominant factor in redistricting.[185]

Similarly, the administration of an affirmative action plan becomes more problematic within a multicultural setting. In the biracial context, whites had discriminated and blacks had been discriminated against. In our multicultural society, many racial or ethnic groups can lay claim to being victimized in the past, underrepresented in the present, or simply dispossessed.

Although African Americans have experienced more discrimination than have other groups, it is difficult to premise group preferences on such matters of degree. Latinos and Asian Americans have their own grievances in this regard. Latinos still face widespread discrimination in areas such as employment, housing, and education. "[M]ost Hispanics know—even if they have not experienced discrimination personally—that discrimination in this country is not dead. Its roots run as deep as the oil in Texas, and the legacy of discrimination still taints the lives of many Hispanics."[186]

Asian Americans can point to a history of state-sponsored discrimination.[187] And despite being labeled the "model minority," Asian Americans still suffer discrimination in terms of income, employment, and education.[188]

How social planners will juggle all these claims for racial recompense is anything but clear. The real problem, however, is that there are such stark differences within groups that affirmative action plans habitually lump into the same preference category. For example, there are wide disparities between poor and middle-class African Americans. The Latino population can be divided between different nationalities and between recent immigrants and families that have been in the United States for many generations. Asian Americans also can be divided into an American-born and an increasingly foreign-born segment that includes Chinese, Filipinos, Japanese, Indians, Koreans, and Vietnamese, among others.

One suspects, in fact, that the differences between individuals within the same racial group are as striking as the differences between individuals of different races. This being the case, an affirmative action plan cannot rest on the stereotypical assumption that members of a given racial or ethnic group in New America are, at least for purposes of preferences, the same.

In a multicultural setting, race becomes an impossible thicket. The Rehnquist Court thus typically expressed the ideal of race neutrality in an unqualified fashion. The strict scrutiny of racial classifications, it held, was "not dependent on the race of those burdened or benefited by a particular classification."[189] Rather, all races would be governed by a single legal standard. Should an exception to this simple and sweeping pronouncement have been made for African Americans? Should preferences for this one group be revived under a less rigorous Fourteenth Amendment standard? It was, after all, African Americans whose path the Court blocked in the *Dred Scott* and *Plessy* decisions. And the legacy of injustice to this particular minority lingers to this very day. Glenn Loury has noted:

> The race problem that deserves national attention concerns the bottom third of the black population, which is locked in ghettos at the center of our great cities and remains shut out from access to the engines of social mobility in our society. Consider that 42 percent of black children lived in poverty in 1995, a rate that has remained essentially unchanged for a quarter-century. And, while patterns of unwed childbearing among blacks are a principal cause of this depressing reality, the fact remains that a great many black youngsters never really have a chance to properly develop their God-given talents.[190]

Even conservative columnist Charles Krauthammer echoes that "opponents of affirmative action should not protest too loudly if the whole structure of preferences that has metastasized into mindless 'diversity' were dismantled and replaced with a simple single preference for the black underclass, the most bereft and isolated minority in America."[191]

So the great piece of unfinished racial business in the United States pertains to the plight of the black underclass. One can accept the full truth and burden of that statement without believing that the Rehnquist Court should have honored racial preferences for black citizens alone. The squalor of the ghetto or the barrio or the reservation merits our attention as a matter of the human predicament, not as a question of race. The creation of opportunity must be a matter of national pride, not of racial guilt.

Our moral obligations run to individuals, not to races. And our sense of patriotism encompasses all Americans who suffer the blight of hopelessness, be they white or brown or yellow or black. If in fact, the problems of poverty become no more than the problem of someone else's race, they will soon become the subject of indifference and neglect. The race of the nine-year-old child in the urban ghetto may be different than our own. But his citizenship and his humanity are the same. A legal standard based on race stresses only the differences among Americans. Solving our problems requires those in political life to celebrate the ways in which we are the same.

The dangers of singling out African Americans for special treatment would not end there. Even though an objective assessment might confirm that the degree of disadvantage among blacks and discrimination against blacks as a group to be unique, many individual black citizens have had great advantages in the United States and many nonblack citizens have suffered acute disadvantages and discrimination of their own. The greatest disservice, however, of a special equal protection standard would be to African Americans themselves. They would be marked as a group as special wards of the state. Their legitimate accomplishments would be wrongly tarnished by the widespread perception of special treatment. They would become objects of resentment from the rest of society, and the subject of stereotypical assumptions that would cause prejudice against them to endure.

The Rehnquist Court was right to avert this tragedy and to impose race neutrality in the law. "[A]ny person, of whatever race," wrote Justice O'Connor for the Court in *Adarand*, "has the right to demand that any governmental actor subject to the Constitution justify any racial classification subjecting that person to unequal treatment under the strictest judicial scrutiny."[192]

If the Rehnquist Court refused to qualify the color-blind ideal for African Americans, should it have varied the standard of review according to the context of a particular case? Are race-based preferences more justifiable, for example, in educational admissions than in employment? Should race-based discharges be subject to more rigorous scrutiny than race-based hiring on the theory that individuals depend more on the jobs they already have than on the ones they have yet to get? The possibility that public employers might seek to achieve racial diversity in hiring but not in firing was set to come before the Court in the celebrated case of *Taxman v. Board of Education*.[193] There, Sharon Taxman, a white teacher in Piscataway, New Jersey, was dismissed instead of Debra Williams, an equally qualified and equally tenured black teacher, when the school board decided to reduce its staff.[194] The board relied on its affirmative action policy and Williams's race in retaining her instead of Taxman.[195]

The purpose, however, of the race-based layoff was not to remedy past underrepresentation by blacks in Piscataway's teaching ranks but instead to achieve diversity in the teaching staff.[196] The Third Circuit found this nonremedial use of race to violate Title VII.[197]

Taxman became the Supreme Court case that never was. In November 1997, in a surprising move, the NAACP Legal Defense and Educational Fund and other civil rights groups helped finance the case's settlement before the Court could even hear argument.[198] The groups contributed approximately 70 percent of the $433,500 necessary to pay Taxman's back salary and legal costs.[199]

Two important lessons can be drawn from the manner in which the *Taxman* case was resolved. First, the message of the Rehnquist Court rang loud and clear across the land: Few doubted the Court would reject the Piscataway school board's use of racial preferences in the context of employee layoffs and many feared it would announce an even broader principle of race neutrality applicable to personnel and school admissions decisions alike.

A second lesson to be learned from the settlement is that the problem of race is a stubborn one; it cannot be solved by the Supreme Court alone. The *Taxman* case, although seemingly within reach of the Court, ultimately eluded it. And although the Supreme Court plays an important role in determining whether we will become a race-based society, the Court cannot chart our nation's path alone. Much will now depend on the actions of Congress and the response of the Executive Branch both as an employer and as a litigator. Much will also turn on the private sector itself, as admissions officers and corporate executives choose policies for selecting individuals to attend and represent their institutions. The truly relevant question thus becomes: What do we want as a nation?[200]

In the final analysis, the standard of race neutrality is not one that can be easily qualified. The law rightly views many questions as ones of nuance and degree, but the wrongness of using race as a means of measuring human beings cannot be winked away. How can courts say that it is permissible to use race in this area but not that? The poison of race, once admitted, will course through the veins of our national system.

The need to reject race as a legal yardstick stems in large part from its contagious nature. The racial explanation for events and the racial justification for actions is one that is all too readily available for every American.

To admit race in our public decisions is to gamble with our future as a nation. When our grandchildren celebrate the tricentennial, they will respect the Rehnquist Court for resisting the road to disunion.

Notes

1. 60 U.S. (19 How.) 393 (1857).
2. 163 U.S. 537 (1896).
3. 347 U.S. 483 (1954).
4. 391 U.S. 430 (1968).
5. 448 U.S. 448 (1980).
6. Id. at 456–92; *Green*, 391 U.S. at 438–41.
7. 467 U.S. 561 (1984).
8. 476 U.S. 267 (1986).
9. 488 U.S. 469 (1989).
10. Id. at 504–08.
11. Id. at 476–77.
12. Brown v. Board of Educ., 349 U.S. 294, 301 (1955).
13. *See* Greenberg, *Crusaders in the Courts: How a Dedicated Band of Lawyers Fought for the Civil Rights Revolution* 380–401 (1994); Wilkinson, *From Brown to Bakke: The Supreme Court and School Integration* 1954–1978, 78–127 (1979).
14. 391 U.S. 430 (1968).
15. Id. at 438–41.
16. Id. at 431–32.
17. Id. at 441.

18. See id.

19. Id. at 437–38.

20. 402 U.S. 43 (1971).

21. Id. at 44-45.

22. Id. at 45–46 (citation omitted); see also Swann v. Charlotte-Mecklenburg Bd. of Educ., 402 U.S. 1, 28 (1971) ("'Racially neutral' assignment plans proposed by school authorities to a district court may be inadequate; such plans may fail to counteract the continuing effects of past school segregation. . . .").

23. 402 U.S. 1 (1971).

24. Id. at 6, 23.

25. Id. at 25; see also *North Carolina State Bd. of Educ.*, 402 U.S. at 46 (explaining that "some ratios are likely to be useful starting points in shaping a remedy").

The Court, however, did not accord blind deference to the use of racial numbers in school desegregation remedies. For example, in Milliken v. Bradley, 418 U.S. 717 (1974), the Court rejected a district court remedy which was premised largely on the belief that "Detroit schools could not be truly segregated . . . unless the racial composition of the student body of each school substantially reflected the racial composition of the population of the metropolitan area as a whole." Id. at 740. The Court found the remedy to be overexpansive because it included numerous school districts for which no findings of de jure segregation, or even segregative effects, had ever been made. Thus, although the Court in *Swann* approved of the use of mathematical ratios, the *Milliken* decision was a reminder that desegregation "does not require any particular racial balance." Id.

26. 401 U.S. 424 (1971).

27. Id. at 436.

28. Id. at 435.

29. 430 U.S. 144 (1971).

30. Id. at 145.

31. Id. at 162 (White, J., plurality opinion).

32. Id. at 163 (White, J., plurality opinion).

33. 438 U.S. 265 (1978) (Powell, J., opinion of the Court).

34. Id. at 271–72 (opinion of Powell, J., announcing the judgment of the Court); id. at 317 (Powell, J., opinion of the Court).

35. Id. at 325. Justice Powell, who was the crucial fifth Justice comprising the majority on the second aspect of the Court's holding, wrote: "In enjoining petitioner from ever considering the race of any applicant, however, the courts below failed to recognize that the State has a substantial interest that legitimately may be served by a properly devised admissions program involving the competitive consideration of race and ethnic origin." Id. at 320.

36. 443 U.S. 193 (1979).

37. Id. at 200–08.

38. Id. at 197.

39. 448 U.S. 448 (1980).

40. Id. at 448, 492.

41. Id. at 482 (Burger, C.J., plurality opinion).

42. United Steelworkers, 443 U.S. at 204 (citation omitted).

43. 467 U.S. 561 (1984).

44. Id. at 566.

45. Id. at 567.

46. See id.

47. Id. at 579.

48. Id.

49. See id. at 587.

50. Id. at 583.

51. 476 U.S. 267 (1986).

52. See id.

53. See id. at 274.

54. Id. at 276 (Powell, J., plurality opinion).

55. See id. at 280–81 (Powell, J., plurality opinion); id. at 287 (opinion of O'Connor, J.).

56. Some early analyses of the Rehnquist Court's decisions in the area of race relations are in Fried, *Order and Law: Arguing the Reagan Revolution—A Firsthand Account* 89–131 (1991); Savage, *Turning Right: The Making of the Rehnquist Supreme Court* (1992); and Simon, *The Center Holds: The Power Struggle Inside the Rehnquist Court* 17–81 (1995). For a thoughtful review of the race discrimination cases of the Rehnquist Court's first five years, see Landsberg, Race and the Rehnquist Court, 66 Tul. L. Rev. 1267 (1992).

57. 488 U.S. 469 (1989).

58. Id. at 477.

59. Id. at 493–511.

60. Id. at 493–94 (O'Connor, J., joined by Rehnquist, C.J., White, and Kennedy, J. J., plurality opinion); id. at 520 (Scalia, J., concurring opinion).

61. Id. at 498 (opinion of the Court) (quoting *Wygant*, 476 U.S. 267, 275 (Powell, J., plurality opinion)).

62. Id. at 507–08 (opinion of the Court).

63. 497 U.S. 547 (1990).

64. See id. at 565–66.

65. Id. at 564–65.

66. See id. at 566.

67. 515 U.S. 200 (1995).

68. Id. at 225 (quoting *Metro*, 497 U.S. at 564).

69. See id. at 225–26.

70. See id. at 225–26, 235.

71. Id. at 227 (emphasis added); see id. at 224.

72. Id. at 227, 235.

73. 509 U.S. 630 (1993).

74. Id. at 633.

75. Id. at 638.

76. Id. at 658.

77. See id. at 650–51.

78. 515 U.S. 900 (1995).

79. See id.

80. See id. at 914–15.

81. 517 U.S. 899 (1996).

82. 517 U.S. 952 (1996).

83. See Hunt, supra note 81, at 901.

84. See id. at 906–07.

85. Id. at 909–10 (citations omitted).

86. See Bush v. Vera, 517 U.S. at 972–76 (O'Connor, J., plurality opinion); see id. at 996 (Kennedy, J., concurring); see id. at 999 (Kennedy, J., concurring).

87. Id. at 985 (O'Connor, J., plurality opinion).

88. Id. at 969 (O'Connor, J., plurality opinion) (emphasis added).

89. Id. at 975 (O'Connor, J., plurality opinion).

90. See id.

91. Id. at 985–86 (O'Connor, J., plurality opinion) (citations omitted).

92. 476 U.S. 79 (1986).

93. See id. at 96–98.

94. 499 U.S. 400 (1991). In 1998, the Court extended *Powers* to the grand jury context, holding that a white defendant had "standing to raise an equal protection challenge to discrimination against black persons in the selection of his grand jury." Campbell v. Louisiana, 523 U.S. 392, 400 (1998).

95. See Powers, 499 U.S. at 416.

96. 500 U.S. 614 (1991).

97. See id. at 631.

98. See id. at 628-29.

99. 505 U.S. 42 (1992).

100. See id. at 55.

101. *Edmonson*, 500 U.S. at 630–31.

102. The Court also extended the nondiscrimination principle in this area beyond the context of race. In J.E.B. v. Alabama ex rel. T.B., 511 U.S. 127 (1994), the Court held that "gender, like race, is an unconstitutional proxy for juror competence and impartiality." Id. at 129.

103. It should be noted that the Rehnquist Court also interpreted Title VII to counter directly the race-by-numbers results in Griggs v. Duke Power Co., 401 U.S. at 434, and United Steelworkers of America, 443 U.S. at 194. In Wards Cove Packing Co. v. Atonio, 490 U.S. 642 (1989), the Court held, inter alia, that a mere showing of racial imbalance in a work force is insufficient to make out a case of disparate impact. Plaintiffs must also demonstrate that a specific employment practice has created the disparate impact. See id. at 656–57. The decision also clarified the proper placement of burdens of proof in disparate impact cases and expanded the grounds for affirmative defenses. See id. at 658–60. These latter aspects of the *Wards Cove* opinion were overruled by the Civil Rights Act of 1991 §105, 42 U.S.C. § 2000e-2(k). Congress, however, appears to have accepted the portion of the Court's holding rejecting mere racial imbalance as insufficient proof of disparate impact. See 42 U.S.C. § 2000e-2(k) (1) (A) (i).

104. 519 U.S. 337 (1997).

105. Relying in part on Title VII precedents, the Court similarly expanded the reach of the Age Discrimination in Employment Act of 1967 (ADEA) in McKennon v. Nashville Banner Publishing Co., 513 U.S. 352 (1995). There, the Court held that an employee discharged in violation of ADEA is not barred from all relief when the employer subsequently discovers evidence of wrongdoing that would have led to the employee's discharge on lawful grounds. See id. at 356–57. And, in Bragdon v. Abbott, 524 U.S. 624 (1998), the Supreme Court confirmed the broad reach of the Americans with Disabilities Act of 1990, holding that infection with asymptomatic human immunodeficiency virus (HIV) constituted a disability under the Act. See id. at 655.

106. 517 U.S. 620 (1996).

107. Id. at 624.

108. Id. at 627.

109. See id. at 627–28.

110. Id. at 623 (quoting *Plessy v. Ferguson*, 163 U.S. 537, 559 (1896) (Harlan, J., dissenting)).

111. See id.

112. Romer v. Evans, 517 U.S. 620, 632 (1996).

113. 518 U.S. 515 (1996).

114. See id. at 577–78.

115. Id. at 540–46.

116. Id. at 545.

117. See id. at 547–48; Romer, 517 U.S. at 635–36.

118. 42 U.S.C. § 2000e (1964).

119. See, e.g., Bush v. Vera, 517 U.S. 952 (1996) (Stevens, J., dissenting); City of Richmond v. J. A. Croson Co., 488 U.S. 469, 529 (1989) (Marshall, J., dissenting).

120. 488 U.S. 469 (1989).

121. 515 U.S. 900 (1995).

122. 517 U.S. 620 (1996).

123. Id. at 636. (Scalia, J., dissenting).

124. See id.

125. Bush v. Vera, 517 U.S. 952, 1041 (Stevens, J., dissenting).

126. See City of Richmond v. J.A. Croson Co., 488 U.S. 469, 529 (1989) (Marshall, J., dissenting).

127. Id.

128. See Griggs v. Duke Power Co., 401 U.S. 424 (1971).

129. See Bush v. Vera, 517 U.S. 952 (1996).

130. See United States v. Virginia, 518 U.S. 515 (1996).

131. See Romer v. Evans, 517 U.S. 620 (1996).

132. 443 U.S. 193 (1979).

133. 448 U.S. 448 (1980).

134. Id. at 472 (Burger, C.J., plurality opinion).

135. Id. at 483 (Burger, C.J., plurality opinion).

136. Sometimes the Burger Court upheld far-reaching remedial decrees in school desegregation cases, see, e.g., Swann v. Charlotte-Mecklenburg Bd. of Educ., 402 U.S. 1 (1971), and invalidated employment tests that failed to admit sufficient numbers of minorities into the private work force. See e.g., Griggs v. Duke Power Co., 401 U.S. 424 (1971).

137. S. 1085, 104th Cong. (1995); H.R. 2128, 104th Cong. (1995).

138. See id.

139. S. 950, 105th Cong. (1997); S. 952, 105th Cong. (1997); H.R. 1909, 105th Cong. (1997).

140. Proposition 209, California Civil Rights Initiative (enacted as Cal. Const. art. I, § 31).

141. See Coalition for Econ. Equity v. Wilson, 946 F. Supp. 1480, 1491 (N.D. Cal. 1996), *vacated*, 110 F.3d 1431 (9th Cir.), *amended on denial of reh'g by* 122 F.3d 692 (9th Cir.), *cert. denied*, 118 S. Ct. 397 (1997).

142. See Coalition For Economic Equity v. Wilson, 122 F.3d 692 (9th Cir.), *cert. denied*, 118 S. Ct. 397 (1997).

143. See Coalition For Economic Equity v. Wilson, 110 F.3d 1431, 1437 (1997).

144. 78 F.3d 932 (5th Cir.), *cert. denied*, 518 U.S.1033 (1996).

145. "The Cold Truth About Racial Preferences," *Wash. Times*, July 29, 1997, at A16.

146. See id.

147. See id.

148. See id.

149. Applebome, "Minority Numbers Plunge at Some Law Schools After Affirmative Action Banned," *Sunday Patriot-News* (Harrisburg), June 29, 1997, at A13 (quoting Professor Marjorie Shultz).

150. 5 U.S. (1 Cranch) 137 (1803).

151. See, e.g., United States v. Fourdice, 505 U.S. 717 (1992) (Mississippi); Richmond v. J.A. Croson Co., 488 U.S. 469 (1989) (Virginia).

152. Voting Rights Act of 1965, 42 U.S.C. § 1973(b) (1998).

153. See Lawyer v. Department of Justice, 521 U.S. 567 (1997); Johnson v. DeGrandy, 512 U.S. 997 (1994).

154. See Abrams v. Johnson, 521 U.S. 74 (1997); Miller v. Johnson, 515 U.S. 900 (1995).

155. See Shaw v. Hunt, 517 U.S. 899 (1996); Shaw v. Reno, 509 U.S. 630 (1993).

156. See Bush v. Vera, 517 U.S. 952 (1996).

157. See Abrams v. Johnson, 521 U.S. at 81; Lawyer v. Department of Justice, 521 U.S. at 568, 570, 576; Shaw v. Hunt, 517 U.S. at 905, 914; Bush v. Vera, 517 U.S. at 957, 960–61; Miller v. Johnson, 515 U.S. at 903, 906–07; Johnson v. DeGrandy, 512 U.S. at 1000, 1002; Shaw v. Reno, 509 U.S. at 644.

158. *Croson*, 488 U.S. at 552 (Marshall, J., dissenting).

159. Metro Broadcasting, Inc. v. FCC, 497 U.S. 547, 603 (O'Connor, J., dissenting).

160. 512 U.S. 997 (1994).

161. See, e.g., Patterson v. McLean Credit Union, 491 U.S. 164 (1989), *overruled in part by* Civil Rights Act of 1991, § 101(2)(b), 42 U.S.C. § 1981(b); Watson v. Fort Worth Bank & Trust, 487 U.S. 977 (1988); Goodman v. Lukens Steel Co., 482 U.S. 656 (1987).

162. See, e.g., United States v. Fourdice, 505 U.S. 717 (1992).

163. 91 F.3d 1547 (3d Cir. 1996) (en banc), *cert. granted*, 521 U.S. 1117, *cert. dismissed*, 118 S. Ct. 595 (1997).

164. 509 U.S. 630 (1993).

165. See Hansen & Faber, *Current Population Reports:The Foreign-Born Population: 1996*, at 1 fig. 1 (U.S. Bureau of the Census, P20-494, 1997).

166. See id. at 2 tbl. A.

167. See id.

168. See Healy, "Changes in Law Lead to 27% Hike in Legal Immigration," *L.A. Times*, Apr. 23, 1997, at A4.

169. Dewar, "U.S. in 50 Years—Not Black or White, but Everything Else," *Houston Chronicle*, Apr. 27, 1997, at 1 (quoting Philip Nyden).

170. See Day, *Current Population Reports: Population Projections of the United States by Age, Sex, Race, and Hispanic Origin: 1995 to 2050*, at 13 & tbl. J (U.S. Bureau of the Census, P25-1130, 1996); Lawrence, "Political Battlegrounds of the Future," *USA Today*, Aug. 8, 1997, at 6A.

171. See Lawrence, supra note 170, at 6A.

172. See Day, supra note 170, at 13 tbl.J.

173. See Lawrence, supra note 170.

174. *Morning Edition: U.S. Latinos*, NPR radio broadcast, Aug. 11, 1997, available in Westlaw, MORNED File.

175. Nichols, "Taking Off: Houston's Asian Communities Growing Rapidly," *Dallas Morning News*, June 29, 1997, at 45A (quoting Glenda Joe, a publicist and Asian community leader).

176. See id.

177. *See Morning Edition: Latinos in North Carolina*, NPR radio broadcast, Aug. 15, 1997, available in Westlaw, MORNED File.

178. See *Morning Edition: U.S. Latinos*, supra note 174.

179. Booth, "One Nation Indivisible: Is It History?," *Wash. Post*, Feb. 22, 1998, at A1; Branigin, "The Myth of the Melting Pot: Immigrants Shunning Idea of Assimilation," *Wash. Post*, May 25, 1998, at A1.

180. Booth, supra note 179, at A18.

181. Id. (quoting Todd Gitlin, a professor of culture and communications at New York University).

182. Plessy v. Ferguson, 163 U.S. 537, 559 (1896) (Harlan, J., dissenting).

183. See Loury, "Double Talk," *New Republic*, Aug. 25, 1997, at 23. The Census Bureau's Current Population Survey documents that, as of 1995, approximately 2.5 percent of our nation's total married couples—over 1.3 million couples—are interracial. U.S. Bureau of the Census, *Interracial Married Couples: 1960 to Present* (last modified Sept. 20, 1996) <http://www.census.gov/population/socdemo/ms-la/95hiso4.txt>.

184. Miller v. Johnson, 515 U.S. 900, 925 (1995).

185. Id. at 920–27.

186. Fleming, "The Faces of Discrimination," *Hispanic*, June 1994, at 22; see also 140 Cong. Rec. S12,933 (1994) (statement of Sen. Riegle) ("It is estimated that one in every four Hispanic-American families lives in poverty. Only about half of the adults hold high school diplomas and fewer than 10 percent have graduated from college. And at a time when U.S. concern over illegal immigration is high, Hispanic-Americans are frequently the targets of racial discrimination."). Id.

187. See Chinese Exclusion Act, ch. 126, 22 Stat. 58 (1882) (repealed 1943) (suspending immigration of Chinese laborers to the United States for ten years); Korematsu v. United States, 323 U.S. 214 (1944) (upholding exclusion order); Hirabayashi v. United States, 320 U.S. 81 (1943) (upholding curfew order).

188. 143 Cong. Rec. S2619–20 (daily ed. Sept. 14, 1997) (statement of Sen. Akaka); see also Tyson, "Asian Americans Spurn Image as Model Minority," *Christian Sci. Monitor*, Aug. 26, 1994, at 6.

189. Adarand Constructors, Inc. v. Pena, 515 U.S. 200, 224 (1995) (quoting City of Richmond v. J.A. Croson Co., 488 U.S. 469, 494 (1989)).

190. Loury, supra note 183, at 23.

191. Krauthammer, "Diversity Trap," *Wash. Post*, Aug. 15, 1997, at A25.

192. *Adarand*, 515 U.S. at 224.

193. 91 F.3d 1547 (3d Cir. 1996), *cert. granted*, 521 U.S. 1117, *cert. dismissed*, 118 S. Ct. 595 (1997).

194. See id. at 1551.

195. See id.

196. See id. at 1563.

197. See id. at 1567.

198. *See* Biskupic, "Rights Groups Pay to Settle Bias Case," *Wash. Post*, Nov. 22, 1997, at A1.

199. See id.

200. I have tried to explore this question in my book *One Nation Indivisible: How Ethnic Separatism Threatens America* (1997). The concern over the future of America's identity is certainly not mine alone. See, e.g., Lind, *The Next American Nation: The New Nationalism and the Fourth American Revolution* (1995); Schlesinger, *The Disuniting of America: Reflections on a Multicultural Society* (1991).

5

THE FIRST FREEDOM AND
THE REHNQUIST COURT

JOHN T. NOONAN, JR.

I must begin this chapter with a dissent—a dissent from the rubric under which the conference has placed the presentation: "Church and State."[1] We don't have a Church in the United States. We have churches, mosques, synagogues, temples, zen sanctuaries. We have religions, at least 1,400 of them.[2] We have believers, 167 million of them.[3] We have consciences, 273 million of them.[4] It is in relation to the 1,400 religions, the 167 million believers, the 273 million consciences that the activities of government stand. And we have units of government, not a State. We have a federal government, all three of whose parts, not excluding the judiciary, act upon religions, believers, and consciences. We have fifty states also divided into parts. We have thousands of school boards, municipalities, counties, zoning agencies, state universities, city transit systems, and so on, all of whose operations may impinge upon the fundamental constitutional freedom that is the first freedom secured by the Bill of Rights. Let us banish for good the obsolete European usage of speaking of Church and State.

Certain as I am that the rubric is wrong, I am far from being so certain on the topic itself, whose most central element, at least for Christians, Jews, and Moslems, involves the relation of human beings to an invisible, impalpable Being, unseen but not unreal, without vocal chords but not silent, who is experienced by many not as a projection but as a presence. The crude, categorizing methods of the law are intrusive in their attempts to capture or channel this relation. The judges, who are called on occasion to treat of it, grope uncertainly, necessarily reflecting their own experience.

Only sporadically does this elusive subject engage the Justices of the Supreme Court. The Rehnquist Court's total oeuvre on religion is no more than twenty cases. Published opinions on the topic make up about 1.6 percent of its published opinions.[5] Making an assessment of the efforts of the Rehnquist Court, one must acknowledge the sincerity that has attended them; one must admit the intractability of some questions; and one must concede that no criticisms are beyond criticism.

Religion has not fared badly in the Rehnquist Court, or so it might be argued. In the eyes of a majority of the Court, the classic case in which free exercise should come into play is one in which the government targets a specific religion and legislates specifically against it. Such was in 1993 the case of *Church of the Lukumi Babalu Aye v. City of Hialeah*.[6] Santeria, a religion that cultivated the spirits by the sacrifice of a variety of animals and birds, from chickens to sheep, was unwelcome in Hialeah. The city council passed three ordinances couched in general terms but circumstantially shown to be aimed at the Santeria sacrifices. All Justices agreed that the ordinances were unconstitutional. Outright persecution was out. On that capital point, no hesitation was shown; no compromise was necessary; no qualifications were made.

In several other cases, the overtly religious position lost because it was too tightly embraced by the governmental unit involved. Although none of these cases were cut and dried and although the Chief Justice dissented in each, each case involved governmental sponsorship of a religious message. In *Edwards v. Aguillard*,[7] the Louisiana legislature prescribed the teaching that God created the world from nothing; public high schools had to provide this account as an alternative if evolution was taught. In *County of Allegheny v. American Civil Liberties Union*,[8] the county put a creche at Christmas on the central stairway of the county courthouse with an angel bearing a banner proclaiming "Gloria in excelsis Deo" written above the manger. In *Lee v. Weisman*,[9] school officials arranged for prayers at graduation and oversaw the prayers chosen. In each instance specific religious pronouncements were made by agencies of government.

In contrast, when the legislature has accommodated religion, not endorsed a doctrine, the Court has rejected the claim that a religion has been established. The first of these cases, decided in 1987, is *Corporation of the Presiding Bishop of the Church of Jesus Christ of Latter-Day Saints v. Amos*,[10] upholding the exemption in the Civil Rights Act of 1964 [11] of religious employers discriminating on religious grounds in hiring even for a nonreligious job, in this case engineer for a church-run gymnasium. All Justices concurred in the judgment.

The next such case was more divisive. Writing for a majority of five in *Bowen v. Kendrick*,[12] the Chief Justice sustained the constitutionality of the Adolescent Family Life Act of 1981[13] permitting grants to religious organizations, as well as other charities, to provide counseling on adolescent sex and pregnancy. The enlistment of religious organizations in this secular health measure was held neither to advance religion nor to excessively entangle government with religion.[14] The dissenters focused on the specifically Catholic teaching on marriage and procreation that formed part of the program of one grantee.[15] In *Zobrest v. Catalina Foothills School District*,[16] the Chief Justice, again writing for a majority of five, upheld the application of the Individuals with Disabilities Education Act[17] to provide a sign-language interpreter to a child attending a Catholic high school. Justice Blackmun's dissent objected to allowing "a public employee to participate directly in religious indoctrination."[18]

Climatically, in 1997, in *Agostini v. Felton*,[19] the Rehnquist Court revisited a twelve-year-old decision of the Burger Court and found it inconsistent with the new cases. The Elementary and Secondary Education Act of 1965[20] gave grants to local school boards so that they could provide remedial education in reading and mathematics, guidance and job counseling to poorly performing students in low-income areas. The New York Board of Education gave parochial school students such help on the premises of the parochial schools. In 1985, the Supreme Court held the practice unconstitutional.[21] Now, in 1997, *Zobrest* had created "fresh law."[22] Neither religious indoctrination nor a symbolic union of government with religion would be created by secular counselors, federally funded, carrying out their functions at parochial schools; nor would there be "excessive entanglement."[23] Justice Souter wrote for four dissenters. The program provided services to the religious schools and relieved the schools of a burden that was theirs; it was aid directly given to the schools.[24]

The teaching of the last three of these cases is that religion is not established when a religious organization is aided to perform a perfectly secular mission. Alternatively, all four cases could be read as incorporating the Supreme Court's general respect for federal legislation. Although free exercise is formulated in terms of a negative on Congress, the Supreme Court has never invalidated a federal law for violating free exercise. Now the Court showed a similar deference to Congress in determining what did or did not constitute an establishment.

The prototype of these cases was *Bradfield v. Roberts*,[25] holding that the District of Columbia and the Surgeon General of the Army could constitutionally contract for services for the sick with Providence Hospital, run by the Sisters of Charity. *Bradfield* involved federal authority and a specific secular service provided by nuns. The line from *Bradfield* to *Agostini* is not beyond debate but holds firm if the deference to Congress, implicit but not articulated in the cases, is taken into account.

A different line of nonestablishment holdings goes back to the 1981 decision *Widmar v. Vincent*.[26] Here the meetings of an evangelical student group were treated as speech and so could not be excluded, on account of their religious content, from a place in the public forum that the University of Missouri had created for all student groups.[27] The only dissenter was Justice White, who observed that if the majority was right in its treatment of acts of worship as speech, the university should be able to offer "Sunday Mass" as a course.[28]

In 1984 Congress extended the reasoning of *Widmar* to public schools. It passed the Equal Access Act,[29] applicable to any school receiving federal financial aid. If such a school created a "limited open forum" for student meetings during noninstructional time, the school could not deny access "on the basis of the religious, political, philosophical, or other content of the speech at such meetings."[30] An Omaha, Nebraska public school that recognized thirty student clubs denied access to a proposed Christian club that would read and discuss the Bible, have fellowship, and pray. In 1990, in *Board of Education of the Westside Community Schools v. Mergens*,[31] the Rehnquist Court upheld the constitutionality of the Equal Access Act and held that the school had violated the law. Justice Stevens dissented.

In 1993 Justice White became the author of the opinion in *Lamb's Chapel v. Center Moriches Union Free School District*, holding that a school board violated the right to free speech of an evangelical church that wanted to use school property, after school hours, to show films promoting "Christian family values."[32] The school board could not constitutionally discriminate against a religious viewpoint. *Widmar* controlled.

All Justices agreed with the result, although Justice Scalia would have used the case as an occasion to bury *Lemon v. Kurtzman*.[33] This legacy of the Burger Court hung on as a ghost with its law clerks' language of a three-pronged test for establishment an embarrassment effectively nonfunctional but not formally discarded.

Widmar and *Lamb's Chapel* were the operative precedents for Justice Scalia, writing for a plurality that included the Chief Justice, in *Capitol Square Review and Advisory Board v. Pinette*.[34] The plaza surrounding the state capitol in Columbus, Ohio, was a forum for the discussion of public matters. The Ku Klux Klan sought to put up a cross on the square during the Christmas season. The cross had been excluded by the square's review board, not because of the Klan's sponsorship but because of its religious character. The Court agreed that *Lamb's Chapel* was dispositive; the cross could be erected.[35]

The same reasoning was followed by Justice Kennedy, writing in 1995 for a five to four majority, in *Rosenberger v. Rector and Visitors of the University of Virginia*.[36] The university collected a mandatory student fee from which student publications were funded but not those publications that primarily promoted or manifested "a particular belief in or about a deity or an ultimate reality."[37] The university, the majority concluded, had created a limited public forum from which it could not exclude a religious viewpoint. *Lamb's Chapel* spoke to the situation. The evangelical students' magazine, *Wide Awake: A Christian Perspective at the University of Virginia*, was entitled to university money. Justice Souter, writing for the four dissenters, saw the Court as approving the state funding "of core religious activity."[38] For the dissenters, subsidy of the publication of overtly religious messages was different from providing "a street corner" or its analogues.[39] Intuitively, they saw the state paying for printing as different from the state providing a pavement.

Rosenberger is the controversial climax of the line of cases governed by the logic of *Widmar*. It is plain that religion does well, in the context of litigation, when it is classified as speech. For any advocate of a religious cause the message is obvious: appeal to free speech, not free exercise. Doing so provides the advantage of the Supreme Court's current precedents and avoids, or at least diminishes, the secularists' suspicion of anything religious. There is no preference for religion, only equality, thereby eliminating the invidiousness of a claim of privilege for religion. Above all, this means that over one's cause is the banner of the most cherished liberal value. The "freedom of thought, and of speech"—thought and speech being treated as a unit—has been identified by Justice Cardozo as "the matrix, the indispensable condition, of nearly every other form of freedom."[40] When religion can be presented as part of this indispensable matrix, it has the greatest chance of achieving judicial recognition. It enters a constitutional domain that is richly developed and marked by many subtle gradings and fine distinctions.

Should this identification of religion with speech be accepted or cultivated by a court? It is easy to do. The teaching of religion normally depends on speech. The expression of worship normally requires speech. The performance of ritual can be read as symbolic speech. Religion for most persons consists in communications to, or from, a divine being, or communications about that being. Religion can, therefore, be considered a subdivision of speech.

Treating it as such for purposes of the Bill of Rights has three disadvantages.

First, it ignores the text of the First Amendment, which begins its enumeration of freedoms with that of religion before recognizing the freedoms of speech and of the press. Second, it ignores the history of the First Amendment, some of whose most active supporters were evangelical Christians desirous of protection not of speech as such but of their conscientious response to God. Third, it cuts away the foundation of religious freedom, the creature's duty to the Creator, and substitutes a secular equality of all communications. The move to catalogue religion under speech is a sensible tactic in litigation; it must be resisted in judicial and academic analysis.

When religion is at stake in the *Widmar* sort of situation, three issues are always involved: Does inclusion of religion establish religion? Does exclusion of religion offend equality in speech? Does exclusion of religion violate free exercise? The Court has created a problem by continuing an approach, now probably beyond correction, of treating what it calls "the Establishment Clause" as a separate clause in tension with what it terms "the Free Exercise Clause."

James Madison is the Founding Father most often invoked by the Court. The theological foundation of Madison's position is often overlooked. It is, as he expresses it in the *Memorial and Remonstrance*, as follows: the duty we owe our Creator "is precedent both in order of time and in degree of obligation to the claims of civil society."[41] A Madisonian approach would see the protection of free exercise as fundamental, the prevention of an establishment as important and auxiliary, a means that should not subvert the end of each person freely responding to the Creator by conscientious exercise of belief.

In Madisonian perspective, a burden on free exercise is a separate burden from a burden on free speech. The reiteration of Madison's protest against using taxes to teach religion—a feature of Justice Souter's dissent in *Rosenberger* [42]—does not do full justice to Madison's thought if it omits Madison's insistence on the precedence of the obligations of conscience.

As to how Madison would vote in a case like *Rosenberger*, an historical answer may, perhaps, exist. He was never confronted with the University of Virginia paying for an evangelical journal, but he was given by Thomas Jefferson the task of selecting theological treatises for the university library. Neither he nor Jefferson, the founder of the university, thought it wrong to spend the state's money on books that not only manifested belief about the deity but actively promoted it.

Madison's selection included many of the Christian writers identified as Fathers of the Church; the great scholastic theologians Thomas Aquinas and Duns Scotus; and both Protestant and Catholic controversialists of the Reformation, such as Bellarmine, Calvin, Chillingworth, Erasmus, and Socinius.[43] No work by Hume or Paine or Voltaire was nominated. Madison's list was that of an ecumenically minded Christian. The state was to pay for such works that not only promoted a belief about God but specifically promoted a Christian theology of God. Madison, if this analogy holds any force, would have let state-collected funds subsidize *Wide Awake* not because it was speech but because the students of the University of Virginia should not be deprived of Christian or, for that matter, any religious literature.

Madison, however, is not the tutelary patron of the Rehnquist Court on religion. Madison held the belief that the free exercise of religion flowing from his fundamental postulate must, given the nature of government, be approached asymptotically.[44] The maximum free exercise possible is the Madisonian ideal that I take as a measure. From that standpoint, after the U.S. Supreme Court began belatedly, in 1940, to find a role in the protection of free exercise, there are several milestones:

> *Cantwell v. Connecticut*, treating free exercise as trumping a state statute of general application against disorder in the streets and a state statute of general application requiring the registration of solicitors for charity.[45]
> *Murdock v. Pennsylvania*, where free exercise in the distribution of religious literature led to exemption of the distributors from a license tax on all door-to-door distributors.[46]
> *West Virginia State Board of Education v. Barnette*, where the "fixed star in our constitutional constellation" is proclaimed that prohibits a school from requiring the salute of the flag from children whose religious belief views the salute as idolatry.[47]
> *Sherbert v. Verner*, holding that a Seventh Day Adventist's refusal to work on Saturday, her Sabbath Day, was not a valid reason for denying her unemployment benefits.[48]
> *Wisconsin v. Yoder*, teaching that the highest function of a state is the education of its citizens but holding that even this function must be subordinated to the religious imperative that keeps Old Order Amish children from high school of any kind lest they be conformed to the world.[49]

Cantwell, Murdock, Barnette, Sherbert, and *Yoder*—these are the cases asymptotically approaching Madison's ideal. It is in terms of them that I measure the Rehnquist Court.

The Chief Justice's first opinion as Chief Justice on free exercise struck the note that preferred secular orderliness to recognition of the requirements of the spirit. In *O'Lone v. Shabazz*,[50] delivered in June 1987, the Court upheld, five to four, a regulation of New Jersey Leesburg State Prison that prevented Muslim prisoners, assigned to outside work, from attending the Friday communal prayer service commanded by the Koran.

The Chief Justice emphasized that "the respect and deference that the United States Constitution allows for the judgment of prison administrators."[51] No portion of the Constitution was cited for this proposition. This respect and deference, nonetheless, eclipsed the free exercise right of the Muslims, an explicit constitutional right that the Court acknowledged they retained in subordinated fashion.

The next year, in an opinion by Justice O'Connor, the Rehnquist Court held, six to two, that a logging road projected by the Forest Service prevailed over the free exercise rights of the Yurok, Karok, and Tolowa Indians, for whom the burial lands affected were an "indispensable part" of their religious practice.[52] The road, the Court assumed, would "virtually destroy the . . . Indians' ability to practice their religion."[53] But the Court knew of no principle in the Constitution preventing this result.[54]

In 1989 the Supreme Court, six to three, struck down as an unconstitutional establishment of religion Texas's exemption from sales tax of periodicals promulgating the teaching of a religious faith and of books consisting wholly of writings sacred to a religious faith.[55] The apparently contradictory precedent of *Murdock* was brushed aside in Justice Brennan's plurality opinion.

The Chief Justice joined Justice Scalia's dissent pointing to the widespread practice of the states of not taxing such publications and to the existence of many other tax exemptions specific to religiously identified uses.[56] A "new strain of irrationality," the dissent observed, was being added to the Court's treatment of religion.[57]

The strain intensified with *Employment Division v. Smith* in 1990.[58] In an opinion by Justice Scalia, the Rehnquist Court, five to four, rejected the free exercise claim of two members of the Native American Church, fired by the state of Oregon for ingesting peyote as part of the ritual of their religion. The majority explicitly embraced the proposition that a neutral, generally applicable law might burden the free exercise of religion and would be constitutionally valid unless some other principle was also offended.[59] *Cantwell, Murdock, Sherbert* and *Yoder* were explained in terms of offense to another principle.[60] *Barnette* was neglected, except that *Minersville School District v. Gobitis*, which *Barnette* had overruled, was quoted as if *Gobitis* were still good law.[61]

Justice O'Connor wrote for the minority, contending that precedent required a "compelling" state interest to override a claim of free exercise.[62] Looked at in terms of what had been considered a compelling interest—prison housekeeping, a logging road—the difference in practice between the minority and the majority was trivial. Looked at in terms of rhetoric and in terms of following precedent, the difference showed a real split in the Court with the Chief Justice on the side of Justice Scalia.

In 1994, the Satmar Hasidim, practitioners of a form of Judaism as aloof from the world as the Amish, found their free exercise of religion treated as an establishment of religion by a six to three majority of the Court, the Chief Justice and Justice Scalia being among the dissenters.[63] The Satmar all lived in the village of Kiryas Joel and sent their children to their own religious schools, which had no services for handicapped children. Handicapped Satmar children experienced trauma in the regular public schools.

The New York legislature designated Kiryas Joel as a special school district, which then functioned only to run a special education program for the handicapped Satmar, not offering any religious instruction at all. The fact that the voters of Kiryas Joel were all Satmar was enough to condemn it as a legislatively created school district. As the dissent observed, on this theory, schools in any community overwhelmingly of one denomination were of doubtful constitutionality.[64] The Satmar were denied the right to practice their religion, live in a single community, and at the same time get public assistance for their handicapped school-age offspring.

In 1993, Congress passed the Religious Freedom Restoration Act (RFRA).[65] The law prohibited any unit of government, state or federal, from burdening a person's exercise of religion unless the government could prove that the burden was in furtherance of a compelling governmental interest and that imposition of the burden was the least restrictive means of furthering that interest.[66] In *City of Boerne v. Flores*, the Court, six to three, invalidated RFRA as applied to the states.[67] It exceeded Congress's power under Section 5 of the Fourteenth Amendment, the Court held, to legislate so generally to protect a liberty guaranteed by that amendment.[68] Congress, the Court said, could only enforce the amendment, not define its meaning.[69]

Moreover, the Court added, Congress's response lacked "proportionality or congruence between the means adopted and the legitimate end to be achieved."[70] For these reasons, a zoning ordinance of a Texas town protecting an historic district took precedence over the need of a Catholic parish to replace a Mission-style church built in 1923 with a larger structure to accommodate its burgeoning congregation. The minority followed Justice O'Connor's dissent in *Smith*, the division reflecting the Court's split in *Smith*.

What generalizations do these six cases afford about the Rehnquist Court and the First Freedom? They stand in sharp contrast to that Court's accommodation of the funding of the secular services provided by churches, the religious exemption upheld in *Amos*, and the acceptance of religious activity classified as speech. The Rehnquist Court has not been unsympathetic to religion. What moves it here?

First, the majority of these cases (*Texas Monthly* and *Kiryas Joel* are exceptions) are cases in which two different currents in the courts reinforce each other—the current putting a high value on clear law and an orderly society and the current disinclined to enlarge the benefits accorded religion. The embodiment of the first current is Justice Scalia, whose *Smith* opinion breathes an abhorrence of the anarchy of individual consciences trumping statutes.[71] The embodiment of the second is Justice Stevens, who has gone so far as to say that RFRA sets up an establishment by giving religion special privileges.[72]

The conjunction of the two currents has led to the institutional posture most prominent in *Boerne*, where the intervention of Congress in a fight within the Court is treated as lèse majesté, and Congress is bluntly told to butt out.[73] The message is emphasized by the invention of a new standard for judging the constitutionality of an act of Congress—the proportion between the end sought and the means used. Outside of the Eighth Amendment, such a test is unknown. If the federal courts were to employ it regularly, federal legislation would be subject to massive factual challenges. Its use in *Boerne* evinces consensus on protecting the Court's jurisprudence with a heavy institutional club.

Boerne is further remarkable as the first decision by the Supreme Court to invalidate federal legislation affecting free exercise. The First Amendment, after all, says that *Congress* shall not prohibit the free exercise of religion. It was the Supreme Court which, in 1940, extended the amendment to the states.[74] In *Boerne*, the Court finds Congress incompetent to legislate in further extension of this freedom in the states.[75] Neither the text of the First Amendment nor the text of the Fourteenth Amendment supports this restriction. The institutional allergy to congressional poaching on turf the Court has, so to speak, created is very strong.

Second, the cases are insensitive to discrete, insular minorities which happen to be practicing a nonmainstream religion—the Muslims in Leesburg, the Indian tribes with sacred grounds, the Native Americans in Oregon, the Satmar in New York. Religious freedom was first established in the jurisprudence of the Supreme Court by such a discrete, insular minority—the Jehovah's Witnesses. Religious freedom was confirmed by the victories of other small minorities, the Adventists and the Old Order Amish. Part of the secret of their success might have been thought to have been their helplessness, their need for judicial protection. If so, this reason for success no longer held.

Third, the cases cumulatively are a repudiation of the Madisonian ideal. Madison, indeed, is never quoted in the opinion of the Court in any of these cases. The cases are equally a repudiation of the asymptotic approximation attempted in *Cantwell, Murdock, Barnette, Sherbert,* and *Yoder.* The basic religious premise of these cases is replaced by secular premises. In two instances, the replacement is not even by reference to a constitutional text. In *Smith,* Justice Scalia invokes parental rights, unmentioned in the Constitution, to explain *Yoder*[76] and refers to "individualized exemptions," a bureaucratic practice, to explain *Sherbert.*[77] The religious foundation of the plaintiffs' case in *Barnette,* and *Barnette* itself, is ignored, while the eminently secularist spirit of *Gobitis* is revived by quotation.[78]

The willingness to ignore or radically reinterpret precedent has led William Ball, that experienced veteran of Supreme Court battles over religion, to remark that in this area the Court makes up the rules as it goes along.[79] It is not quite that chaotic. The Rehnquist Court has become the settled opponent of James Madison's foundational proposition.

Notes

1. Editor's Note: Judge Noonan's presentation at the Rehnquist Conference was part of a series of talks on the "Constitutional Corpus" of the Rehnquist Court's decisons. His topic was framed initially as "Church and State."

2. Melton, *The Encyclopedia of American Religions,* xv (1989).

3. Finke & Stark, *The Churching of America,* 1776–1990, 25 (1992).

4. U.S. *Population Estimate* (U. S. Census Bureau, June 3, 1999).

5. Found by dividing the number of Supreme Court cases on religion since 1986 — twenty — by the total number of cases the Rehnquist Court has decided. The total number of cases was compiled from the *Harvard Law Review's* annual November issues on the Supreme Court, which list the number of cases decided each term. See, e.g., "The Supreme Court, 1988 Term-Leading Cases," 103 *Harv. L. Rev.* 394 (1989); "The Supreme Court, 1997 Term-Leading Cases," 111 *Harv. L. Rev.* 431 (1997).

6. 508 U.S. 520 (1993).

7. 482 U.S. 578 (1987).

8. 492 U.S. 573 (1989).

9. 505 U.S. 577 (1992).

10. 483 U.S. 327 (1987).

11. Civil Rights Act of 1964 § 702, 42 U.S.C. § 2000e-1 (1998).

12. 487 U.S. 589 (1988).

13. Adolescent Family Life Act of 1981, 42 U.S.C. § 300z (1998).

14. *Bowen,* 487 U.S. at 605.

15. Id. at 625.

16. 509 U.S. 1 (1993).

17. Individuals with Disabilities Education Act of 1991 § 601, 20 U.S.C. § 1400 (1998).

18. *Zobrest,* 509 U.S. at 18.

19. 521 U.S. 203 (1997).

20. Elementary and Secondary Education Act of 1965 § 1001, 20 U.S.C. § 6301 (1998).

21. School Dist. of Grand Rapids v. Ball, 473 U.S. 373 (1985).

22. *Agostini,* 521 U.S. at 225.

23. Id. at 205.

24. Id. at 252.

25. 175 U.S. 291 (1899).

26. 454 U.S. 263 (1981).

27. Id. at 267.

28. Id. at 287.

29. Equal Access Act of 1984 § 801, 20 U.S.C. § 4071 (1998).

30. 20 U.S.C. § 4071(a).

31. 496 U.S. 226 (1990).

32. 508 U.S. 384, 394 (1993).

33. Id. at 398 (Scalia, J., concurring) (citing Lemon v. Kurtzman, 403 U.S. 602 (1971).

34. 515 U.S. 753 (1995).

35. Id. at 760.

36. 515 U.S. 819 (1995).

37. Id. at 819.

38. Id. at 863.

39. Id. at 889.

40. Palko v. Connecticut, 302 U.S. 319, 327 (1937).

41. Madison, *A Memorial and Remonstrance*, (reprinted in Everson v. Board. of Educ. of Ewing, 320 U.S. 1, 64 (1947)) (appendix to dissent of Rutledge, J.)

42. *Rosenberger*, 515 U.S. at 868.

43. James Madison to Thomas Jefferson, September 4, 1824, Madison, *Writings*, 9: 203–07.

44. See Noonan, *The Lustre of Our Country* 86–7 (1998).

45. 310 U.S. 296 (1940).

46. 319 U.S. 157 (1943).

47. 319 U.S. 624, 642 (1943).

48. 374 U.S. 398 (1963).

49. 406 U.S. 205 (1972).

50. 482 U.S. 342 (1987).

51. Id. at 350.

52. Lyng v. Northwest Indian Cemetery Protection Assoc., 485 U.S. 439, 442 (1988).

53. Id. at 451.

54. Id. at 452.

55. Texas Monthly v. Bullock, 489 U.S. 1 (1989).

56. Id. at 32.

57. Id. at 45.

58. 494 U.S. 872 (1990).

59. Id. at 883.

60. Id. at 877.

61. Id. at 879.

62. Id. at 894.

63. Board of Educ. of Kiryas Joel Village School Dist. v. Grumet, 512 U.S. 687 (1994).

64. Id. at 736.

65. Religious Freedom Restoration Act of 1993 § 2, 42 U.S.C. § 2000bb (1998).

66. 42 U.S.C. § 2000bb-1(b).

67. 521 U.S. 507 (1997).

68. Id. at 524–25.

69. Id. at 519.

70. Id. at 532–33.

71. See *Smith*, 494 U.S. at 886.

72. See *Boerne*, 521 U.S. at 537.

73. Id. at 536.

74. *Cantwell,* 310 U.S. at 296.

75. See *Boerne,* 521 U.S. at 530–31.

76. *Smith,* 494 U.S. at 881.

77. Id. at 884 (quoting Bowen v. Roy, 476 U.S. 693, 708 (1986)).

78. Id. at 879.

79. Ball, *Mere Creatures of the State? Education, Religion, and the Courts: A View from the Courtroom* 3–4 (1994).

· 6 ·

CONFESSIONS, SEARCH AND SEIZURE, AND THE REHNQUIST COURT

YALE KAMISAR

Police Interrogation and Confessions

About the time William Rehnquist ascended to the Chief Justiceship of the United States, two events occurred that increased the likelihood that *Miranda* would enjoy a long life.

In *Moran v. Burbine*,[1] a six to three majority held that a confession preceded by an otherwise valid waiver of a suspect's *Miranda* rights should not be excluded either (1) because the police misled an inquiring attorney when they told her they were not going to question the suspect she called about or (2) because the police failed to inform the suspect of the attorney's efforts to reach him.

Although *Burbine* has been criticized by a number of commentators,[2] I think it is a plausible and defensible reading of *Miranda*.[3] I find it hard to believe that the *Miranda* Court would consider the now-familiar warnings inadequate when—even though a suspect has been warned of his or her *Miranda* rights and has effectively waived them—a lawyer whose services the suspect has never requested and whose existence the suspect is unaware of has contacted the police on his or her behalf.[4]

Whether or not I am right, more important than *Burbine*'s specific holding, I think, is the way the Court that decided *Burbine* looked back at and characterized *Miranda*. Justice O'Connor spoke for six Justices (including Chief Justice Burger and soon-to-be Chief Justice Rehnquist) when she told us that *Miranda* "as written" struck "the proper balance" between law enforcement interests and a defendant's Fifth Amendment rights.[5]

Unlike most critics of the landmark case, the *Burbine* Court viewed *Miranda* as a case that "embodies a carefully crafted balance designed to fully protect *both* the defendant's and society's interests."[6] The *Burbine* Court also reminded us that *Miranda* had rejected "the more extreme position" advocated by the ACLU that nothing less than "the *actual presence* of a lawyer" (as opposed merely to police warnings to a suspect about his rights) is needed to dispel the coercion inherent in custodial interrogation.[7] Instead, the *Miranda* Court had concluded, to quote the *Burbine* Court again, that "the suspect's rights could be adequately protected by less intrusive means."[8]

Until this point, neither Justice O'Connor nor any of the Justices who joined her opinion in the *Burbine* case could be called friends or admirers of *Miranda*. Nevertheless, what they had to say about *Miranda* was what most of *Miranda's* supporters had been saying about the case for the previous twenty years.

There is another noteworthy event that, I believe, provides a useful background for the Rehnquist Court's treatment of *Miranda*. This event started out quite ominously for the famous case but ultimately turned out well.

Some four months after Justice Rehnquist had become Chief Justice, a division of the Department of Justice released a 120-page report endorsed by Attorney General Edwin Meese III, a report that sharply attacked *Miranda* as an illegitimate decision.[9] Shortly thereafter, "Meese's minions," as then Solicitor General Charles Fried called them, took up the cry and "proclaimed it a Department objective to get the Supreme Court to overrule *Miranda*."[10]

As Professor Stephen Schulhofer notes, the Meese-endorsed report on the law of pretrial interrogation "triggered a spate of new articles confirming support for *Miranda* in the law enforcement community."[11] As for Attorney General Meese's campaign inside the Department of Justice against *Miranda*, Solicitor General (now Massachusetts Justice) Fried resisted on various grounds. For one thing, "not a single Justice had indicated any interest in overruling *Miranda*, while the substantive law [confining the *Miranda* rule] was getting better and better."[12] Moreover, Fried's impression was that "most professional law enforcement organizations had learned to live with *Miranda*, and even to love it to the extent that it provided them with a safe harbor."[13]

After considering Solicitor General Fried's objections, the Attorney General backed off. For the rest of Fried's time in office, "the *Miranda* issue was laid to rest."[14] I think it no exaggeration to say that the time to overrule *Miranda* had come and gone.

Miranda: *Its Bases and Its Legitimacy*

Have I spoken too quickly? What about the fact that starting with Justice Rehnquist's opinion for the Court in *Michigan v. Tucker*,[15] the post-Warren Court has repeatedly distinguished between *actual* coercion by physical violence or threats of violence and *inherent* or *irrebutably presumed* coercion (the basis for the *Miranda* rules). The post-Warren Court has also drawn a line between statements that are *actually* "coerced" or "compelled" and those obtained *merely* in violation of *Miranda's* "procedural safeguards" or "prophylactic rules."[16]

Thus, although a statement found to be "involuntary" under pre-*Miranda* standards is inadmissible *for any purpose*, a statement obtained in violation of *Miranda* may be used to impeach a defendant's testimony if he subsequently takes the stand in his own defense.[17] Because a police officer may find the distinction somewhat mystifying, one witty commentator has suggested that the author of a police training manual might explain the situation as follows: "The Supreme Court has said that pre-*Miranda* voluntariness standards are part of the 'real' Constitution. *Miranda* is part of the Court's 'just pretend' Constitution."[18]

Ironically, the language in the *Miranda* opinion that the post-Warren Court used in *Tucker* and other cases to deconstitutionalize *Miranda* is language Chief Justice Warren inserted at the suggestion of Justice Brennan. Commenting on an early draft of the *Miranda* opinion, Justice Brennan wrote Warren:

> [W]e are justified in policing interrogation practices only to the extent required to prevent denial of the right against self-incrimination as we defined that right in *Malloy* [v. *Hogan*]. I therefore do not think, as our draft seems to suggest, that there is only a single constitutional solution to the problems of testimonial compulsion inherent in custodial interrogation. I agree that, largely for the reasons you have stated, all four cases must be reversed for lack of any safeguards against denial of the right. I also agree that warnings and the help of counsel are appropriate. But should we not leave Congress and the States latitude to devise other means (if they can) which might also create an interrogation climate which has the similar effect of preventing the fettering of a person's own will?[19]

Chief Justice Warren reworked his draft opinion of *Miranda* to accommodate Justice Brennan's suggestions. The new language caught William Rehnquist's attention even before he ascended to the Supreme Court.[20] And when he wrote the opinion of the Court in *Michigan v. Tucker* maintaining that the *Miranda* Court itself had "recognized" that the *Miranda* rules were "not themselves rights protected by the Constitution" but only "procedural safeguards designed to "insure that the right against compulsory self-incrimination was protected,"[21] Justice Rehnquist again relied on the language in *Miranda* that the author of the opinion had added at Justice Brennan's request.[22]

In addition to arguing that the post-Warren Court has ignored important language in the *Miranda* opinion,[23] defenders of *Miranda* would maintain more generally that the privilege against self-incrimination, along with other constitutional rights, needs "breathing space."[24] What the *Miranda* Court did, they would maintain, was to try to ensure that no confession *actually* compelled would be admitted into evidence by establishing conclusive presumptions and related forms of "prophylactic" rules to "implement" or to "reinforce" the privilege against self-incrimination—in order to guard against *actual* constitutional violations. Is this improper?

Yes, retorts a leading critic of the Warren Court, Joseph Grano. As the Court *now* characterizes what it did in *Miranda*, maintains Professor Grano, that case is an "illegitimate" decision.[25] To permit federal courts to impose "prophylactic rules" on the states, (i.e., rules that may be violated without directly violating the Constitution), contends Grano, is "to say in essence that federal courts have supervisory power over state courts."[26] According to him, the Court lacks constitutional authority to overturn state convictions when the Constitution has not actually been violated.

A provision of the federal criminal code enacted in 1968, Section 3501, title 18, of the U. S. Code, purports to "repeal" *Miranda* and reinstate the due process— "totality of the circumstances"—"voluntariness" test for the admissibility of confessions. The validity of Section 3501 may turn on whether or not Professor Grano's characterization of *Miranda* is sound.

As Justice Scalia pointed out recently, Section 3501 "has been studiously avoided by every Administration . . . since its enactment more than 25 years ago."[27] Justice Scalia sharply criticized the Justice Department's "repeated refusal to invoke Section 3501," a refusal that has "caused the federal judiciary to confront a host of '*Miranda*' issues that might be entirely irrelevant under federal law."[28] Scalia has also maintained that because Section 3501 "is a provision of law directed *to the courts*, reflecting the people's assessment of the proper balance to be struck [in this area], [w]e shirk our duty if we systematically disregard that statutory command simply because the Justice Department declines to remind us of it."[29]

The failure of the Justice Department to invoke Section 3501 did not discourage two conservative legal groups, the Washington Legal Foundation and the Safe Streets Coalition. Led by the indefatigable Paul Cassell, a Utah Law School professor who has become the nation's leading critic of *Miranda*,[30] these groups repeatedly urged the federal courts to inject Section 3501 into their cases.

Recently, after the Fourth Circuit upheld a district court's ruling suppressing defendant's confession on the ground that the confession had been obtained in violation of *Miranda*,[31] these organizations moved to proceed as *amici curiae*, maintaining that the confession should have been admitted, despite the *Miranda* violation, unless it failed to satisfy the more lenient standard for admissibility set forth in Section 3501. To the surprise of many, the Fourth Circuit then issued an order directing the parties to consider the effect of Section 3501 on the admissibility of defendant's confession.

Because the government had not pressed Section 3501 before the district court or the court of appeals as a basis for a determination that defendant's confession was admissible, the Fourth Circuit declined to rehear the appeal. But the court voiced strong disagreement with the Justice Department's view that *Miranda* "remains binding on lower federal courts notwithstanding Section 3501 unless or until it is modified by the Supreme Court."

A year later, in *United States v. Dickerson*,[32] the Fourth Circuit gave the Washington Legal Foundation and the Safe Streets Coalition a stunning victory. Although the dissenting judge protested that the ruling was made "without the benefit of any briefing in opposition" and "against the express wishes of the Department of Justice,"[33] a two to one majority held that the pre-*Miranda* voluntariness test set forth in Section 3501, rather than the famous *Miranda* case, governs the admissibility of confessions in the federal courts. Therefore, the district court had erred when it had suppressed a voluntary confession simply because it was obtained in violation of *Miranda*.

The reasoning of the Fourth Circuit may be summarized quite briefly: Congress has the power to "overrule" rules of evidence and procedure that are not required by the Constitution. The *Miranda* rules are not constitutionally required; they are only "prophylactic" rules designed to implement or reinforce the underlying constitutional right. Therefore, Section 3501 is a valid exercise of congressional authority to override judicially created rules not part of the Constitution.

I must disagree with the reasoning of the Fourth Circuit panel. I do not believe that the Warren Court lacked constitutional authority to overturn state convictions resting on statements that were not shown to be "involuntary" or "coerced" in the pre-*Miranda* sense of these terms.

I share Stephen Schulhofer's view that the conclusive presumption of compulsion adopted by the *Miranda* Court was "a responsible reaction to the problems of the voluntariness test, to the rarity of uses in which compelling pressures are truly absent, and to the adjudicatory costs of case-by-case decisions in this area."[34] And I agree with Schulhofer's colleague, David Strauss, that prophylactic rules are a "a central and necessary feature of constitutional law."[35]

Suppose *Miranda* had established a *rebuttable* presumption that any incriminating statement obtained in a custodial setting without the *Miranda* safeguards (or equally effective procedures) is compelled, but that this presumption could be overcome if the suspect were a police officer, lawyer, law student or a person with a doctorate in criminology. Such a presumption would produce the same result a *conclusive* presumption would in the great bulk of cases. But as far as I know, everybody agrees that a court's responsibility to achieve accurate fact finding permits it to assign burdens of proof and to adopt rebuttable presumptions. As Professor Strauss argues, if it is legitimate for a court to decide that evidence of voluntariness is legally immaterial in some cases (where the evidence is insufficient to overcome a rebuttable presumption), why should it be improper for a court to extend this approach to all cases.[36]

A "prophylactic" rule is not a dirty word. Sometimes such rules are necessary and proper. The privilege against self-incrimination, no less than other constitutional rights, needs "breathing space." And prophylactic rules may be the best way to provide it.

Miranda is based on the realization that case-by-case determination of the "voluntariness" of a confession in light of the totality of the circumstances was severely testing the capacity of the judiciary and that institutional realities warranted a conclusive presumption that a confession obtained under certain conditions and in the absence of certain safeguards was compelled. The pre-*Miranda* "voluntariness" test was too mushy, subjective, and unruly to provide suspects with adequate protection.[37] And it was too time-consuming to administer. As Justice Hugo Black expressed it during the oral arguments in *Miranda*: "If you are going to determine the admissibility of a confession each time on the circumstances . . . if the Court will take them one by one . . . it is more than we are capable of doing."[38]

In 1966, after years of struggling with the "voluntariness" test, a majority of the Supreme Court had arrived at the same conclusion that this traditional test was woefully inadequate and simply unworkable. Something else was needed, something easier to administer. That "something else" turned out to be *Miranda*. Under any sensible approach to constitutional interpretation, the Supreme Court must be allowed to take into account its own fact-finding limitations.

Establishing presumptions and prophylactic rules is inherent in the art of judging—in the effort to make constitutional rights more meaningful. The Fourth Circuit panel that decided *Dickerson* did a lot more than try to deal *Miranda* a fatal blow. Its approach to constitutional decision making restricts the ability of the Rehnquist Court—and every Court—to interpret constitutional provisions in light of institutional realities.

A good example of how the Court promulgates a "prophylactic rule" in order to compensate for its fact-finding limitations is *North Carolina v. Pearce*.[39] A number of defendants had successfully overturned their original convictions only to have the judge give them a heavier sentence for the same crime when they were re-tried and reconvicted. There was reason to think that in some of these cases, at least, sentencing judges were "punishing" defendants for having succeeded in get-ting their first convictions set aside. As the Court noted, however, "[t]he existence of a retaliatory motivation would . . . be extremely difficult to prove in any indi-vidual case."[40]

What did the *Pearce* Court do? It established what has "come to be called a 'presumption of vindictiveness'":[41] "In order to assure the absence of [a retaliatory] motivation" it held that "whenever a judge imposes a more severe sentence upon a defendant after a new trial, the reasons [for] doing so must affirmatively appear [and] must be based upon objective information concerning identifiable conduct on the part of the defendant occurring after the time of the original sentencing pro-ceeding."[42] Absent such a showing, vindictiveness against the defendant for having successfully attacked his first conviction is to be presumed and the sentence he re-ceived on retrial struck down as a violation of due process.

The Court subsequently made plain that *Pearce* had created a "prophylactic rule" and that "prophylactic" was not a dirty word. Speaking for a seven to two major-ity (one that included Chief Justice Burger and Justice Rehnquist), Justice White ex-plained *Pearce* as a case in which, "[p]ositing that a more penalty after reconviction would violate due process [if] imposed as purposeful punishment for having success-fully appealed," the Court concluded that "such untoward sentences occurred *with sufficient frequency* to warrant the imposition of a prophylactic rule. . . ."[43]

A year later, again speaking for a seven to two majority that included Burger and Rehnquist, Justice Powell (who has never been accused of being enthused about the Warren Court's revolution in criminal procedure), explained and de-fended "the *Pearce* prophylactic rules" by analogizing them to the *Miranda* rules:

> By eliminating the possibility that [improper considerations] might occasion en-hanced sentences, the *Pearce* prophylactic rules assist in guaranteeing the propriety of the sentencing phase of the criminal process. In this protective role, *Pearce* is analogous to *Miranda*, [in] which the Court established rules to govern police practices during custodial interrogations in order to safeguard the rights of the ac-cused and to assure the reliability of statements made during these interrogations. Thus, the prophylactic rules in *Pearce* and *Miranda* are similar in that each was de-signed to preserve the integrity of a phase of the criminal process.[44]

Justice Powell and the six Justices who joined him seemed untroubled by the fact that in many instances application of the *Pearce* rule would benefit defendants whose rights had not *actually* been violated—who had not actually been the vic-tims of vindictiveness.[45] This was a good reason for not applying *Pearce* retroac-tively to resentencing proceedings that took place prior to the *Pearce* decision[46] (just as *Miranda* had not been applied retroactively),[47] but it was not a valid reason for failing to apply the rule prospectively. It is "an inherent attribute of prophylactic constitutional rules" that their application will benefit "some defendants who have suffered no constitutional deprivation."[48]

In still another case applying *Pearce*, even Chief Justice Burger seemed unper-turbed by its "prophylactic" nature. Speaking for a majority of the Court that included Justice vindictiveness from entering into a decision and to allay any fear on the part of a defendant that an increased sentence is in fact the product of vindictiveness, the [*Pearce*] Court fashioned what in essence is a "prophylactic rule."[49] But the Court did not say this disapprovingly.

Neither the Chief Justice nor any other member of the Court complained that the *Pearce* rule had enabled federal courts to exercise their "supervisory power over state courts." Nobody seemed troubled that a defendant who had received an increased sentence on retrial could establish a due process violation without showing *actual* vindictiveness. Nor did anybody suggest that *Pearce* was an "illegitimate" decision.

North Carolina v. Pearce is usually classified as an "appeals" case or a "double jeopardy" case. But one need not stray from the field of confessions to find other examples of "prophylactic rules" whose legitimacy has been accepted or at least assumed. Indeed, one need go no further than *Miranda*'s own progeny.

Marking one of the few times the post-Warren Court has read *Miranda* rather broadly, *Edwards v. Arizona*[50] held that when a suspect effectively asserts his right to a lawyer (as opposed to his right to remain silent)[51] the suspect may not be subjected to further police questioning *until* counsel has been made available to him *unless* he himself initiates further conversation with the police.[52] This means that the police cannot try to change the suspect's mind—not even if they give him a fresh set of warnings at the outset of a new interrogation session. Rather, they must wait to see whether the suspect changes his mind on his own initiative.

Edwards held, in effect (in a forceful opinion by Justice White, and a surprising one considering his angry dissent in *Miranda*), that when a custodial suspect invokes his right to counsel, there is a *conclusive presumption* that any subsequent waiver of rights that comes at police instigation, not at the suspect's own behest, is compelled. To put it somewhat differently, *Edwards* in effect established a new "prophylactic rule" that built on and reinforced *Miranda*'s "prophylactic rules."

It will not do to say that the *Edwards* rule was *required by* the *Miranda* decision. Six years prior to *Edwards*, the Court had held that if a suspect asserts his "right to silence" (as opposed to his right to counsel) the police *may*, if they cease questioning on the spot, "try again"—and succeed at a subsequent interrogation.[53] The Court could have plausibly held that invocation of the right to counsel should be treated no differently than assertion of the right to silence. Indeed, as I have maintained elsewhere, I do not think it makes much sense to draw a distinction based on which *Miranda* right a suspect happens to trigger.[54]

Why, then, did the Burger Court establish, and the Rehnquist Court reaffirm and expand, what the Court has recently called "the bright-line, prophylactic *Edwards* rule?"[55] In *Minnick v. Mississippi*,[56] a seven to two majority of the Rehnquist Court (only Justice Scalia, joined by Rehnquist, C. J., dissenting) told us the following:

> The [*Edwards*] rule ensures that any statement made [by a suspect who has previously asserted his right to counsel] is not the result of coercive pressures. *Edwards* conserves judicial resources which would otherwise be expended in making difficult determinations of voluntariness. . . .[57]

Is this not an explanation and defense of *Miranda* itself as well as *Edwards*? To be sure, as Professor Grano once said to me in a debate about *Miranda's* legitimacy, the fact that the Rehnquist Court has reaffirmed and expanded the *Edwards* rule does not conclusively refute the argument that *Miranda* is an "illegitimate" or extraconstitutional decision—that the Rehnquist Court may also have transgressed proper boundaries does not change the fact that the Court lacks constitutional authority to overturn state convictions when the Constitution has not *actually* been violated. That may be so, but it sure makes it unlikely that the Rehnquist Court will overrule *Miranda* on this ground. It also makes it unlikely that the Rehnquist Court will uphold Section 3501 on this ground.

Further evidence that prophylactic constitutional rules are not to be demeaned is provided by *Withrow v. Williams*.[58] When the Court held that a state prisoner afforded a full and fair opportunity to litigate a Fourth Amendment claim could not obtain federal habeas relief on the ground that illegally seized evidence was used against him in the state prosecution,[59] many assumed that a similar restriction on the exercise of federal habeas jurisdiction would apply to a state prisoner's claim that his conviction rested on statements obtained in violation of *Miranda*. For there was little reason to think that the post-Warren Court had a warmer spot in its heart for *Miranda* than it did for the search and seizure exclusionary rule. But the *Withrow* Court confounded the prognosticators.

The government argued in *Withrow* that because the *Miranda* rules "are not constitutional in character, but merely 'prophylactic,'" federal habeas review should not extend to claims based on violations of these rules.[60] A majority of the Court was not impressed; it accepted the government's characterization of the *Miranda* safeguards, for purposes of the case, but not the government's conclusion. Justice Souter, who wrote the opinion of the Court in *Withrow*, did not deny that "we have sometimes called the *Miranda* safeguards 'prophylactic' in nature"[61] (because, explained Souter, violation of these safeguards might lead to the exclusion of statements that would not be found "involuntary" under pre-*Miranda* standards). But this, he noted, is a "far cry" from putting *Miranda* in the same category as the search and seizure exclusionary rule or from rendering *Miranda* subject to the same restrictions on the exercise of federal habeas jurisdiction that apply to in search and seizure cases.[62]

The Fourth Amendment exclusionary rule, observed the Court, cannot "be thought to enhance the soundness of the criminal process by improving the reliability of evidence introduced at trial,"[63] but *Miranda* differs in this respect: "'Prophylactic' though it may be, *in protecting* a defendant's Fifth Amendment privilege against self-incrimination, *Miranda* safeguards 'a fundamental *trial* right.'"[64] It "brace[s] against 'the possibility of unreliable statements in every instance of in-custody interrogation,'" and thereby "serves to guard against 'the use of unreliable statements at trial.'"[65]

Other Threats to Miranda

Assuming arguendo that I am right—that the Court will reject the argument that Section 3501 "overrules" *Miranda*—that famous case is not out of danger. The Rehnquist Court may still deal *Miranda* some heavy blows.

For one thing, the Court may uphold the use for impeachment purposes of statements obtained in violation of *Miranda* even when the police *deliberately* violate a suspect's rights for the very purpose of obtaining evidence for impeachment purposes. For another thing, the Court may permit the government to use all the clues and physical evidence obtained as a result of a *Miranda* violation. Still worse, the Court may allow the government to do so even when the police *deliberately* commit a *Miranda* violation for the very purpose of obtaining clues and other derivative evidence.

As Professor Carol Steiker has pointed out, in discussing the Warren Court and its successor Courts it is helpful to distinguish between "conduct" rules (those addressed to law enforcement officials) and "decision" rules (those addressed to courts regarding the consequences of unconstitutional conduct).[66] Although they have left the Warren Court's "conduct" rules relatively intact, the Burger and Rehnquist Courts have "wag[ed] counter-revolutionary war" against the Warren Court's "decision" rules.[67] And they have done so by developing a number of what Professor Steiker calls "inclusionary rules"—rules that permit the use at trial of admittedly unconstitutionally obtained evidence or that let stand criminal convictions based on such evidence."[68]

These "inclusionary" rules, Steiker persuasively argues, "represent a departure from the Warren Court's understanding of the judicial consequences of constitutional violations by the police that is much more dramatic than the changes made in police-conduct rules over the same period of time."[69] Good examples of "inclusionary" rules are the post-Warren Court doctrines regarding the use of statements obtained in violation of *Miranda* for impeachment purposes and the use of evidence *derived from* statements obtained in violation of *Miranda* (i.e., the admissibility of the "fruit of the poisonous tree").

The first blow the post-Warren Court struck *Miranda* was *Harris v. New York*,[70] which held that statements preceded by defective warnings, and thus inadmissible in the government's case in chief, could still be used to impeach the defendant's credibility if he chose to take the witness stand. Four years later, in *Oregon v. Hass*,[71] the Court went a considerable step further. In this case, after being advised of his rights, the suspect had asserted his right to counsel. But the police had continued to question him. The Court ruled that in this situation, too, the resulting statements could be used for impeachment cases. However, there is, I think, an important distinction between the facts in *Harris* and those in *Hass*.

Many suspects make incriminating statements even after being given a full set of warnings. Therefore, *Harris* might have been explained (and contained) on the ground that permitting impeachment use of statements obtained without complete warnings would not significantly encourage the police to violate *Miranda*. However, now that *Hass* is on the books, when a suspect *asserts* his right to counsel, the police seem to have virtually nothing to lose and something to gain by *continuing* to question the suspect in violation of *Miranda*.

The *Hass* Court took notice of this argument, but dismissed it as a "speculative possibility."[72] It is not easy to establish, but if and when it can be established that the police deliberately ignored a suspect's assertion of his rights for the very purpose of obtaining impeachment evidence, are we *still* in the realm of speculation?

The *Hass* Court saw no need to bar the impeachment use of statements obtained in violation of *Miranda* because "there is sufficient deterrence when the evidence is made unavailable to the prosecution in its case in chief."[73] (Now *that is* speculation.) But how can a court maintain that position when it is clear that the fact that the statements could not be used in the government's case in chief failed to deter the officer? When the officer deliberately violated *Miranda* in order to secure impeachment evidence?

This is why it was so discouraging when last year the California Supreme Court rejected the argument that *Hass* was based on the assumption that a purposeful or deliberate violation of *Miranda* and *Edwards* would not occur.[74] I can only hope that the U.S. Supreme Court rejects the California court's remarkable conclusion that evidence of "a purpose to violate the suspect's rights in order to secure [impeachment] evidence" only "call[s] into question" the accuracy of the U.S. Supreme Court's assumption in the impeachment cases that "police misconduct will be deterred adequately by excluding improperly obtained evidence from the prosecution's case-in-chief, but such evidence does not render the [impeachment exception] inapplicable."[75]

Why not? What does it take to demolish the unexamined and unsupported assumption that "sufficient deterrence" is provided so long as statements obtained in violation of *Miranda* are inadmissible in the prosecution's case in chief?

Oregon v. Elstad[76] represents an even more serious threat to *Miranda* than do the impeachment cases. Indeed, short of flatly overruling *Miranda* or upholding the federal statute purporting to "repeal" it, *Elstad* poses the greatest danger of all.

In that case, in the course of ruling that the fact that the police had obtained a statement from the defendant in violation of *Miranda* when they questioned him earlier at his home did not bar the admissibility of a second statement, made at the stationhouse, when this time the police had complied with *Miranda*, the Court indicated that the "fruit of the poisonous tree" doctrine does not apply to *Miranda* at all.[77] If so, *all* the "fruits" of, or evidence derived from, a *Miranda* violation would be admissible, whether they are a second confession, a prosecution witness, or physical evidence.

Elstad can plausibly be read very narrowly. For one thing, the failure to advise Elstad of his *Miranda* rights seemed to be inadvertent. If, for example, Elstad had invoked his right to counsel at the first meeting and the police had refused to honor that right, the result might have been different.[78] Moreover, as dissenting Justice Brennan pointed out in *Elstad*, the majority "relies heavily on individual 'volition' as an insulating factor in successive-confession cases"—a factor "altogether missing in the context of inanimate evidence."[79]

However, at several places in her majority opinion, Justice O'Connor tells us that the poisonous tree doctrine assumes the existence of an underlying constitutional violation—for example, a violation of the Fourth Amendment or "police infringement of the Fifth Amendment itself."[80] And it is plain that the *Elstad* majority did not believe that a *Miranda* violation qualifies as a "constitutional violation."[81]

The Court has never explicitly addressed the question whether physical or non-testimonial evidence derived from a *Miranda* violation is admissible. However, I have to say that there is a good chance that it will answer that question in the affirmative. In the meantime, ever since *Elstad* was decided, "federal and state courts have almost uniformly ruled that the prosecution can introduce nontestimonial fruits of a *Miranda* violation in a criminal trial."[82]

"It has been said," observed Judge Henry Friendly some thirty years ago, "that 'what data there are' suggest that the obtaining of leads with which to obtain real or demonstrative evidence or prosecution witnesses is more important than getting statements for use in court."[83] A good deal more recently, another commentator similarly noted that "[e]xpert interrogators have long recognized, and continue to instruct, that a confession is a primary source for determining the existence and whereabouts of the fruit of a crime such as documents or weapons."[84]

Therefore, a ruling that *all types* of evidence derived from a *Miranda* violation are admissible would strike the landmark case a grievous blow. How could we possibly expect the police to comply with *Miranda* if the courts barred *only* the use of incriminating statements obtained in violation of that doctrine, but none of the leads or clues or evidence these statements brought to light?

A decade ago, in order to underscore the potential cumulative effect of the various exceptions to *Miranda* that the post-Warren Court had carved out, Professor Albert Alschuler discussed the various ways to get around *Miranda* that a hypothetical unscrupulous police training instructor might teach young officers.[85] However, it is now clear that we are no longer dealing with hypothetical police instructors or imaginary police training materials.

In 1998, we learned that lawyers seeking to prohibit officers in two California police departments from questioning custodial suspects after they have asserted their *Miranda* rights had come upon police training materials that instruct officers to "go 'outside *Miranda*,'" that is, *to continue to question* someone who has invoked his rights (e.g., clearly asserted his right to counsel) so that the police may learn the whereabouts of physical evidence the prosecution may use, or so that the police may acquire the names of other witnesses the prosecution may call, or so that the police may obtain statements the prosecution can use if the defendant takes the stand in his own defense.[86]

The deputy district attorney who made the training videotape is not unaware that some police officers may feel a bit uncomfortable deliberately violating *Miranda*. He reassures these fastidious officers as follows:

> When you violate *Miranda*, you're not violating the Constitution . . . [There's] no law says you can't question people "outside *Miranda*". . . .
> [When we question someone who has invoked his *Miranda* rights] [a]ll we lose is the statement taken in violation of *Miranda*. We do not lose physical evidence that resulted from that. We do not lose the testimony of other witnesses that we learned about only by violating his *Miranda* invocation.[87]

Unfortunately, the deputy district attorney is right about the testimony of other witnesses whose whereabouts are learned only by violating *Miranda*. He may be right about the use of physical evidence as well. But the Court has not yet made it clear that physical evidence discovered as a result of a *Miranda* violation may also be used by the prosecution. However, there is a distinct possibility that the Court will so hold in the near future. If it does, we can be sure that police training instructors would call it to the attention of their students. Indeed, if the recently discovered California police training videotape is any indication, police officers are *already* being instructed that if a custodial suspect invokes his *Miranda* rights, what the officers can "legally do" is continue to question him because "[a]ll we lose is the statement taken in violation of *Miranda*. We do not lose physical evidence that resulted from that."

I am painfully aware that a number of Justices view *Miranda* as occupying a lowly position in the hierarchy of rights. Nevertheless, I cannot believe this Court would admit the fruits of a *Miranda* violation obtained pursuant to a police department policy of violating *Miranda* for the very purpose of obtaining derivative evidence. If it turns out I am wrong about this, we should simply give *Miranda* a "respectful burial."[88]

Coerced Confessions and the "Rule of Automatic Reversal"

As Professor Steiker has noted, not only has the post-Warren Court "promulgat[ed] 'inclusionary rules' that make possible the admission of evidence that has been obtained through unconstitutional conduct of law enforcement agents," by changing rules governing the standard of review on appeal and on federal habeas corpus it has made it harder for the erroneous admission of unconstitutionally obtained evidence at trial to lead to the overturning of convictions.[89] To be sure, it was the Warren Court that first recognized a doctrine of harmless constitutional error.[90] (Prior to the 1960s, it was generally assumed that constitutional error could never be regarded "harmless error.") But the Court was careful to note that some constitutional rights — it specifically mentioned the right against admission of a coerced confession — "are so basic to a fair trial that their infraction can never be treated as harmless error."[91]

However, as Judge Harry Edwards recently observed, the post-Warren Court has "dramatically expanded the list of constitutional violations that are subject to harmless-error analysis" and has "subtract[ed] one" from the list of those errors thought to be "per se reversible."[92] In *Arizona v. Fulminante*[93] (a case about which another participant in the University of Tulsa Conference, Justice Stanley Mosk, had some understandably harsh things to say),[94] a five to four majority of the Rehnquist Court overruled a long line of cases[95] and held that the improper admission of a coerced confession *was* subject to harmless-error analysis.[96]

The *Fulminante* majority, per Chief Justice Rehnquist, drew—and relied heavily on—a distinction between (1) "trial errors," which may be "quantitatively assessed" in the context of other evidence presented, and (2) "structural defects in the constitution of the trial mechanism" which pervade the entire conduct of the trial and thus "defy analysis by 'harmless-error' standards." (The Chief Justice viewed the other two constitutional violations referred to in *Chapman* as reversible per se—total deprivation of the right to counsel at trial and trial before a judge who in not impartial—as "structural defects.")[97]

Two decades earlier, a five to four majority of the Burger Court had held that even though a postindictment confession made to a police officer posing as defendant's "cellmate" should have been excluded on Sixth Amendment-*Massiah* grounds, any error was harmless.[98] Moreover, during the 1970s and 1980s, the great majority of lower courts had applied the harmless-error rule to the erroneous admission of statements obtained in violation of *Miranda*.[99]

This led Chief Justice Rehnquist to say in *Fulminante* that "the evidentiary impact of an involuntary confession, and *its effect* upon the composition of the record, is indistinguishable from that of a confession obtained in violation of the Sixth Amendment"[100] —or one inadmissible *for any other reason*. The Chief Justice would have us believe that for harmless-error purposes an inadmissible confession is an inadmissible confession. But this is not so.

The magnitude of the police illegality in a case such as *Oregon v. Elstad*,[101] where the police briefly questioned a suspect in his own living room without first giving him the *Miranda* warnings, is not of the same order as the magnitude of the police misconduct in cases such as *Malinski* (where police interrogation stripped off defendant's clothes and kept him naked for several hours)[102] and *Payne* (where the chief of police threatened to turn a young black over to a mob waiting outside the jailhouse unless he confessed)[103] and *Rogers* (where, in order to get the defendant to confess, the police threatened to "bring in" his wife for questioning).[104] It was in *Malinski*, *Payne*, and *Rogers* and cases like them that the Court firmly established the "rule of automatic reversal" —and it was driven to do so, I think it fair to say, by the felt need to *condemn* police methods that violated fundamental values and offended a civilized system of justice.[105]

That they coerced a confession out of a suspect is about as bad a thing one can say of the police. When such a confession is erroneously admitted at trial it casts a dark shadow on the integrity of the criminal process that led to a conviction. That is why I think when the Court adopted and first applied the "rule of automatic reversal" in such cases it said in effect: Regardless of other evidence of guilt, a coerced confession deeply stains the criminal process. This is not an occasion for speculation about the impact of the confession on the trier of fact. Do it over again— without the confession.[106]

To be sure, the police misconduct in *Fulminante* was not as egregious as it had been in many of the earlier coerced confession cases. While in prison, the defendant had been befriended by another inmate, Sarivola, who, unknown to the defendant, was a paid informant for the FBI masquerading as an organized crime figure. On hearing a rumor that defendant had killed his stepdaughter, Sarivola told the defendant that he was receiving and would continue to receive "tough treatment" from other inmates because of the rumor, but that he, Sarivola, would protect him from the other prisoners if defendant told him the truth about the murder. At that point, defendant confessed to Sarivola that he had committed the murder.

In overturning the rule of automatic reversal for improperly admitted coerced confessions, Chief Justice noted that "there are no allegations of physical violence on behalf of the police."[107] But what exactly is his point?

Some forty years ago, the Court pointed out that "coercion can be mental as well as physical and [that] the blood of the accused is not the only hallmark" of a coerced confession.[108] Having found it "impossible to create a meaningful distinction" for harmless-error analysis—those are Chief Justice Rehnquist's words—

between coerced confessions and confessions inadmissible on other grounds[109]—surely the Chief Justice is not prepared to create a meaningful distinction, for harmless-error purposes, between coerced confessions marked by physical violence and those not so marked—between *barely* or *mildly coerced* confessions and *egregiously* coerced ones.[110]

If all *inadmissible* confessions are to be treated alike for harmless-error purposes, and that is the best reading of *Fulminante*, then surely all *coerced* confessions are to be treated alike. In this context, at least, a coerced confession is a coerced confession. Henceforth, *all* coerced confessions, even those beaten out of a suspect, will be subject to harmless-error analysis.

Constitutional violations not subject to harmless error now include not only a total deprivation of the right to counsel at trial and a biased judge but racial discrimination in the selection of a grand jury.[111] However, if a defendant has been found guilty beyond a reasonable doubt by a properly constituted *petit* jury at a trial on the merits free of any other error, how can the error that occurred in the selection of the grand jury be classified, as the Chief Justice does in *Fulminante*, as a "structural defect affecting the framework within which the trial proceeds"?[112]

A grand jury proceeding merely decides whether there is a prima facie case against a defendant. Thus, "any possible prejudice to the defendant" resulting from racial discrimination in the selection of a grand jury "disappears" when a constitutionally valid trial jury later finds him guilty beyond a reasonable doubt.[113] It hardly follows, therefore, as the *Fulminante* majority would have us believe, that *whenever* racial discrimination takes place in selecting a grand jury the reliability of the determination of guilt is suspect.[114]

The best explanation for automatic reversal when there has been racial discrimination in the selection of grand jurors is *not* that a structural error has occurred whose effects are inherently indeterminate but that a constitutional error of large magnitude has taken place—one that "strikes at the fundamental values of our judicial system and our society as a whole."[115] The same, I think, can be said when the police extract a confession from a person and that confession is then used against him at his trial. The use of a coerced confession at one's trial, no less than discrimination in the selection of a grand jury, "destroys the appearance of justice and thereby casts doubt on the integrity of the judicial process."[116]

I believe there is a good deal to be said for Judge Harry Edwards's view: "We have come a long way from the brutal beating with whips and leather straps used to extract a confession in *Brown v. Mississippi*, or the thirty-six uninterrupted hours of questioning under bright lights employed in *Ashcraft v. Tennessee*, but we have done so only because the reversal of a conviction was the sure penalty for these actions."[117]

In rejecting the argument that harmless-error analysis should govern instances of racial discrimination in the selection of grand jurors, the Court, per Marshall, J., called such discrimination "a grave constitutional trespass" and noted that if it "becomes a thing of the past, no conviction will ever again be lost on account of it."[118] Again, the same may be said for the erroneous admission of coerced confessions.

More than sixty years after the Wickersham Commission exposed the ugly facts of the "third degree" and more than thirty years after the Court decided *Miranda*, are there still so many confessions being coerced and so many being improperly admitted into evidence that we need a harmless-error doctrine to excuse some of them?

Search and Seizure

As Justice Stewart pointed out, in lectures he delivered shortly after stepping down from the High Court,[119] there are two principal ways to reduce the impact of the search-and-seizure exclusionary rule: by narrowing the thrust of the exclusionary rule and by shrinking the scope of the Fourth Amendment itself, thereby giving the police more leeway to investigate crime. Although not all post-Warren Court search-and-seizure rulings have been in favor of the government, in the main the Court has significantly reduced the impact of the exclusionary rule in *both* respects.

Narrowing the Thrust of the Exclusionary Rule

Although one would gain little inkling of this from the majority opinions of the Burger and Rehnquist Courts, originally and for much of its life the federal exclusionary rule, first promulgated in the famous 1914 *Weeks* case,[120] rested on what might be called a "principled basis."[121] The reasons for excluding evidence obtained in violation of the Fourth Amendment were to avoid "sanctioning" or "ratifying" the police misconduct that produced the evidence, to keep the courts from being contaminated by partnership in police misconduct, to prevent the government whose agents had violated the Constitution from being in a better position than the government whose officers had obeyed the Constitution, and—ultimately—to assure the police and the public alike that courts take constitutional rights seriously.[122]

I believe this is the dominant theme of *Mapp v. Ohio*,[123] the case that touched off the Warren Court's revolution in U.S. criminal procedure by imposing the federal exclusionary rule on the states as a matter of Fourteenth Amendment due process.[124]

Evidently Justice Clark, author of the majority opinion in *Mapp*, felt obligated to refute *all* the arguments critics of the exclusionary rule had made over the years—one of which was that the rule was not an effective deterrent or not markedly superior to "other methods" in this regard.[125] Thus, at one point Justice Clark did discuss whether or not exclusion of the illegally obtained evidence is a more effective deterrent than "other means of protection" (Clark thought it was).[126] But when one considers the totality of Justice Clark's opinion the dominant message of *Mapp* is fairly clear: Although not explicitly provided for in the text of the Fourth Amendment, the exclusionary rule is a *command* of the Constitution.

Part I of the *Mapp* opinion emphasizes that the exclusionary rule is not "a mere rule of evidence" or an exercise of the Court's "supervisory powers" but a "constitutionally required" doctrine.[127] In Part III, the Court "hold[s] that all evidence obtained by searches and seizures in violation of the Constitution is, *by that same authority*, inadmissible in a state court."[128] Part IV concludes with the assurance that "no man is to be convicted on unconstitutional evidence."[129] And the fifth and last part of the opinion refers to "our holding that the exclusionary rule is an essential part of both the Fourth and Fourteenth Amendments"[130] and observes that the constitutional prohibition against unreasonable searches and seizures "is enforceable in the same manner and to like effect as other basic rights secured by the Due Process Clause."[131]

In short, the majority opinion in *Mapp* reaffirms what I have called the "original understanding" of the exclusionary rule, as explained in *Weeks* and its progeny: The rule is constitutionally required. Its survival does not depend on proof that it significantly affects police conduct (although Justice Clark was convinced that it does, as am I). Nor does its application to various fact situations turn on such proof.

However, ways of thinking about the exclusionary rule soon changed. In the post-Warren Court era, the "deterrence" rationale and "cost-benefit" analysis gained ascendancy. This approach bloomed in *United States v. Calandra*,[132] the most important exclusionary rule case of the 1970s. The *Calandra* majority, per Justice Powell, characterized the exclusionary rule—one might say disparaged it—as a "judicially created remedy designed to safeguard Fourth Amendment rights generally through its deterrent effect, rather than a personal constitutional right of the party aggrieved."[133] Thus, whether the exclusionary rule should be applied "presents a question not of rights but of remedies"—a question to be answered by weighing the "likely 'costs'" of the rule against its "likely 'benefits.'"[134]

The post-*Mapp* way of thinking about the exclusionary rule enabled critics of the rule to gain some important victories. This is hardly surprising. The "costs" of the exclusionary rule are immediately apparent—the "freeing" of a "plainly guilty" drug dealer[135]—but the "benefits" of the rule are hard to grasp.

One *could* say that the benefits "involve safeguarding a zone of dignity and privacy for every citizen, controlling abuses of power [and] preserving checks and balances."[136] And one *could* regard these goals as "pretty weighty benefits, perhaps even invaluable ones."[137] But the Court has not done so. Instead, it has viewed the benefits of the rule "as abstract [and] speculative."[138]

On the other hand, the Court has underscored what it thinks are the severe *costs* of the rule. Thus, it has called the rule a "drastic measure,"[139] an "extreme sanction,"[140] a rule that "exacts a costly toll upon the ability of courts to ascertain the truth in a criminal case,"[141] and one whose application is "contrary to the idea of proportionality that is essential to the concept of justice."[142]

Given the Court's characterization of the "costs" and "benefits" to be balanced, the outcome is quite predictable. Indeed, although cost-benefit analysis sounds objective, even scientific, it is hard to avoid the conclusion that in search-and-seizure cases, at least, it simply gives back the values and assumptions the Court feeds into it.

During the cost-benefit analysis era, the exclusionary rule lost numerous times, for example, in *United States v. Calandra* (declining to apply the rule in grand jury proceedings),[143] *Stone v. Powell* (greatly limiting the circumstances under which Fourth Amendment claims can be raised in federal habeas corpus proceedings),[144] *United States v. Janis* (rule inapplicable in federal civil tax proceedings),[145] and *INS v. Lopez-Mendoza* (rule inapplicable in civil deportation proceedings).[146]

The cost-benefit approach to the search-and-seizure exclusionary rule culminated in *United States v. Leon*,[147] the case that adopted a so-called good-faith exception (actually a "reasonable mistake" exception) to the exclusionary rule. According to the *Leon* majority, the "marginal or nonexistent benefits" produced by the exclusionary rule when the police reasonably but mistakenly rely on a search warrant that turns out to be invalid "cannot justify the costs of exclusion."[148]

The earlier cases using the cost-benefit approach had assumed that the exclusionary rule was fully applicable in a criminal prosecution against the direct victim of a Fourth Amendment violation and had maintained that the rule *need not also* be applied in certain "collateral" or "peripheral" settings because "no significant *additional* increment of deterrence [was] deemed likely."[149] But *Leon*, for the first time, used cost-benefit analysis to narrow the scope of the exclusionary rule in the prosecution's case in chief against those whose rights have been violated.

In *Leon*, the officers relied on a search warrant. Is the "reasonable good faith" exception limited to the warrant setting? Some language in *Leon* supports such a limitation; other language indicates that *Leon* should apply *whenever* the police are acting in objective good faith.

I must say that at the time *Leon* was decided, I did not believe it would be limited to the warrant setting. For one thing, the Court, and individual Justices in separate opinions, had voiced serious doubts "the extreme sanction of exclusion," as the Court called it in *Leon*,[150] could "pay its way" in *any* setting, let alone one in which the Fourth Amendment violations were neither deliberate nor substantial. For another thing, I found it hard to believe that after many years of talk about a "good-faith" or "reasonable-mistake" exception to the exclusionary rule, the Court would finally adopt such an exception only to limit it to the tiny percentage of police searches conducted pursuant to warrants.

The Rehnquist Court is yet to say that the same cost-benefit analysis that led to the result in *Leon* supports a good-faith exception across the board. But the Rehnquist Court has extended *Leon* to other fact situations.

Thus it has upheld the admissibility of evidence where (1) the police act in reasonable reliance on a statute authorizing the search in question even though the statute turns out to be in violation of the Fourth Amendment[151] and (2) the police make an invalid arrest, but one attributable to negligent recordkeeping by a court clerk.[152]

As illustrated by the case of *Pennsylvania Board of Probation v. Scott*,[153] the Rehnquist Court has also continued to decline to apply the exclusionary rule to proceedings other than criminal prosecutions. But the reasoning of the Court leaves a good deal to be desired.

In *Scott*, the officers who conducted the warrantless and apparently suspicionless search of Scott's home because they thought he might be keeping firearms there, a violation of one of the conditions of his parole as well as a crime, knew that Scott was a parolee. They themselves were parole officers. If Scott did turn out to possess firearms (and he did), the officers probably contemplated a revocation proceeding rather than a criminal prosecution. For, as the Supreme Court observed a quarter-century ago,[154] a parole revocation "is often preferred to a new prosecution because of the procedural ease of recommitting the individual on the basis of a lesser showing by the State."

The Pennsylvania Supreme Court had drawn a distinction between situations such as *Scott* and cases in which the searching officers are unaware of the suspect's status as a parolee. In the latter situation, the Pennsylvania Court saw no reason to apply the exclusionary rule in a parole revocation hearing because the officers probably had a criminal prosecution in mind and knew that the exclusionary rule applied in such a proceedings. Thus, reasoned the state court, in such a situation applying the exclusionary rule in a revocation proceeding is unlikely to act as a significant *additional* deterrent to illegal government behavior.[155]

However, maintained the state court, "a different balance exists" when the officer knows or has reason to believe that the suspect *is* a probationer or parolee. In this situation, because the officer probably only has a revocation hearing in mind, there *is* a need to apply the exclusionary rule in the revocation proceeding. Otherwise, there will often be *nothing else* to deter the officer from conducting an illegal search.[156]

I happen to think that the Pennsylvania Supreme Court was right. But I don't have any votes. Justice Clarence Thomas does. On this occasion he had five — five who disagreed with the state court.

The *Scott* majority begged the question, I venture to say, by claiming that application of the exclusionary rule in the revocation hearing would only provide "marginal deterrence."[157] As Justice Souter pointed out for the dissenters, when the searching officers know that the subject of their search is a parolee (or probationer), there is *nothing* "marginal" or "incremental" about application of the exclusionary rule. For the officers probably assume that the revocation hearing will be *the only proceeding* in which the evidence will be offered.[158]

According to the *Scott* majority, the relationship of parole officers to their parolees is "more supervisory than adversarial" and "the failure of the parolee is in a sense a failure for his supervising officer."[159] (At this point, I guess, we are supposed to picture parole officers who look like Pat O'Brien or Barry Fitzgerald.) This relationship, continued the majority, means that "the harsh deterrent of exclusion is unwarranted, given such other deterrents as departmental training and discipline and the threat of damage actions."[160]

As the dissenters responded, however, while parole officers *sometimes* serve as counselors for parolees, they "often serve as both prosecutors and law enforcement officials" in their relationships with them.[161] As for "departmental training and discipline" being a sufficient deterrent, observed the dissenters, the very same thing could be said about the police generally — but that argument was rejected in *Mapp v. Ohio* (as it had been three decades earlier in the *Weeks* case).[162]

Moreover, added the dissenters, the majority did not refer to any specific departmental training regulation. Nor did it cite a single instance of discipline imposed on a Pennsylvania parole officers for conducting an illegal search of a parolee's home. Nor did it mention a single lawsuit brought by a parolee for an illegal search.

The *Scott* decision is hardly surprising — given the many uncomplimentary things the Court had said about the exclusionary rule in the 1970s and 1980s — most of which Justice Thomas repeated in his majority opinion. *Scott* may be viewed as another case in a long list of cases declining to apply the exclusionary rule to proceedings *other than* criminal prosecutions. *The only thing really surprising* about

Scott is that as many as four Justices dissented. Justice Stevens reiterated his view that the Fourth Amendment required the exclusion of illegally seized evidence.[163] And, in a separate dissent, Justice Souter, joined by Justices Ginsburg and Breyer, challenged the way the majority had worked out its cost-benefit analysis.

The costs of applying the exclusionary rule in the revocation hearings, maintained Souter, are surely no greater than the costs of applying the rule in a criminal prosecution.[164] Nor are the benefits any less. For in a case such as *Scott* a parole revocation hearing usually takes the place of a criminal trial, making it *the only* proceeding in which illegally obtained evidence will be used against a parolee.[165]

Taking a Grudging View of What Constitutes a Search or Seizure

Police practices need not be based on individualized suspicion or conducted pursuant to search warrants—indeed, are not covered by the Fourth Amendment at all—if they do not constitute "searches" or "seizures" within the meaning of the Amendment. Thus, another way to diminish the protection against unreasonable search and seizure—and a way the post-Warren Court has made considerable use of—is to take a narrow, stingy view of what amounts to a "search" or "seizure."

The Burger Court took a grudging view of the key terms "searches" and "seizures" in a number of cases. Recall, for example, *United States v. Miller* (because bank depositor "takes the risk" that information revealed to the bank will be conveyed to the government, transfer of information to the government is not a "search" or "seizure"),[166] *Smith v. Maryland* (because one who uses the phone "assumes the risk" the phone company will tell the government the number she dialed, the government's use of a pen register, a device that records all numbers dialed from a given phone and the time they were dialed, is not a "search" or "seizure"),[167] *Oliver v. United States* (although one takes sufficient precautions to render entry on his private land, situated beyond the curtilage, a criminal trespass under state law, police entry on and examination of that land not a "search"),[168] and *California v. Ciraolo* (police aerial surveillance of fenced-in backyard not a "search"; evidently defendant should have placed an opaque dome over his backyard).[169]

The Rehnquist Court has continued the trend. A trash bag is a common repository for personal effects and a search of such bags can reveal intimate details about one's business dealings; political activities, associations and beliefs; consumption of alcohol; sexual practices, health and personal hygiene. Nevertheless, the Rehnquist Court held that the police may tear open the sealed opaque trash bags one leaves at the curb for garbage pickup and examine their contents for evidence of crime without engaging in a "search."[170]

The police had some information that Mr. Greenwood might have been engaged in drug trafficking. But the way the opinion is written, this does not matter. The Court would have reached the same result if the police had no reason whatever to believe that Greenwood was violating the drug laws.

This is what it means to say, as the *Greenwood* Court did, that the examination of a person's sealed garbage is not a "search" or a "seizure" and thus not restricted in any way by the Fourth Amendment.

To say that the use of a police investigatory technique (e.g., police aerial surveillance, police use of a pen register, or police examination of one's garbage), is not a "search" is a drastic move, for it means the police investigatory technique is completely uncontrolled by the Fourth Amendment. However, to conclude that a particular investigatory technique *is* a "search" is not a drastic move, for such a conclusion does not ban the investigative technique at issue altogether.

The expectation of privacy with respect to one's trash is considerably less intense and consistent than the expectation of privacy or to one's home. Thus, one could classify the examination of the contents of sealed trash bags as a "search" yet plausibly conclude that it is not bounded by the same limitations applicable to a search of one's dwelling. One might conclude, for example, that, although a "search," police examination of sealed trash requires *neither* a search warrant *nor* traditional probable cause.

Unfortunately, when deciding whether a particular police investigative practice is a "search" or "seizure" the Rehnquist Court (as well as its immediate predecessor) has failed to heed the advice of our two greatest commentators on the law of search and seizure, Professors Anthony Amsterdam and Wayne LaFave. According to them, the fundamental inquiry in a case such as *Greenwood* ought to be whether, if the particular police investigative practice at issue is allowed to go "unregulated by constitutional restraints," our privacy "would be diminished to a compass inconsistent with the aims of an open and free society."[171]

I, for one, think the answer to that question is yes. A society in which law enforcement officials have *carte blanche* to rummage through people's trash for evidence of crime, and inevitably come upon information pertaining to intimate aspects of their personal lives, is a society whose privacy has been diminished to a degree inconsistent with the aims of a free and open society.

The Rehnquist Court has not only taken a cramped view of what constitutes a "search," it has also given the crucial term "seizure" a narrow reading. In *Florida v. Bostick*, [172] the Court told us that if armed police board an interstate bus at a scheduled intermediate stop, announce their mission is to detect drug traffickers, randomly approach a passenger, ask to see his bus ticket and driver's license, and then ask the passenger to let him search his luggage, no "seizure" has taken place. Under these circumstances, with one or two husky officers towering over him and one officer "in his face," we are supposed to believe that a reasonable person would feel free to terminate the encounter or to ignore the police presence and continue to do what he was doing—return to the crossword puzzle he was doing or just go to sleep.

Does anybody really believe this? I can think of a few, a very few, people who might react this way—but I would not call any of them "reasonable persons."

Insulating Arbitrary Police Action

New York Times columnist William Safire may have exaggerated a bit, but not by much, when he maintained that "a strong reason must exist for commuters to go into hock to buy a car, to sweat out traffic jams [and] to groan over repair bills" and that that reason is "the blessed orneriness called privacy."[173] Evidently the post-Warren Supreme Court does not agree. For the privacy the Fourth Amendment affords motorists diminished a good deal in the 1970s and 1980s and it diminished still further during the era of the Rehnquist Court.

First, some background. Two major exceptions to the search warrant requirement arise in an automobile setting: (1) the search incident to a lawful arrest and (2) the *Carroll* doctrine,[174] once called the "moving vehicle" exception.

In *New York v. Belton*,[175] the Burger Court adopted a "bright-line rule" that greatly broadens the search-incident exception, at least in automobile settings. *Belton* holds that whether or not there is probable cause to believe a car contains evidence of crime, as long as there are adequate grounds to make a lawful custodial arrest of the car's occupants, even though the occupants are handcuffed and standing outside the car, the police may conduct a warrantless search of the entire interior or passenger compartment of the car. (This search includes closed containers found within that zone.) Thus, warned Justice Stevens, an arresting officer may find reason to take a minor traffic offender into custody "whenever he sees an interesting looking briefcase or package in a vehicle that has been stopped for a traffic violation."[176]

In a typical automobile search, the "search incident to arrest" exception and the *Carroll* doctrine overlap. The two exceptions to the warrant clause are conceptually distinct, however. As it was originally understood and for most of its life, the *Carroll* doctrine permitted the police to search a car without the warrant only when there were *both* probable cause to believe that the car contained evidence of crime *and* "exigent circumstances" making it impractical to obtain a warrant. However, the Burger Court significantly expanded the doctrine by virtually eliminating the exigent circumstances requirement.

Thus, in essence, the *Carroll* doctrine became simply a "probable cause" exception to the warrant requirement for automobiles. Even cars that had been removed to a police station could be subjected to warrantless searches. The Burger Court implicitly recognized that it had extended, or transformed, the *Carroll* doctrine by offering new rationales for the doctrine—once called the "moving vehicle exception"—such as the lesser expectation of privacy in a car.

In the 1982 *Ross* case,[177] the Burger Court further extended the *Carroll* doctrine using it to sustain the warrantless search of a "moveable container" found in a locked car trunk. The Burger Court drew a distinction between cases such as *Ross*, where the police had probable cause to search the entire vehicle for drugs, not just a *particular* container inside the vehicle, and cases in which the police had focused on a particular package or suitcase even before it was placed in the vehicle and whose presence in the car was merely coincidental or purely fortuitous.[178] The police could dispense with a search warrant in the former case—that was an "automobile search" case—but not in the latter—that was only a "suitcase search" case.

Dissenting in *Ross*, Justice Marshall, joined by Justice Brennan, protested that even though the police encounter a closed container when they have probably cause to search the entire vehicle, that closed container is no less private than the container the police came upon when they are specifically searching for it—when probable cause is focused exclusively on it and not on the vehicle generally.[179] A closed container, the *Ross* dissenters said in effect, is a closed container is a closed container; *therefore*, whether the police have probable cause to search the entire vehicle or probable cause to search a specific container only, they should have to obtain a warrant to search the container in *either* case.

A decade later, in the *Acevedo*[180] case, the Rehnquist Court agreed with much of the *Ross* dissenters' reasoning—but not their conclusion. The *Acevedo* Court agreed that a closed container *is* a container *is* a container. Therefore what? Therefore, concluded *Acevedo*, whether the probable cause has focused exclusively on a particular container that just happens to be in a vehicle or whether the police have probable cause to search the entire vehicle and come upon the container, the police *should not have to bother with* a warrant in either case.[181]

Acevedo may be read as a case which simply tidied up, or sought to tidy up, the law governing searches of closed containers in vehicles. I think this would be an unduly narrow reading of the case.

If the *Acevedo* Court eliminated one anomaly (the different Fourth Amendment treatment of closed containers *in* a vehicle), it preserved another—the different Fourth Amendment treatment of closed containers depending on whether they are *inside* or *outside* vehicles. That suitcases, briefcases, and other closed containers should receive the protection of the warrant requirement when found *outside* an automobile but lose that protection when placed inside seems bizarre. Surely a person demonstrates *a stronger expectation* of privacy (at least one unfamiliar with the *Carroll* doctrine) when he locks a suitcase or briefcase in the trunk of his car than when he does not.

I fear that someday the reasoning of *Acevedo* will apply (or extend) to closed containers *outside* a vehicle. Indeed, in *Acevedo*, Justice Scalia concurred in the result on the ground that a "probable cause" search of a closed container *anywhere*, as long as it is "outside a privately owned building," is "not one of those searches whose Fourth Amendment reasonableness depends upon a warrant."[182] It would not be the first time that a Scalia concurring opinion presaged a major development in criminal procedure.

In 1996, when the Rehnquist Court handed down its decision in *Whren v. United States*,[183] one's privacy in one's car diminished further. In *Whren* a surprisingly unanimous Court, per Justice Scalia, held that a traffic stop or arrest is permissible as long as an officer in the same circumstances *could have* made the stop or arrest (because the officer had observed a traffic violation) *regardless* of whether a reasonable officer *would have* made the stop or arrest *had there not been* some reason or motivation beyond the traffic offense (such as a hunch that the driver had drugs or guns in his possession).

The defendants in *Whren* did not deny that they had violated certain provisions of the local traffic code. But they argued that, given the great multitude of traffic and vehicular equipment regulations and the ease with which the police may find *anybody* violating one or more of them, allowing mere observation of a minor traffic offense automatically to justify a stop or arrest gives the police the kind of arbitrary power that the Fourth Amendment is supposed to prohibit.

Because the use of vehicles is so heavily and minutely regulated, total compliance is virtually impossible.[184] This situation, maintained the defense, creates the great temptation to use traffic enforcement as a means of investigating other, more serious, violations, as to which *no individualized suspicion exists*. Probable cause as to a minor traffic violation can be so easily come by that its existence provides no effective protection against arbitrary police action.

Moreover, there is reason to think that the police use *the pretext* of traffic enforcement to harass motorists because of the length of their hair, the style of their clothing, or the color of their skin.[185]

In a more recent case, *United States v. Roberson*,[186] the defense's contention that the traffic stop was a mere pretext to search for drugs was supported by this particular trooper's remarkable record—in the past five years he had arrested 250 people on drug charges—*all* after traffic stops or arrests. (How many motorists were stopped and induced to consent to searches of their cars in order to produce that remarkable record? And *who* were the people stopped?)

I think the *Whren* Court should have adopted the *"would have"* test, under which a traffic stop or arrest satisfies the Fourth Amendment *only if* a reasonable police officer *would have* been motivated to stop the car or arrest the motorist by a desire to enforce the traffic laws or—to put it another way—police action violates the Fourth Amendment if a reasonable officer would not have taken the action she did, but for an underlying purpose or motivation that, *standing alone*, could not provide a lawful basis for the police action.

Applying this test to the facts of the *Whren* case would have been easy. The arresting officers were *plainclothes vice squad* in unmarked cars, patrolling what they call a "high drug area" of Washington, D.C.[187] District of Columbia police regulations permit plainclothes officers in unmarked cars to enforce traffic laws *only when* the violation is "so grave as to pose an *immediate threat* to the safety of others"[188]— and that is a far cry from the minor violations that occurred in *Whren*.

But the Court rejected this approach. It held that a traffic stop supported by adequate grounds to believe that a violation occurred satisfies the Fourth Amendment *whatever* the motives of the police, *whatever* internal police regulations may have to say about enforcing the traffic laws, and *whatever* the usual or routine practice of the police department. In short, *Whren* tells us that there is *no such thing* as a pretext traffic stop.

A year after *Whren*, the Rehnquist Court handed down two more decisions that expand police powers when dealing with motorists and car passengers: *Ohio v. Robinette*[189] and *Maryland v. Wilson*.[190]

The *Robinette* case featured Deputy Sheriff Newsome. He testified that it was his routine practice to ask permission to search a motorist's car during a traffic stop. When asked in another case why, he replied: "I need the practice."[191] He had a *lot* of practice. In one year alone he requested, and obtained consent to, a search incident to a traffic stop more than 750 times.[192]

The *Robinette* case arose as follows: After stopping defendant for speeding in a construction zone, issuing a verbal warning, and returning his license, Deputy Newsome added: "One question before you get gone. Are you carrying any illegal contraband in your car? Any weapon of any kind, drugs, anything like that?"[193]

When the defendant replied in the negative, the deputy asked whether he could search the car. The defendant consented. The search turned up a small amount of drugs.

The Ohio Supreme Court held that the evidence should have been excluded

because the defendant's consent to the search was obtained during an illegal detention (*after* every aspect of the traffic stop had been brought to a conclusion) and the
drugs found were a product of that unlawful detention.[194]

The Ohio court ruled that unless the situation were clarified by the officer,
most motorists in Robinette's situation would believe when asked to consent to a
search of their cars that they were still validly in police custody. This being so, to
prevent the police from turning a routine traffic stop "into a fishing expedition for
unrelated criminal activity," and to ensure that the encounter immediately following the completion of the business relating to the traffic stop is truly consensual,
when the police have completed the business of the traffic stop, any attempt to search
a vehicle about an unrelated crime must be preceded by a police warning: "At this
time you are legally free to go" (or words to this effect).[195]

The state of Ohio and the attorneys general of thirty-six other states warned the
U.S. Supreme Court that the prophylactic rule promulgated by the Ohio Supreme
Court would "hamstring efforts to ferret out illegal drug trafficking and use."[196]
The U.S. Solicitor General's office, which filed an *amicus* brief on behalf of Ohio,
assured the Supreme Court that "a reasonable person in [Mr. Robinette's] situation
would have understood that he was free to leave."[197]

If this is so, I cannot help asking: If a motorist knows, or a reasonable person in
his shoes *would* know, that he is "free to leave," how or why is requiring the police
to tell him this—to tell him what he *already* knows (or what every reasonable person in his shoes *would* know)—going to "hamstring efforts" to combat drug traffic? I
may be missing something, but it strikes me that warning a motorist in Robinette's
situation that he is "free to leave" would *only* have an adverse effect on law enforcement if and when it informs a motorist who *does not think* he is free to leave the
scene that he *is*.

To almost no one's surprise, the U.S. Supreme Court reversed. Chief Justice
Rehnquist, who wrote the majority opinion, thought it would be "unrealistic" to require police officers to tell motorists detained for traffic violations that they are "free
to go" before asking them whether they would consent to a search of their cars.[198]

Why would it be impractical? Keep in mind that Deputy Newsome, and many
other officers as well, routinely ask motorists who have been stopped for a traffic
violation and are about to leave whether they are carrying drugs or weapons and
(after receiving the usual negative answers) whether they will consent to a search
of their cars. This is sometimes called the "oh-by-the-way" routine. It is hard to
see why advising a once-detained motorist that he is free to leave is any more time-
consuming or any more burdensome than the technique Newsome and other officers use in *working their way up* to asking a motorist to consent to a search.

In rejecting the position taken by the Ohio court, Chief Justice Rehnquist
noted that the Court has consistently eschewed bright-line rules.[199] In fact, however, the post-Warren Court has promulgated a number of bright-line rules *expanding* police power.

For example, *New York v. Class*[200] permits an officer to reach into the passenger compartment of a vehicle to move papers obscuring the vehicle identification
number after its driver has been stopped for a traffic violation and has left the vehicle *even though* there is no reason to think the driver has committed any offense

other than the traffic violation. *New York v. Belton*[201] holds that even though there is no basis for believing that a car contains contraband or any evidence of crime, as long as there are adequate grounds for making a custodial arrest of the car's driver, the police may conduct a warrantless search of the entire interior *or passenger* compartment of the car, including closed containers found within that zone.

Moreover, *Pennsylvania v. Mimms*[202] allows an officer to order a driver out of a validly stopped vehicle absent any particularized suspicion that the driver is armed or dangerous. Indeed, only a short three months after telling us that it had consistently avoided bright-line rules in the search-and-seizure area, the Court adopted still another bright-line rule in *Maryland v. Wilson*,[203] holding that the aforementioned *Mimms* rule applies to *the passenger* in a lawfully stopped vehicle as well as to the driver.

Taken together, *Whren, Wilson,* and *Robinette* give the police a great deal of discretionary power. If they follow him or her long enough, the police can stop almost any driver for a traffic violation. Once stopped, drivers can be intimidated or misled or "sweet-talked" into consenting to searches of their cars. (Some experienced officers report that they have *never* failed to get a motorist to consent to a search of his or her car.)

Robinette demonstrates that the Rehnquist Court seems unwilling or uninterested in requiring the police to clarify the situation in which a person finds herself when the police seek her consent to a search of her car. And *Maryland v. Wilson* enables the police to order passengers out of the car as a matter of course.

As Professor David A. Harris has observed, as a result of *Whren, Robinette,* and *Wilson*:

> [F]or all practical purposes, the venerable Fourth Amendment principle that the police need a reason—call it probable cause, reasonable suspicion, or whatever— to interfere with a citizen in his or her daily activity has all but vanished for anyone who drives or rides in a car. Traffic stops have become both the occasion and the legal justification for a new kind of criminal investigation: one that features suspicionless investigation on an individual level, without any special governmental need beyond ordinary law enforcement.[204]

As already mentioned, surprisingly no Justice dissented in *Whren*. But Justice Kennedy may be having second thoughts about the case. Dissenting in *Wilson*, he pointed out: "The practical effect of our holding in *Whren*, of course, is to allow the police to stop vehicles in almost countless circumstances. When *Whren* is coupled with today's holding, the Court puts tens of millions of passengers at risk of arbitrary control by the police. If the command to exit were to become commonplace, the Constitution would be diminished in a most public way."[205]

Some Final Thoughts

The reasoning used by the Burger and Rehnquist Courts in the criminal procedure cases outruns the results these Courts have reached to date. (But the Rehnquist Court may yet achieve these results before its era ends.)

If, as the Court has repeatedly told us, a mere violation of *Miranda* is not a violation of the Constitution, then didn't the Supreme Court go awry in the *Miranda* case itself when it imposed the new confession doctrine on the states? For if a confession obtained without giving a suspect the *Miranda* warnings does not infringe on the self-incrimination clause *unless it is accompanied by actual coercion*, why are the state courts not free to admit all confessions are not the product of actual coercion?

By disparaging the *Miranda* warnings, by viewing them as only second-class prophylactic safeguards and *Miranda* violations as only second-class wrongs, language in various Burger Court cases[206] seem to have prepared the way for the overruling of *Miranda* itself—or at least prepared the way to uphold the constitutionality of Section 3501, which purports to "repeal" *Miranda*. But the Rehnquist Court has yet to take that next step. Instead it has reaffirmed, reinvigorated, and spoke approvingly of the "bright-line prophylactic *Edwards* rule."[207]

On the search-and-seizure front, too, the post-Warren Court has not been led by the logic of its principles and assumptions to a conclusion one would have expected. If, as the Court told us a decade and a half ago in *Leon*, any rule that excludes reliable evidence must "pay its way" by deterring official lawlessness,[208] and if, as it also told us more than two decades ago, the deterrent effect of the exclusionary rule has never been established,[209] then why stop with a good faith modification of the exclusionary rule? Why not abolish the rule altogether?

One reason, ironically, is that a "shrunken" Fourth Amendment and a narrower exclusionary rule has made the rule a good deal more livable and defensible. After thirty years of the Burger and Rehnquist Courts, the scope of the Fourth Amendment and its exclusionary rule has been so downsized, the need to act pursuant to a search warrant so reduced, the probable cause standard so softened, and the occasions on which the police may act on the basis of "reasonable suspicion," or no individualized suspicion at all, so increased that nowadays if the criminal goes free it is because the constable has *flouted* the Fourth Amendment, *not* because he had made an *honest* blunder.[210]

This may well be the price we have had to pay for the exclusionary rule. I think it is the price we would have had to pay for an *effective* tort remedy or any other Fourth Amendment remedy that *actually worked*. But that price *has been* paid.

When we talk about the Rehnquist Court, we are talking about a moving target. The Rehnquist Court era might extend another five or ten years. Depending on the mood of the country and the views of future Justices, the Rehnquist Court may yet carry the post-Warren Court's characterization of *Miranda* and the search-and-seizure exclusionary rule to "the limits of its logic."[211] Then again, it may not.

Whether or not the Rehnquist Court does sustain Congress's 1968 "repeal" of *Miranda* or does expand the so-called good-faith exception to the Fourth Amendment exclusionary rule—or ultimately abolishes the exclusionary rule altogether—may well tell us more about the Rehnquist Court and criminal justice than any ruling this Court has handed down to date.

Much remains to be seen. At present, I think there are four Supreme Court Justices who are fairly sensitive to the rights of those accused or suspected of crime:

Stevens, Souter, Ginsburg and Breyer. Sometimes this foursome will be joined by Justice Kennedy. On rare occasions, such as *Chandler v. Miller*,[212] this foursome will be joined by everybody except Chief Justice Rehnquist. A good deal may turn on whether this foursome grows or shrinks—on whether a new Justice replaces, say, Rehnquist or, say, Stevens—and on who makes the appointment.

In short, we will not be able to evaluate fully "The Rehnquist Court and Criminal Justice" until the Rehnquist Court era comes to an end. And we may not be able to do it even then. A complete evaluation may have to await a quarter-century retrospective—just as, on this very campus, I did a quarter-century retrospective on "The Warren Court and Criminal Justice" several years ago.[213]

However, if the University of Tulsa College of Law does hold a conference at which it invites someone to present a paper on a quarter-century retrospective on "The Rehnquist Court and Criminal Justice," I'm afraid it will have to ask someone else.

Notes

1. 475 U.S. 412 (1986).

2. See, e.g., Stuntz, "Self Incrimination and Excuse," 88 *Colum. L. Rev.* 1227, 1267–68 (1988); Notes, 100 *Harv. L. Rev.* 125 (1986); 23 *N. Eng. L. Rev.* 151 (1988).

3. Miranda v. Arizona, 384 U.S. 436 (1966). To say that *Miranda* as originally written does not require the result sought by the defendant in *Burbine* is not to deny that it may be forcefully argued that a rule *complementing* the *Miranda* doctrine should bar the admissibility of a confession obtained in *Burbine*-like circumstances.

4. A footnote in the *Miranda* opinion, 384 U.S. at 465 n. 35, does seem to say that preventing an attorney from consulting with his client would constitute a violation of the Sixth Amendment right to counsel, but at this point the *Miranda* Court is discussing Escobedo v. Illinois, 378 U.S. 478 (1964), a case in which the suspect had *repeatedly asked* to speak to his lawyer. Moreover, Escobedo *was aware* of the fact that his lawyer was trying to talk to him and that the police were preventing the lawyer from doing so. This realization may well have underscored the police domination of the situation and undermined Escobedo's resolve.

5. Moran v. Burbine, 475 U.S. at 433 n. 4 (emphasis in the original).

6. Id. at 433 n. 4 (emphasis in the original).

7. Id. at 426 (emphasis added).

8. Id.

9. Office of Legal Policy, U.S. Department of Justice, *Report to the Attorney General on the Law of Pre-Trial Interrogation* (reprinted in 22 *U. Mich. J. L. Ref.* 437 (1989). Although the report was written in February 1986, it contains an addendum written in January 1987 and was not released to the public until that month. Although the report states that it does not represent the view of any division of Justice other than the Office of Legal Policy, the release of the report was accompanied by an announcement that the Attorney General had endorsed it. See Schulhofer, "Reconsidering *Miranda*," 54 *U. Chi. L. Rev.* 435 n. 2 (1987).

10. Fried, *Order and Law* 46 (1991).

11. Schulhofer, supra note 9, at 456 n. 53.

12. Fried, supra note 10, at 47.

13. Id. See also Special Comm. on Criminal Justice in a Free Society, Criminal Section, ABA, *Criminal Justice in Crisis* 28–29 (1988): "A very strong majority of those

surveyed—prosecutors, judges, and police officers—agree that compliance with *Miranda* does not present serious problems for law enforcement."

14. See Fried, supra note 10, at 47.

15. 417 U.S. 433 (1974), discussed in text infra notes 25–28 and in accompanying footnotes.

16. See especially New York v. Quarles, 467 U.S. 649 (1984); Oregon v. Elstad, 470 U.S. 298 (1985).

17. See Oregon v. Hass, 420 U.S. 714 (1975); Harris v. New York, 401 U.S. 222 (1971).

18. Alschuler, "Failed Pragmatism: Reflections on the Burger Court," 100 *Harv. L. Rev.* 1436, 1443 (1987).

19. For a discussion of, and substantial extracts from, Justice Brennan's lengthy memorandum to the Chief Justice (including the extract that appears in the text of this chapter), see Weisselberg, "Saving *Miranda*," 84 *Cornell L. Rev.* 109, 123–25 (1998). In Malloy v. Hogan, 378 U.S. 1 (1964), the Court, per Justice Brennan, told us that the Fifth Amendment privilege against self-incrimination applies to the states to its full extent and that the "voluntariness" of a confession "is controlled by [the self-incrimination] portion of the Fifth Amendment." Id. at 6.

20. As noted in Herman, "The Supreme Court, the Attorney General and the Good Old Days of Police Interrogation," 48 *Ohio State L.J.* 733, 738–39 n. 44 (1987), in June 1969, the Department of Justice sent to all U.S. attorneys a memorandum characterizing the *Miranda* warnings as "not themselves constitutional absolutes," but "a protective measure," "a means, suggested by the Court, by which the accused's Fifth Amendment privilege may be safeguarded." At the time the memorandum appeared, future Justice William Rehnquist headed the Justice Department's Office of Legal Counsel. It would not be surprising if the Office had been consulted about or, in fact, contributed to the writing of the memorandum.

21. *Tucker*, 417 U.S. at 444.

22. See Weisselberg, supra note 19, at 128–29.

23. As Weisselberg points out, Justice Rehnquist's statement is misleading. The *Miranda* Court did point out that the Constitution does not "require adherence to *any particular solution* for the inherent compulsions of the interrogation process (384 U.S. at 467) (emphasis added), but it made clear that "unless we are shown other procedures which are *at least as effective* in apprising accused persons of their [rights] and in assuring a continuous opportunity to exercise [them], the [*Miranda* warnings] must be observed." Id. (emphasis added).

24. Chief Justice Marshall, joined by Justice Brennan, dissenting in Weatherford v. Bursey, 429 U.S. 545, 565 (1977). In *Bursey*, a codefendant (actually an undercover agent) attended a pretrial meeting between defendant and his lawyer. Although a majority of the Court rejected the argument that such an intrusion into the attorney–client relationship constituted a per se violation of defendant's right to effective counsel regardless of the agent's purpose in attending the meeting (the district court found that the agent accepted an invitation to attend the meeting to avoid raising suspicion that he was an informant) and regardless of whether the agent reported anything he learned at the meeting to his superiors or to the prosecution (the district court found that the agent had revealed nothing said or done at the meeting), *Bursey* sheds light as when and why a prophylactic rule should be used. As dissenting Justice Marshall observed:

[E]ven if I were to agree that unintended and undisclosed interceptions by government witness-employees affect neither the fairness of trials nor the effectiveness of defense counsel, I still could not join in upholding the practice [of having a government agent attend a meeting of the defense team at which defense plans are reviewed]. For in my view, the precious constitutional rights at stake here, like other constitutional rights, need "breathing space to survive," *NAACP v. Button*, 371 U.S. 415, 433 (1963), and a prophylactic prohibition on all intrusions of this sort is therefore essential. A rule that offers defendants relief only when they can prove "intent" or "disclosure" is, I fear, little better than no rule at all. Establishing that a desire to intercept confidential communications was a factor in a State's decision to keep an agent under cover will seldom be possible, since the State always can argue plausibly that its sole purpose was to continue to enjoy the legitimate services of the undercover agent. Proving that an informer reported to the prosecution on defense strategy will be equally difficult. . . .

Id. at 565.

25. See Grano, *Confessions, Truth and the Law*, 174, 185–98 (1993).

26. Id. at 191.

27. Davis v. United States, 512 U.S. 452, 464 (1994) (concurring opinion).

28. Id. at 465.

29. Id.

30. See, e.g., Cassell, "*Miranda*'s Social Costs: An Empirical Reassessment," 90 *Nw. U. L. Rev.* 387 (1996); Cassell, "All Benefits, No Costs: The Grand Illusion of *Miranda*'s Defenders," 90 *Nw.U. L. Rev.* 1084 (1996); Cassell & Fowles, "Handcuffing the Cops? A Thirty-Year Perspective on *Miranda*'s Harmful Effects on Law Enforcement," 50 *Stan. L. Rev.* 1055 (1998).

31. United States v. Leong, 116 F.3d 1474 (4th Cir. 1997). The discussion of the proceedings in *Leong* is based on an account of the case set forth in Kamisar, LaFave, and Israel, *Modern Criminal Procedure* 70–74 (1998 Supp.) which, in turn, is based heavily on materials about the case provided by Paul Cassell. Professor Cassell served as counsel for Amici Curiae Washington Legal Foundation and Safe Streets Coalition in *Leong*.

32. Dickerson v. United States, 166 F.3d 667 (4th Cir. 1999), rev'd 530 U.S. 428 (2000). Editor's note: The Supreme Court applied the reasoning suggested by Professor Kamisar in his Chapter. *Miranda* was and is "constitutional" in character and not merely "prophylactic.").

33. Id. at 695.

34. Schulhofer, "Reconsidering *Miranda*," 54 *U. Chi. L. Rev.* 435, 453 (1987).

35. Strauss, "The Ubiquity of Prophylactic Rules," 55 *U. Chi. L. Rev.* 190 (1988).

36. Id. at 194.

37. See discussion in Kamisar, "A Dissent from the *Miranda* Dissents" (1966), in *Police Interrogation and Confessions* 41, 69–76 (1980).

38. Id. at 75.

39. 395 U.S. 711 (1969).

40. Id. at 725 n. 20.

41. Whitebread & Slobogin, *Criminal Procedure* 762 (3d ed., 1993).

42. Pearce, 395 U.S. at 726.

43. Colten v. Kentucky, 407 U.S. 104, 116 (1972) (emphasis added).

44. Michigan v. Payne, 412 U.S. 47, 53 (1973).

45. See discussion in *Payne*, 412 U.S. at 53–4.

46. Michigan v. Payne, 412 U.S. 47 (1973), so held.

47. Johnson v. New Jersey, 384 U.S. 719 (1966).

48. *Payne*, 412 U.S. at 53.

49. Wasman v. United States, 468 U.S. 559, 564 (1984).

50. 451 U.S. 477 (1981).

51. See Michigan v. Mosley, 423 U.S. 96 (1975).

52. See Edwards, 451 U.S. at 484–85.

53. Michigan v. Mosley, 423 U.S. 96 (1975).

54. See Choper, Kamisar & Tribe, *The Supreme Court: Trends and Developments* 1982–83 153–58 (1984) (remarks of Kamisar).

55. Arizona v. Roberson, 486 U.S. 675, 682 (1988).

56. 498 U.S. 146 (1990).

57. Id. at 151.

58. 507 U.S. 680 (1993).

59. Stone v. Powell, 428 U.S. 465 (1976).

60. See *Withrow*, 507 U.S. at 690.

61. Id. at 690.

62. See id. at 691.

63. Id.

64. Id.

65. Id. at 692.

66. Steiker, "Counter-Revolution in Constitutional Criminal Procedure? Two Audiences, Two Answers," 94 *Mich. L. Rev.* 2466, 2469–71 (1996).

67. Id. at 2470.

68. Id. at 2469.

69. Id. at 2504.

70. 401 U.S. 222 (1971).

71. 420 U.S. 714 (1975).

72. Id. at 723.

73. Id. at 722.

74. People v. Peevy, 73 Cal. Rptr. 2d 865 (1998).

75. Id. at 876.

76. 470 U.S. 298 (1985).

77. Id. at 307–08.

78. At one point in her majority opinion, Justice O'Connor distinguished cases such as *Elstad*, where the police failed to advise a suspect of his *Miranda* rights at their first meeting, from cases "concerning suspects whose invocation of their rights . . . were flatly ignored while police subjected them to continued interrogation." Id. at 313 n. 3.

79. Id. at 347 n. 29.

80. Id. at 309; see also id. at 304–05, 308.

81. See id. at 307–08.

82. Wollin, "Policing the Police: Should *Miranda* Violations Bear Fruit?," 53 *Ohio St. L.J.* 805, 835 (1992).

83. Friendly, "A Postscript on *Miranda*," in Benchmarks 266, 282 (1967).

84. Wollin, supra note 82, at 845.

85. Alschuler, supra note 18, at 1442–43.

86. The full transcript of the California police training videotape discussed in this text is reprinted in the appendix to Weisselberg, supra note 19. Substantial extracts from the training tape appear in Kamisar, LaFave, and Israel, supra note 31, at 93.

87. Weisselberg, supra note 19.

88. Cf. Gideon v. Wainwright, 372 U.S. 335, 348 (1963) (Harlan, J., concurring).

89. See Steiker, supra note 66, at 2527–28.

90. There may be some constitutional errors, concluded the Warren Court in Chapman v. California, 386 U.S. 18, 22 (1967), "which in the setting of a particular case are so unimportant and insignificant that they may, consistent with the Federal Constitution, be deemed harmless, no requiring the automatic reversal of the conviction." But the Court

went on to say that the error in *Chapman* (permitting the prosecutor to comment on the defendant's failure to take the stand) was not "harmless." Because of its repeated references to defendant's failure to take the stand, the state could not possibly demonstrate that the error was "harmless beyond a reasonable doubt" (i.e., prove beyond a reasonable doubt that the error did not contribute to the conviction).

91. *Chapman*, 386 U.S. at 23 & n. 8.

92. Edwards, "To Err is Human, But Not Always Harmless; When Should Legal Error Be Tolerated?," 70 N.Y.U. L. Rev. 1167, 1176–77 (1995). For strong criticism of the expansion of the harmless error doctrine, see Goldberg, "Harmless Error: Constitutional Sneak Thief," 71 J. Crim. L. & Criminology 421, 427 (1980); Stacy & Dayton, "Rethinking Harmless Constitutional Error," 88 Colum. L. Rev. 79–81 (1988).

93. 499 U.S. 279 (1991).

94. As noted earlier, the papers of speakers at the Conference held on September 17, 1998 at the University of Tulsa on the Rehnquist Court formed the basis for this volume. One speaker at the Conference whose paper was not included in this volume was the Honorable Stanley Mosk, Justice of the Supreme Court of California [now deceased]. In his paper, titled "Justice Rehnquist and Federalism," Justice Mosk said the following about *Arizona v. Fulminante*: "This decision has been deplored by legal scholars and editorial writers alike, and for good reason." After citing extensively from these writers, Justice Mosk quoted his dissent in *People v. Cahill*, 5 Cal.4th 478 (1993), a case in which a majority of the California Supreme Court followed *Fulminante* under its state constitution and in which he dissented: It has been said that fundamental truth is the first casualty of war. Now a fundamental principle of justice has become a casualty of the synthetic war on crime." Id. at 511. He then continued, "I adhere to that view."

95. The rule of automatic reversal for improperly admitted coerced confessions dates back to Malinski v. New York, 324 U.S. 401, 404 (1945). See Kamisar, "Betts v. *Brady* Twenty Years Later: The Right to Counsel and Due Process," 61 Mich. L. Rev. 219, 236 (1962); Ogletree, Jr., "Arizona v. Fulminante: The Harm of Applying Harmless Errror to Coerced Confessions," 105 Harv. L. Rev. 151, 152 (1991).

96. However, a five to three majority of the Court concluded that, under the circumstances, the admission of Fulminante's confession was not harmless beyond a reasonable doubt.

Chapman maintained that a constitutional error could be viewed as harmless only if the prosecution "prove[d] beyond reasonable doubt that the error did not contribute to the evidence obtained." But Harrington v. California, 395 U.S. 250 (1969), seemed to say that the error could be deemed harmless is the remaining untainted evidence of guilt was "overwhelming." See also Milton v. Wainwright, 407 U.S. 371 (1972); Schneble v. Florida, 405 U.S. 427 (1972). As Judge Edwards has noted, supra note 92, at 1186–87, "the *Harrington* approach to harmless-error analysis—one of looking to whether the record evidence adequately demonstrates the appellant's guilt, rather than whether the error contributed to the verdict—has become standard practice for many appellate panels considering both constitutional and nonconstitutional error." But *Arizona v. Fulminante*, discussed immediately below, seems to mark a return to the *Chapman* approach and to be "far removed from the guilt-based version of harmless error found in *Harrington*." Id. at 1190.

97. *Fulminante*, 499 U.S. at 307–10. For powerful criticism of the distinction between "trial errors" and "structural defects," see Ogletree, supra note 95, at 162–64.

98. Milton v. Wainwright, 467 U.S. 371 (1972). The reference in the text is to Massiah v. United States, 377 U.S. 201 (1964).

99. See Steiker, supra note 66, at 2527–28.

100. *Fulminante*, 499 U.S. at 310 (emphasis added).

101. See the discussion in the text at supra notes 76–79.

102. Malinski v. New York, 324 U.S. 402 (1945).

103. Payne v. Arkansas, 356 U.S. 560 (1958).

104. Rogers v. Richmond, 365 U.S. 534 (1961).

105. As Justice O'Connor observed for a majority in Miller v. Fenton, 474 U.S. 104, 109 (1985), the Court has "long held that certain interrogation techniques . . . are so offensive to a civilized system of justice that they must be condemned under the Due Process Clause. . . "

106. Dissenting in *Chapman*, 386 U.S. at 45–51, the case that first recognized that some constitutional errors could be harmless, Justice Harlan observed that one reason that some constitutional errors fall into the "automatic-reversal" category is that they are so contrary to fundamental values or so undermine public respect for the integrity of the criminal process that our society cannot (or should not) "tolerate" acceptance of a judgment tainted by such an error. I share the view that this is why for so many years the Court applied a "rule of automatic reversal" to coerced confessions. See LaFave & Israel, *Criminal Procedure* § 26.6 (d) (1984) and Whitebread & Slobogin, *Criminal Procedure* 778–79 (3d, ed. 1993).

107. *Fulminante*, 499 U.S. at 311. There are three parts to the Court's decision in this case; (1) a 5–4 majority, per Justice White, agreed with the state supreme court that the confession was coerced; (2) a 5–4 majority, per Chief Justice Rehnquist, held that the erroneous admission of a coerced confession was subject to "harmless error" analysis; and (3) still another 5–3 majority, per Justice White, concluded that the admission of Fulminante's confession was not harmless beyond a reasonable doubt.

108. Blackburn v. Alabama, 361 U.S. 199, 206 (1960).

109. See *Fulminante*, 499 U.S. at 312.

110. I must say I do not understand why the Chief Justice finds it *"impossible"* to distinguish between coerced confessions and other inadmissible confessions for harmless-error purposes. The Court has had little difficulty in making this very distinction in other contexts. See discussion in text supra, at notes 70 through 82 on the use of confessions obtained in violation of *Miranda* for impeachment purposes and, in order to acquire derivative evidence.

111. Vasquez v. Hillery, 474 U.S. 254 (1986).

112. *Fulminante*, 499 U.S. at 310.

113. Justice Stewart, joined by Justice Rehnquist, concurring in Rose v. Mitchell, 443 U.S. 545, 575 (1979).

114. See *Fulminante*, 499 U.S. at 309–10.

115. Vasquez v. Hillery, 474 U.S. 254, 262 (1986) (Marshall, J.) (quoting from Justice Blackmun's opinion of the Court in Rose v. Mitchell, 443 U.S. 545, 556 (1979)).

116. Rose v. Mitchell, 443 U.S. 543, 555–56 (1979) (explaining why racial discrimination is "especially pernicious in the administration of justice").

117. Edwards, supra note 92, at 1197. The references are to Brown v. Mississippi, 297 U.S. 278 (1936), and Ashcraft v. Tennessee, 322 U.S. 143 (1944). Judge Edwards continues: "While I do not expect to see a resurrection of such tactics in the law-enforcement community, I do fear that unbridled judicial infatuation with harmless error could lead to more subtle, but equally dangerous, adverse effects on the integrity of our system of justice."

118. Vasquez v. Hillery, 474 U.S. 254, 262 (1986).

119. Stewart, "The Road to *Mapp v. Ohio* and Beyond: The Origins, Development and Future of the Exclusionary Rule in Search-and-Seizure Cases," 83 *Colum. L. Rev.* 1365, 1397 (1983).

120. Weeks v. United States, 232 U.S. 383 (1914).

121. See the discussion of *Weeks* and other early search-and-seizure cases in Kamisar,

"Does (Did) (Should) the Exclusionary Rule Rest on a 'Principled Basis' Rather than an 'Empirical Proposition'"?, 16 *Creighton L. Rev.* 565, 598–604 (1983).

122. See id.

123. 367 U.S. 643 (1961) (overruling Wolf v. Colorado, 338 U.S. 25 (1949)).

124. As a close student of the Warren Court has observed, although some may argue that the Warren Court's revolution began with Griffin v. Illinois, 351 U.S. 12 (1956) (a case that dealt with the appellate rights of indigent defendants), "it was perhaps not until 1961 and [the *Mapp* decision] that a majority of the bench began consistently to reflect those positions that one today considers distinctive of the Warren Court." Allen, "The Judicial Quest for Penal Justice: The Warren Court and the Criminal Cases," 1975 *U. Ill. L.F.* 518, 519.

125. This was a major premise of Wolf v. Colorado, 338 U.S. 25 (1949), the case *Mapp* overruled.

126. See *Mapp*, 367 U.S. at 651–53.

127. See id. at 645–50.

128. Id. at 665 (emphasis added).

129. Id. at 657.

130. Id.

131. Id. at 660.

132. 414 U.S. 338 (1974) (ruling that grand jury witnesses may not refuse to answer questions on the ground that the questions are based on the fruits of an unlawful search).

133. Id. at 348.

134. Id. at 348, 354, 349.

135. However, are the costs any different than those that would be exacted by any equally effective alternative remedy? Doesn't a society whose police comply with the Fourth Amendment *in the first place* "pay the same price" as the society whose law enforcement officials cannot use the evidence they obtained because they violated the Fourth Amendment? Don't both societies convict fewer criminals?

136. Schulhofer, "The Constitution and the Police: Individual Rights and Law Enforcement," 66 *Wash. U.L. Q.* 11, 19 (1988).

137. Id.

138. Id.

139. United States v. Janis, 428 U.S. 433, 459 (1976).

140. United States v. Leon, 468 U.S. 897, 926 (1984).

141. United States v. Payner, 447 U.S. 727, 734 (1980).

142. Stone v. Powell, 428 U.S. 465, 489 (1976).

143. See supra notes 132–34 and accompanying text.

144. 428 U.S. 465 (1976).

145. 428 U.S. 433 (1976).

146. 468 U.S. 1032 (1984).

147. 468 U.S. 897 (1984).

148. Id. at 922.

149. LaFave, *Search and Seizure: A Treatise on the Fourth Amendment* 56 (3d ed., 1996).

150. See supra note 140 and accompanying text.

151. Illinois v. Krull, 480 U.S. 340 (1987).

152. Arizona v. Evans, 514 U.S. (1995).

153. 524 U.S. 357 (1998).

154. Morrissey v. Brewer, 408 U.S. 471, 479 (1972).

155. See Scott v. Pennsylvania Bd. of Probation, 698 A.2d 32, 38 (Pa. 1997).

156. See id.

157. *Pennsylvania Bd. of Probation*, 524 U.S. at 2022.

158. See *Pennsylvania Bd. of Probation*, 524 U.S. at 2025.

159. See *Pennsylvania Bd. of Probation*, 524 U.S. at 2022.

160. Id.

161. Id at 2025.

162. Weeks v. United States, 232 U.S. 383 (1914).

163. See *Pennsylvania Bd. of Probation* 524 U.S. at 2022–23.

164. See *Pennsylvania Bd. of Probation* 524 U.S. at 2026–27.

165. See *Pennsylvania Bd. of Probation* 524 U.S. at 2025, 2027.

166. 425 U.S. 435 (1976).

167. 442 U.S. 735 (1979).

168. 466 U.S. 170 (1984).

169. 476 U.S. 207 (1986).

170. California v. Greenwood, 486 U.S. 35 (1988). It is unclear to what extent the decision in *Greenwood* is grounded on the notion that one has no legitimate expectation of privacy in materials one voluntarily turns over to a third person or to what extent the decision turns on the fact that Mr. Greenwood left his garbage bags for collection on the curb—outside the curtilage of his home.

171. Amsterdam, "Perspectives on the Fourth Amendment," 58 *Minn. L. Rev.* 349, 403 (1974), quoted with approval in LaFave, supra note 106, at 393.

172. 501 U.S. 420 (1991).

173. Quoted in Katz, "Automobile Searches and Diminished Expectations in the Warrant Clause," 19 *Am. Crim. L. Rev.* 557, 571 n. 79 (1982). See also the discussion of how private automobile transportation has shaped American society in Harris, "Car Wars: The Fourth Amendment's Death on the Highway," 66 *Geo.Wash. L. Rev.* 556, 576–78 (1998).

174. The *Carroll* doctrine gets its name from Carroll v. United States, 267 U.S. 132 (1925).

175. 453 U.S. 454 (1981).

176. Id. at 452 (concurring in the judgement in *Belton* and dissenting in the companion case of Robbins v. California, 453 U.S. 420 (1981)).

177. United States v. Ross, 456 U.S. 798 (1982).

178. See id. at 809–25. See also the discussion of *Ross* in California v. Acevedo, 500 U.S. 565, 570–75 (1991).

179. See *Ross*, 456 U.S. at 839–42.

180. California v. Acevedo, 500 U.S. 565 (1991).

181. See id. at 579–80.

182. Id. at 584–85.

183. 517 U.S. 806 (1996).

184. As Professor David A. Harris has observed, supra note 173, at 559–60: "['Moving violations'] only begin the catalog of possible offenses. There are traffic infractions for almost every conceivable aspect of vehicle operation, from the distance drivers must signal before turning, to the times of day and weather conditions that require drivers to turn on their lights. Some of these offenses are not even clearly defined, giving officers the discretion to stop drivers who are operating vehicles in ways and under conditions that are not 'reasonable and prudent.' And if regulation of driving is pervasive, legal requirements concerning vehicle equipment may be even more so."

185. See Davis, "Race, Cops and Traffic Stops," 51 *U. Miami L. Rev.* 425 (1997); Harris, "'Driving While Black' and All Other Traffic Offenses: The Supreme Court and Pretextual Traffic Stops," 87 *J. Crim. L. & Criminology* 544 (1997); Sklansky, "Traffic Stops, Minority Motorists, and the Future of the Fourth Amendment," 1997 *Sup. Ct. Rev.* 271. See also Kennedy, *Race Crime and the Law* 137, 158–60 (1997); Maclin, "'Black and Blue Encounters—Some

Preliminary Thoughts about Fourth Amendment Seizures: Should Race Matter?," 26 *Val. U. L. Rev.* 243 (1991); Johnson, "Race and the Decision to Detain a Suspect," 93 *Yale L.J.* 214 (1983).

186. 6 F.3d 1088 (5th Cir. 1993).

187. *Whren*, 517 U.S. at 803.

188. Id. at 815.

189. 519 U.S. 33 (1997).

190. 519 U.S. 408 (1997).

191. State v. Retherford, 639 N.E.2d 498, 502 (Ohio App. 1994)

192. See id. at 503 n. 3.

193. *Robinette*, 519 U.S. at 35–36.

194. State v. Robinette, 653 N.E.2d 695, 698–99 (Ohio 1995).

195. Id. at 696, quoted in *Robinette*, 519 U.S. at 36.

196. Brief of Amicus Curiae States of Alabama, California, Colorado, et al, p. 8.

197. Brief for the United States as Amicus Curiae Supporting Petitioner, p. 24

198. *Robinette*, 519 U.S. at 40.

199. Id. at 39.

200. 475 U.S. 106 (1986).

201. See text supra notes 175–76.

202. 434 U.S. 106 (1977).

203. 519 U.S. 408 (1997).

204. Harris, supra note 173, at 565.

205. *Wilson*, 519 U.S. at 423.

206. See Michigan v. Tucker, 417 U.S. 433 (1974); New York v. Quarles, 467 U.S. 649 (1984); Oregon v. Elstad, 470 U.S. 298 (1985).

207. Arizona v. Roberson, 486 U.S. 675, 682 (1998). See also Minnick v. Mississippi, 498 U.S. 146 (1990).

208. See *Leon*, 468 U.S. at 907 n. 6.

209. See United States v. Janis, 428 U.S. 433, 449–53 & 450 n.22 (1976); Stone v. Powell, 428 U.S. 465, 492 & n. 32 (1976).

210. Cf. Judge (later Justice) Cardozo's oft-quoted criticism of the exclusionary rule, People v. Defore, 242 N.Y. 13, 21, 150 N.E. 585, 587 (1926): "The criminal is to go free because the constable has blundered."

211. See the observation of Justice Holmes in Hudson County Water Co. v. McCarter, 209 U.S. 349, 355 (1908).

212. Chandler v. Miler, 520 U.S. 305 (1997). In *Chandler*, an eight to one majority, per Justice Ginsburg, struck down a Georgia statute requiring candidates for various state offices (e.g., governor, attorney general, appellate judges, district attorneys, and state legislators) to certify that they had tested negative for drug use within thirty days prior to qualifying for nomination or election. The state had relied on the U.S. Supreme Court's three prior drug-testing cases, all of which had upheld the challenged drug-testing programs: National Treasury Employees Union v. Von Raab, 489 U.S. 656 (1989) (sustaining drug tests for U.S. Customs Service employees seeking transfer or promotion to certain positions); Skinner v. Railway Labor Executives Ass'n, 489 U.S. 602 (1989) (sustaining drug and alcohol tests for railroad employees involved in train accidents or who violate certain safety rules); Vernonia Sch. Dist. 47 J v. Acton, 515 U.S. 646 (1995) (upholding random drug testing of public school student athletes). These cases, especially *Von Raab*, can plausibly be read quite broadly or quite narrowly (limiting them to their special facts). In *Chandler* the Court read its drug-testing precedents quite narrowly.

The state's primary argument in *Chandler* was that unlawful drug use is incompatible with holding high office: drug use undermines public confidence and trust in elected officials, calls into question their judgment and integrity, and jeopardizes antidrug law enforcement efforts and other public functions. The Georgia statute, maintained the state, deters unlawful drug users from becoming candidates and thus stops them from attaining high state office.

It is possible to read *Von Raab* broadly as supporting the state's argument in *Chandler*— as standing for the proposition that warrant*less* and suspicion*less* drug testing may be based on the government's need to maintain the "integrity" and "public image" of its employees. But the *Chandler* Court emphatically rejected this rationale for random drug testing, 520 U.S. at 318, 321–22:

> Our precedents establish that the proffered special need for drug testing must be substantial—important enough to override the individual's acknowledged privacy interest, sufficiently vital to suppress the Fourth Amendment's normal requirement of individualized suspicion. Georgia has failed to show . . . a special need of that kind.

> . . . Georgia asserts no evidence of a drug problem among the state's elected officials, these officials typically do not perform high-risk, safety-sensitive tasks, and the required certification immediately aids no interdiction effort. The need revealed, in short, is "symbolic," not "special," as that term draws meaning from our case law.

> However well meant, the candidate drug test Georgia has devised diminishes personal privacy for a symbol's sake. The Fourth Amendment shields society against that state action.

213. See Kamisar, "The Warren Court and Criminal Justice," in *The Warren Court: A Retrospective* 116 (Bernard Schwartz ed., 1996).

THE REHNQUIST COURT AND
ECONOMIC RIGHTS

LINO A. GRAGLIA

William H. Rehnquist was appointed an Associate Justice of the United States Supreme Court by President Nixon in 1972, replacing John Marshall Harlan. He was promoted to Chief Justice by President Reagan in 1986, replacing Warren E. Burger and inaugurating the "Rehnquist Court." He, in turn, was replaced as an Associate Justice by Antonin E. Scalia. The remaining members of the Court were William J. Brennan, Jr., Thurgood Marshall, Byron R. White, Harry A. Blackmun, Lewis F. Powell, Jr., John Paul Stevens, and Sandra Day O'Connor. He thus headed a Court to which all members but two—White, appointed by President Kennedy, and Marshall, appointed by President Johnson—were appointed by Republican presidents. Justice Powell was replaced by Justice Anthony M. Kennedy in 1988, Justice Brennan by Justice David H. Souter in 1990, Justice Marshall by Justice Clarence Thomas in 1992—at which point eight of the nine Justices were Republican appointees. Justice White was replaced by Ruth Bader Ginsburg in 1993, and Justice Blackmun by Stephen G. Breyer in 1994, returning the Court to a seven to two Republican–Democrat division.

The Warren Court's Constitutional Revolution

The Rehnquist Court, like its immediate predecessor, the Burger Court, and all later Courts for the foreseeable future, can only be appraised in reference to the Warren Court, the defining Court of the twentieth century. The Warren Court, and more specifically its 1954 decision in *Brown v. Board of Education*,[1] redefined the role of the Court in our system of government, creating the governmental regime under which we now live.

Judicial Review, Contemplated as a Conservative Force

Constitutional law is, for most practical purposes, the product of "judicial review," the power of courts, and ultimately the United States Supreme Court, to disallow policy choices made by other officials and institutions of government on the ground that they are prohibited by the Constitution. The central question of constitutional law, the only question common to the myriad subjects considered under that rubric, is how, if at all, is it possible to justify such a power in a supposedly democratic, federalist system. The three pillars of the Constitution are republicanism (i.e., representative self-government; federalism—decentralized policymaking power—and separation of powers), with lawmaking assigned exclusively to Congress.[2]

Policymaking by the Supreme Court—by majority vote of a committee of nine lawyers, unelected and effectively holding office for life, making policy for the nation as a whole from Washington, D.C.—is the antithesis of the constitutional system.

The official justification for judical review, the only justification ever offered by the Justices, is of course, that they do no more than interpret and enforce the restrictions on policy choices imposed by the Constitution.[3] That this answer is fictional should be obvious enough from the fact that the Constitution, a short document, places few restrictions on policy choices by the federal government in the exercise of its enumerated powers and even fewer on policy choices by the states. Further, they are restrictions that American legislators—all American citizens living in the United States—ordinarily have little occasion or temptation to violate. Most important, short as the Constitution is, little of it is even purportedly involved in most constitutional cases.

The vast bulk of constitutional cases concern state, not federal, law, and nearly all of the Court's invalidations of state policy choices purport to be based on a single constitutional provision, one sentence of the Fourteenth Amendment and, indeed, ultimately on four words, "due process" and "equal protection."[4] No jurisprudential sophistication is required to understand that the Justices do not decide a vast array of difficult issues of social policy by studying those four words. No question of interpretation in any meaningful sense was in fact involved in any of the Court's controversial so-called constitutional cases of recent decades.

What do you suppose the Court "interpreted" in *Roe v. Wade*,[5] the abortion decision, for example, the word "due" or the word "process"? The Justices have made of the Fourteenth Amendment a warrant for their enactment of their notions of good social policy. If it could be returned to its intended meaning—a guarantee of basic civil rights to blacks, or given any specific meaning—constitutional law would largely go away.

Surely the most extraordinary fact about judicial review, initially, is that it is not explicitly provided for and spelled out in the Constitution, unlike the somewhat analogous veto power of the President, which is carefully specified with provision made, as one would expect, for the ultimate decision to be made by Congress.[6] Given, in addition, that judicial review was an innovation in the science of government, unprecedented in the British system, and its obvious potential for abuse, one may doubt that the issue was thought through and deliberately decided upon by the framers and ratifiers of the Constitution. That much-debated question is not, however, of much importance. There is no doubt, in any event, that the framers did not intend the Supreme Court to be a policymaking institution.

If judicial review were in practice what it is in theory—judicial enforcement of constitutionally prohibited policy choices—occasions for its exercise to declare laws unconstitutional would be so rare as to make the power a matter of little more than academic interest.[7]

Judicial review, very narrowly defined, was defended by Alexander Hamilton, who favored a totally centralized constitutional monarchy, in the *Federalist Papers*.[8] It was established by his fellow Federalist Party partisan and nationalist, Chief Justice John Marshall in 1803 in *Marbury v. Madison*,[9] on the basis of arguments no one has since found convincing.[10] Hamilton and Marshall, ardent defenders of property and contract rights, undoubtedly contemplated that judicial review, exercised by successful and wealthy lawyers such as themselves, would be a conservative force, a corrective for the redistributive and leveling tendency that may be an inherent defect of democratic government.

For 150 years, the first three-quarters of our life as a nation, they were basically right: judicial review served as an antiegalitarian defender of the status quo, a brake on radical change. The most significant constitutional limitation on state power prior to the Civil War was the Contracts Clause,[11] a prohibition of debtor-relief legislation, which Chief Justice Marshall, having little else to work with, carried to extremes.[12]

The Contracts Clause shows that the framers of the original Constitution were indeed concerned to protect individual rights from majority rule, but primarily the rights of bankers.

It is fair to say that the history of judicial review, at least until more recent times, has not been a glorious one. Perhaps, like the medical profession, which has surely killed more people than it has cured through most of its history,[13] it has come into its own only lately. The first significant use of the power to invalidate a federal statute was in *Dred Scott v. Sandford*[14] in 1857, fifty-four years after *Marbury*, holding, with no basis in the Constitution, that Congress could not limit the extension of slavery and that a state could not make even a free black a citizen. The result, apparently, was to give us the Civil War, with its more than 600,000 battlefield deaths, more than in all our other wars combined. Those deaths, one might think, should weigh heavily in appraising the value of judicial review.

The Court's most significant use of the power following the Civil War was to invalidate the 1875 Civil Rights Act's prohibition of racial discrimination in places of public accommodation,[15] thereby giving us segregation for another eighty-nine years, until Congress prohibited it again in the 1964 Civil Rights Act.[16] The Court next held, in a series of cases, that although a state could not constitutionally prohibit,[17] it could constitutionally require,[18] segregation in public transportation.

The Court's most important use of judicial review against federal law in the twentieth century was to invalidate statutes limiting child labor[19] and bring to a halt President Franklin Roosevelt's New Deal.[20] From the 1890s until 1937, judicial review was used primarily to disallow state and federal regulation of business and economic affairs.[21] During this era it was liberals, of course, who attacked judicial review, quite correctly, as usurpation by judges of policymaking power.[22] In 1937, however, the Court, under threat of President Roosevelt's so-called Court-packing plan, suddenly and totally reversed direction, withdrawing from all further interference with economic and business regulation.[23]

President Roosevelt finally got to make Supreme Court appointments during his second term, with the result that the Constitution never gave the New Deal, or any state or federal economic regulation, the least bit of trouble again. The Court renounced its former activism as constitutionally baseless and swore never again to act as a "super legislature."[24]

Brown v. Board of Education: *Judicial Review as an Engine of Social Change*

There is no way, however, that human beings, and least of all lawyers, can have the power, even if not the authority, to have their personal policy preferences prevail and be expected to refrain from using it. The Justices' resolution to confine themselves to enforcing the terms of the Constitution proved, therefore, to be short-lived. President Roosevelt's appointees no longer disallowed business and economic regulation—which they tended to favor rather than oppose—but they quickly reasserted their power to reject policy choices that they did not favor. The Court would continue to usurp policymaking power, but now for the purpose of advancing rather than impeding egalitarianism.[25]

The culmination of this new judicial policy came, of course, in *Brown*, holding school racial segregation and, it soon appeared, all racial discrimination by government[26] unconstitutional. In one bold stroke and a short opinion, the Court undertook to overthrow a long-standing basic social policy of one-third of the nation. That the Court had the power to do this was uncertain enough at the time, however, that the Court declined to issue a decree and announced the following year that the newly declared constitutional right did not have to be enforced at once but only "as soon as practicable" and with "all deliberate speed,"[27] another innovation in constitutional law. The Court thereafter made no serious effort to enforce the decision for ten years,[28] making it possible to argue, indeed, that segregation might have ended more quickly in the deep South if *Brown* had never been decided.

The *Brown* decision only became effective when the principle of no racial discrimination by government was adopted and ratified (and extended even to private discrimination in public accommodations and employment) by Congress in the 1964 Civil Rights Act.[29] What had seemed a risky and dubious venture ten years before now appeared to be a triumph.

As important as *Brown* was for what it held, it proved far more important for the change in perception it produced, especially among judges, as to the appropriate role of courts in our system of government. It seemed to demonstrate for many people, and especially liberal academics, the superiority of policymaking by electorally unaccountable Supreme Court Justices on the basis of "principle" and "morality" to policymaking by mere politicians subject to popular control. If the Court could bring about the clear moral goal of ending racial segregation in the South by merely pronouncing it unconstitutional—as many people believed, although it was the 1964 Civil Rights Act that ended it—what was it that the Court could not do? And if the Court could bring about further advances in morality and justice by simply issuing constitutional commands, why should it not do so?

The unquestionable moral triumph attributed to *Brown* wrapped the Court's later and much more questionable innovations in a cloak of invulnerability. To argue thereafter that it was a perversion of our system of government for the Court to decide a vast array of social policy issues for the nation as a whole in the name of the Constitution was only to invite the response, "So, you disagree with *Brown?*" As it was not permissible, politically or academically, to disagree with *Brown*, opponents of government by the judiciary were reduced to silence.

With *Brown*, the Court went from being the brake on social change contemplated by Hamilton and Marshall to being the nation's primary engine of change, in effect a continuing constitutional convention.

The result was to make the Court the most important institution of government in terms of domestic social policy, the source of virtually all the dramatic changes that have taken place in our society since *Brown*. The Court has decided issues literally of life and death, such as abortion[30] and capital punishment;[31] issues of public morality, such as pornography,[32] public nudity,[33] and homosexuality;[34] and issues of public order, such as street demonstrations[35] and vagrancy control.[36] The Court has ordered the reapportionment of all legislatures, state and federal, except for the United States Senate, on the basis of one person, one vote.[37]

It has prohibited the states from providing for prayer or Bible reading in the public schools[38] while also forbidding most government aid to religious schools[39] and most displays of religious symbols in public places.[40] The Court has remade both state and federal systems of criminal procedure, creating rights for the criminally accused unknown to any other system of law and a criminal law system of such complexity and cost as to make enforcement often seem not worthwhile.[41] The Court has remade and largely abolished the law of libel,[42] disallowed most distinctions on the basis of sex,[43] legitimacy,[44] and alienage,[45] and so on almost endlessly.

Contemporary Constitutional Law: A Cover for Judicial Enactment of a Left-Liberal Agenda

Only two things must be understood to fully understand constitutional law since *Brown*. First, it has almost nothing to do with the Constitution, as is evident enough from the fact, already noted, that there is so little that the Court even purports to interpret. It is further demonstrated by the fact that there was a time that "the Constitution" permitted racial assignment of children to public schools,[46] a time when it prohibited such assignment,[47] and a time, the present, when such assignment is often required.[48] That covers all the possibilities, yet in all that time the Constitution was not changed in any relevant respect. A scientific observer would have no difficulty in concluding that the Constitution is not the relevant variable.

Abortion, to cite another example, formerly restricted in all states, did not become a constitutional right in 1973[49] because the Court suddenly discovered in the Fourteenth Amendment a prohibition no one had noticed during the amendment's previous 105 years, but only because unrestricted abortion had become a fundamental tenet of elite opinion, and the Court had become the mirror and mouthpiece of that opinion. If the abortion right was created out of whole cloth, the Court's religion decisions can be seen, if possible, as even worse, not only without support in but in defiance of the Constitution.

The religion clauses of the First Amendment,[50] meant to guarantee the states freedom from federal interference in matters of religion,[51] are the very provisions relied on by the Court, an arm of the federal government, in assuming control of the states in matters of religion.

The second and final thing necessary to an understanding of constitutional law since *Brown* is recognition that the Court's rulings of unconstitutionality have not been random in their political impact. The long (though only partial) list of decisions recited earlier have only one thing in common. In every instance, the effect was to move public policy to the left. It would be only a small exaggeration to say that the American Civil Liberties Union (ACLU), the paradigmatic voice of liberalism and the prime constitutional litigator of our time, never lost in the Supreme Court even though it did not always win.

It either obtained a policy choice—for example, elimination of state-sponsored prayer in the schools or removal of restrictions on pornography—that it could not obtain in the ordinary political process because opposed by a majority of the American people, or it was left where it was to try again on another day. Connecticut's anticontraception law, for example, was invalidated only on the third try.[52]

For defenders of conservative or traditional views, the situation was precisely reversed. They almost never won even though they did not always lose. For opponents of abortion, for example, a positive victory comparable to the liberal victory in *Roe v. Wade* would be a decision not merely overruling *Roe v. Wade* and returning the issue to the political process but a decision prohibiting the practice of abortion. Even the overruling of *Roe* has proved to be more, of course, despite ten consecutive Republican appointments to the Court, than opponents of abortion have been able to obtain.

The Burger and Rehnquist Courts: Counter-Revolutions That Weren't

The American people face no more urgent question than whether and to what extent this new constitutional system and radically altered form of government will be allowed to continue. How, if at all, is it possible to reduce the policymaking role assumed by the Supreme Court and return to the constitutional scheme of representative self-government in a federalist system?

There appear to be several ways to limit the Court's power, including constitutional amendment, impeachment, and limitation of jurisdiction, but for various reasons in practice they have proved to be more theoretical than real.[53] It is revealing that President Roosevelt did not turn to any of them in his struggle with the Court but resorted instead to an attempt, perfectly constitutional, to appoint additional justices. The only real hope for a change in the role of the Court in our system of government, it seemed then and still seems, is by a change in personnel.

President Roosevelt did not succeed in increasing the number of Justices on the Court, but he did finally, in his second and later terms, get to appoint replacements as Justices resigned, which proved sufficient to turn the Court around on the constitutionality of the New Deal. It was confidently expected that President Nixon, who ran on a program of "strict construction" and opposition to judicial policymaking, would, if given appointments, be equally successful in regard to the Warren Court.

It was possible to see the Warren Court as an historical accident, the result of such chance factors as the longevity of Black and Douglas, holdovers from the New Deal, still on the court more than a third of a century later to be joined by Brennan and Marshall, vestiges of the countercultural euphoria of the 1960s. Further, many of the most controversial Warren Court decisions, such as *Miranda v. Arizona*,[54] were by a closely divided Court and issued over strong dissents.

Surely, it seemed, the appointment of two or three Justices less committed to the policy preferences of the ACLU or more committed to the democratic political process would drastically turn things around. President Nixon, it happened, was extremely fortunate in that he got to make four appointments, including the Chief Justice, in his first term, and President Ford, who completed Nixon's second term, made one more.

Thus, recent appointments (Brennan, appointed in 1956, was also a Republican appointee) by supposedly conservative Republican presidents then accounted for a majority of the Court. Presidents Nixon and Ford did not, however, replicate President Roosevelt's success. One of the most surprising and significant facts of our recent history is that so major a change in personnel made so little difference in the Court's direction.

The expectation that the Warren Court's constitutional revolution would be met by a counter-revolution was quickly seen to be baseless. As the subtitle of a well-known book on the subject put it, the Burger Court, the Warren Court's immediate successor, proved to be "The Counter-Revolution That Wasn't."[55] Not only did it fail to overrule a single controversial Warren Court decision — not *Miranda*, not the prohibition of state-sponsored prayer in schools — but it produced some possibly even more controversial decisions of its own, as on abortion,[56] sex[57] and alienage[58] discrimination, and busing for school racial balance.[59] The Warren Court had worked such a thorough change in the nation's understanding of the proper role of the Court, it seemed, as to make its position in the vanguard of social change unalterable.

If the hopes of opponents of liberal (or any) policymaking by judges were dashed by Presidents Nixon and Ford and the Burger Court, they were revived by the election of President Reagan. Surely he, at least, could be trusted to find Supreme Court appointees willing to terminate, if not reverse, the role of the Court as the enacting arm of the ACLU. President Reagan was not as fortunate as President Nixon in that, in addition to appointing a new Chief Justice, promoting Associate Justice Rehnquist, he was able to make only three new appointments in his two terms, Justices O'Connor, Scalia, and Kennedy.[60] Reagan's successor, President Bush, was able to make two more appointments in his one term, Justices Souter and Thomas. At this point, eight of the nine Justices were Republican appointees, and Republican Presidents had made ten consecutive appointments. Even that proved not to be enough, however, to make a fundamental change in the role of the Court established by the Warren Court.

The Rehnquist Court has proved to be another counter-revolution that wasn't. Not a single one of the revolutionary decisions of the Warren Court, or any of the additional revolutionary decisions of the Burger Court, has been reversed.

How can we explain, then, the general belief and frequent academic complaint that we now have a "conservative Court"? Indeed, the current Court is so conservative that the ACLU has been reduced, it complains, to appealing to legislators rather than judges for enactment of its political agenda. The Court is thought to be conservative, however, only because to be "conservative" according to academics and the media it is not necessary that a Court enact conservative instead of liberal policy preferences; it is enough that it enacts liberal policy preferences less frequently or reliably. A Court that actually took away a past liberal victory, as by overruling *Miranda* or *Roe v. Wade*, would be seen not merely as conservative but reactionary. A Court that gave conservatives positive victories—by *prohibiting* abortion, for example, or *requiring* states to provide for prayer in the schools or to suppress pornography—would be denounced as tyrannical and cries would go up for measures to limit the Court's power and return us to self-government.

The Rehnquist Court has not only failed to overturn; but it has expressly reaffirmed the basic holding of *Roe v. Wade*,[61] generally seen as the ultimate expression of liberal activism. It has also reaffirmed the Warren Court's prohibition of prayer in schools, holding that a state may not permit a prayer by a speaker at a high school graduation ceremony.[62] Worse, the Court has not only failed to deprive liberals of their past victories; it continues to award them new major victories.

The Court has found constitutionally prohibited, for example, Virginia's operation of an all-male military college,[63] Colorado's adoption of an amendment to the state constitution precluding the grant of special rights to homosexuals,[64] Congress's attempt to restrict child pornography on the Internet,[65] and state statutes imposing political term limits.[66] It is possible to label as conservative a Court that continues to produce such extraordinary liberal victories only because that has come to be seen as the norm, the Court's ordinary function; it is only any departure from this norm that is seen as noteworthy.

Two Exceptions: Judicial Activism of the Right

There have, however, been some departures from the norm by the Rehnquist Court, possible examples of judicial activism of the right. Judicial activism can be simply and most usefully defined as a court's holding unconstitutional a policy choice that the Constitution does not clearly prohibit[67]—"clearly" because in a democracy the opinion of elected legislators should prevail in cases of doubt. Because, as noted previously, the Constitution wisely restricts few policy choices and legislators are rarely inclined or tempted to violate these restrictions, virtually all rulings of unconstitutionality are the result of activism, and the vast majority of such rulings, at least 90 percent, continue to favor liberal causes. Further, the Rehnquist Court's few decisions giving conservatives positive victories have been mostly by close votes and are therefore of uncertain stability.

The most important Rehnquist Court decisions favoring conservative policies have undoubtedly been in the area of so-called affirmative action, that is, the use of racial preferences or other racial discrimination to increase racial integration or otherwise attempt to benefit blacks. In *Richmond v. J.A. Croson*[68] in 1989 and *Adarand v. Peña*[69] in 1995, the Court invalidated state and federal "set-aside" programs that gave preference in awarding government contracts to members of certain racial groups. Similarly, in a series of cases beginning with *Shaw v. Reno*[70] in 1993, the Court has disallowed the drawing of political district lines on the basis of race in order to facilitate the election of black candidates.

Because the purpose of the Fourteenth Amendment, the basis of the decisions invalidating state laws, was to guarantee certain basic civil rights to blacks, it is hardly credible that it was meant to preclude state efforts to assist blacks. That the Due Process Clause of the Fifth Amendment was meant to preclude such efforts is, if anything, even less credible.

It is equally incredible, however, that the Fourteenth Amendment was meant to prevent school racial segregation, as held in *Brown*.[71] We have, therefore, an issue as to where analysis is to begin, of what, as is said in philosophy, is to be taken as "the given." If *Brown* is taken as a given, assumed to be correctly decided and understood, as it should be and as it was by Congress in enacting the 1964 Civil Rights Act, to establish the principle that all racial discrimination by government is prohibited, then *J.A. Croson, Adarand,* and *Shaw v. Reno* were also correctly decided. These conservative victories can be seen, therefore, not as activist but as rare examples of rulings of unconstitutionality that are constitutionally justified.

A second possible example of judicial activism of the right, an unjustified ruling of unconstitutionality that enacts a conservative policy preference, is presented by the Court's recent decisions on the Just Compensation or "Takings" Clause of the Fifth Amendment,[72] which provides that "private property" shall not "be taken for public use, without just compensation."[73] The Court was unusually active in this area of the law in 1987, one year into the Rehnquist Court, handing down four significant decisions.

Although the takings claimant lost the first decision,[74] succeeding claimants, probably for the first time in history, then won three in a row.[75] Are these rulings of unconstitutionality examples of judicial activism of the right or were they clearly required by the Constitution?

This question, too, like the question of the constitutionality of racial preferences, depends on where analysis is to begin, on what is taken as given. There is no doubt that the Fifth Amendment, including the Takings Clause, was meant, like the rest of the Bill of Rights, to apply only to the federal government.[76] The notion that it was made applicable to the states by reason of "incorporation" in the Fourteenth Amendment by the Due Process Clause is purely fictional, an expression of the judges' urge, warned against by Jefferson, toward the expansion of their jurisdiction. The preposterousness of the notion should be sufficiently clear from the fact that the Fifth Amendment also contains a Due Process Clause, along with the Takings Clause. It would be odd, to say the least, if the Due Process Clause includes the Takings Clause in the Fourteenth Amendment although it obviously does not in the Fifth.[77]

As already noted, although the Fourteenth Amendment has become our second Constitution, the putative basis of almost every ruling of unconstitutionality against state law, its original purpose, to guarantee certain basic civil rights to blacks, is not seriously in doubt.[78] It is not credible that the states that ratified the Fourteenth Amendment understood that they were thereby subjecting themselves to federal, and particularly Supreme Court, supervision of an array of their basic social policy choices. In addition, the Takings Clause, even as applied to the federal government, was understood, like most provisions of the Bill of Rights, to have a limited application.

In essence, a taking was understood to occur only when government seized or caused the physical occupancy of property, not when government regulations lessened property values.[79] Here as elsewhere, however, the Constitution has little to do with constitutional law.

From the earliest days, Supreme Court Justices, particularly Chief Justice Marshall, were unable to resist invalidating laws with which they strongly disagreed, especially, at first, laws violating what they saw as sacred rights of property, on extraconstitutional grounds. At first they simply cited "natural law" or the social compact.[80] In the late nineteenth and early twentieth centuries, however, when the Justices succumbed to the pleas of lawyers to protect the property of railroads from increasing state regulation, natural law and social compact theories had gone out of fashion and there was a felt need to cite constitutional text. The justices therefore turned to the Due Process Clauses, which did at least include the word "property," and invented the oxymoronic notion of "substantive due process."[81]

The Fifth and Fourteenth Amendments provide that no person shall be deprived of "life, liberty, or property, without due process of law." The literal and historical meaning of due process was simply that no one was to be criminally punished except in accordance with established legal procedures.[82] Through the magic of lawyerly reasoning, the Supreme Court converted this procedural protection into a prohibition of any law, regardless of procedure, that restricted liberty or property rights in a way of which the Justices disapproved. Restrictions on the use of property that the Court considered unreasonable were found to be either simply prohibited or prohibited in the absence of compensation.[83] Justice Holmes, the skeptic, and Justice Brandeis, the liberal, saw that there was no basis for substantive due process, but because the doctrine was well established as a protection for property, they argued that it should be extended to protect speech as well. "The general principle of free speech, it seems to me," Holmes wrote dissenting in *Gitlow v. New York*, "must be taken to be included in the Fourteenth Amendment, in view of the scope that has been given to the word 'liberty' as there used."[84]

Ironically, today the situation has been precisely reversed. Post-New Deal Courts have had little interest in protecting property and a keen interest in protecting and expanding rights of speech,[85] along with the rights of the criminally accused,[86] and others seen as socially oppressed.[87] The Warren Court sought to find support for this view of the Court's role by declaring almost all of the Bill of Rights applicable to the states by reason of "incorporation" into the Fourteenth Amendment.[88]

First Amendment and criminal procedure rights flourished extravagantly, but as property owners were not seen as requiring the Court's protection, the Takings Clause became an embarrassment that almost vanished from sight.[89]

As judicial activism overwhelmingly advances liberal causes in the modern era, it is overwhelmingly favored by liberals. Conservatives such as Chief Justice Rehnquist and Justice Scalia, on the other hand, generally favor a more limited role for the Court. Because, however, it is apparently firmly established that the Fourteenth Amendment incorporates almost all Bill of Rights provisions, expansively interpreted, there would seem to be little reason why the Takings Clause of the Fifth Amendment should be excluded.

If the Court is going to create doctrines to protect property, Holmes and Brandeis once argued, it should apply them also to protect speech; if the Court is going to create doctrines to protect speech and the criminally accused, Rehnquist and Scalia have in effect reversed the argument, it should apply them also to protect property. As Chief Justice Rehnquist put it in a recent opinion for the Court: "We see no reason why the Takings Clause of the Fifth Amendment, as much a part of the Bill of Rights as the First Amendment or Fourth Amendment, should be relegated to the status of a poor relation. . . ."[90]

The Rehnquist Court's Taking Decisions

The Rehnquist Court has clearly sought to expand constitutional protection of economic rights by reinvigorating the Takings Clause. What has been and is likely to be the result of its efforts? As has already been noted, historically a taking within the meaning of the clause was understood to require a government assertion of title to or physical occupancy of property.[91] A loss of value because of government restrictions on use was not enough. For example, no taking was found when value was greatly lessened by a prohibition law that precluded the use of a brewery[92] or by laws that prohibited the continued use of land for a stable,[93] a brickyard,[94] or a quarry[95] when urban growth made such use, previously legitimate and appropriate, inconsistent with the best use of adjacent land.

Pennsylvania Coal

Takings law apparently underwent a drastic change in 1922, however, with Justice Holmes's opinion for the Court in *Pennsylvania Coal v. Mahon*,[96] easily the most cited and discussed case in the area. Individuals and a municipality had purchased and paid for only the surface right to certain lands owned by the coal company. The company expressly retained the right to mine the coal under the land without liability for the fact that this might cause the surface to subside or collapse. The state, however, then passed a law requiring that the coal be left in the ground when necessary for surface support, thereby seeking to obtain by regulation what it had declined to obtain by purchase.

Justice Holmes, a hard-headed skeptic with a keen nose for dishonesty, saw this as little other than an act of theft. Because coal has value only if it can be mined, he said, the requirement that coal be left in the ground to support streets and dwellings was effectively its appropriation for a public use, requring compensation. It would not have been acceptable for Holmes to give as an explanation simply that the chicanery involved was too obvious and offensive, but even he could come up with no other explanation than that "while property may be regulated to a certain extent, if regulation goes too far it will recognized as a taking."[97] This explanation was difficult to accept or even understand for many reasons, including that in prior cases regulations reducing the value of land by more than 90 percent were not found to go "too far" and therefore require compensation.[98]

Pennsylvania Coal established that restrictions on the use of land could constitute a taking requiring compensation, but it provided no real guidance as to when such a taking was to be found. The Court dealt with this problem over the next several decades by the simple expedient of never again finding a so-called regulatory taking, even when it was clear that government was using regulation to obtain benefits for which it was unwilling to pay. The Court expressly acknowledged that it was unable to state any rule as to regulatory takings; each case, it said, turned on "essentially ad hoc factual inquiries."[99]

Applying a so-called balancing test — that is, a ruleless utilitarian calculus — the Court found in every case that the public interest served by the restriction on the use of plaintiff's property outweighed the resulting loss in value. In fact, it seemed to be enough that the restriction could "rationally" be thought to serve some public purpose, as almost all restrictions do. That is, there seemed to be little difference, if any, in the test used in takings cases compared to the "rational basis" test used in economic substantive due process cases. This is a test that is virtually impossible to fail, the true function of which is to make clear that the Court has no interest in intervening in the area of law involved.[100]

Keystone

In 1987, however, we suddenly saw the remarkable spectacle of Takings Clause plaintiffs prevailing in three consecutive cases. These victories were all the more remarkable in that the year began with a decision that seemed to put the final nail into the idea of a regulatory taking. *Keystone Bituminous Coal Association v. DeBenedictis*[101] was, amazingly, essentially a replay of *Pennsylvania Coal v. Mahon*. As before, individuals and towns had entered into contracts with coal companies expressly purchasing only surface rights to land and leaving the companies free to mine the underlying coal. The Pennsylvania legislature again enacted a statute prohibiting, with no provision for compensation, mining that deprived the surface of support. This time, the Court, in a five to four decision, upheld the statute, overruling *Pennsylvania Coal* in all but name.

In a long and ingenious opinion for the Court, Justice Stevens declared that Justice Holmes's opinion in *Pennsylvania Coal* was merely "advisory" in important respects and that everyone's understanding of the case for the past sixty-five years was mistaken.[102] According to Stevens, compensation was required in *Pennsylvania Coal* only because the statute was not found to serve any public, but only a private, purpose — it did not pass even the rational basis test — and because the coal company was left without any economically viable use of its property. In *Keystone*, however, the Court found, the requirement of support did serve a public purpose, and the restriction on mining, although it deprived plaintiffs of the value of 27 million tons of coal, left them with plenty of other coal to mine.[103] Chief Justice Rehnquist, joined by Justices Powell, O'Connor, and Scalia, dissented on the ground that *Pennsylvania Coal* was controlling. The distinctions the Court purported to find between the cases, he said, "verge on the trivial."[104]

Although *Keystone* effectively overruled the only Supreme Court decision ever to uphold a regulatory taking claim, three other 1987 decisions, all victories for plaintiffs, seemed to reflect a very different stance by a Court majority toward takings claims. In *Hodel v. Irving*,[105] the Court unanimously (although with several concurring opinions)[106] invalidated a federal statute that attempted to increase the productivity of Indian lands—allotted to individual tribe members but held in trust by the United States—by consolidating the ownership of small undivided shares of a tract. The statute provided that individual shares of less than 2 percent of the acreage of a tract could not be transferred by intestacy or devise but would, instead, escheat to the tribe upon the death of the individual owner. The statute terminated only a limited property right, the right to have an ownership interest pass to heirs upon death. Although the Court had upheld the abolition of more important property rights in other cases, such as the right to sell, it now held that the "total abrogation" of the rights of descent and devise could not be upheld without compensation.[107]

A principal objection seemed to be that permitting the property interest to pass by intestacy or devise would not lead to fractioning in all cases, and that the statute therefore should have provided an exception for such cases. Although clearly of limited significance, the decision did seem to indicate that despite *Keystone*, something other than a rational basis test would sometimes be applied in Takings Clause cases.

First English

The Court's next decision, *First English Evangelical Lutheran Church of Glendale v. City of Los Angeles*,[108] is potentially of greater importance, especially to land use planning. After all buildings on plaintiff's property were destroyed by flood, Los Angeles, as a health and safety measure, adopted an ordinance prohibiting further construction on the property. The California courts held that even if the ordinance constituted a taking because it deprived plaintiff of all use of the land, plaintiff's only remedy was a suit to invalidate the ordinance, not a suit for damages.

The Supreme Court disagreed, holding that even if the ordinance proved to be only temporary because later invalidated, plaintiff was entitled to compensation for losses incurred while it remained in effect. Although not all regulations restricting the use of property constitute compensible takings, unlike all physical occupancies, losses incurred by temporary regulatory takings are as fully compensable as losses caused by a temporary physical takings. Despite *Keystone*, it thus appeared, the regulatory takings doctrine still had more than a breath of life.

Nollan

The third and final 1987 victory for a Takings Clause claimant, in *Nollan v. California Coastal Commission*,[109] is potentially the most significant. The Nollans sought to replace a dilapidated bungalow on their beachfront property with a much larger house. This could not be done without the permission of the California Coastal Commission, which agreed to grant a permit only on condition that the Nollans cede to the public an easement to cross their property along the ocean front on dry sand (i.e., above the mean high tide line). This would facilitate passage between public beaches on either side of the Nollans' property. The commission found that the proposed larger building would impede the public's view of the sea, and the easement would compensate for this loss of visual access, the Commission argued, by providing a different form of access.

The Nollans challenged the conditional easement requirement as a taking, and the Supreme Court, in an opinion by Justice Scalia, agreed. Scalia saw the case as involving a physical taking, not a mere use restriction, because members of the public were granted a permanent right to traverse the property. If the Commission had simply required the Nollans to grant an easement to the public, it would clearly have been a taking. But here the requirement was made a condition of the grant of a construction permit which the commission, the Court assumed, could properly deny.

The condition, however, Scalia objected, did nothing to alleviate the problem, the impairment of public visual access, that justified the requirement of a permit. He said:

> It is quite impossible to understand, how a requirement that people already on the public beaches be able to walk across the Nollans' property reduces any obstacle to viewing the beach created by the new house. . . . [The] lack of nexus between the condition and the original purpose of the building restriction converts that purpose into something other than what it was.[110]

The permit requirement thus became simply a means of obtaining an easement without paying for it, an impermissible taking.

The significance of *Nollan* lies less, however, in the nexus requirement it established[111] than in the Court's demonstrated willingness to invalidate a state's land regulation scheme. Scalia recited and purported to accept the orthodox and apparently extremely deferential proposition that "land-use regulation does not effect a taking if it 'substantially advance[s] legitimate state interests' and does not 'den[y] an owner economically viable use of his land.'"[112]

Few government regulations of land use cannot be shown, at least arguably, to serve a legitimate state interest, that is, to advance the public welfare in some way, and few, if any, deprive the land of all economic value.

Scalia significantly qualified his deferential statement, however, by stating in a footnote that there is reason to believe that takings challenges to property restrictions are tested by a standard different from that applicable to challenges based on the Due Process or Equal Protection Clauses. A regulation challenged under the Takings Clause must be shown to "substantially advance" a legitimate state interest, not merely to have some "rational" relation to that interest.[113] The distinction between "substantial" and "rational" may seem subtle, but "rational" is a constitutional term of art.

By rejecting a mere "rational basis" requirement, Scalia clearly announced that the Court's long-standing abdication of review in economic substantive due process and equal protection cases is not applicable to regulatory takings cases.

The Court, however, is closely divided on the issue of intervention in regulatory takings cases—Justices Brennan, Marshall, Blackmun, and Stevens dissented in *Nollan*—as it is on many other contentious issues. Scalia may be eager to intervene but his majority is precarious, and despite the promise of *Nollan,* no other decision upholding a regulatory taking claim was handed down for five years.

Lucas

The regulatory takings issue next came to the Court in 1992 in *Lucas v. South Carolina Coastal Council.*[114] Plaintiff Lucas had paid $975,000 for two residential lots on the Isle of Palms, a barrier island off Charleston, South Carolina, with the intention of building single-family homes. Two years later the South Carolina legislature passed a statute that effectively prohibited construction on the lots. The result, a South Carolina trial court found, was to render the property valueless. The South Carolina Supreme Court held, nonetheless, that there had been no taking, only a valid restriction of land use for ecological and other purposes.

The United States Supreme Court reversed and, again in an opinion by Justice Scalia, announced a seemingly dramatic per se rule. Government regulation that prohibits "all economically beneficial or productive use of land" is categorically a taking requiring compensation;[115] the Court's typical ruleless balancing approach is inapplicable.

Two factors, however, weaken, if not eliminate, the seeming clarity and importance of the *Lucas* rule. First, whether a restriction on the use of property totally destroys its value depends entirely on how the property is defined. For example, prohibiting mining of a certain amount of coal reduces the market value of that coal by 100 percent but reduces the value of all the coal in the mine by a much smaller percentage.

Pennsylvania Coal and *Keystone* reached different conclusions simply by defining the relevant property differently: *Pennsylvania Coal* looked at the value of the coal that could no longer be mined and *Keystone* looked at the value of the coal that still could. The issue is to determine the totality, the denominator of a fraction, with which the loss of value is to be compared, and it is not clear how that is to be done. Scalia himself recognized this, stating with typical candor, "regrettably, the rhetorical force of our 'deprivation of all economically feasible use' rule is greater than its precision, since the rule does not make clear the 'property interest' against which the loss of value is to be measured."[116]

The Court gave little guidance as to how to answer this question, and the facts of the case shed little light on it because it seemed clear that the relevant totality was simply the two lots, which the regulation supposedly "took" completely.

The *Lucas* rule that a regulation destroying all economically beneficial use of land is a taking is also qualified by the fact that compensation is nonetheless not required, Scalia agreed, if "inquiry into the nature of the owner's estate shows that the proscribed use interests were not part of his title to begin with."[117] That is, compensation is not required if the challenged regulation merely prohibits a use that preexisting state law had already prohibited. Takings law had always purported to turn on a distinction between regulations that merely prohibit "noxious" uses of land—for example, uses that produce pollution—which do not require compensation, and regulations that seek to obtain a public benefit from the land, as to which compensation is required.[118]

It happens, unfortunately, that this harm/benefit distinction is easily manipulated. The regulation in *Lucas*, for example, Scalia pointed out, could be described as preventing harm to "South Carolina's ecological resources" or, instead, as achieving the benefits of an "ecological preserve."[119]

Scalia, therefore, purported to reject the harm/benefit distinction as one often existing only "in the eye of the beholder."[120] The distinction he substituted, however, between use interests that are or are not part of the owner's title to begin with turns out not to be very different. Scalia's approach requires a court to look to a state's property law to determine what is included in plaintiff's title, but what is included largely depends on the state's law of "nuisance," which excludes "noxious" uses of land. Such uses, therefore, are not part of an owner's title.

A state's nuisance law, however, will not only often be indefinite but will likely turn on the supposed harm/benefit distinction. The distinction is thus brought back into the takings calculus even under Scalia's approach. Scalia's approach is likely, nonetheless, to have a restrictive effect in that it should serve to limit the power of state legislatures to create new noxious use categories as particular occasions demand in order to avoid paying compensation for restrictions of land uses that were previously permissible.

The significance of *Lucas*, like the significance of *First English* and *Nollan*, is difficult to gauge. On the one hand, its per se rule would seem to have very little application, as Scalia explicitly recognized, even apart from the denominator and scope of title problems. Regulations that leave property valueless by prohibiting all economically beneficial use are rare. Government regulators should almost always be able to see that use-restricted land retains some value, at least if "value" is broadly defined. On the other hand, it makes little sense, as Justice Stevens argued in dissent, to say that a total devaluation of property is a taking per se but that a near-total devaluation must be subject to a balancing test that, on the basis of such decisions as *Keystone*, would almost certainly result in no taking being found.

As long as the attitude reflected in Scalia's *Lucas* opinion prevails, however, there will be pressure to find that less than a "total" loss of value is sufficient to constitute a taking. Indeed, it is doubtful that the loss of value was truly total in *Lucas*; petitioner could still use the property, as Justice Blackmun pointed out in dissent,[121] to "picnic, swim, camp in a tent, or live on the property in a moveable trailer." To argue this, however, seems like a bad joke. The lower court's finding, not questioned in the Supreme Court, that the property was valueless was probably realistic, even if not literally true. In any event, and perhaps most important, the decision demonstrated again the Court's willingness to intervene, even if only very occasionally, in the area of land use regulation.

Dolan

The Rehnquist Court's next major pronouncement on takings law came two years later in *Dolan v. City of Tigard*.[122] Plaintiff Dolan owned a one-and-two-thirds-acre lot alongside a creek in downtown Tigard, a suburb of Portland, Oregon. The city agreed to permit Dolan to expand her hardware store on the lot and pave additional parking spaces on two conditions. The first was that she dedicate to the city for use as part of a public greenway the portion of her property that was within the flood plain of the creek.

The second was that she dedicate an additional fifteen-foot-wide strip adjoining the flood plain to be used as a pedestrian and bicycle pathway. Plaintiff had already been precluded from building on the flood plain, and the pathway dedication, which accounted for about 10 percent of the property, would be counted in meeting a previous requirement, not challenged, that businesses set aside 15 percent of their property for open space and landscaping.

The case was essentially a replay of *Nollan*, except that now the *Nollan* requirement of a nexus between the condition imposed on grant of a permit and the purpose of the use restriction was found to be met and yet a taking was found. The additional paving of the property would increase water runoff and contribute to the flooding problem that justified limiting development in the flood plain. The required dedication of a pedestrian/bicycle pathway was justified as relieving the additional traffic problem that the expanded store would cause. The question, therefore, the Court said, in an opinion by Chief Justice Rehnquist, was not merely whether there was a connection but rather whether there was "the required degree of connection between the exactions imposed by the city and the projected impacts of the proposed development."[123] This was not a case, like *Nollan*, the Court said, where the city was "simply trying to obtain an easement through gimmickry, which converted a valid regulation of land use into 'an out-and-out plan of extortion.'"[124]

The Court reviewed a number of state court decisions on the issue of the required degree of connection. Some state courts, it said, accepted "very generalized statements as to the necessary connection between the required dedication and the proposed development."[125] This standard, the Court found, was "too lax."[126] Other state courts apply a "specifi[c] and uniquely attributable" test, requiring that the exaction be "directly proportional to the specifically created need."[127]

The Court rejected this too, doubting that the federal Constitution "requires such exacting scrutiny."[128] Still other state courts had adopted an "intermediate position," demanding that the required dedication of property have some "reasonable relationship" to the need created by the development.[129] The Court felt that this standard was closest to the "federal constitutional norm," but it rejected the term "reasonable relationship" because it "seems confusingly similar to the term 'rational basis' which describes the minimal level of scrutiny under the Equal Protection Clause of the Fourteenth Amendment."[130] The Court therefore adopted, instead, the term "rough proportionality," which requires "some sort of individualized determination that the required dedication is related both in nature and extent to the impact of the proposed development."[131]

The Court thus made much more explicit than in *Lucas* its rejection of the "rational basis" test in regulatory taking cases. The "rational basis" test meant in effect that the Court had abandoned review of business regulations, but "simply denominating a governmental measure as a 'business regulation,'" Chief Justice Rehnquist insisted, "does not immunize it from constitutional challenge on the grounds that it violates a provision of the Bill of Rights."[132]

He could "see no reason why the Takings Clause of the Fifth Amendment, as much a part of the Bill of Rights as the First Amendment or Fourth Amendment, should be relegated to the status of a poor relation. . . ."[133] If the extremely activist stance adopted by the Warren and later Courts in regard to the First and Fourth Amendments was now to be adopted as to the Takings Clause, the clause will indeed assume a prominent role in our constitutional jurisprudence.

The Court then turned to the facts of the case before it and found that neither of the city's permit conditions met its newly announced standard. The city could properly prohibit development in the flood plain to control flooding, but flood control could not justify requiring dedication of plaintiff's flood plain property to serve as part of a greenway system. It was "difficult to see," the Court said, "why recreational visitors trampling along petitioner's flood plain easement"—which was the practical effect of requiring a dedication—"are related to the city's legitimate interest in reducing flooding problems."[134] Under this reasoning, however, as pointed out by Justice Souter in dissent, the flood plain dedication condition was found invalid simply because it failed to meet the nexus requirement of *Nollan* (i.e., there was *no* connection between dedication and the flooding problem) not because there was any lack of "rough proportionality" as required by *Dolan*.

The Court's treatment of the permit condition requiring dedication of a pedestrian/bicycle footpath, however, clearly achieved new heights of activism in a takings case, apparently fulfilling the Court's promise that the Takings Clause would be treated like the First and Fourth Amendments. The city undertook to show, without contradiction, that the expanded store would generate roughly 435 additional trips per day in the central business district. Nor did Dolan or the Court dispute the city's contention that the pathway "could offset some of the traffic demand . . . and lessen the increase in traffic congestion."[135] This undeniable nexus between the condition imposed on the permit and a problem caused by the development was found insufficient, however, to sustain the condition. Although the pathway clearly "could" offset some of the increased traffic demand, the Court conceded, the city failed to show that "it will, or is likely to do so."[136]

The city's obligation, the Court said, was to "make some effort to quantify its findings in support of the dedication for the pedestrian/bicycle pathway beyond the conclusory statement that it could offset some of the traffic demand generated."[137] When a conditional permit is challenged as a taking, the defendant governmental unit has the burden of justifying its regulatory scheme to the satisfaction of a majority of the Justices, and justification, it would appear, will not be easy. This is indeed a rejection of the rational basis test; it would seem, as Justice Stevens, joined by Justices Blackmun and Ginsburg, pointed out in dissent, to return the Court at least in the conditional permit context, to the type of close and skeptical "substantive due process" review of state economic regulations that is epitomized by *Lochner v. New York*.[138]

Return to *Lochner?*

So where are we now on the takings issue? *Dolan* is a remarkably activist decision that has no doubt, as intended, thrown the fear of God, or at least of the Supreme Court, into land use planners. It seems unlikely, however, that the Court will proceed much further in that direction. Justice Ginsburg joined Justices Stevens,

Blackmun, and Souter in a vigorous dissent, giving Chief Justice Rehnquist a bare majority that may not be entirely reliable. There have been no further such decisions since 1994. That Justice Breyer has replaced Justice Blackmun will probably not make a difference on this issue, but it is highly doubtful that the *Dolan* approach could survive one or two additional appointments to the Court by another liberal president like Clinton.

Liberal victories, the Court's usual and expected product, applauded by academia, tend to grow and flourish; conservative victories, freakish deviations from the norm, tend to be limited and short-lived.

To accuse a decision of being a return to *Lochner* is, in contemporary constitutional law, the ultimate perjorative. But why so, what exactly was wrong with *Lochner*? The *Lochner* era Court invalidated licensing requirements, price and wage controls, and other regulations of business that most economists would agree today are not in the public interest. The Court was probably more right than wrong in seeing the regulations it invalidated as socially harmful.

It is more difficult to criticize the *Lochner* era decisions for the policies the Court imposed than for the fact that the Court felt authorized to impose them. All one can confidently say against those decisions is that, right or wrong on the policy issues, the Court had no constitutional authority to make them, that the right of self-government must include the right to make and, it may be hoped, learn from mistakes.

This objection does not sit well, however, in the mouths of the *Dolan* dissenters or of most of today's constitutional law professors. It is based on a faith in government by the people through elected representatives that they do not share.

Constitutional scholars and other members of our cultural elite show little evidence of this faith when it comes to the Court intervening on other issues. On the contrary, the nightmare of the cultural elite is that policymaking may fall into the hands of the American people—who, after all, favor such unenlightened policies as capital punishment, effective enforcement of the criminal law, prayer in schools, suppression of pornography, and the assignment of public school children to neighborhood schools. The function of constitutional law as the cultural elite sees it is to prevent that from happening, to keep the ultimate decision on basic issues of social policy in the hands of the Supreme Court Justices, themselves members and generally representative of the cultural elite.

As activist as *Dolan* may be, it is certainly not more so than *Roe v. Wade*,[139] *Romer v. Evans*,[140] *United States v. Virginia*,[141] or an endless array of Supreme Court enactments of liberal policy preferences.

Chief Justice Rehnquist was entirely correct in insisting in *Dolan* that the Takings Clause applies to the states fully as much as the First and Fourth Amendments by reason of incorporation in the Fourteenth Amendment. It is too bad, indeed tragic, that we apparently lack the means or the will to reject the incorporation doctrine as a power-usurping fiction and have allowed the constitutional scheme of self-government in a federalist system to degenerate into government by majority vote of nine unelected lawyers. As long as the Court is permitted to make social policy in any area of the Justices' choosing, however, it is difficult to accept that conservative Justices should permit the Court to make an exception where property rights are concerned. Indeed, there may well be more justification, on both textual and policy grounds, for judicial intervention in this area than in many others.

Notes

1. 347 U.S. 483 (1954).
2. U.S. Const. art. I, § 1 ("All legislative Powers herein granted shall be vested in a Congress of the United States").
3. See, e.g., Justice Owen Roberts's classic statement in United States v. Butler, 297 U.S. 1, 62 (1938) ("It is sometimes said that the court assumes a power to overrule or control the action of the people's representatives. This is a misconception. The Constitution is the supreme law of the land ordained and established by the people. All legislation must conform to the principles it lays down. When an act of Congress is appropriately challenged in the courts as not conforming to the constitutional mandate the judicial branch of the Government has only one duty—to lay the article of the Constitution which is invoked beside the statute which is challenged and to decide whether the latter squares with the former.").
4. U.S. Const. amend. 14: "No State shall . . . deprive any person of life, liberty, or property, without due process of law; nor shall any State deny to any person within its jurisdiction the equal protection of the laws."
5. 410 U.S. 113 (1973).
6. U.S. Const. art. I, § 7.
7. Examples of clearly unconstitutional laws are difficult to find. The clearest, if not the only, example found in most constitutional law casebooks is the Minnesota Mortgage Moratorium Act of 1933, a debtor-relief law challenged in Home Building & Loan Ass'n v. Blaisdell, 290 U.S. 398 (1934). Missing probably its best, if not its only, opportunity to hold unconstitutional a law that really was, the Court, in the depths of the Great Depression, upheld the law by a five to four vote.
8. See *The Federalist No. 78*, 464 (Clinton Rossiter ed., 1961) (According to Hamilton, the power would be only to invalidate laws "contrary to the manifest tenor" (id. at 466) of and in "irreconcilable variance" (id. at 467) with the Constitution. Judges would have no "arbitrary discretion," he argued, because they must "be bound down by strict rules and precedents which serve to define and point out their duty in every particular case that comes before them. . . ." (id. at 471).).
9. 1 Cranch 137 (1803).
10. See, e.g., Van Alstyne, "Critical Guide to *Marbury v. Madison*," 1969 *Duke L. J.* 1.
11. U.S. Const. art. I, § 10 ("No State shall . . . pass any . . . Law impairing the Obligation of Contracts . . .").
12. See, e.g., Dartmouth College v. Woodward, 17 U.S. (4 Wheat.) 518 (1819) (holding that the Contracts Clause protected Dartmouth's charter of incorporation against legislative infringement); Ogden v. Saunders, 25 U.S. (12 Wheat.) 213, 332 (1827) (Marshall dissenting—his only dissent on a constitutional issue—from the Court's decision upholding a state bankruptcy law that applied only prospectively).
13. See, e.g., Haggard, *Devils, Drugs, and Doctors* (1929).
14. 19 How. 393 (1857).
15. Civil Rights Cases, 109 U.S. 3 (1883).
16. 78 Stat. 241, 42 U.S.C. § 1971 et seq. (1964).
17. Hall v.De Cuir, 95 U.S. 485 (1877).
18. Plessy v. Ferguson, 163 U.S. 537 (1896).
19. Hammer v. Dagenhart, 247 U.S. 251 (1918) (invalid under the commerce power); Bailey v. Drexel Furniture Co., 259 U.S. 20 (1922) (invalid under the taxing power).

20. See, e.g., Carter v. Carter Coal, 298 U.S. 238 (1936) (invalidating the Bituminous Coal Conservation Act of 1935); United States v. Butler, 297 U.S. 1 (1938) (invalidating the Agricultural Adjustment Act of 1933).

21. See, e.g., Lochner v. New York, 198 U.S. 45 (1905) (working hours of bakery employees); Coppage v. Kansas, 236 U.S. 1 (1915) (laws prohibiting refusal to hire union members); New State Ice Co. v. Liebmann, 283 U.S. 262 (1932) (licensing).

22. See, e.g., Commager, *Majority Rule and Minority Rights* (1943); Boudin, *Government by Judiciary* (1968).

23. See, e.g., NLRB v. Jones & Laughlin Steel Corp., 301 U.S. 1 (1937); Wickard v. Filburn, 317 U.S. 111 (1942); United States v. Darby, 312 U.S. 100 (1941).

24. See, e.g., Ferguson v. Skrupa, 372 U.S. 726 (1963); Olsen v. Nebraska, 313 U.S. 236 (1941).

25. See United States v. Carolene Prod., 304 U.S. 144, 153 n. 4 ("presumption of constitutionality" may have a "narrower scope" when legislation may reflect prejudice against "discrete and insular minorities"); Skinner v. Oklahoma, 316 U.S. 525 (1942) (invalidating sterilization law); Griswold v. Connecticut, 381 U.S. 479 (1965) (invalidating anticontraception law).

26. See, e.g., Mayor and City Council of Baltimore City v. Dawson, 350 U.S. 877 (1955) (public beaches); Holmes v. City of Atlanta, 350 U.S. 879 (1955) (municipal golf courses); Gayle v. Browder, 352 U.S. 903 (1956) (buses).

27. Brown v. Board of Educ., 349 U.S. 294, 300–301 (1955).

28. But see Cooper v. Aaron, 358 U.S. 1 (1958) (Little Rock) (reaffirming *Brown*).

29. 78 Stat. 241, 42 U.S.C. § 1971 et seq. (1964)

30. See, e.g., Roe v. Wade, 410 U.S. 113 (1973).

31. See, e.g., Furman v. Georgia, 408 U.S. 238 (1972).

32. See, e.g., Roth v. United States, 354 U.S. 476 (1957); Miller v. California, 413 U.S. 15 (1973).

33. See, e.g., Barnes v. Glen Theatre, Inc., 501 U.S. 560 (1991).

34. See, e.g., Bowers v. Hardwick, 478 U.S. 186 (1986).

35. See, e.g., Cox v. Louisiana, 379 U.S. 536 (1965); Texas v. Johnson, 491 U.S. 397 (1929) (flag burning).

36. See, e.g., Clark v. Community for Creative Non-Violence, 468 U.S. 288 (1984); Papachristou v. City of Jacksonville, 405 U.S. 156 (1972).

37. See, e.g., Reynolds v. Sims, 377 U.S. 533 (1964); Lucas v. Colorado Gen. Assembly, 377 U.S. 713 (1964).

38. See, e.g., Engel v. Vitale, 370 U.S. 421 (1962) (prayer); Abington School Dist. v. Schempp, 374 U.S. 203 (1963) (Bible reading).

39. See, e.g., Lemon v. Kurtzman, 403 U.S. 602 (1971).

40. See, e.g., Allegheny County v. ACLU, 492 U.S. 573 (1989).

41. See, e.g., Miranda v. Arizona, 384 U.S. 436 (1966) (exclusion of confessions); Mapp v. Ohio, 367 U.S. 643 (1961) (exclusion of physical evidence).

42. New York Times v. Sullivan, 376 U.S. 254, 279–80 (1964); Gertz v. Robert Welch, Inc., 418 U.S. 323 (1974) (recovery only for false and injurious statements made with "actual malice").

43. See, e.g., Craig v. Boren, 429 U.S. 190 (1976).

44. See, e.g., Levy v. Louisiana, 391 U.S. 68 (1968).

45. See, e.g., Graham v. Richardson, 403 U.S. 365 (1971).

46. See, e.g., Plessy v. Ferguson, 163 U.S. 537 (1896); Gong Lum v. Rice, 275 U.S. 78 (1922).

47. Brown v. Board of Educ., 347 U.S. 483 (1954).

48. See, e.g., Dayton Bd. of Educ. v. Brinkman, 443 U.S. 526 (1979).

49. Roe v. Wade, 410 U.S. 113 (1973).

50. U.S. Const., amend. I, "Congress shall make no law respecting an establishment of religion, or prohibiting the free exercise thereof. . . ."

51. See, e.g., Cord, *Separation of Church and State: Historical Fact and Current Fiction* (1982).

52. Griswold v. Connecticut, 381 U.S. 479 (1965).

53. The Constitution is extremely difficult to amend, impeachment has come to be seen as improper except for criminal acts, and statutes limiting jurisdiction are subject to the Catch-22 of requiring Supreme Court approval.

54. 384 U.S. 436 (1966).

55. *The Burger Court: The Counter-Revolution That Wasn't* (V. Blasi ed., 1983).

56. Roe v. Wade, 410 U.S. 113 (1973).

57. Craig v. Boren, 429 U.S. 190 (1976).

58. Graham v. Richardson, 403 U.S. 365 (1971).

59. Swann v. Charlotte-Mecklenburg Bd. of Educ., 402 U.S. 1 (1971).

60. President Reagan made a serious mistake in choosing Scalia ahead of Robert Bork, instead of vice versa, in making Supreme Court appointments. Bork, denied confirmation by a Democrat-controlled Senate, would almost surely have been confirmed by the Republican-controlled Senate that confirmed Scalia unanimously, while Scalia—the first Italian-American appointee—whose judicial philosophy is much the same as Bork's, would have been confirmed at any time.

61. Planned Parenthood v. Casey, 505 U.S. 833 (1992).

62. Lee v. Weisman, 505 U.S. 577 (1992).

63. United States v. Virginia, 518 U.S. 515 (1996).

64. Romer v. Evans, 517 U.S. 620 (1996).

65. ACLU v. Reno, 521 U.S. 844 (1997).

66. U. S. Term Limits, Inc. v. Thornton, 514 U.S. 779 (1995).

67. It is difficult—except perhaps on federalism issues, where, however, judicially enforceable standards are lacking, see Graglia, "*United States v. Lopez*: Judicial Review Under the Commerce Clause," 74 *Tex. L. Rev.* 719 (1996)—to find examples of the Court upholding policy choices that the Constitution clearly forbids. An example is Home Building & Loan Ass'n v. Blaisdell, 290 U.S. 398 (1934). Such decisions would seem, in any event, inactivist rather than activist, inasmuch as they permit the results of the political process to prevail.

68. 488 U.S. 469 (1989).

69. 515 U.S. 200 (1995).

70. 509 U.S. 630 (1993).

71. See Gragllia, *Disaster by Decree: The Supreme Court Decisions on Race and the Schools* 21 (1976).

72. A third possible example is the Court's recent invalidation of congressional acts on federalism grounds; see, e.g., United States v. Lopez, 514 U.S. 549 (1995); New York v. United States, 505 U.S. 144 (1992); Printz v. United States, 521 U.S. 898 (1997).

73. U.S. Const. amend. V.

74. Keystone Bituminous Coal Ass'n v. Debenedictus, 480 U.S. 470 (1987).

75. Hodel v. Irving, 481 U.S. 704 (1987); First English Evangelical Lutheran Church v. City of Los Angeles, 422 U.S. 304 (1987); Nollan v. California Coastal Comm'n, 483 U.S. 825 (1987).

76. Barron v. Mayor and City Council of Baltimore, 7 Pet. (32 U.S.) 243 (1833).

77. Similarly, the fact that the framers of the Fourteenth Amendment explicitly included a Bill of Rights provision, the Due Process Clause, makes it unlikely they meant oth-

ers to be included by implication in the Fourteenth Amendment's Privileges or Immunities Clause.

78. See, e.g., Berger, *Government by Judiciary* (1977).

79. See, e.g., Treanor, "The Origins and Original Significance of the Just Compensation Clause of the Fifth Amendment, 94 *Yale L J.* 694 (1985). Interestingly, the Takings Clause was the only provision of the Bill of Rights that was not requested by any state during ratification of the Constitution. It was uniquely a contribution by James Madison, added to his compilation of state requests for amendments that became the Bill of Rights.

80. See, e.g., Fletcher v. Peck, 6 Cranch (10 U.S.) 87 (1810); Terrett v. Taylor, 19 Cranch (13 U.S.) 43 (1815).

81. See Corwin, *Liberty Against Government* (1948).

82. Ibid.

83. See, e.g., Missouri Pac. Ry. Co. v. Nebraska, 164 U.S. 403 (1896).

84. Gitlow v. New York, 268 U.S. 652, 672 (1925).

85. See, e.g., New York Times v. Sullivan, 376 U.S. 254 (1964).

86. See, e.g., Miranda v. Arizona, 324 U.S. 436 (1966).

87. See, e.g., Levy v. Louisiana, 391 U.S. 68 (1968) (illegitimates).

88. See, e.g., Duncan v. Louisiana, 391 U.S. 745 (1968).

89. See, e.g., Goldblatt v. Hempstead, 369 U.S. 590 (1962).

90. Dolan v. City of Tigard, 512 U.S. 374, 392 (1994).

91. It was not universally accepted in the eighteenth century that even government seizure and occupancy of land, as for the building of highways, required compensation; it was often assumed that the value added to the adjoining land would be compensation enough. Schwartz, A *History of the Supreme Court* 373 (1993).

92. Mugler v. Kansas, 123 U.S. 623 (1887).

93. Reinman v. City of Little Rock, 237 U.S. 171 (1915).

94. Hadacheck v. Sebastian, 239 U.S. 394 (1915).

95. Goldblatt v. Hempstead, 369 U.S. 590 (1962).

96. 260 U.S. 393 (1922).

97. Id. at 415.

98. E.g., Hadicheck v. Sebastian, 239 U.S. 394 (1915).

99. Penn Cent. Trans. Co. v. New York City, 438 U.S. 104, 124 (1978).

100. See, e.g., Williamson v. Lee Optical, 348 U.S. 483 (1955); Railway Express Agency v. New York, 366 U.S. 106 (1949).

101. 480 U.S. 470 (1987).

102. Id. at 484.

103. Whatever the difficulties and uncertainties of the Takings Clause, there could be no real doubt that the Pennsylvania statute violated the Contracts Clause, prohibiting states from "impairing the Obligations of Contracts." The state's contract with the coal companies specifically provided that the companies would not be liable for surface damage caused by mining. Justice Stevens's opinion dismissed this objection with the statement, "the Commonwealth's interests in the legislation are more than adequate to justify the impact of the statute on petitioners' contractual agreements." Contract obligation may be impaired, that is, when it is in the state's interest to do so, because "it is well settled," Stevens said, "that the prohibition against impairing the obligation of contracts is not to be read literally." The majority's disdain for property rights, Stevens made clear, could hardly have been more complete.

104. *Keystone*, 480 U.S. at 508.

105. 481 U.S. 704 (1987).

106. Concurring opinions were filed by Justice Brennan, joined by Justices Marshall

and Blackmun, by Justice Scalia, joined by Chief Justice Rehnquist and Justice Powell, and by Justice Stevens (concurring only in the judgment), joined by Justice White.

107. Id. at 717.

108. 482 U.S. 304 (1987). Justice Stevens filed a dissenting opinion, joined in part by Justices White and O'Connor.

109. 483 U.S. 825 (1987).

110. Id. at 837.

111. Indeed, as Professor William K. Jones has pointed out, in perhaps the most useful discussion one can find of the takings issue, there seems little doubt that the Commission could have accomplished its purpose if it had simply proceeded in two steps rather than one. The Commission, Scalia noted, could have validly conditioned grant of the permit on height or width limitations. It could even have required that "the Nollans provide a viewing spot on their property for passersby with whose sighting of the ocean their new house would interfere" (id. at 836). If the Commission had first imposed a viewing spot requirement, however, the Nollans would almost surely have gladly traded it for a requirement of beach access:

> The viewing spot does the public little good, absent related parking facilities and beach access; but its occasional use is highly intrusive on the Nollans' privacy; viewers wander past the ground floor windows of the Nollan house at all hours of the day and night. On the other hand, lateral access across the Nollan beach would be highly valued by bathers at adjacent public beaches, and traversals by them along the beach would be largely invisible from the Nollan house, because the beach in issue was only about ten feet wide and there was a seawall eight feet high between the beach and the house. It is hard to imagine that the Supreme Court would interpose its authority to block the second step, an exchange advantageous to both the Nollans and the public. If this analysis is correct, then the victory of the Nollans cannot be attributed to any sturdy constitutional safeguard.

Jones, "Confiscation: A Rationale of the Law of Takings," 24 *Hofstra L. Rev.* 1 (1995).

112. *Nolan*, 483 U.S. at 834 (quoting Agins v. Tiburon, 447 U.S. 255, 260 (1980)).

113. Id. at 836.

114. 505 U.S. 1003 (1992).

115. Id. at 1015. Justice Kennedy concurred only in the judgment, Justices Blackmun and Stevens filed dissenting opinions, and Justice Souter would have dismissed the writ as improvidently granted.

116. Id. at 1016.

117. Id. at 1027.

118. See Sax,"Takings and the Police Power," 74 *Yale L.J.* 36 (1964).

119. Lucas, 505 U.S. at 1024.

120. Id.

121. Id. at 1044.

122. 512 U.S. 374 (1994). See also Suitum v. Tahoe Regional Planning Agency, 520 U.S. 725 (1997).

123. Id. at 377.

124. Id. at 387 (quoting Nollan v. California Coastal Comm'n, 483 U.S. 825, 837 (1987)).

125. Id. at 389.

126. Id.

127. Id.

128. Id. at 390.

129. Id.

130. Id. at 391.
131. Id.
132. Id at 392.
133. Id.
134. Id. at 393.
135. Id. at 395.
136. Id. at 395. (quoting Dolan v. City of Tigard, 317 Ore. 110, 127, 854 P.2d 437, 447 (1993)).
137. Id. at 395.
138. Id. at 406 (citing Lochner v. New York, 198 U.S. 45 (1905)). Justice Souter also dissented.
139. 410 U.S. 113 (1973).
140. 517 U.S. 620 (1996).
141. 518 U.S. 515 (1996).

· II ·

A
BROADER
PERSPECTIVE

· 8 ·

THE REHNQUIST COURT
Some More or Less Historical Comments

LAWRENCE M. FRIEDMAN

Giving a historical account of the Rehnquist Court is peculiarly difficult, and in some ways not even possible. For one thing, the story is not over. Rehnquist is very much alive; and the Court is very much a living, ongoing institution.

Still, the Rehnquist Court has been an entity for a number of years. Rehnquist became Chief Justice in 1986. Many aspects of the Court since then have been pawed over by scholars. There is an enormous literature, parsing, dissecting, assessing every Justice and every crucial decision. Enough is known, then, about the Court so that we can put its work, its ways of thinking, and its influence into something of a historical framework, at least in a preliminary way.

The Vanishing Supreme Court

One striking feature of the Rehnquist Court is the radical reduction of the caseload. The Court in the 1990s is deciding many fewer cases than before. Erwin Chemerinsky titled his article on the 1988–1989 Supreme Court Term, in the *Harvard Law Review*, "The Vanishing Constitution."[1] A more apt title, today, might be the vanishing Supreme Court. In the term Chemerinsky commented on, there were 143 full opinions of the Court, eighty-eight concurrences and 116 dissents.[2] For the 1996 term, the Court wrote eighty-six opinions; there were forty concurrences, and sixty dissents.[3] This is an extraordinary drop in the output of the Court.

There have been several theories about why the caseload has shrunk so drastically; none of them seems entirely convincing. Is the Court so fractured that it cannot agree on what to hear? Some people sense a kind of constitutional exhaustion—an impulse to dampen the ardor of the Court, mute its shrill voice, cut its role down to a more manageable size. The majority of the Court, and certainly the Chief Justice is among them, *would* like to dismantle some of the Court's pretensions—do less, decide less, get the Supreme Court out of the headlines.

The majority of the Justices also seem to want to show more deference to the states than earlier Courts. The Court, for example, surprised everybody by breathing a bit of life into the corpse of the Commerce Clause as a limitation on the power of Congress.[4]

The Court, very definitely, would like to get the federal judiciary out of the death penalty business, as much as possible, and leave all this to the tender mercies of the states. Rehnquist, for one, never seems to find *any* procedural errors in even the most slapdash trials, as long as they resulted in a death sentence. Some members of the Court clearly feel that the Justices of the Warren Court grabbed too much power for themselves; that the Burger Court did nothing or not enough to put a stop to this usurpation; and that it is time to call a halt to liberal activism or even to put the engine in reverse. All this of course is well-known. And all this surely influences the sheer size of the Court's workload. In the minds of some, that Court is best which does the least.

The Eye of the Hurricane

The job of cutting the Court down to size is not an easy one. It runs up against one crucial aspect of the Court's work and its position in society: the Court is a *political* institution, like it or not—political not in the sense of electoral politics but in the sense of politically meaningful and important. Because the Court has an acutely political function, and because of the significance of law, the legal order, and litigation in American life, the Court attracts litigants and problems the way flames attract moths.

The political role of the Court, and the visibility this engenders, is unlikely to change in the predictable future. The fuss over the Bork nomination was a symptom (though not a cause) of the Court's political visibility. The Clarence Thomas hearings made matters worse. Of course, not every nomination sets off so many sparks. And, it must be admitted, the Court has been in the center of controversy almost since its inception. Certainly, cases such as *Dred Scott*,[5] the income tax cases,[6] *Brown v. Board of Education*,[7] and *Roe v. Wade*,[8] have pushed the Court into the limelight at many points in its history. It may be that the Court is *more* controversial than ever before; this would be hard to prove one way or another. But the Court is certainly an extremely visible institution, and it is likely to remain that way.

I say visible even though the Court is quite secretive and shies away from publicity. In this regard, the Court is an anomaly. This is an age of mass media. The President's face is on TV every day. His wife, his daughter, his dog—everything about him gets chronicled. Leaders like the President are in fact *celebrities*, and the Justices of the Supreme Court are, in a minor way, celebrities themselves, whether they like it or not. In a media-driven, celebrity-mad society,[9] government is both a prisoner of the media and a manipulator of news and images in the media. It makes use of all the black arts of public relations.

Yet the Supreme Court in the main acts differently. It keeps its secrets.[10] It resists television. It does not hold press conferences, and the Justices try to stay out of the limelight—more or less. The Court has maintained, more than any other Washington institution, a kind of curtain of privacy. But all this is relative to the rest of the government. Compared to its own past history, the Court is undoubtedly more exposed, more naked to the public than before. One sign of this is the appearance—and popularity—of books which purport to crack open its secret doors.[11] Another was the Bork and Thomas nominations, which were particular sensations in their day.

The Fractured Court

The basic structure of the Court as an institution has been slowly changing over the years. The Court is no longer a truly collegial body, a panel of judges who work together and hammer out compromises. Justices still have to work to build a majority, but it is probably more accurate to refer to the Court as an uneasy union of nine separate law offices. There is a famous description of the Court, sometimes ascribed to Oliver Wendell Holmes, Jr., as nine scorpions in a bottle.[12] They may still be scorpions, but each one now seems to have his or her own bottle. Partly this is because of the growth of staff: Justices did not have (official) law clerks before 1922;[13] now they have three or four. There are not nine Justices but nine "chambers."

Whether the Justices work together, and how much they collaborate, is hard to know. There is mounting evidence from the papers of Justices, from the clerks themselves, and from judicial biographies, that the Court is a very fractured body.[14] And of course we have the evidence of their printed and written opinions. These clearly show a deeply divided, somewhat quarrelsome Court. In each case, somebody has to cobble together a majority opinion, and the Justices do talk and confer. They may even be, for the most part, friends. But more and more the Justices seem to insist on their own say in the actual business of deciding cases and writing opinions. The result is a bewildering and confusing array of concurrences and dissents and partial concurrences and dissents, all jumbled together so that in many cases it is impossible to say *what* the Court actually decided, if anything.

A 1993 case, not especially noteworthy, *Saudi Arabia v. Nelson*,[15] can be taken as an example. Scott Nelson worked at the King Faisal Specialist Hospital in Riyadh, in Saudi Arabia. He was, he claimed, arrested after he tried to blow the whistle on some suspicious goings-on. The Saudis, he said, then threw him into jail, where he was shackled, tortured, and beaten in "an overcrowded cell area infested with rats." He sued the Saudis for damages, and the defense was sovereign immunity.

Souter delivered the Court's opinion; four Justices joined. Kennedy joined "except for the last paragraph of Part II." White wrote an opinion concurring in the judgment (Blackmun joined him). Kennedy concurred in part and dissented in part, and Blackmun and Stevens joined "as to Parts I-B and II." Blackmun then wrote an opinion "concurring in the judgment in part and dissenting in part," and Stevens wrote his own separate dissent.

This sort of thing is becoming increasingly common. The Justices agree and disagree in bits and pieces. They defer much less to each other's judgment, even when they agree on the actual results. Each Justice is concerned with building up and maintaining a separate identity, ideology, and body of opinions. Under such circumstances, what comes out are not collegial products, at least not to the extent they once were, and the Court becomes nine separate power centers—nine sovereignties.

This may or may not go along with a decline in civility and trust among Justices. Certainly Scalia is an exceptional case, with his biting and vitriolic attacks on other Justices, his heavy sarcasm. His dissent in *Kiryas Joel* is just one example out of many in which he expresses something close to contempt for his fellow Justices.[16]

It is abundantly clear that the Rehnquist Court is divided into hostile blocs; that the blocs do not trust each other; that there is at times a good deal of anger and vitriol on all sides.[17] Whether there is more of this kind of acrimony than in the past is hard to say—the velvet curtain was drawn much more tightly in past generations. There are well-known historical instances of Justices who simply did not speak to each other. There are well-known instances of bloc voting on the Court— the famous "four horsemen" of the early 1930s, for example.[18] But the situation today may be worse than ever before—if not on the level of personalities then at least on the level of work product.

The *Casey* Case

In many ways, the noted case of *Planned Parenthood of Southeastern Pennsylvania v. Casey*, decided in 1992,[19] illustrates how fractured and acrimonious the Court has become.[20] O'Connor, Kennedy, and Souter (writing together) announced the judgment of the Court "and delivered the opinion of the Court with respect to Parts I, II, III, V-A, V-C, and VI, an opinion with respect to Part V-E, in which Justice Stevens joins, and an opinion with respect to Parts IV, V-B, and V-d."

The fundamental question in this case was whether to hold on to *Roe v. Wade*[21] or overrule it. As we know, a bare majority of the Court voted, in the end, not to overrule. This too is (so far) emblematic of the work of the Rehnquist Court. For all its conservatism, it has yet to make a single move that would radically change or unsettle existing constitutional doctrine. It has hacked away here and there and nibbled here and there around the edges. It has gotten rid of some doctrines of the Warren Court and marginalized others. A lot of this is quite significant, but none of it is truly revolutionary.

Not only is *Roe v. Wade* still standing, bloody but unbowed, but so are *Brown*,[22] *Miranda*,[23] and most of the other icons of Warren liberalism. To quote a title from a book about the Rehnquist Court: the "center holds."[24] As far as (say) Scalia is concerned, the Court's inability to work a revolution is not for lack of trying, but even before the appointment of Ginsburg and Breyer, there were clear limits beyond which the Court seemed unwilling, or unable, to go.[25]

Casey also stimulated one of Justice Scalia's harsh and intemperate dissents. Scalia tosses around words such as "fabricated," "contrived," and worse to describe the joint opinion, and he ends by describing a portrait of Roger Brooke Taney, painted in 1859, which shows Taney sitting in an armchair, his "right hand hanging limply," his eyes vacant and staring, with an "expression of profound sadness and disillusionment." The point is that Taney was (in Scalia's eyes) a broken man, defeated and depressed because of his fatal misstep in *Dred Scott*. This, he implies, is the fate that might be in store for the Justices in *Casey*. And he ends his dissent by saying that the Court "should get out of this area," that is, abortion, where "we have no right to be."[26]

Note that Scalia's last words are not a demand for a different way of framing a certain doctrine but a demand to "get out of this area," that is, to renunciate, to shrink the role of the Court. (We will return to this aspect of Scalia's philosophy.) And the Court has done its share of renunciating—in death penalty cases, for example, where it has bowed to the will of Congress, and the howls of the public, and cut down its role in overseeing state processes. The Court has also (as we saw) dramatically cut down on its output.

But renunciation in the largest sense is not really possible for the Supreme Court. It is inconsistent with the Court's actual role in American society, a role one commentator has compared to the priests of a (civil) religion.[27] It would be a long and complicated story to explain exactly how the Court reached this position. One point, however, should be made. The Court is obviously, and necessarily, a creature of its period. Its docket and its work reflect factors and forces from outside its marble chambers, outside the legal order altogether, and which reflect the general culture.

Lawyers are extremely keen on procedural justice—due process and the like. They have constructed whole philosophies around the notion of fairness in procedures. The public does not disagree, of course, about the value of fair procedures. But the definition of freedom that the public holds, I believe, is strongly *substantive*. People believe very much in "rights," and not just the old, classic rights—freedom of speech, freedom to vote, freedom of religion. They also feel strongly about many of the new "privacy" rights, rights to make important life choices free of government interference. This is why *Griswold v. Connecticut*[28] is so sacrosanct. It is why so many people were willing to oppose Bork to the bitter end. People look to the Courts for vindication of their rights; and for this reason all the arguments about "countermajoritarianism" seem quite beside the point—politically at least.

Scalia argues that *Roe v. Wade*, far from solving the problem of abortion, made the problem worse: Before *Roe*, he says, "national politics were not plagued by abortion protests, national abortion lobbying, or abortion marches on Congress."[29] In other words, *Roe* had a polarizing effect; it "fanned into life an issue that has inflamed our national politics."[30]

Of course, we have no way of knowing whether this is so or not—no way to guess how abortion politics would have played out without *Roe*. I think, however, we can concede this point—at least somewhat—to Scalia. But it is also true that the right of women to control their bodies, to decide whether or not to have a baby, was an issue before the case was decided; and a sharply contested and divisive one. The case, after all, did not arise in a vacuum.[31] But even if we grant Scalia's point, doesn't it prove too much? The same argument could be made about *Brown v. Board of Education*; it definitely fanned a flame. It encouraged a militant civil rights movement; it led to a period of "massive resistance;" it set off a rancorous, sometimes violent debate. Indeed, the point *has* been made about *Brown*.[32]

Rights-consciousness—and particularly the sense that there are fundamental, inborn, inherent, basic rights, which legislatures should not touch—is a strong *social* aspect of twentieth-century opinion in Western countries. One consequence of this fact is an inevitable increase in the role of Courts, which are after all the guardians and interpreters of these fundamental rights.[33]

The joint opinion in *Casey* spoke about a "realm of personal liberty," a "right to define one's own concept of existence, of meaning, of the universe, and of the mystery of life."[34] It is possible to snort and howl at this sentiment as a matter of constitutional *law*, and Scalia certainly would, but the sentiment resonates profoundly with postulates of modern American culture.[35]

As has always been true, the Supreme Court does not run into political difficulties simply because it is powerful, or even because it chooses to exercise that power. Nobody would really care if the Court was "activist" or not (except perhaps a few academics) if people approved of the *results* of its activities. The public is result-oriented; no question. The issue is, for what ends is the power used? Who gains and who loses? Liberals howled with rage at the behavior of the Supreme Court in the days of *Lochner*.[36] The right howled with equal rage at the doings of the Warren Court. What evokes rage is not the style, the writing of opinions, the legal logic, or even the fact of "activism" itself (which in any event is not easy to define). Not one out of a thousand of the people who picket abortion clinics and denounce *Roe v. Wade* has the foggiest notion of the *legal* issues in the case. Results, consequences, winners and losers—these are all that matter in society.

In short, the public judges the Court in terms of what it does and not in terms of how it reasons. The public also generates a set of expectations. The Court rises in the eyes of this or that segment of the public if it meets those expectations. If not, its popularity suffers. Legal ideology, attitudes toward "activism," the craftsmanship and logical coherence of opinions, and so on, are rarely if ever decisive.

An instructive example is the way *Griswold v. Connecticut* [37] has become a sacred cow. I think it is fair to say that this is one of the Court's most feeble efforts, from the standpoint of legal reasoning or the structure of argumentation or what-have-you.[38] Yet the case's place in history is rock-solid. Those who mounted the (legal) attack on *Roe v. Wade* were often extremely careful to tiptoe around *Griswold*. When Charles Fried argued for the government in *Webster v. Reproductive Health Services*,[39] he insisted that *Roe* should be overturned but spoke of *Griswold* with respect: the government, he said, was "not asking the Court to unravel the fabric of . . . privacy rights" in cases like *Griswold*; the government was merely "asking the Court to pull this one thread" out of the fabric.[40] At the end of the century, the idea of a law against the sale of condoms and other contraceptive devices seems patently absurd to the vast majority of the population. *Griswold* (or its result) has become genuinely popular—unassailable, in fact. *Roe v. Wade*, of course, is much less solid—but not for technical reasons, and not because it is poorly reasoned, or even because its holding has so weak a basis in the Constitutional text.

The public has no interest in or knowledge of the debates over originalism, use of legislative history, and the like. People do, however, have substantive opinions. What doomed Robert Bork's nomination was his radical failure to understand what the public wants, or even to *care* about this issue. Of course, in theory, Bork was right: a Justice is not supposed to worry about mere public opinion. But this platitude no longer applies, if it ever did, at the point at which a Justice is appointed.

The issue of public opinion relates to the *legitimacy* of the Court and what it does—a subject of endless speculation, and (frequently) dire warnings from dissenting opinions. "Legitimacy" is an extremely slippery concept, a concept of multiple meanings. There is, to begin with, a normative or philosophical meaning. But this is not the meaning I am concerned with here.

A second meaning refers to a public sense, a kind of feeling or opinion, that an institution, rule, doctrine or arrangement is right, lawful, proper, and should be obeyed. In this sense, legitimacy is an empirical question—a question, indeed, of what people out there actually think and believe.[41]

Polls suggest that the Supreme Court is, in fact, extremely well thought of. The public considers it, on the whole, fair, impartial, and committed to justice. They think of the Court as (relatively) free from partisan politics. Even the uproar over *Roe v. Wade* does not seem to impair this feeling. Even in the days of "impeach Earl Warren," the Court seemed to lead a charmed life, and McCarthyite threats to impeach William O. Douglas got nowhere. Indeed, one might read the fate of Roosevelt's Court-packing plan as a warning. A supremely popular President could not work his will on the Supreme Court—even though the Court had come down with a flock of exceedingly unpopular decisions.[42]

The Court itself seems to worry about the issue inordinately. The question of legitimacy was a powerful factor (if we can believe what we read) in the joint opinion written in *Casey*.[43] Legitimacy is a constant theme in Scalia's work. Scalia is constantly nagging and warning about impending loss of legitimacy (he is not the only one, of course).

In *Cruzan v. Director, Missouri Department of Health*,[44] a "right to die" case, Scalia, in his concurrence, said he "would have preferred that we announce, clearly and promptly, that the federal Courts have no business in this field" (there are no end of "fields" Scalia thinks the Court has no business in).[45] He added that the Court "need not, and has no authority to, inject itself into every field of human activity where irrationality and oppression may theoretically occur, and *if it tries to do so it will destroy itself*."[46] There is, of course, not a shred of evidence for this last, apocalyptic prophecy.

It is, to be sure, possible in theory for the Court to do something so outrageous, so against the public will, that it will in fact destroy itself. The historical record suggests that this is in practice extremely unlikely. *Dred Scott*[47] came as close as any case had come, but it too did not destroy the Supreme Court. The Court has, of course, has made some highly unpopular decisions. Huge majorities (according to the polls) would like to see prayer in the public schools, for example. But the Court sticks to its guns on this point;[48] it survives, and flourishes in fact.

In part this is because the Court on most issues does not wander *that* far from "public opinion," or at least from views that have *some* basis in the opinion of *some* significant group. The Rehnquist Court may be doing a better job of hewing to the public line than the Warren Court. The Court has certainly been tougher on crime than the Warren Court—too much so, in my opinion, and in the opinion of some others.[49]

This is especially true of death penalty cases. The majority of the Court is clearly fed up with the endless writs, petitions, and delays; they seem to want to clean out death row as quickly as possible and hustle these killers off to their fate. This may be an accurate reading of the public mind on this particular issue; at any rate, legislative policy has also been traveling in this direction.

The central core of the Court is also probably right in the way it reads the public mind on issues of privacy. This is why contraception is a total nonissue. Whatever one thinks about the craftsmanship of *Griswold*—probably not much—this case has sunk fairly deep roots in the soil. Abortion[50] and gay rights [51] are another matter. They are at the contested frontier of social norms, and consequently at the contested frontier of public policy. The country is (obviously) deeply divided on these issues, and so is the Court.

What happens when Courts do come down with decisions that seem to fly in the face of public opinion? The Rehnquist Court itself has provided a good example—the flag-burning case, decided in 1989.[52] The Texas statute in this case made it a crime to deface or damage the flag "in a way that the actor knows will seriously offend one or more persons likely to observe or discover his actions." The defendant burned an American flag, as part of a demonstration. He was convicted, and appealed. The Supreme Court overturned his conviction, five to four, on free speech grounds. This led to an epidemic of tub thumping, posturing, and flag waving in Congress—admittedly in response to a blizzard of letters, state legislative resolutions, and public opinion polls that showed a rate of disagreement with the Court as high as 85 percent.[53]

There were also the usual calls for a constitutional amendment. This did not succeed. But Congress quickly passed a Flag Protection Act. In 1990, the Supreme Court struck this statute down, again by a five to four margin.[54] This led to more speeches, letters, manifestoes, and yet another attempt to amend the Constitution. The proposed amendment died in the House of Representatives (it got a majority, but not two-thirds).

And then the whole issue seemed to expire; it simply vanished from the radar screens. Polls still showed high support for a constitutional amendment, but there was no salience, no intensity. People were apparently bored with the issue, and it had become "very much like a summer television rerun, a formula notorious for killing public interest."[55]

Of course, the Court could not know that the flag-burning issue would die out—any more than it could have guessed, realistically, that the fuss over *Roe v. Wade* would *not* prove to be a flash in the pan. But the Justices are surely aware that some, perhaps many, of the decisions that arouse fury lose their bite when the dust settles (school prayer, for one). Flag burning touched on people's momentary passions, but not their vital interests, economic or otherwise. Perhaps this explains why the issue had no staying power.

The majority of the Court also claims to be very concerned about federal–state relations; about preserving the constitutional balance, and about returning power to the localities. I doubt that the public knows or cares very much about the subject— certainly not as a matter of theory. Some of the same people who shout "states' rights" when it comes to matters of race relations, would be only too happy to see federal laws on pornography, crime control, and limits on cantankerous tort juries. As always, it is outcome and substance that matter.

Nor is the public (I would guess) in love with little procedural niceties, and of course it knows nothing and cares less about federal jurisdiction, the scope of habeas corpus, and so on. The Court seems inordinately fond of these issues, especially when it comes to turning down appeals from men on death row. The majority of the Court seems annoyed at the gall of the attorneys for condemned men, with their constant demands for delays, stays of executions, and so on.

The public, as I said, wants to be tough on crime. Nonetheless, I wonder whether people would consider it right to sentence a man to life imprisonment without possibility of parole for possessing 672 grams of cocaine—a punishment more severe than the punishment for the average murderer.[56] I suspect that most would find this punishment cruel and unusual. And I think people would be shocked to learn that three members of the Court (Rehnquist, Scalia, and Thomas) are of the view that putting an innocent man to death does not violate his constitutional rights.[57] In one notorious case, *Coleman v. Thompson*,[58] a lower Virginia court denied the habeas corpus petition of Roger Coleman, who sat on death row. Coleman tried to appeal to the Virginia Supreme Court. He filed his appeal a few days late, under Virginia rules. The Virginia Supreme Court, playing hardball, refused to hear his case on the merits. Coleman then turned to the federal courts for relief, but the Supreme Court was deaf to his entreaties.

Sandra Day O'Connor's opinion began with the words, "This is a case about federalism." If Virginia wanted to be tough and deny Coleman's petition, why, that was their privilege under our system. The delay, the mistake in filing, of course was not Coleman's but his attorney's, but it was Coleman, not his attorney, who was later put to death. There is a strong case—a *very* strong case—that Coleman was in fact innocent of the crime for which he paid the ultimate price.[59]

A Conservative Court?

The points just made bear on the question of just how "conservative" the Rehnquist Court really is. In some ways, the Rehnquist Court is obviously a conservative Court; it has a working majority of conservatives, and a three-man bloc (Rehnquist himself, Scalia, and Thomas) that is *very* conservative, perhaps radically conservative.[60] This is by way of contrast, quite obviously, with the Warren Court, and it is even somewhat different from the Burger Court.[61]

The case for conservatism is not hard to make out: the Court favors states over the federal government, is extremely tough on crime, likes the death penalty, is suspicious of affirmative action—the list could go on, but all this is quite familiar. The Court may claim that it is politically neutral—indeed, that it merely abides by time-honored "principles"—but that is surely a mirage.[62]

In many regards, the majority of the Court is firmly, even aggressively conservative.[63] But in the history of the Supreme Court as a whole, the Rehnquist Court takes on a rather different aspect. The labels, "liberal" and "conservative," are tricky and can be misleading. The Supreme Court, from the Civil War on, usually represented forces and ideas which we, today, would identify as on the right rather than on the left. The Court that struck down civil rights laws,[64] that upheld segregation[65] and labor injunctions, that refused to allow Congress to ban from commerce products made with child labor,[66] that voided big hunks of the New Deal[67]—this was not a Court that was popular with progressives of various stamps. From this standpoint, the Warren Court was the aberration, and the Rehnquist Court is simply regressing to the mean.

Clearly, compared to these past Courts, the present Court is in one sense not conservative at all. Most commentators on the work of the Supreme Court are obsessed with *comparing* Justices, and clearly Scalia and Thomas, not to mention Rehnquist himself, are much, much more conservative than, say, Ruth Bader Ginsburg, or, certainly, more conservative than departed Justices such as Brennan and Marshall. But the Court does not exist in a vacuum. The Court exists in a specific place, and at a specific time. The whole Court has shifted *dramatically* to the "left," compared to, say, the Court of the 1890s. On race relations, the most conservative Justice today is far more liberal than John Marshall Harlan, the most "left" of the Justices on race issues in the 1890s.

The Court is conservative, therefore, but only by comparison with other contemporaries. If we compare the Court with its ancestors, we get a different picture entirely. The Supreme Court in 1896 voted eight to one for race segregation. Today's Court would vote nine to zero against de jure segregation, but the issue is not even on the agenda any longer.

The Court necessarily works with its own, modern agenda. An example or two might be instructive. Take another sharply divisive case of 1992, *Lee v. Weisman*.[68] This care posed an issue of church and state. Deborah Weisman graduated from Nathan Bishop Middle School, a public school in Providence, Rhode Island. She was 14 years old. She and her father objected to prayers at the graduation ceremony. The Supreme Court, five to four, decided that the Establishment Clause forbade the practice that had been followed in Providence. It affirmed an injunction issued against the school district. The school could no longer offer prayers at its graduations.

Scalia wrote one of his characteristic, stinging dissents (Rehnquist, White, and Thomas joined him).[69] The majority opinion, Scalia said, was "bereft of any reference to history;" it "lays waste a tradition that is as old as public-school graduation ceremonies themselves;" the decision was, in general, an offense against deep-rooted American custom. The majority had worried about "psychological coercion" of students; Scalia sneered at this, and excoriated this line of reasoning as an "instrument of destruction," a "bulldozer" which the Court used to carry out what he called "social engineering."

The case, he says, shows why the Constitution cannot be allowed to rest on "the changeable philosophical predilections of the Justices." No, constitutional interpretation "must have deep foundations in the historic practices of our people."[70] At the end of his opinion, Scalia appends a little essay about the wonderful results that come from people voluntarily praying together; the "simple and inspiring prayers" offered at this graduation would do no harm—in fact these prayers might "inoculate" their listeners from "religious bigotry and prejudice." It was therefore "senseless" to "deprive our society of that important unifying mechanism."[71]

In his dissent, Scalia invokes history and tradition—in general these are big themes with this particular Justice.[72] But in an important way he is quite wrong in his reading of history and tradition. Scalia does have a point—but it is a point about today, not about history or tradition or yesterday. The most interesting aspect of the case is the actual text of the prayers and the identity of the clergyman who recited this text.

The school principal had, in fact, invited a rabbi, Leslie Gutterman, to give the prayer. The principal also handed Rabbi Gutterman a pamphlet, "Guidelines for Civil Occasions," prepared by the National Conference of Christians and Jews, to help him get prepared for his stint at the graduation. The pamphlet talked about how to give nonsectarian prayers—prayers of "inclusiveness and sensitivity." In his prayer at graduation, Rabbi Gutterman referred to the "legacy of America where diversity is celebrated and the rights of minorities are protected."[73]

The public schools of the nineteenth century—the schools of Scalia's "tradition"—would never have invited a Rabbi to offer prayers, or a Catholic priest for that matter, and whatever (Protestant) clergyman the school might have chosen would certainly not have talked about "diversity" or the "rights of minorities." In fact, public schools were so sectarian, consciously or not, that they were one of the factors that led American Catholics to found their own school systems. The Bible was frequently read in nineteenth-century schools, but it was the King James Bible, and this was deeply offensive to Catholics.[74]

Thus Scalia's references to history and tradition simply do not hold water. There *is* an American tradition of prayer, Bible reading, and the like, in the schools, but that tradition was radically different from the practice that was *actually* at issue in the case coming out of Rhode Island.

Yet, on the other hand, Scalia's point about *this* kind of prayer, the Rabbi Gutterman type—that it fosters tolerance and mutual respect—is far from frivolous. Rabbi Gutterman was trying to deliver a kind of pluralist prayer in a pluralist environment—an environment that emphatically did not exist in this form in the nineteenth century, and certainly not when the Constitution was drafted. Stripped of its rancor, Scalia's opinion might be saying that this kind of prayer, is acceptable precisely because it avoids the problems of an establishment of religion, which older generations had not avoided. That is, this sort of prayer is acceptable *because* it is not traditional, because it is a modern kind of prayer; because it is so sensitive to American pluralism and the rights of minorities. And indeed the modernity of the situation, its attempt to balance disparate viewpoints, is what makes the case such a close and difficult one.

I am not suggesting here whether the majority or the minority has the better answer, or whether the whole line of church–state cases starting with *Everson* [75] is a mistake or not.[76] What I am saying is that even the "conservative" dissent here is not conservative in the historic sense. I have no doubt that even Scalia would have joined the majority in striking down a *compulsory* prayer, or a frankly sectarian religious program at graduation or elsewhere in the public system. Even Scalia would balk at the kind of suffocating, intolerant public Protestantism that was the norm in the nineteenth century and for part of the twentieth century, and which has retreated because of social and demographic changes—and, perhaps, because of some decisions of the United States Supreme Court.

Thus the *Lee* decision, though it seems to be an example of sharp divisions within the Court—and it is—also illustrates how much the Court is, in fact, as it must be, molded by the culture of its period, and how the differences among Justices, though real, and deep, mask a greater and deeper similarity of outlook. The Court was split nearly down the middle on the issue whether a state was barred by the First Amendment from regulating nude dancing:[77] can one even *imagine* this as an issue in the nineteenth century, or even in the 1950s, when Earl Warren was Chief Justice?

The Justices themselves "evolve"; they are influenced by events, like the rest of us. They change radically over time—over their own lifetimes, too. Rehnquist himself is not the Rehnquist of the 1950s. At that time, as a young clerk (to Justice Jackson), he was (despite his later denials) almost certainly opposed to *Brown v. Board of Education*; he wrote a memo to that effect.[78] No question, he remains conservative on issues of race, affirmative action, criminal justice, the establishment clause, and the like, but there is no reason to think he remains stuck fast in the same opinions that he held during the 1950s.

The Court is, of course, deeply divided on issues of race. But what it divides about are *contemporary* issues of race. Take, for example, *Shaw v. Reno*.[79] In this case, the Court (five to four) struck down an "unconstitutional racial gerrymander." North Carolina had carved out two congressional districts, with weird shapes, to guarantee two seats in Congress for black representatives. Sandra Day O'Connor wrote the majority opinion; she also wrote the opinion striking down an ordinance of Richmond, Virginia, which created a quota for minority contractors.[80] But at the time of *Plessy v. Ferguson*,[81] there were no black districts in North Carolina; the period of *Plessy* was a period in which the South was in the process of systematically depriving blacks of their right to vote, by hook, crook, and by force. And blacks at the turn of the century had little or no political influence in Richmond, Virginia.

O'Connor's racial "conservatism" is real enough and distressing to many African Americans and their allies. Nonetheless, it is a distinctly *modern* conservatism, a conservatism which is conservative in terms of the facts of life of the 1990s. In the 1990s, blacks have a vastly different role in American life than they did a century before. To the nineteenth century, O'Connor's general views on race would have seemed not conservative but downright radical.

Rehnquist and O'Connor are not alone. Those of us who are old enough remember Strom Thurmond as a Dixiecrat, as a die-hard segregationist. We remember him fulminating against the Supreme Court for daring to attack the "Southern way of life." We did not miss the irony of watching Thurmond in action at the hearings on the confirmation of Clarence Thomas. Thurmond, like the Republicans in general, backed Thomas enthusiastically. Now Thomas was (and is) deeply conservative, of course, but he was also a black man aspiring to a high government position, and what is more, a black man married to a white woman. This would have been anathema to Strom Thurmond the Dixiecrat. The interracial marriage would have been a felony in Thurmond's state before the Supreme Court's decision in *Loving v. Virginia*.[82]

It is possible that the Thurmonds of the world are still the same old racists; that nothing has changed inside of them. But this is, in a way, irrelevant. They have had to change on the outside, for political reasons if for nothing else. That in itself is a momentous sign of the times, and a fact of great social significance. History, as we all know, is a river that flows only in one direction, and whether we want to or not, we are borne along with it as it flows. This is true for everybody in society, including the nine Justices who sit on the Rehnquist Court.

Notes

1. Chemerinsky, "The Vanishing Constitution," 103 *Harv. L. Rev.* 44 (1989).

2. "The Supreme Court, 1988 Term-Leading Cases," 103 *Harv. L. Rev.* 394 (1989).

3. "The Supreme Court, 1997 Term-Leading Cases," 111 *Harv. L. Rev.* 431 (1997).

4. United States v. Lopez, 514 U.S. 549 (1995). In *Lopez*, the Supreme Court struck down the Gun-Free School Zones Act of 1990. This law made it a crime to "possess a firearm at a . . . school zone," that is, within 1,000 feet of the grounds of a school. Lopez was arrested for violating the law. A bare majority of the Court felt that the law had nothing to do with interstate commerce, and exceeded the powers of Congress. This was the first time in sixty years that the Court had so ruled. More recently, the Court has expanded the immunity of states and has limited citizen suits against the states. See Alden v. Maine, 119 S. Ct. 2240 (1999).

5. Dred Scott v. Sanford, 60 U.S. 393 (1851).

6. Pollock v. Farmers' Loan & Trust Co., 158 U.S. 601 (1895).

7. 394 U.S. 294 (1954).

8. 410 U.S. 113 (1973).

9. Friedman, *The Horizontal Society* 27–47 (1999).

10. Slotnick, "Media Coverage of Supreme Court Decision-Making: Problems and Prospects," 75 *Judicature* 128 (1991); Katsh, "The Supreme Court Beat: How Television Covers the United States Supreme Court," 67 *Judicature* 8 (1983).

11. Notably, Woodward & Armstrong, *The Brethren: Inside the Supreme Court* (1979), which was a (surprise) best-seller; a more recent and more illuminating example is Lazarus, *Closed Chambers* (1998).

12. Indeed, the phrase was used as the title of a collection of essays by Lerner, *Nine Scorpions in a Bottle: Great Judges and Cases of the Supreme Court* (Richard Cummings ed., 1994).

13. Apparently, Justice Horace Gray hired a law clerk in 1882 but paid this clerk out of his own pocket. Congress appropriated funds for a law clerk for each Justice in 1922. Brown, "Gender Discrimination in the Supreme Court's Clerkship Selection Process," 75 *Or. L. Rev.* 359, n. 12 (1996).

14. See, in particular, Lazarus, *Closed Chambers* (1998). See also, for example, Ball, *A Defiant Life: Thurgood Marshall and the Persistence of Racism in America* 287 (1998).

15. 507 U.S. 349 (1993).

16. Board of Educ. of Kiryas Joel Village Sch. Dist. v. Grumet, 512 U.S. 687 (1994). The village was a small enclave of Orthodox Jews of the Satmar Hasidic sect. In 1989, New York's legislature created a statute which allowed the village to constitute a school district of its own. The point was to allow for a school district, paid for by the state, in which the only students would be kids of the sect who were handicapped and needed special education (the regular students went to private religious schools). The Supreme Court voided the law by virtue of the Establishment Clause of the First Amendment. Scalia's dissent (id.. at 732) drips with sarcasm; he ridicules Souter's (majority) opinion, refers to its "facile conclusion," calls the decision "astounding . . . unprecedented," based on the "flimsiest of evidence," and so on.

17. On this point, Lazarus's *Closed Chambers*, is quite detailed—depressingly so.

18. See, in general, Leuchtenburg, *The Supreme Court Reborn: The Constitutional Revolution in the Age of Roosevelt* (1995).

19. 505 U.S. 833 (1992).

20. To be sure, there are also some unusual features to this case. That the "judgment of the Court" was announced by *three* Justices, who wrote a common opinion, is highly unusual.

21. 410 U.S. 113 (1973). There is, of course, an enormous literature on this case. See, in particular, Garrow, *Liberty and Sexuality: The Right to Privacy and the Making of Roe v. Wade* (1994).

22. Brown v. Board. of Educ., 394 U.S. 294 (1954).

23. Miranda v. Arizona, 384 U.S. 436 (1966).

24. Simon, *The Center Holds: The Power Struggle Inside the Rehnquist Court* (1995).

25. Of course, the final word is not yet in. Clinton's term of office runs out in the year 2000; he is unlikely to get a chance to make another appointment to the Supreme Court, and much may depend on who takes the White House in 2000.

26. 505 U.S. at 1002.

27. Semonche, *Keeping the Faith: A Cultural History of the U.S. Supreme Court* (1998). The Court operates "within a civil religion," whose "theology" supplies the justices "with certain fundamental moral assumptions that they bring to the task of interpreting the words of the holy writ." Id. at 402.

28. 381 U.S. 479 (1965).

29. *Casey*, 505 U.S. at 995.

30. See id.

31. See, e.g., Reagan, *When Abortion Was a Crime: Women, Medicine, and Law in the United States, 1876–1973* (1997).

32. See Klarman, "*Brown,* Racial Change, and the Civil Rights Movement," 80 *Va. L. Rev.* 7 (1994).

33. See Shapiro, "The Globalization of Law," in 1 *Indiana J. Global Legal Studies* 37, 45–50 (1993); Tate, *The Global Expansion of Judicial Power* (Torbjörn Vallinder ed., 1995).

34. *Casey*, 505 U.S. at 833.

35. On this point, see Friedman, *The Republic of Choice: Law, Authority, and Culture* (1990).

36. Lochner v. New York, 198 U.S. 45 (1905), struck down a New York statute regulating (among other things) the hours of labor of bakery workers. The case came to be a symbol of a recalcitrant, conservative Supreme Court.

37. 381 U.S. 479 (1965).

38. Douglas's opinion in particular has been derided, with its talk about "penumbras" and "emanations" from the Bill of Rights, its citation of the Third Amendment (quartering of soldiers in private houses is forbidden), and its reference to the "sacred precincts of marital bedrooms."

39. 492 U.S. 490 (1989).

40. Lazarus, supra note 11, at 397.

41. See Tyler, *Why People Obey the Law* (1990); Friedman, *The Legal System: A Social Science Perspective* 112–120 (1975).

42. See Leuchtenberg, supra note 18.

43. Overruling *Roe* "would seriously weaken the Court's capacity to . . . function." The "substance" of the Court's "legitimacy" is the "warrant for the Court's decisions. . . . The Court must take care to speak and act in ways that allow people to accept its decision on the terms the Court claims for them, as grounded truly in principle, not as compromises with social and political pressures. *Casey*, 505 U.S. at 833.

44. 457 U.S. 261 (1990).

45. Id. at 293.

46. Id. at 261, 301 (emphasis added).

47. Dred Scott v. Sandford, 60 U.S. (19 How.) 393 (1857).

48. The original decision was Engel v. Vitale, 370 U.S. 421 (1962). Attempts to overturn the decision through constitutional amendment failed in Congress, but the issue did not

die. The Reagan administration revived the issue in the early 1980s—at this time, a "public opinion survey indicated that more than four-fifths of the public had heard of the prayer amendment . . . and 79% [of those] favored it." But the prayer amendment failed again. *Kyvig, Explicit and Authentic Acts: Amending the U.S. Constitution, 1776–1995,* 379–385, 451–53(1996). And in 1985, in Wallace v. Jaffree, 472 U.S. 38 (1985), the Court confronted an Alabama statute allowing schools to set aside one minute at the beginning of the school day "for meditation or voluntary prayer." The Court struck it down.

49. See generally Smith, *The Rehnquist Court and Criminal Punishment* (1997).

50. Compare Roe v. Wade, 410 U.S. 113 (1973) with Planned Parenthood of Southeastern Pia. v. Casey, 505 U.S. 833 (1992).

51. Compare Bowers v. Hardwick, 478 U.S. 186 (1986) with Romer v. Evans, 517 U.S. 620 (1996).

52. Texas v. Johnson, 491 U.S. 397 (1989).

53. Goldstein, *Burning the Flag: The Great 1989–1990 American Flag Desecration Controversy* 113–122 (1996).

54. The Flag Protection Act, 103 Stat. 777 (Act of October 28, 1989); the case overturning it was United States v. Eichman, 486 U.S. 310 (1990).

55. Goldstein, supra note 53, at 334.

56. Harmelin v. Michigan, 501 U.S. 957 (1991). This was another 5–4 decision. Scalia (but hardly any of the other Justices) does not think there is any requirement of "proportionality" imposed by the Eighth Amendment. See Smith, supra note 49, at 50–56. *Smith* also points out a doctrinal irony. In a later case, Austin v. United States, 509 U.S. 602 (1993), the defendant, convicted of possessing cocaine with intent to distribute it, forfeited his mobile home and auto body shop. The Court unanimously remanded for a determination whether the forfeiture violated the Excessive Fines clause of the Eighth Amendment.

57. Herrera v. Collins, 506 U.S. 390 (1993).

58. Coleman v. Thompson, 501 U.S. 722 (1991).

59. The case is discussed in Tucker, *May God Have Mercy: A True Story of Crime and Punishment* (1997).

60, Of course, one can argue endlessly about what "conservative" means. The Court—or its majority—is not "conservative" in the sense of slavish adherence to precedent. It is, in many ways, quite as "activist" as the Warren court. See Smith and Jones, "The Rehnquist Court's Activism and the Risk of Injustice," 26 *Conn. L. Rev.* 53 (1993).

61. *Roe v. Wade*, after all, was a Burger court decision.

62. Here I must disagree with Suzanna Sherry's views, in Sherry, "All the Supreme Court Really Needs to Know It Learned from the Warren Court," 50 *Vanderbilt L. Rev.* 459 (1997), that "many of the current Court's so-called conservative cases and doctrines are direct descendants of Warren Court cases and doctrines." Obviously, the same sort of point could be made about the Warren Court: just the Marshall or Taney or Lochner court in slightly different dress.

Rebecca Brown, responding to Professor Sherry, begins by saying that "if one compares the genetic structure of humans to those of dogs, one finds that ninety-six percent of the DNA in the two species is identical." Brown, "Formal Neutrality in the Warren and Rehnquist Courts: Illusions of Similarity," 50 *Vanderbilt L. Rev.* 487 (1997). The analogy is perhaps even better than Professor Brown thinks. If one compares humans *and* dogs with sponges or mushrooms, the 96 percent overlap does not look at all strange. In many ways, the Rehnquist Court, at its most conservative, is still more like the Warren Court than, say, it is like John Marshall's Court, or medieval English courts, or the courts of the Trobriand Islanders, for obvious reasons.

63. For an interesting attempt to measure the work of the Court empirically, see

Rosche, "How Conservative Is the Rehnquist Court? Three Issues, One Answer," 65 *Fordham L. Rev.* 2685 (1997).

64. See Civil Rights Cases, 109 U.S. 3 (1883).

65. See Plessy v. Ferguson, 163 U.S. 537 (1896),

66. See Hammer v. Dagenhart, 247 U.S. 251, 269 (1918).

67. See Cushman, "Rethinking the New Deal," 80 *Va. L. Rev.* 201, 210, 230 (1994).

68. 505 U.S. 577 (1992).

69. Id. at 631.

70. Id. at 632.

71. Id. at 646.

72. See, e.g., Michael H. v. Gerald D., 491 U.S. 505 (1989), where the Court faced the question of the rights of a biological father. California law provided that a child born to a married woman was conclusively presumed to be the legitimate child of that woman and her husband. The "real" father wanted visitation rights; and said the statute was unconstitutional. A bare majority upheld the statute. Scalia argued, for the majority, that the biological father had to show "an interest traditionally protected by our society"; and an "adulterous natural father" had no such interest.

73. Id. at 582

74. Tyack et al., *Law and the Shaping of Public Education, 1798-1954*, 68–69 (1987).

75. Everson v. Board of Educ. of Ewing Township, 330 U.S. 1 (1947).

76. For interesting discussions of this point, see Everson *Revisited: Religion, Education, and Law at the Crossroads* (Jo Renée Formicola and Hubert Morken eds., 1997).

77. Barnes v. Glen Theatre, Inc., 501 U.S. 560 (1991).

78. See Schwartz, "Chief Justice Rehnquist, Justice Jackson, and the *Brown* Case," 1988 *Supreme Ct. Rev.* 245; Ray, "A Law Clerk and His Justice: What William Rehnquist Did Not Learn from Robert Jackson," 29 *Ind. L. Rev.* 535, 554–558 (1996).

79. Shaw v. Reno, 509 U.S. 630 (1993).

80. Adarand Constructors, Inc. v. Pena, 515 U.S. 200 (1995).

81. 163 U.S. 537 (1896).

82. 388 U.S. 1 (1967).

· 9 ·

A JOURNALIST'S PERSPECTIVE

DAVID SAVAGE

Most people think of books as being more solid and profound, deeper, and certainly more permanent when compared to a speech, a panel discussion, or a newspaper article. This perception is true of readers as well as writers of all sorts. On occasion, I have chatted with Chief Justice Rehnquist about writing and books—he always seems to have one in the works—and he has commented he writes books because they offer a more lasting record for history.[1]

As a newspaper reporter, that is certainly my view, but I was taken aback somewhat to learn it was his too. I was tempted but did not ask: What does that say about all your Supreme Court opinions?

In its first twelve years, the Rehnquist Court has been the subject of at least three books.[2] The definitive work surely would have been written by Bernard Schwartz.[3] As it is, we are left with three pretenders.

The books published so far describe a work in progress. That is, they offer a thesis or a way of understanding a Supreme Court that is still at work, still changing, and still, if Justices Scalia and Thomas will forgive me, evolving. Opinions about the Court are evolving too, to judge by these three books. However, as Henry Adams famously observed, the United States Presidency evolved from George Washington to Ulysses Grant,[4] proving beyond doubt that evolution and progress are not the same.

The first of the books, *Turning Right*,[5] appeared in the spring of 1992. Written by a journalist[6] who covered the Court,[7] it seeks to explain what it all means. The thesis of this book, such it is, was captured by its title, *Turning Right: The Making of the Rehnquist Supreme Court*. Beginning with Richard Nixon's 1968 campaign, Republican Presidents had publicly proclaimed their intent to change the Supreme Court: to bring it back from the advance guard of liberal activism and, in particular, to make more conservative in the areas of criminal law and the death penalty.[8] If anything, Ronald Reagan and his legal advisers were even more committed to this cause.[9]

Reagan did not accept the Court's rulings that protected abortion[10] and banned school prayer.[11] As he understood the Constitution, the opposite made more sense: protect prayer and ban abortion.

As governor of California, Reagan had been burned by several of his choices for the California Supreme Court who, to his surprise, voted to end the death penalty.[12] As President, he was determined not to make the same mistake when appointing new Justices. Compiling lists of reliable jurists to elevate to the higher Courts became something of a preoccupation of the Reagan Justice Department.[13]

President Reagan added three new Justices to the Supreme Court,[14] and of course, elevated Nixon's most conservative appointee to be Chief Justice.[15] And Reagan's chosen successor, George Bush, filled two more seats.[16]

The result of these appointments was that by 1992, every new Supreme Court appointee for a generation, dating back to 1967, had been appointed by a conservative Republican President. But, of course, at the Supreme Court, unlike at the White House, all the occupants do not change suddenly on a designated day after the election. There is no "Out with the old, in with the new" rule. One new Justice arrives to fill the seat of one recently departed.[17]

Change is gradual. But during the first five years of the Rehnquist Court, the change moved only in one direction—older and more liberal justices were replaced by those who were younger and more conservative.

The shift along this giant ideological fault line—and the resulting grinding and shuddering, the dust it kicked up and the fear it set off among some—was the true subject of *Turning Right*. The old liberals had blocked the use of the death penalty, supported affirmative action as well as forced busing to desegregated the schools, and insisted that religion had no role in public schools and government had no business in the area of abortion. They favored broad federal power as a progressive force.[18]

The conservatives, heirs to the antifederalists, sought to rein in federal power and to strengthen the states as sovereigns. With a five-member majority, they swept aside the broad challenges to the death penalty[19] and ruled that racial preferences by government are unconstitutional.[20] They allowed the states more freedom to regulate abortion[21] and gave students new freedom to read the Bible and pray privately at school.[22] The Reagan Revolution was winning in the Supreme Court.

In June 1992, a funny thing happened. The conservative Justices, having marched in step steadily and confidently toward the right, suddenly stopped, as if they had reached a cliff and seen the abyss below. What they saw was stark indeed. They had pushed to allow the states more authority to regulate the practices of abortion, for example, by requiring teenagers to get their parents' permission.[23] Now, they were faced with a more profound question. Should they overturn the right to abortion set in *Roe v. Wade* and again let the states make abortion a crime? And would they go back on the school prayer decisions of the 1960s and again permit organized prayer to again become part of public school life? The answer from Justices Anthony Kennedy, Sandra O'Connor, and David Souter was *no*.[24]

In *Lee v. Weisman*,[25] the five to four majority said it was unconstitutional for a public school to have a rabbi invoke the name of God at a graduation ceremony. And, in *Planned Parenthood v. Casey*,[26] the five to four majority affirmed the basic right of women to choose abortion.

The abortion decision is easily the most dramatic story in the years I have covered the Court. *Roe v. Wade* [27] had appeared to be doomed. In 1989, Rehnquist had four votes essentially to throw out the right to abortion (*Webster v. Reproductive Health Services*).[28] Besides his own, they included Byron White, Antonin Scalia, and Anthony Kennedy. In the next two years, the Court's leading liberals, William Brennan and Thurgood Marshall, retired and were replaced by Bush's appointees, David Souter and Clarence Thomas. Surely, on the abortion question, the Chief Justice that spring looked to have five or six votes to overturn the right to abortion. The only question was whether a decision would come then, or later.

At the conference on the Pennsylvania case, seven Justices voted to uphold the state's new abortion regulations, and the Chief Justice planned to write the opinion for the Court.[29] But Justices O'Connor and Souter, later joined by Justice Kennedy, decided to write a separate concurring opinion that affirmed the basic right to abortion.

For Kennedy in particular, it meant "'crossing the Rubicon." He had been appointed by President Reagan after Ed Meese's Justice Department signed off on him as a reliable conservative.[30] As a Catholic, he had a personal aversion to abortion. Yet, he was determined to be a nonideological judge, not a sure vote for the right wing.[31] He was always convinced of the existence of the "liberty" clause of the Constitution.[32] And for him, as with Justice Souter, precedent carried a high premium. It was one thing to reject a right to abortion at first glance in 1973; quite another to overturn the right nearly twenty years later. Still, until the last moment, Kennedy remained torn. Kennedy crossed the Rubicon that day, and the Court has never been the same since. Of course, this development caused some difficulties for the author of a book titled *Turning Right*. On one program, a smiling TV person looked over at me, his expression suggesting he had come up with a trick question.

"Well, Mr. Savage, is the Court still turning right?," he asked.

"No, it is not," I replied simply.

He paused and looked thunderstruck, as though I had just admitted the copies of my book immediately should be pulled from the bookstore shelves.

Three years later appeared *The Center Holds* by former reporter and now New York Law School Professor James Simon.[33] The book proclaimed in its first sentence: "This is the story of a conservative judicial revolution that failed." He observed, "The center held largely because liberal justices were able to attract support from their more moderate brethren who refused to join the ideologically committed conservatives on the right wing of the court."

The theme of this book was drawn from a fine newspaper story that Linda Greenhouse wrote for the front page of the *New York Times* in late June of 1992. It featured photos of Justices O'Connor, Kennedy, and Souter and held them up as something of a moderate triumvirate that had taken control of the court. Her story was nicely timed and explained the surprise outcomes in the religion and abortion cases. But it was a newspaper story, not a book.

The Center Holds came out in the spring of 1995, just in time for a series of powerful conservative rulings. All came on a five to four vote, with loud dissents from the more liberal faction, including Justice Souter. In *United States v. Lopez*,[34] the Court for the first time in sixty years threw out a federal law on the grounds that Congress had exceeded its constitutional authority under the Commerce Clause. Congress can regulate economic activity that has a "substantial link" to interstate commerce, the Chief Justice said, but the Federal Gun-Free Schools Zones Act regulates the possession of guns near schools, which is not economic activity and is not related to interstate commerce.

In *Adarand Constructors v. Pena*,[35] the Court said all racial classifications by the federal government are presumptively unconstitutional. In *Missouri v. Jenkins*,[36] it sounded the death knell for a Court-ordered school desegregation program in Kansas City. And in *Rosenberger v. University of Virginia*,[37] the Court said Christian students who publish a campus magazine are entitled to same state subsidies given other student publications. In dissent, Justice Souter said it was the first time the Court had condoned direct state funding of core religious activities.

I do not know how Professor Simon has explained the Court's failure to follow his prescription, although I am sure he said more than me. As I understand it, he asserted the Court's decisions in 1995 were not all that conservative.

The next book on the Rehnquist Court, *Closed Chambers*, written by former clerk Edward Lazarus,[38] was "an indictment" of the Rehnquist Court as a genuinely awful place, torn by "destructive pathologies" of deceit and partisanship.

"The toxic combination . . . of partisanship and lack of character has crept into the delicate ecosystem of the court," he writes. The Justices have split into "self contained ideological factions who exchange increasingly harsh accusations of hypocrisy and illegitimacy." They do not respect precedent and "twist the court's internal rules to attain narrow advantage." They "resort to transparently deceitful and hypocritical arguments and factual distortions."

"The story of the Court in the late 1980s and early 1990s is of this spirit of faction and recrimination," he concludes. The "warping factors of polarization and a failure of integrity profoundly affected the court's decisions," he says. "The current Court remains a place shattered, one lacking not only a center but a leader and a shared sense of purpose."

Lazarus's book received a fair amount of attention in early 1998, and not because of his rather hyperbolic account of life there. He or his publisher successfully seized on a tried-and-true promotional gimmick: This was to be the "inside story"—revealing the secrets and the gossip from inside a close-knit organization.

This promotional gimmick always sells in the publishing world, even if it rarely delivers for the reader. *The Brethren*,[39] the best known book on the Supreme Court, was a huge best-seller because it promised an inside look at a secret institution. As I recall, it recounted various little stories about how Chief Justice Burger insisted on using his silverware at lunch, showing him to be a pompous character.[40] Woodward seemed to know little about the law and cared less, so his book did not get bogged down in telling the reader much about what it is Court does. Instead, he reported on personal mannerisms and stray comments about the Justices—that is, the inside story.

About seven or eight years ago, I ran into Lazarus (the author of the clerk's book on the Court) at the Library of Congress. We were looking through the Marshall papers, searching for signs of intelligent life. My book had recently been published,[41] and he had just signed a contract to write a Court book for a huge advance. One newsmagazine used the figure of $300,000, if I recall correctly. We chatted for just a moment, but I remember thinking he must have promised the publisher a "clerk-reveals-secrets" book on the Court.

Why else pay all that money to a novice writer? This may have presented something of an ethical dilemma for Lazarus, because the clerks are supposed to keep confidential what they learn at the Court. He seems to have finessed the matter in the usual way: by promising much on the book cover and by delivering relatively little.

The cover proclaims: "'The First Eyewitness Account of the Epic Struggles Inside the Supreme Court." This deserves special recognition in the annals of promotion hype. The words "first," "eyewitness," "epic," and "inside" would lead one to think he was going to read an account of someone who went along with first explorers to reach the South Pole or a Manhattan Project scientist who was there at the birth of nuclear weapons, not the collected opinions of a clerk at court.

Lazarus ran into another, now familiar problem. He denounced the Court as hopelessly divided. The "pure poison" of partisanship has afflicted Rehnquist Court so deeply, he says, that it could not perform its judicial duties. This diagnosis landed in the bookstores during a term that was marked by unanimous decisions and a remarkable show of consensus on several very difficult issues.

The term began with a nine to zero ruling in *State Oil v. Khan*[42] overturning the thirty-year-old ban on the setting of maximum retail prices. Justice O'Connor explained that economic thinking had changed so much as to entirely discredit the earlier holding.

A few weeks later, the Court considered whether someone who says "no" and simply denies an accusation can be charged with lying later if his answer is not true. In two decisions nicely timed for the national appearance of Monica Lewinski, the court announced that lies, even small ones, can be prosecuted as separate crimes.[43]

Does the Double Jeopardy Clause forbid the government from imposing a civil fine after a criminal prosecution for bank fraud? No, the Court said unanimously. The Chief Justice explained that the Double Jeopardy Clause forbids only a second prosecution, not a second punishment, for the same offense.[44]

Can the police be sued for undertaking a reckless high-speed chase through the city streets that results in the death of a sixteen-year-old motorcyclist? No, the court said unanimously in *County of Sacramento v. Lewis*. The Due Process Clause of the Fourteenth Amendment protects against deliberate and intentional deprivations of liberty, not accidents, Justice Souter said.[45]

Can Congress require the National Endowment for the Arts to take "decency" into account when awarding its grants. Yes, the court said on a eight to one vote in *NEA v. Finley*.[46]

By a nine to zero vote in *Oncale v. Sundowner Offshore Services*,[47] the Court said a man who was sexually harassed by male supervisors can file a suite under federal law.

In the last week of the 1997 term, the Court handed down two major rulings on sexual harassment. A seven-member majority agreed on a common framework for handling these issues. Employers are presumptively liable for harassment perpetrated by one of their low-level supervisors, even if they did not know of it, the Court said. However, they can successfully defend themselves by proving they had an effective policy against harassment and a complaint procedure which the victim could have, but did not, follow (*Faragher v. City of Boca Raton* and *Burlington In-*

dustries v. Ellerth).[48] And, remember, this followed a term in which the Court unanimously rejected the notion of a constitutional right to assisted suicide[49] and unanimously ruled that President Clinton could be forced to stand trial in a civil suit.[50]

On the last week of the 1997 term, President Clinton won one and lost one. In the case of Vince Foster's lawyer and his notes, the Court in a six to three vote rebuked independent counsel Kenneth Starr and upheld the traditional lawyer-client privilege of confidentiality. Chief Justice Rehnquist wrote the majority opinion and he was joined by Justices Stevens, Souter, Kennedy, Ginsburg, and Breyer (*Swidler & Berlin v. United States*).[51] The next day, the Court struck down the president's line-item veto authority. This time Justice Stevens wrote the majority opinion and was joined by Rehnquist, Kennedy, Souter, Thomas, and Ginsburg.[52]

If this is a Court that is hopelessly divided into warring ideological factions, I have missed the story again.

What can be said about these three books on the Rehnquist Court? First, if one is upset about a trend seen in the current court, write a book about it. One can bring about instant change, usually before he has completed his book tour.

Second, books describing the current court—as well as academic articles, speeches, and panel discussions—should include the small-print warning that accompanies the giant-size ads in which mutual funds tout their money-making prowess: "Past performance does not guarantee future results."

And finally, if someone wants to keep up with what is really taking place at the Supreme Court, he or she should consider subscribing to a good newspaper.

Notes

1. See, e.g., Rehnquist, *All the Laws But One: Civil Liberties in Wartime* (1998); Rehnquist, *Grand Inquests: The Historic Impeachment of Justice Samuel Chase and President Andrew Johnson* (1992); Rehnquist, *The Supreme Court: How It Was, How It Is* (1987).

2. Lazarus, *Closed Chambers: The First Eyewitness Account of the Epic Struggles Inside The Supreme Court* (1998); Simon, *The Center Holds: The Power Struggle Inside The Rehnquist Court* (1995); Savage, *Turning Right: The Making of the Rehnquist Supreme Court* (1992).

3. Compare *The Warren Court: A Retrospective* (Bernard Schwartz ed., Oxford University Press 1996); Schwartz, *The Ascent of Pragmatism: The Burger Court In Action* (1990).

4. Adams, *The Education of Henry Adams: an Autobiography Illustrated with Gravures by Samuel Chamberlain and with an Introduction by Henry Seidel Canby* 247 (1942)

5. Savage, *Turning Right: The Making of the Rehnquist Supreme Court* (1992).

6. Editor's Note: David G. Savage, the author of this article, joined the *Los Angeles Times* in 1981 as an education writer and moved to the Washington bureau in 1986 as a Supreme Court correspondent..

7. In the spring of 1986, my editors in Los Angeles agreed to send me back to Washington to take over the Supreme Court beat. Our long-time court reporter Phil Hager was anxious to return to California, so we switched coasts. The first week in June, Phil said he had set up a lunch with Associate Justice Rehnquist who, despite a public reputation as a strident conservative and no friend of the press, was friendly with many reporters. He remains one of the most friendly and approachable members of the Court. On that day, over his usual

lunch, the Justice lived up his billing as a remarkably down-to-earth, unaffected person. He asked about my children and what schools they would attend. We talked a bit about the newspaper business and politics.

Hager had mentioned that we should ask about his retirement. The perennial rumor was that Rehnquist planned to leave the Court early and not stay to his doddering old age. He had witnessed the sad spectacle of Justice William O. Douglas, the one-time liberal lion disabled by a stroke but still unwilling to retire. In 1986, Rehnquist was approaching his 62nd birthday, time at which he could take a full retirement. But when Hager brought up the subject, the Justice said little and moved to other topics. A few days later, I realized why. There he was standing in the White House Press Room as President Reagan announced that he would replace Warren Burger as Chief Justice of the United States. Thus, I can claim to have been there at the birth of the Rehnquist Court.

8. Aitken, *Nixon: A Life* 391 (1993); Greene, *The Presidency of Gerald Ford* 98 (1995); Smith & Hensley, "Unfulfilled Aspirations: The Court-Packing Efforts of Presidents Reagan and Bush," 57 *Alb. L. Rev.* 1111, 1117–20 (1994).

9. Witt, *A Different Justice: Reagan and the Supreme Court* 100 (1986).

10. "Reagan Still Opposed to Ruling on Abortion," *San Diego Union & Trib.*, June 12, 1986, at A3.

11. Witt, supra note 9, at 131.

12. Parker & Hubbard, "The Evidence for Death," 78 *Cal. L. Rev.* 973, 976 n. 15 (1990); see Thompson, "Judicial Retention Elections and Judicial Method: A Retrospective on the California Retention Election of 1986," 61 *S. Cal. L. Rev.* 2007 (1988).

13. de Lama, "Reagan Facing Political Risk in Filling Vacancy," *Chi. Trib.*, June 27, 1987, at 1.

14. Ciolli, "Getting Set for the George Bush Area: A Chance to Push Right, *Newsday*, Nov. 13, 1988, at 6.

15. Schieffer & Gates, *The Acting President* 274 (1989).

16. Marshall, "High Court Liberal and Its Only Black, to Retire Judiciary: Justice Cites Health, Advancing age. Bush Has the Opportunity to Put a Conservative Stamp on the Court That Could Last for Decades," *L.A. Times*, June 28, 1991, at A1.

17. Savage, supra note 5, at 453.

18. See generally Henry, "The Players and the Play," in *The Burger Court: Counter-Revolution or Confirmation* 13 (Bernard Schwartz ed., 1998).

19. See, e.g., McClesky v. Kemp, 481 U.S. 279 (1987).

20. See, e.g., City of Richmond v. J.A. Croson Co., 488 U.S. 469 (1989).

21. See, e.g., Webster v. Reproductive Health Serv., 492 U.S. 490 (1989).

22. See Wallace v. Jaffree, 472 U.S. 38 (1985).

23. See Ohio v. Akron Center for Reproductive Serv., 497 U.S. 502 (1990).

24. Wiessler, "Minds of Their Own, Conservative Justices Demonstrate Their Independence," *Houston Chron.*, July 1, 1992, at A1.

25. 505 U.S. 577 (1992).

26. 510 U.S. 1309 (1994).

27. 410 U.S. 113 (1973).

28. 492 U.S. 490 (1989).

29. Simon, "Speech: Politics and the Rehnquist Court," 40 *N.Y.L. Sch. L. Rev.* 863, 870 (1996).

30. "Sacramento Jurist Is Court Nominee; Reagan Calls Judge Kennedy Fair But to," *San Diego Trib.*, Nov. 11, 1987 at A1.

31. "Daily Briefing Kennedy's High Court Decisions Stem From Belief in Precedent," *San Francisco Chron.*, July 1, 1992, at A4.

32. Hyde, "Contemporary Challenges to Catholic Lawyers," 38 *Cath. Law.* 75, 83 (1998).

33. Simon, *The Center Holds: The Power Struggle Inside The Rehnquist Court* (1995).

34. 514 U.S. 549 (1995).

35. 515 U.S. 200 (1995).

36. 515 U.S. 70 (1995).

37. 515 U.S. 819 (1995).

38. Lazarus, *Closed Chambers: The First Eyewitness Account of the Epic Struggles Inside the Supreme Court* (1998).

39. Woodard & Armstrong, *The Brethren: Inside the Supreme Court* (1979).

40. Id. at 153, 269.

41. *Turning Right*, supra note 5.

42. 118 S. Ct. 275 (1997).

43. LaChance v. Erickson, 118 S. Ct. 753 (1997); Brogan v. United States, 118 S. Ct. 805 (1997).

44. Hudson v. United States, 118 S. Ct. 488 (1997).

45. 118 S. Ct. 1709 (1998).

46. 524 U.S. 569 (1998).

47. 523 U.S. 75 (1998).

48. Faragher v. City of Boca Raton, 524 U.S. 775 (1998); Burlington Indust. v. Ellerth, 524 U.S. 742 (1998).

49. Washington v. Glucksberg, 521 U.S. 2258 (1997).

50. Clinton v. Jones, 520 U.S. 681 (1997).

51. 524 U.S. 399 (1998).

52. Clinton v. City of New York, 118 S. Ct. 2091 (1998).

10

THE REHNQUIST COURT AND
THE LEGAL PROFESSION

JEROME J. SHESTACK

The Supreme Court's place in our profession has no parallel in any secular assembly. Whether we applaud or deplore particular opinions, the Court represents the pinnacle of our profession and enjoys our veneration.

That very tradition of veneration makes it difficult to assess the Court's impact on the legal profession. It is especially difficult to appraise a current era when our view may be affected by the passions and alliances of the day, and not yet tempered by the objectivity derived from distance in time. Any appraisal here includes that caveat.

Strikingly, history, for the most part, has paid slight attention to the Court's Chief Justices. John Marshall, of course, was an exception. In lesser measure, but still winning history's cognizance, are Taney, Hughes, and Warren, for their commanding roles in charting the course of the Court during their eras.[1]

Other Chief Justices have won historic recognition by virtue of their leadership in advancing the administration of justice. Here, Taft and Burger are leading examples.[2]

But memory does not go much further. There may have been appraisals aplenty at the time, but today, few, others than Court scholars, recall the impact of Ellsworth, or Waite, or Fuller, or White, or Vinson.

Appraisal of an era named after a Chief Justice is all the more difficult when we recall that even when a Chief Justice is as commanding as Earl Warren—much of the credit often goes to another. More than 70 percent of all Associate Justices outlive the Chief Justice serving when they were appointed, and many have had seminal influence on the Court. Justice William Brennan once hailed Hugo Black as the architect of the Warren years. And many believe that it was Brennan (during the Warren Court years) "who, by and large, formulated the principles, analyzed the precedents, and chose the words that transformed the ideal into law."[3]

Even with a commanding Chief Justice, the makeup of the Court is crucial. John Marshall's influence over the Court was diminished by dint of Andrew Jackson's appointments and Roger Taney's because of Lincoln's. Warren needed Black, Douglas, and Brennan but also Goldberg, and later, Marshall and Fortas, to command a majority. It is intriguing, though not cheering, to speculate whether *Brown v. Board of Education* would have been unanimous if Scalia, Thomas, or Rehnquist had been sitting with Warren at that time.[4]

The difference a Justice or two can make is monumental.[5] At times, Rehnquist's Court was called the "Powell Court," when Justice Powell was the swing vote. Today, Rehnquist's Court is often called the "Kennedy Court," or the "Kennedy–O'Connor Court," because their votes frequently determine whether the Chief Justice's often predictable vote will be on the high or low side of a five to four decision.[6]

I make this point not to detract from the influence of the Chief Justice on a Court era but to underscore that virtually all the Justices come to the Court with a well-molded legal philosophy. Each is proud of his or her independent judgment. Each holds life tenure during good behavior. Each is mindful of past decisions. Each knows the need to command a majority. And, each presumably would rather find common ground than be confined to a dissenting opinion. In their final determinations, Chief Justice Rehnquist has said, using an odd simile, Justices are as "independent as hogs on ice."[7]

Chief Justice Rehnquist often illustrates the point with an anecdote about a time when Justice McReynolds was late for a Court conference. Then Chief Justice Hughes sent a messenger to McReynolds's chambers to importune him to hurry. The messenger soon returned and the Chief Justice asked whether his message had been communicated to Justice McReynolds. The messenger affirmatively replied that he had. To the Chief Justice's next question, the messenger replied, "He said to tell you that he doesn't work for you."[8]

The autonomy of Associate Justices aside, the influence of a forceful Chief Justice is considerable. The Chief Justice enjoys a decided advantage by being the first in the conference presentation, by assigning opinions, and by virtue of the respect accorded his position. And where—as in the case of Chief Justice Rehnquist—he possesses great intellectual strength and enjoys the friendship of his colleagues, his influence is formidable.

Moreover, beyond a Chief Justice's influence on his colleagues, he is the spokesman for the Court and, indeed, for the entire judiciary. Prior to becoming Chief Justice, Rehnquist said that on occasion, the Chief Justice "is given the opportunity to strike a blow for the cause, an opportunity which is simply not accorded even the most gifted of his associates." And he said, to strike a blow for the cause "affords some measurement of the men who have sat in the center chair of the Court."[9] Let us keep the Chief Justice's own standard in mind as we review his tenure.

My observations on the impact of the "Rehnquist Court" on the legal profession address three areas: the court jurisprudence, the administration of justice, and the collegiality and relationships with the organized bar.

I need hardly add that my comments, though informed by contacts with the bar, are nevertheless subjective. It could hardly be otherwise in analyzing the impact of the Court on a highly diverse profession, with lawyers on every point of the political spectrum, and where difference of opinion has the sanctity of sacrament!

The Court's Jurisprudence

Most lawyers do not deal with the constitutional issues considered by the Supreme Court and are largely unaffected by the clash of circuit court decisions triggering certiorari. And because veneration of the Court is ingrained, they hesitate to criticize the Justices openly. But, lawyers are neither apathetic toward nor ignorant of Supreme Court decisions. Lawyers like to follow the Court and peruse major decisions. They feel affinity with their profession through familiarity with the decisions that affect constitutional democracy and the justice system. Also significant is that the Court creates mainstream legal thinking and culture. In measures large and small, direct or indirect, lawyers' attitudes and aspirations on societal, as well as legal, issues are affected by the Court.

Let me then begin not with the current Rehnquist era but with the start of Chief Justice Earl Warren's term in 1953—which coincided with my own entry into practice. As a person concerned with the ideals of equal justice and individual rights, the world I found at that time was not a heartwarming sight. In the south, Jim Crow reigned. Blacks were segregated, forbidden access to places of public accommodation, excluded from juries, and denied voting rights. McCarthyism stifled dissent. States frequently fostered religious practices. Legislatures were gerrymandered. Free speech doctrine was muddy. Capital trials proceeded without counsel for the accused. Criminal procedure was virtually the exclusive domain of state law. Convictions turned upon illegally seized evidence or coerced confessions.[10] As Lawrence Sager once put it, the Constitution was "under-enforced."[11]

During the Warren era, most of these failings were redressed. In a series of landmark cases, the First, Fourth, Fifth, Sixth, and Fourteenth Amendments all became more relevant to the states and were given a generous presence in our justice system. The Court made commitments to individual rights. What Brennan described as "human dignity"[12] became embodied in constitutional law.[13] The Court decreed changes not only in the justice system, but in the larger society. For example, the desegregation cases reordered large regions in our society, the reappointment cases upset established political arrangements, and, the school prayer cases banished a practice familiar to generations of students.[14]

Warren Burger thought he could reverse the liberal tide. Justice Douglas relates in his biography that shortly after Burger became Chief Justice, he told the conference that the Court should override a number of Warren decisions, particularly *Gideon*[15] and *Miranda*.[16] But, much as Burger might have wished to do so, the tide of change could not be reversed. The majority of the Justices, many still from the Warren era, were unwilling to retract the seminal advances of that era.[17] Indeed, as Judge Henry has incisively written, in some measure, the liberal direction was extended in areas of free speech, abortion, women's rights, and capital punishment.[18]

How did the legal profession react to these constitutional advances? The bar was going through its own metamorphosis. When Warren became Chief Justice, the bar reflected the social condition in the nation. Neither blacks nor women had a role at the bar. The bar was apathetic toward civil rights. Legal services to the poor were hardly more than a token gesture. Criminal justice standards of fairness were negligible. Human rights initiatives were nonstarters in bar conferences. The bar was elitist, smug, and largely uninvolved in the issues that were occupying the Warren Court.[19]

Starting with the mid-1960s and through the 1970s, the bar changed substantially—becoming much more progressive. A variety of factors spanned the change: more vibrant leadership; the influx of younger lawyers; changes in societal mood; the inspirational vigor of the Warren Court. Or, perhaps it was simply catching up with what was happening in America: an America marked by the civil rights revolution, campus unrest, Vietnam protests, the war against poverty, and the Kennedy challenge of asking, "what you can do for your country."[20]

Certainly, the Warren era helped create a new mainstream in the profession's culture and its moral outlook. Perhaps *Brown v. Board of Education* [21] was the striking beginning of a slow awakening. It led, in the early 1960s, to the bar addressing civil rights. *Miranda v. Arizona*[22] became a beacon of fairness in criminal law. *Gideon v. Wainwright*[23] uplifted public defenders. These and other decisions resurfaced in the mid-1960s, prompting the bar to endorse legal services to the poor under the leadership of Lewis Powell, president of the American Bar Association (ABA). They also led to ABA consideration of criminal justice standards. [24]

There were other cases, such as *Griswold v. Connecticut*,[25] which upgraded privacy, and *New York Times v. Sullivan*,[26] which gave a new dimension to free speech. Gender and racial bias began to be seriously addressed in the profession.[27] The bar endorsed affirmative action and advocated human rights treaties.[28]

The landmark constitutional cases of the period between 1956 and 1976 were favorably received not only in academia but also in meetings of bar associations, particularly the American Bar Association. As the Warren era proceeded and extended into the Burger era, lawyers became more and more affirming and embracing of the Court's advances in the Bill of Rights area and of its moral stance for human dignity as a fundamental constitutional value. Warren, Black, Douglas, Goldberg, and Brennan, in particular, became heroes of the profession, or at least much of it.

To use Tony Lewis's words, it was "an age of judicial heroism."[29] Many lawyers have told me that it was the Warren era that inspired them to go to law school. It was a period during which public interest law firms began to flourish. Many of their cases resulted in landmark decisions. It was before the era of the mushrooming of law firms and the frenzied drive for the higher bottom line. Some of the best and the brightest young lawyers went from law school to public interest and legal services posts. It was the post-World War II generation that had beaten back the forces of darkness and looked to the future with optimism. As David Halberstam put it, the Warren era "allowed a generation of us who love freedom to love our country that much more."[30]

In 1972, President Nixon appointed William Rehnquist to the Court as an Associate Justice. At the time, questions were raised about his views on race. In hindsight, it is clear that his confirmation hearing testimony about his views on *Brown v. Board of Education*, while he was a law clerk to Justice Jackson, did not exactly sparkle with candor.[31] But his patent brilliance captured the votes needed for confirmation.[32] As Rehnquist's background suggested then, and as his dissenting opinions confirmed during his years of Court service prior to becoming Chief Justice, he would have reversed many if not most of the Warren Court's constitutional gains for individual rights.[33] But the votes were not there to do so; Brennan, Marshall, Blackmun, and Stevens were still on the Court and upheld the Warren tradition.

By the time Rehnquist became Chief Justice in the mid-1980s and shortly thereafter, the Court's composition changed. Justices O'Connor and Scalia were now on the Court, soon to be joined by Justice Kennedy, all appointed by Republican Presidents. The Chief Justice could reasonably have anticipated a conservative majority with which he could lead a judicial counter-revolution. His agenda was never a secret. It included subordinating the Commerce Clause to states' rights, lowering the wall between church and state, essentially abandoning affirmative action, restricting habeas corpus, diminishing defendants' rights in criminal cases, and undoing or chipping away at *Roe v. Wade.* [34] Given the new composition of the Court, his agenda seemed achievable. As Justice Thurgood Marshall put it, the new makeup of the Rehnquist Court sent "a clear signal that scores of established constitutional liberties are now ripe for reconsideration," and that "Power, not reason, is the new currency of this Court's decision making."[35] And reconsideration and conservative revision did take place, although not wholly in the counter-revolutionary mode the Chief Justice envisioned.

As it turned out, first Powell, and then Kennedy and O'Connor, were often reluctant to take the Court as far to the right as the Chief Justice desired. Souter, for the most part, took the more moderate, and at times liberal position, as did Justice Stevens and, more recently, Justices Ginsburg and Breyer. Hence, in important constitutional cases, the core of the so-called Rehnquist Court often consisted only of the Chief Justice, Scalia and White (until 1993) and Thomas (since 1991). The Chief Justice had to scramble for the fifth vote and sometimes for the fourth and fifth. For the Chief Justice's view to prevail, generally Kennedy and O'Connor had to be persuaded; yet they showed a predilection to wrestle, often agonize, in reaching their determinations and ultimately to be guided more by fact-driven, pragmatic considerations than by a politically rooted philosophy.[36] In pursuit of their vote, the Chief Justice often endorsed a more moderate position than he preferred.

But whatever the nuances, and however it was done, the fact is that a good portion of the Rehnquist agenda has, indeed, been accomplished, and his stamp on the Court's jurisprudence is unmistakable. To be sure, many of the landmark decisions of the Warren–Burger era are still standing. But many have been maimed and hobbled, worn down, and given what Brennan gently termed a "cramped interpretation."[37] Thus, in *Planned Parenthood v. Casey,*[38] the Chief Justice's attempt to overrule *Roe v. Wade,* failed, but he was able to guarantee that much more state regulation of abortion would pass constitutional muster. A series of decisions emasculated affirmative action, leaving it largely a vestigial remainder in Supreme Court jurisprudence. *Miranda* and *Mapp* have become shadows of their former selves.[39] *Lopez* [40] and its progeny shrunk the Constitution's Commerce Clause to a lower condition than at any time since the pre-Roosevelt era.[41] The expansion of the Bill of Rights and the Fourteenth Amendment has come to an almost full stop. Only the free speech portion of the First Amendment remains reasonably vigorous. Statistically, Rehnquist produced a majority for his agenda in approximately two-thirds of the controversial cases in which there was a five to four split. For the present, that statistic alone establishes the Court as the "Rehnquist Court."[42]

What has been the overall impact of Rehnquist Court decisions on the legal profession? Most of whatever storm blows over the Court is generated by academics, not lawyers. Votes are counted; internal memoranda are dissected; motives are attributed. Some say the opinions reflect the temper of the times; others say they do not reflect the temper of the times. The opinions are searching and careful; they are glib and result oriented. The conservative tide has won out; it has not won out. The Court, as Mr. Dooley claimed, follows the "illection returns"[43]; the Court does not follow the "illection returns." The center holds; the center fails to hold. It is the worst of times; it is as good as it will get.[44]

And no academic consensus emerges. But academic debate aside, what is the impact of the Rehnquist Court on the practicing and organized bar?

The profession, of course, is far from monolithic, which precludes any definitive answer. Lawyers may address particular cases or trends in their areas of expertise, but they generally do not write on the Court's philosophy or jurisprudential approach. But lawyers do understand, and so do trial courts, that criminal defendants now have less constitutional protection than before; that the death penalty is alive and well; that death row inmates have only one shot at a federal court; that no one has to worry much about affirmative action; that religion preaches again in the public arena; that states' rights have been given a dose of judicial Viagra. Lawyers and lower courts try to take these shifts in stride.

But there is more. There is a symbiotic relationship between the Court and the profession. And I sense a troubled mood among many of our profession who think deeply about the Court.

For many lawyers, perhaps even most, the Court has always been the profession's moral compass and the Chief Justice its moral exponent. Whether or not one agrees with a high Court decision, lawyers want the Court's decisions to be principled and based on fealty to law, justice, and constitutional values—not to political ends.

I believe that the Warren Court was seen as following a moral compass that pointed directly to the essence of our Constitution, expressed in its preamble: "to form a more perfect union," and commanding "justice" and the "blessings of liberty" for ourselves and our posterity.[45] The Warren Court translated these goals of our Constitution into the moral principle of human worth and dignity, [46] and that vision comported with the mission of a profession whose daily work was often advancing individual rights, giving status to claims and bringing to people fairness and the dignity of justice. Not all agreed with the direction taken or the level of its activities, but there was no doubt that the Warren Court's moral compass was, for the most part, unwavering.[47]

Rejecting the direction in which the Warren Court's compass pointed, conservatives wrapped themselves in the banners of neutrality, deference, *stare decisis*, judicial restraint, and majoritarianism. These principles were supposedly unwavering and immune to political tempests and the evils of judicial activism. The conservative compass pointed to a course that could be defended on principled grounds.

But what now seems to have gone awry is the calibration of the conservative moral compass. It is so not so much that the compass points in a different direction. It is that its points waiver back and forth, as if blown by political winds, with principles more like accomplices than guides.

Thus, the Chief Justice and his principal conservative colleagues extol the virtues of *stare decisis*, a hallmark of judicial restraint. But when precedent runs counter to their desired result, their activism is rampant and they are quite willing to consign the precedent if not to the morgue then to life supports.[48] They profess fealty to majoritarianism—judicial deference to decisions of democratically elected officials. But that principle is cast aside to hallow states' rights, with hardly a tremor for overriding congressional enactments.[49] So it is with original intent, with textualism, with strict construction, with judicial restraint—all the declared moral principles of conservativism are given lip service but then subverted to conservative driven results.[50]

The moral structure is further assailed by revelations about the once hidden world of internal correspondence, memoranda, and draft opinions within the Court, particularly during the Rehnquist era.[51] These revelations generally have a time lag. Still, it is disturbing to learn of the internal manipulation, maneuvering, and stealth is by which the constitutional corpus is wounded, as Professor Schwartz put it. We have all heard Bismarck's *bon mot* that one should never see how law or sausages are made. But it is disconcerting to find that mean-spirited aphorism applied to Supreme Court decision making.

So what is to be said about the "Rehnquist Court?" Not all decisions, to be sure, but certainly many are affected by the Chief Justice—decisions in which the terms "political," "regressive," "result oriented," or even "hypocritical" often seem more fitting than principled or moral. Constitutional vitality now seems diminished. And there is no vision one can happily embrace. I find that sad.

I do not apply these evaluations to Justices O'Connor and Kennedy, who continue to be the critical arbiters in a five to four or a six to three decision, sometimes seeming to struggle to sustain the enlightened decisions of the Warren Court, yet often dipping into the luggage of conservatism they brought with them to the Court. Nor to Justice Stevens, who continues to resist the categorizers even as he generally inclines toward a liberal direction. Nor to the newer Justices—Souter, Ginsburg, and Breyer, all of whom seem to be in a slow process of developing a philosophy of cautious constitutional interpretation, but one that accords modern vitality to the Bill of Rights and which, as Brennan put it, may be fitting for the times.[52]

It has been observed that the struggle [53] for the ideological soul of the Rehnquist Court is fierce and by no means over. Perhaps one of the lures of Supreme Court watching comes from not knowing what will evolve. But for now, in a substantial portion of its five to four jurisprudence, the Supreme Court can be viewed as "the Rehnquist Court," and it is likely to stay that way into the first years of the next millennium. For those of us who delighted in the Warren era, there is now little joy on the first Monday of October or during the last week in June.

Professional Standards

Few of the Court's cases directly affect professional conduct, and in recent years, there is little here to excite the profession.

The Burger Court gave full leeway to lawyer advertising, much to the dismay of Chief Justice Burger himself. The Rehnquist Court has drawn in the reins slightly, but not enough to make a difference.[54] Surely, the Court should now understand how advertising has hurt the legal profession. Yet, it seems little inclined to circumscribe lawyer advertising except in minute increments.

During this past term, the Court affirmed maintenance of the attorney-client privilege after death.[55] Scores of amicus briefs supported upholding the privilege, and none was opposed. The case was a no-brainer.

More notable, the *Philips* case addressed the constitutionality of the Texas Interest on Lawyers Trust Accounts (IOLTA) program.[56] The Chief Justice seemed eager to hold that setting aside minute accumulations of interest in these attorneys' accounts to serve legal services for the poor was an unconstitutional taking.[57] But that position could not muster five votes. The taking issue was not decided. So the Court sent the case back to the lower courts. But the holding that such interest money had to be considered property still nearly devastated IOLTA. Both Justices Souter and Breyer dissents showed a realistic appreciation of the purpose and working of the Texas IOLTA plan; their opinions make good sense but still could not garner five votes.

For a long time, appointments to the Court have not been made from the trial bar or even the trial courts. Not since Lewis Powell resigned more than a dozen years ago has the Court had a member with substantial practice as a trial lawyer anywhere close to the time of ascending to the Court. The lack of experience is evident in the Court's opinions.

In a number of areas involving complex areas of practice in which the law has been muddled and the lower courts inconsistent (sex and age discrimination cases, class action standards, punitive damages, etc.) the Court has valiantly tried to set bright lines for practitioners. But the bright line often turns out to be faded and fuzzy when lower courts try to apply it, requiring more cases or legislation to clarify impractical or murky opinions. How many times have I heard trial lawyers sigh that the Court does not understand what happens in a trial.

A high-profile case, where I believe more trial experience would have provided perspective the Court did not display, is the infamous *Paula Jones* case. There, the Court ruled that allowing litigation against President Clinton to proceed during his term of office would not unduly impose on the time necessary to fulfill his presidential duties.[58] One of the Justices subsequently noted that the unanimity of that decision shows that in a case with political dimension, the Court is cohesive and principled. One wonders why the observation was necessary and whether a converse conclusion is to be drawn in cases with a political dimension, where the Court is divided? Unanimous or not, experienced trial lawyers could have foretold that the *Paula Jones* decision was impractical and at odds with the workings of motion and trial practice. And so time has proved.

The Court's lack of familiarity with lawyers' day-to-day practice is sometimes illustrated by anecdotes that members of the bar share with each other after appearing before the Court. In one argument, two of the Justices displayed lack of awareness of how a lawyer referral system worked.[59] In the IOLTA case, the Chief Justice misunderstood how a "retainer" worked. In another case, the Chief Justice gave a tasteless antilawyer quip about fees.[60] During one oral argument, Scalia commented: "I'm certainly glad that I never passed through the sage of being a lawyer to get where I am." To which Breyer commented: "Well, it might have helped, actually."[61]

The Rehnquist Court and the Administration of Justice

The administration of justice is part of the ministry of the legal profession, and the profession looks for guidance to the leader of the ministry. In the federal system, that would be the Supreme Court, and its guidance, and particularly that of the Chief Justice, is vital with respect to access, efficiency, speed, court and case management, judicial education and morale, and other elements of the administration of justice.

Yet, few Chief Justices have given serious and sustained attention to improving the administration of justice. Perhaps they should not be faulted for this. After all, *judging* is the first order of a judge's business, and judicial administration and reform divert time and energy from that task. But another view is that *justice* is really the first order of a judge's business, and justice is affected by the way it is administered.

In modern history, only two Chief Justices in particular have been seen as passionate about improving the administration of justice. Chief Justice William Howard Taft was the most determined occupant of the center chair fostering improvement in our justice system. As President of the American Bar Association in 1913, he crusaded for judicial reform. As President of the United States, his first address on the State of the Union proclaimed that "reducing litigation expenses and expediting decisions" was the greatest need in our American institutions,[62] and he spurred the Supreme Court to modernize the federal rules of equity. As Chief Justice, he presided over the newly created Conference of Senior Circuit Judges, later to become the Judicial Conference, and made it into an effective body to deal with the quantity and quality of justice in federal trial courts. He laid the groundwork for the Federal Rules of Civil Procedure and was the central force behind the Act of 1925, which released the Court from the unqualified right to appeal from courts below and substituted enlarged certiorari jurisdiction. In all these reforms he pursued, he forged an effective partnership with the organized bar.[63]

Chief Justice Warren Burger also devoted himself to improving the administration of justice.[64] He initiated an Institute for Court Management to train multitudes of court administrators. He obtained legislation for the Office of Circuit Executives to allow chief judges of those courts more time to perform their judicial functions. He advanced the Federal Judicial Center with programs of research and continuing education for judges and court personnel. He also used his position to advance state courts, helping to bring about the National Center for State Courts and the National Judicial College. In all these efforts, he formed a partnership with the American Bar Association, viewing the organized bar as "a force for enormous, almost unlimited, good with respect to every problem in the administration of justice."[65] He spoke regularly at ABA meetings on the causes of dissatisfaction with the justice system. He supported ABA initiatives to reduce costs in class actions and in appeals; he encouraged an ABA commission to deal with unnecessary discovery; he was an early supporter of federal funded legal services to the poor and much more.[66]

Chief Justice Rehnquist publicly displays no such passion about the administration of justice. However, the sound administration of the courts does seem to be a matter of concern to the Chief Justice. His practice is to delegate most of the tasks of reform and improvements in the administration of justice to the Judicial Conference and its Executive Committee. The Chief Justice presides over these meetings efficiently and fairly, making decisions promptly, if curtly. Although he generally conserves his powers, he uses them when needed. Thus, he has beneficially involved himself in disputes between the Federal Judicial Center and the Administrative Office, in disputes over rules promulgated by the Conference Executive Committee, and in situations in which the executive branch seems to encroach on judicial independence.

In addition, there are many ongoing projects in judicial administration which, I am told, have his quiet support,[67] such as needed revisions of Rules of Civil Procedure, and the Judicial Conference's Long Range Plan,[68] which can effect major reforms in judicial administration. The Office of Administration also has many beneficial programs, as does the Federal Judicial Center. One wishes the Chief Justice was more outgoing about such programs. He is the spokesman for the judiciary, and for the public to have the perception that the Chief Justice is directly concerned and involved in judicial reform would be no small matter.

One of the items that usually does command the attention of the bar and the public is the Chief Justice's annual reports to Congress on the federal judiciary. Here, in recent years, the Chief Justice has principally focused his reports on four themes: limiting habeas corpus, decrying expanded jurisdiction of the federal courts, filling judicial vacancies, and raising judicial compensation.[69]

The reduction of appeals under writs of habeas corpus has been a particular focus of the Chief Justice.[70] He brings to the issue the enthusiasm of a crusader — not a particularly laudable quality in this case. For example, in 1988, an Ad Hoc Committee appointed by the Chief Justice recommended that death-row inmates be limited to one habeas corpus petition and that the review process have shorter time limits. The Judicial Conference deferred decision on the proposal so that it could be considered by the various circuits. But the Chief Justice submitted the proposal to Congress without waiting for the Conference. In an unprecedented rebuke, a majority of the judges on the Judicial Conference sent a letter to Congress disavowing the proposal and stating that the proposal did not represent the views of the federal judiciary.[71]

The 1997 Antiterrorism and Effective Death Penalty Act established one-year deadlines for filing petitions, limited successive petitions, limited access to the federal habeas corpus review, and savaged long-standing habeas corpus jurisprudence. The Chief Justice praised the Act exuberantly, declaring that these "reforms" reflected the wisdom of Alexander Hamilton's observation that "the nation and state system are to be regarded as a whole."[72]

On the brighter side, the Chief Justice has been effective in addressing the delay in filling judicial vacancies in the federal courts. In recent years the Senate Judiciary Committee has unconscionably delayed acting on many judicial nominations, the usual pretense for the delay being that some of the nominees were activists who had to be carefully screened. Many of the delays have been politically motivated, in part to get the President to share power in appointments, in part to derail more liberal candidates, in part to create a backlog that would not be cleared up during this administration. The result for a considerable period of time was a severe strain on the judges especially in certain courts with a high percentage of vacancies, such as the Second and Ninth Circuits.

In his annual message at the end of 1997, the Chief Justice criticized the delay in filling vacancies and described the consequences of such delay.[73] His message received wide attention. It was rightfully interpreted as criticism of the Senate Judiciary Committee and had substantial impact. Editorials throughout the nation used the Chief Justice's remarks to chastise the Senate delay.

For many months, the ABA had been urging the Senate Judiciary Committee to vote on vacancies—up or down—and not to hold nominees hostage to political manipulations.[74] But the Chief Justice's statement likely had more impact than other importunings. The pace of hearings and confirmations increased, substantially highlighting the influence that the Chief Justice can have in areas affecting judicial independence and the administration of justice.

Another area of the Chief Justice's concern has been judicial salaries, long linked to congressional salaries. Though congressmen may have political reasons for not increasing their own salaries, there is no good reason not to raise judicial salaries. Congressional failure to do so, even with respect to cost-of-living adjustments, has been shameful. The Chief Justice, in his annual messages to Congress, has spoken bluntly about the need to raise judicial salaries.[75]

Federal jurisdiction has been a particular target in addresses by the Chief Justice. He has consistently inveighed against congressional action to give the federal courts jurisdiction over various crimes. In his 1998 message, he scolded Congress for investing federal jurisdiction over a series of crimes better dealt with by states. His position here makes good sense. But he also regularly urges reduction in diversity jurisdiction[76] which, although it would lighten the federal judicial workload, has little appeal for lawyers prey to the vagaries of state judges selected by election rather than by a merit system.

Apart from these items, most of the Chief Justice's annual reports follow a familiar pattern: summaries of statistics on workload and caseload, reports on the activities of the Administrative Office of the United States Courts and the Federal Judicial Center, and calls for cooperation between the Court and Congress, inserting from time to time, messages on the importance of separation of powers and independence of the judiciary.[77] Although the Chief Justice may feel keenly about the need to redress many continuing deficiencies in the administration of justice, his messages do not convey nearly as much as they might to highlight his concerns.

Internal Court Administration

Judicial administration also encompasses administration within the Court. Chief Justice Warren was considered by his colleagues to be an ideal leader. By contrast, Chief Justice Burger, whose work in furthering the administration of the justice system was praiseworthy, received poor grades for his internal administration of the Court. His conferences were often long and tedious, and he is said to have bullied colleagues, manipulated assignments, and punished slights.[78]

Chief Justice Rehnquist gets high marks from his colleagues for his internal administration. He is efficient, not without humor, sparing of the Justices' time, reasonably even-handed in assigning opinions, and personally considerate of his colleagues. The number of cases heard each term is at a level that pleases most of the Court.[79]

In recent years, the bar has paid particular attention to civility, not only in collegial relationships but as an end in itself, as Justice Kennedy put it.[80] One assumes that collegiality and civility are beneficial for the Court. Collegiality among the Courts' Justices is said to be high these days and is often adverted to by the Justices themselves. Court members have publicly hailed the Court's civility, but the sharpness that some Justices display to colleagues in opinions gives a somewhat superficial cast to the claim.[81] Some of Justice Scalia's splenetic dissents, for example, serve as the very model of incivility. In *Romer v. Evans*,[82] he derided Justice Kennedy's position as "preposterous" and "comical" and dismissed the holding as "terminal silliness."[83] In *Webster v. Reproductive Health Services*, he dismissed Justice O'Connor's analysis as one "that cannot be taken seriously."[84] A colleague noted that his insults have "deeply wounded Justice O'Connor."[85] In one case, Justice Scalia suggested that following the Chief Justice's position in that case was cause for a lawyer to be disbarred or committed.[86] Justice Souter's opinions too, sometimes throw darts at colleagues.[87]

The Rehnquist Court and Outreach to the Organized Bar

Good relationships between the Court and the bar are of mutual benefit. If, as Holmes affirmed, the life of the law is experience,[88] it follows that the Court should not be isolated from the endeavors, initiatives, and experience of the profession. Justice Breyer put it in simple terms when he told the ABA House of Delegates that "in our legal culture, judges and lawyers work together outside the courtroom to improve the quality of the rules that govern what happens inside the courtroom, and that is a very good thing."[89] Breyer sees the organized bar as having a mandate "to make law work better for the people whom it is meant to serve,"[90] and he sees the Court as part of that common endeavor.

Even apart from the impact on substantive law and the administration of justice, the Justices—and particularly the Chief Justice—have the potential to serve as exemplars of the profession's ideals and to inspire the bar to live up to the highest values of our profession.[91] Justices who have been heroes in the profession in this century—Holmes, Brandeis, Cardozo, Hughes, Warren, Brennan, and Marshall— have unquestionably educated, influenced, and inspired the profession.

Justice Brennan was the most recent Justice who inspired the bar, not only through his opinions but by his appearances and speeches.[92] I heard him speak many times. His ideals for the profession, his passionate delivery, his call for lawyers to serve the public good, would cause lawyers to yearn—and to strive—for higher ground. We may never see his equal in our time.

Chief Justice Warren Burger also invested much of his energy in raising professional standards. In address after address, he called on the bar to enforce strict professional standards, to enhance Alternate Dispute Resolution (ADR), to impose strict discipline, to condemn advertising, and to play down the adversary system.[93] He gave more attention to raising professional standards than any Chief Justice before or since, and he clearly had a significant impact in energizing the organized bar to advance the standards he advocated.

Unlike his predecessor, Chief Justice Rehnquist is not a familiar figure at bar association conferences. During his twelve years as Chief Justice, he has probably appeared at ABA annual and midyear meetings less than any Chief Justice these past fifty years.

ABA leaders have met from time to time with members of Judicial Conference Committees, including its Executive Committee, but without direct involvement from the Chief Justice.

In his speeches to assemblies of lawyers, the Chief Justice speaks infrequently on matters affecting the judiciary or the profession, and prefers to speak on judicial history—the Marshall Court, the impeachment of Justice Chase and President Andrew Johnson, the trial of Aaron Burr, the Court in Lincoln's era, and other aspects of Court lore.[94] His knowledge of judicial history is comprehensive, indeed awesome. In terms of current relevance, the Chief Justice's expertise on the history of impeachment is widely known. His recent book, *All the Laws But One*,[95] is a splendid historical account of how our nation has handled civil liberties in war time.

The Chief Justice is not an inspirational speaker. His laconic style is not conducive to eloquence. The gold bars on the sleeves of his robe are virtually his only concession to flair.[96] The Chief Justice's annual speeches to the American Law Institute (ALI) have often been on historical subjects, and those on judicial subjects are short and simplistic, lacking the insight or depth ALI members would expect from a Chief Justice.

In speaking to law school graduates, he frequently reminisces about his early days of practice in Arizona, raps billable hours, and urges graduates to consider the lifestyle of working in government offices or small law firms rather than joining large firms practicing in large cities. The message is salutary enough but the context rather simplistic. One of his favorite quotations, to illustrate the importance of choosing the right lifestyle, is from Omar Khayam:

> The wine of life keeps oozing
> drop by drop;
> The leaves of life keep falling
> one by one."[97]

Nor has there been much spark in the few addresses he has given at ABA conferences. For example, in an important ABA Summit Conference on the Justice

System in 1993, his basic message to the audience of bar leaders from around the nation was that the judicial system was underfunded. He left the audience without a stirring or hopeful call.[98]

Of course, there is no requirement that a Chief Justice be an inspirational or engaging public speaker, or that he be involved with the bar and its entities. Yet, the Chief Justice is regarded as the ultimate spokesman for the law, the judiciary, and the legal profession. When he speaks, the public listens and the bar listens. As I noted earlier, the Court and the Chief Justice are the object of our veneration. Surely, the venerated owe something to the venerators.

Of the current Justices, those who have the most meaningful and consistent interaction with the legal profession and the organized bar (particularly the American Bar Association) are Justices Breyer, Ginsburg, and O'Connor and, more recently, Justice Kennedy. The relationship of Justice Stevens is cordial, and when exercised, valuable, but it is not frequent. Justice Souter is uninvolved. The connections of Justices Scalia and Thomas with the organized bar are distant if not outright unfriendly.

In order of seniority, I present miniportraits of the Justices' relationships with the organized bar, particularly the American Bar Association. But the reader should keep in mind the anecdotal and subjective nature of what is presented here, albeit informed by knowledgeable colleagues who share bar leadership.

Justice Paul Stevens

When Justice Stevens was first appointed to the bench, he was a vice president of the Chicago Bar Association. He had more than twenty years of practice in Chicago law firms and six years of teaching experience.[99] His prestige at the bar was high, and lawyers admired and welcomed his elevation to the Court.

Regrettably, Justice Stevens has involved himself little in the affairs or meetings of the organized bar. His only speech to an annual meeting of the ABA was in 1996.[100] Most of the speech was a routine affirmation of judicial fidelity to *stare decisis*. But the latter part of his speech was an inspirational call for integrity and civility, for equal access to representation, and for meritorious judicial selection. These were not novel thoughts, but they were expressed with eloquence and elegance. And he concluded with an impassioned plea for tolerance—quoting Robert Jackson's memorable words,"if there is any fixed star in our Constitutional Constellation it is freedom to differ." The plea for tolerance appears in other of Justice Stevens's speeches, but one wishes he would deliver more of them.

Justice Sandra Day O'Connor

In 1997, the ABA awarded Justice O'Connor its Distinguished Service Medal.[101] The medal is not awarded to Supreme Court Justices as a matter of course. Since initiation of the medal in 1929, only eight Justices have received it.[102] The award to Justice O'Connor was enthusiastically greeted by ABA members. And with good reason.

Any lawyer who encounters Justice O'Connor becomes an admirer. In conversation, she is attentive and responsive, willing to offer counsel when asked, with a gracious and caring manner. Her warmth and manifest decency are cheering, and the generosity of her spirit is unsparing.

Justice O'Connor has chosen one area of the ABA's activities for her central focus: the ABA's Central Eastern European Initiative (CEELI). The purpose of CEELI is to advance the rule of law by supporting law reform efforts in Central and Eastern Europe and the newly independent states of the former Soviet Union. She serves on the ABA CEELI Executive Board and attends its meetings faithfully. She has met with the young CEELI volunteers in Krakow and Kiev and Budapest and Prague mourned with them in Auschwitz. Her relationship with CEELI volunteers in the Eastern and Central European nations is heartwarming.[103]

She is generous in the time she gives to bar leaders who seek her counsel and presence. She speaks at many bar-related events, and no speech is a casual exercise. Her speech on the seventy-fifth Anniversary of the Women's Right to Vote reviews the history of the suffrage movement with learning and grace.[104] A speech in Vienna at the Women in Democracy Conference was insightful and epigrammatic ("The treatment of women in a society is the measure of the civilization").[105] A speech at Northwestern University Law School explained the jurisprudence of the Free Exercise Clause and the Establishment Clause of the First Amendment better than most of the Court's opinions on the subject.[106] Her speech at the University of Wisconsin on "The Life of the Law" expressed a doctrine that Warren or Brennan would gladly have embraced.[107] Her eulogy at the funeral of Justice Powell was elegant and moving. An address to the ABA Standing Committee on Law and National Security on issues facing society at the advent of the twenty-first century was redolent with sobering insights.[108] Listening to this Justice speak is an elevating experience. The bar is fortunate that Justice O'Connor so often participates in its festivals.

Justice Antonin Scalia

The bar expected much from Justice Scalia when he was elevated to the Court. Brilliant in intellect, steeped in constitutional history, humorous and gregarious, benefited by government, academic, and judicial experience, he might have been a leader in the Court and a force in the profession. But other qualities surfaced. A leading constitutional scholar writing in *The New York Times* six years after Scalia's appointment observed, "The verdict is all but unanimous: Scalia is rash, impulsive and imprudent, a Justice who in case after case would rather insult his colleagues' intelligence than appeal to them."[109] One conservative Judge, Alex Kozinski of the Ninth Circuit, has publicly deplored Scalia's inability to forge a conservative consensus.[110]

Justice Scalia does not display much affinity for the organized bar. Part of his disenchantment seems to stem from the time he was nominated for the Court of Appeals and the ABA's Judiciary Committee rated him as "Qualified" rather than "Well Qualified." (He was found "Well Qualified" by the time he was nominated for the Supreme Court.) He also complains that the ABA has taken positions on issues he considers not germane to the profession.[111] He does retain a certain rapport with the ABA Section of Administrative Law, which he once chaired, and with some ultraconservative bar leaders.

When Justice Scalia speaks at a bar conference or to a law school, his speeches are intellectual and witty but often condescending. He is invariably certain about the rightness of his views, which may not be a fault except when it converts into arrogance or incivility. Although Justice Scalia's high intellect and writings on constitutional textual interpretation are respected, his temper and condescending tone diminish an influence on our profession that might have been substantial and felicitous.

Justice Anthony Kennedy

Justice Kennedy does not appear often at bar functions, but when he does, his impact is pronounced. When he speaks at a bar conference or law school he makes himself readily available to the attendees. He is particularly receptive to law schools and has accepted more law school invitations than any of the current Justices. During such visits, he is generous with his time. For example, in 1997, he visited the Vanderbilt Law School. Most visiting dignitaries arrive, deliver a speech, and depart. Justice Kennedy taught two classes, met alumni, lunched with the faculty, and was available for questions and answers.[112] By all accounts, he is always warm and gracious to the bar and students.

His delivery of speeches displays a commanding presence. At the ABA's annual meeting in San Francisco in 1997, he gave a speech—without notes—on civility, which was a tour de force.[113] Eschewing the usual bomides about civility, he presented philosophic insights into civility as an end in itself designed to further human dignity. The speech has been quoted in dozens of bar journals, bar conferences, and judicial writings.[114] It is a prime example of the positive influence a Justice can have.

At an ABA conference in Philadelphia in December 1998, Justice Kennedy delivered a speech on the independence of the judiciary, which again was monumental in learning and insight.[115] His aphorisms are frequently quoted.

Recently, he accepted appointment to an ABA Coordinating Council on Asian initiatives.[116] His increasing receptivity to initiatives of the organized bar has been most welcome and his impact is inspirational.

Justice David Souter

David Souter succeeded to Justice Brennan's seat and reveres him. No one on the Court surpasses David Souter's industry and his singular and intense focus on his opinions. They are written with elegance yet have that uncommon quality of common sense. Souter started on the Rehnquist side of the constitutional scale and now is mostly, though not always, on the opposite side.

To the organized bar, David Souter is the least known of the Justices. His practice is to give speeches rarely, except at periodic appearances at conferences of the First and Third Circuits, which he supervises.[117] Yet, he can speak movingly, as he did at Justice Brennan's 90th birthday celebration,[118] at Brennan's funeral service,[119] and in various introductions of speakers at Supreme Court Historical Society events.[120] He effortlessly exudes intellectual excitement. But, regretfully, unlike his predecessor, Justice Brennan, Justice Souter has chosen largely to disassociate himself from the bar at large.

Justice Clarence Thomas

In relations with the organized bar, Justice Thomas departs from his judicial lock-step march with Justice Scalia. One day in 1997, while serving as President-elect of the ABA, I sat next to Justice Thomas at a luncheon meeting of the Nebraska Bar Association. He invited me to come see him. I accepted, hoping I could further a constructive relationship with the organized bar.

Our meeting lasted for nearly three hours. I presented reasons why I thought he should have a closer relationship to the profession and invited him to speak at some of our meetings. At the end, he said that our dialogue had made him rethink some of his assumptions and he would get back to me. But nothing happened.

Some years ago, the ABA's Section of Individual Rights and Responsibilities had criticized the slow pace of Equal Employment Opportunity Commission decisions while Justice Thomas was Chair of the Commission. He still harbors resentment at that criticism. But his hostility extends further and seem particularly directed against the ABA Standing Committee on the Federal Judiciary. He has accused the Committee of applying a "litmus test" in reviewing prospective nominees to the federal bench. That is sheer nonsense. There is no "litmus test" and no inquiry is made of a prospective nominee's philosophy or politics. The ABA Committee investigates the qualifications of prospective nominees at the request of the President and Attorney General, and its recommendations are based solely on the integrity, judicial temperament, professional experience, and competence of the candidate. The Committee has been a most constructive force in helping to ensure the quality of judicial nominees.

Even apart from savaging the ABA's Judiciary Committee, when Justice Thomas speaks of the ABA in general, he often parrots the diatribes of a small cadre of right-wing ideologues who have long carried on a vendetta against the ABA. The most charitable observation that can be made about Justice Thomas's comments is that they reveal a deplorable ignorance of the ABA's Judiciary Committee and the ABA in general.

Justice Thomas is also scornful of media that have criticized him and to the senators who opposed his nomination. For Justice Thomas, some grudges do not recognize a statute of limitations.

Not too long ago, he spoke to the National Bar Association amidst a storm over the invitation within the NBA itself.[121] His principal theme was that people who accuse him of not thinking for himself and being in Scalia's shadow are racist—a rather odd accusation as many of his most publicized critics are African-American lawyers and judges.[122] Justice Thomas made similar charges of racism against critics at his confirmation hearing. Such complaints seem to come with poor grace from one who has benefited from the affirmative action principles he denounces. Justice Thomas has the potential to interrelate with the profession. It is too bad that he has largely recused himself from the mainstream organized bar and so eagerly embraced radical right ideologues.

Justice Ruth Ginsburg

Before becoming a judge, Justice Ginsburg was already an icon at the bar, particularly among women lawyers, for her long-time advocacy of women's rights, including memorable advocacy at the bar of the Supreme Court. Solicitor General Erwin Griswold once praised an argument she had given before the Supreme Court as among the best he had heard. When President Clinton nominated her to the Court, he aptly called her the Thurgood Marshall of the women's rights movement.[123] Within the ABA, she served on the Council of the pioneering Section of Individual Rights and Responsibilities, which recently awarded her its pretigious Thurgood Marshall Award. Had she not gone on the bench, she surely would have occupied high office in the bar.

Justice Ginsburg is generous in accepting invitations to speak at bar and law school events. Though self-effacing at such events, she is accessible and evidences probing concern about the progress of the bar and the health of the profession. Her speeches resonate with wit, insight, learning, and elegant crafting.[124] She has retained friendships of pre-Court days and is quick to take old friends and new on tours of her rather spectacular chambers, containing an eclectic display of art and memorabilia, indicative of a flair and adventurism seemingly at odds with her normal reserve. Women in the profession idolize her, not only for her past achievements but because of her continuing rapport with women's organizations, which she sustains even from her high place. Her influence on the profession is surely in its ascendency, whether or not she becomes Chief Justice.

Justice Stephen Breyer

By far, the Justice with the greatest rapport with the organized bar is Justice Stephen Breyer. More than any other Justice, I believe he understands the pulse of our profession. At his confirmation hearings, he said that the law had a simple basic purpose: to help Americans "live together productively, harmoniously, and in freedom."[125] It is not surprising that this purpose should strike a responsive chord in the legal profession.

Justice Breyer speaks frequently at ABA functions and mixes easily with the bar. He has spoken to the ABA House of Delegates, and he hosts ABA conferences in the Supreme Court more than any Justice. In his speeches, he encourages lawyers to become involved in the organized bar. He encourages judges to do so as well. He is mindful of the independence of judges but believes that "independence is not isolation."[126]

He writes prodigiously. He presents scholarly issues with ease and grace and can do so spontaneously.[127] He is a Renaissance man, and his insights flow in remarkable profusion. His H. L.A. Hart Memorial Lecture at University College, Oxford on Judicial Review is an incisive analysis of independent judicial review.[128] He has spoken on the interdependence of science and law,[129] architecture,[130] the Zionist ideal,[131] the European Union,[132] the media and the courts,[133] and crimes against humanity.[134] His memorial tributes to friends and colleagues—Donald Turner, Philip Areeda, Louis Jaffe, and others are eloquent and moving.[135] His range is remarkable. Lawyers like him immensely on first meeting and even more so in subsequent ones. He knows nothing of pomposity and everything about fraternity. He is likely to be the Justice with the most significant impact on the organized bar.

Conclusion

At the end of the day, as the expression goes, the principal impact of the Court on the legal profession derives not from the brief encounters of the Court and the organized bar but from the Court's jurisprudence and its influence on our values as lawyers in a learned and noble profession. Earlier, I noted that while an Associate Justice, Rehnquist wrote an article about prior Chief Justices in which he said the following: "The Chief Justice is in many ways merely *prius inter pares*, but on occasion, he is given the opportunity to strike a blow for the cause, an opportunity which is simply not accorded to even the most gifted of his associates."[136]

To strike "a blow for the cause": We lawyers know about causes; we live with them and by them. And I have wondered, which "cause" will mark the Rehnquist Court? The cause of human dignity? The rule of law? Individual rights? Advancing access to justice? A "living Constitution?" Judicial restraint? Precedent? Majoritarianism? None seem to fit.

What then, is the cause? Is it a "crimped interpretation" of the Constitution as Brennan thought? It is reconsideration "of established constitutional liberties," as Marshall predicted. Is it exalting state's "rights" over considerations of national interest? Or, is it to recast the Constitution to accommodate a conservative political agenda? What is "the cause"?

In that same article, Chief Justice Rehnquist said the manner in which a Chief Justice makes use of the opportunities "to strike a blow for the cause affords some measurement of the stature of the men who have sat in the center chair of the Court."[137] After more than a dozen years, I believe the measurement of the stature of which the Chief Justice speaks may be made with respect to the Court's current center chair.

Notes

The author appreciates the research assistance of Elizabeth Vrato, Esquire and Dina Leshetz Bakst, Esquire.

The comments in this chapter were first given at the symposium on the Rehnquist Court held in September 1998. They, therefore, are from the vantage of an observer of the Court at that time.

1. *The Supreme Court and Its Justices* 30–48, 53–64, 98–104 (Jesse H. Choper ed., 1987); *J. Sup. Ct. History* 3–20, 21–34, 79, 111–12, 132 (1998); Johnson, "Chief Justice John Marshall (1801–1835)," 1 *J. Sup. Ct. History* 3 (1998); O'Hara, "Out of the Shadow: Roger Brooks Taney as Chief Justice," *J. Sup. Ct. History* 25 (1985); Schwartz, *Super Chief, Earl Warren and His Supreme Court, a Judicial Biography* (1983); Schwartz, "Chief Justice Earl Warren: Super

Chief in Action," 33 *Tulsa L.J.* 477 (1997); and same title in 1 *J. Sup. Ct. History* 112 (1998); *The Warren Court* (Bernard Schwartz ed., 1996).

2. Morris, "What Heaven Must Be Like: William Howard Taft as Chief Justice, 1921–30," in *Yearbook, Supreme Court Historical Society* 80 (1983); Shestack, "The Burger Court and the Legal Profession," in *The Burger Court* 189–202 (Bernard Schwartz ed., 1998).

3. Irons, *Brennan v. Rehnquist: The Battle for the Constitution*, 323 (1994) (quoting Professor Owen Fiss of Yale Law School). But as Prof. Bernard Schwartz has noted that, "an era of the Supreme Court customarily is designated by the name of its Chief Justice," and Schwartz is quick to emphasize that during the Warren tenure, this designation was more than a mere formality with the Court bearing the mark of its Chief Justice as unmistakenly as the earlier Courts of Marshall and Taney reflected their unique leadership. Schwartz, "Chief Justice Warren and 1984," 35 *Hastings L.J.* 975 (1984).

4. At the time that *Brown v. Board of Education* was before the Court, Rehnquist was a law clerk to Justice Robert Jackson. Rehnquist wrote a memorandum to Jackson concluding with the following: "I think *Plessy v. Ferguson* was right and should be reaffirmed." During Rehnquist's confirmation hearings in 1986, he maintained under oath that the memo represented Justice Jackson's views, not his own. (He was asked by Sen. Edward Kennedy, "Do the I's refer to you Mr. Rehnquist?" "No, I do not think they do," Rehnquist replied.) Richard Kluger, in a monumental book on the *Brown* case found there was "a preponderance of evidence" to suggest the memorandum was an accurate statement of Rehnquist's views, not Jackson's. A fair reading of the evidence, as analyzed not only by Kluger but by other Court scholars, is that Rehnquist's testimony to the Senate Judiciary Committee on this issue did not correspond with the truth. See Kluger, *Simple Justice: The History of* Brown v. Board of Education *and Black America's Struggle for Equality* 609 (1976); Schwartz, "Chief Justice Rehnquist, Justice Jackson and the *Brown* Case," 1988 Sup. Ct. Rev.; Schwartz, "Rehnquist, Runyan, and Jones—The Chief Justice, Civil Rights and *Stare Decisis*," 31 *Tulsa L.J.* 251 (1995); Brenner, "The Memos of Supreme Court Clerk William Rehnquist; Conservative Tracts or Mirror of His Justice's Mind," 76 (2) *Judicature* 77 (1992). *New York Times* columnist Bob Herbert put it harshly: Rehnquist was "apparently lying through his teeth to save his judicial skin in 1986." Herbert, "The Real Disgrace," *N.Y. Times*, Jan. 10, 1999, sec. 4, at 21. The same somewhat more subtly worded suggestion is made by Jeffrey Rosen. See Rosen, "Rehnquist's Choice," *The New Yorker*, Jan. 11, 1999, at 28–29.

5. As Professor Lawrence Tribe has analyzed, many important cases have been decided by one vote, with the Chief Justice not always in the majority. The great *Civil War* cases, the *Prize* cases and the *Test Oath* cases (which tested the boundaries of presidential power) and the *Slaughterhouse* cases of 1873 (the first major attempt to interpret the fourteenth Amendment) were decided by a 5–4 vote. Schwartz, A *History of the Supreme Court* 126–35, 131–32, 158–61, 231–32 (1993). The anti-New Deal decisions in the mid-1930s invalidating the Railroad Retirement Vote were by a 5–4 vote. See Railroad Retirement Fund v. Alton, 295 U.S. 330 (1935); Morehead v. New York, 298 U.S. 587 (1936). When Justice Owen Roberts's famous 1937 "switch in time that saved nine" took place, it was a single vote that sustained the National Labor Relations Act and a Washington minimum wage law. Tribe, What a "Difference a Justice or Two Make," in *The Supreme Court and Its Justices*, supra note 1, at 241. In more recent times, such seminal decisions as Miranda v. Arizona, 384 U.S. 436 (1966) and University of California v. Bakke, 438 U.S. 65 (1978), were decided by one vote. There are many other examples.

6. Garrow, "The Rehnquist Reins," *N.Y. Times*, Oct. 6, 1996, sec. 6, at 65; Rosen, "The Agonizer," (referring to Justice Kennedy), *The New Yorker*, Nov. 11, 1996, at 82.

7. Rehnquist, "Chief Justices I Never Knew," 3 *Hastings Const. L.Q.* 637, (1976). Rehn-

quist has also referred to the Chief Justice as the "interlocutor of the judicial minstrel show, a planner, and occasionally a statesman." Id. at 639.

8. Id. at 637–38.

9. Id. at 655.

10. This scene in the 1950s is vividly painted by Prof. Owen Fiss in Irons, supra note 3, at 337.

11. Sager, "Fair Measure: The Legal Status of Underenforced Constitutional Norms," 91 *Harv. L. Rev.* 1212,1231 (1978).

12. Wermiel, "Law and Human Dignity: The Judicial Soul of Justice Brennan," 7 *Wm. & Mary Bill Rts. J.* 223 (1998).

13. Irons, supra note 3, at Ch. 2. Professor Schwartz put it succinctly: "The Warren Justices saw themselves as present-day chancellors, who secured fairness and equity in individual cases, fired above all by a vision of the equal dignity of man, to be furthered by the Court's value-laden decisions." Schwartz, *The Age of Pragmatism* 411–12 (1990).

14. Cox, "Storm Over the Supreme Court," in *The Eroding Constitution* (Norman Dorsen ed., 1987).

15. Gideon v. Wainwright, 372 U.S. 335 (1963).

16. Miranda v. Arizona, 384 U.S. 436 (1966).

17. Schwartz, *A History of the Supreme Court* 269, 270 (1993).

18. See Henry, The Players and the Play," in *The Burger Court* (Bernard Schwartz ed., 1998), Shestack, supra note 2, at 13. See Chase, "The Burger Court, the Individual and the Criminal Process: Direction and Misdirection," 52 *N.Y.U. L. Rev.* 518 (1977); see also Schwartz, "Chief Justice Earl Warren—Super Chief in Action," 1 *J. Sup. Ct. History*, 123 (1996).

19. Auerbach, *Unequal Justice* 262 (1976).

20. I have discussed the changes in the bar, particularly the American Bar Association, in the thirty-year period from 1960 to 1990 in a number of speeches and articles while President-elect and President of the ABA. See, e.g., Shestack, *The Future of the Legal Profession*, address to Tulsa Bar Association (Aug. 1997); address to Nebraska Bar Association (Oct. 1996); Shestack, *Messages of the President of the ABA, 1997–1998* (ABA publication, 1998).

21. 347 U.S. 483 (1954).

22. 384 U.S. 436 (1966).

23. 372 U.S. 335 (1963).

24. Mayer, *The Lawyers*, 149–222 (1966).

25. 381 U.S. 479 (1965).

26. 376 U.S. 254 (1964).

27. During the early 1970s, the ABA Section of Individual Rights began to propose resolutions supporting gender and racial diversity which were adopted by the ABA House and became ABA policy.

28. As late as 1970, the ABA House of Delegates refused to endorse even the Genocide Convention, despite the urging of the Section of Individual Rights, which I then chaired. By 1976, however, the ABA had endorsed all of the principal United Nations human rights treaties. Podgers, "Praised and Prodded," 84 *A.B.A. J.* 92 (May 1998).

29. Lewis, "The Legacy of the Warren Court," in *The Warren Court* 398 (Bernard Schwartz ed., 1996).

30. Halberstam, "The Common Man as Uncommon Man," in *Reason and Passion* (Joshua Rosenkranz and Bernard Schwartz eds., 1997).

31. See this issue *supra* note 4.

32. Robert Herbert, "The Real Disgrace," *N.Y. Times*, Jan. 10, 1999, sec. 4, at 21.

33. Lardner Jr. and Saferstein, "A Chief Justice-Designate with Big Ambitions Even as a Boy, Rehnquist Hoped to Change the Covenant," *Wash. Post*, (July 6, 1986), at A1; Jenkins, "The Partisan A Talk With Justice Rehnquist," *N.Y. Times* (Magazine), March 3, 1985, at 28, 35; also Garrow, supra note 6.

34. 402 U.S. 941 (1971).

35. Payne v. Tennessee, 501 U.S. 808, 844 (1991) (Marshall J. dissenting). This was Marshall's last dissent before retiring. In *Payne*, issued on the day of Marshall's retirement, Rehnquist announced the decision of the Court declaring victim-impact statements constitutional and reversing two earlier decisions in a blatant, if not cynical, disregard *of stare decisis*. See Rowan, *Dream Makers, Dream Breakers—The World of Justice Thurgood Marshall* 402–05 (1993). See also Simon, *The Center Holds: The Power Struggle Inside the Rehnquist Court* 211 (1996); Schwartz, "The Ten Greatest Justices," 31 *Tulsa L.J.* 155, 200 (1995). Schwartz analyzes Rehnquist's intention to "dismantle" the Warren jurisprudence, noting, "What is not known generally outside the Marble Palace is that Chief Justice Rehnquist has urged even more extreme views on civil rights than have appeared in his published opinions."

36. In an insightful article, Prof. Kathleen M. Sullivan suggests a number of jurisprudential grounded institutional reasons why conservative Justices might vote conservative or liberal. See Sullivan, "The Jurisprudence of the Rehnquist Court," 22 *Nova L. Rev.* 741 (1998); see also Kelso and Kelso, "How the Supreme Court Is Dealing With Precedents in Constitutional Cases," 62 *Brooklyn L. Rev.* 973 (1996). See also Smith and Jones, "The Rehnquist Court's Activities and the Risk of Injustice, "26 *Conn. L. Rev.* 53 (1993); Rosen, supra, note 6.

37. Smith and Jones, note 36.

38. 505 U.S. 833 (1992). See also Webster v. Reprod. Health Serv., 492 U.S. 490 (1989).

39. See Belsky, "Living With *Miranda*: A Reply to Professor Grano," 43 *Drake L. Rev.* 127 (1994). See also Garcia, "Is *Miranda* Dead, Was It Overruled, or Is It Irrelevant," 10 *St. Thomas L. Rev.* 461 (1998); Irons, supra note 3 at 188–211. Judge Louis O. Oberdorfer, commenting on the Fourth Amendment, recently noted that it has become riddled with exceptions and a warrant has become too often "an unnecessary luxury." Judge Louis O. Oberdorfer, *Remarks made on the 35th Anniversary of the Lawyers' Committee for Civil Rights Under Law* (May 1988). See also Simon, supra note 35, at 171–90. Simon describes the change in attitude between Brennan's decisions in criminal cases and Rehnquist's. As noted by Linda Greenhouse of *The New York Times*, Brennan's basic message was that the conviction should be thrown out because of a flagrant violation of the defendant's constitutional rights. In the Chief Justice's presentation upholding a conviction, it is clear that what matters most "is that a crime has been committed, someone must pay." Id. at 173.

40. United States v. Lopez, 514 U.S. 549 (1995); Schwartz, "Symposium: Practitioner's Guide to the October 1994 Supreme Court Term: Term Limits, Commerce and '94 Rehnquist Court," 31 *Tulsa L.J.* 521 (1996). In *Lopez*, Rehnquist authored the majority opinion which struck down the Gun-Free School Zone Act of 1990, a federal statute criminalizing gun possession within 1000 feet of school grounds. See also Seminole Tribe v. Florida, 517 U.S. 44 (1996); Brozonkala v. Virginia Polytechnic Inst. & State Univ., 132 F.3d 1997 (4th Cir. 1997), and 169 F.3d 820 (4th Cir. 1999) (en banc).

41. Before *Lopez*, there were an unbroken line of unsuccessful challenges to exercise of Congressional commerce clause power. See Kelso and Kelso, "How the Supreme Court Is Dealing with Precedents in Constitutional Law," 62 *Brooklyn L. Rev.* 973, 1069 (1996).

42. Simon, "Speech, Politics and the Rehnquist Court," 40 *N.Y.L. Sch. L. Rev.* 863, 865, 866 (1996).

43. Simon, supra note 42, at 864.

44. See, e.g., Simon, supra note 35; *Simon*, supra note 42; Toobin, "Chicken Supreme,"

The New Yorker, Aug. 14, 1995 at 80; O'Brien, "Charting The Rehnquist Court's Course: How the Center Folds, Holds and Shuffles," 40 *N.Y.L. Sch. L. Rev.* 981 (1996); Chemerinsky, "Is the Rehnquist Court Really That Conservative: An Analysis of the 1991–92 Term," 26 *Creighton L. Rev.* 487 (1993); Schwartz, "Rehnquist, Runyon and Jones—The Chief Justice, Civil Rights and *Stare Decisis,*" 31 *Tulsa L.J.* 251 (1991).

45. U.S. Constitution, Preamble.

46. See Irons, supra note 3; *The Burger Court,* supra note 2.

47. Id.

48. See, e.g., Lazarus, *Closed Chambers* (1998); Irons, supra note 3; Simon, supra note 35.

49. Chief Justice Rehnquist wrote that when judges interfere in the decision making of the elected branches of government, judges behave as a small group of fortunately situated people with a tendency to second-guess Congress, state legislatures, and state and federal administrative officers concerning what is best for the country. Rehnquist, "The Notion of a Living Constitution," 54 *Tex. L. Rev.* 693, 698 (1976). Yet this principle of majoritarianism has little effect in practice. On the last day of the 1997 term, for example, the Court found three congressional enactments to be unconstitutional. Schwartz, "A Presidential Strikeout, Federalism, RFRA, Standing, and a Stealth Court, 33 *Tulsa L.J.* 77, 87, 88 (1997).

50. See, e.g., Smith and Jones, supra note 36, at 75 ("the fact that the Rehnquist Court's judicial activism with its powerful affection for outcomes for individual liberties comes from justices who made their names as advocates of judicial restraint raises troubling questions about the hypocrisy detectable in the contradictions between judges' public statements and their actual behavior."). Professor Schwartz, in numerous writings on the Rehnquist Court, delineates the many cases in which Chief Justice Rehnquist and others who share his views have given judicial restraint a variable content. They rarely support judicial restraint when the judiciary is asked to protect civil rights and civil liberties, while they unabashedly favor an energetic activism when it comes to curtailing such rights and liberties, or to promoting business interests. Schwartz, "A Presidential Strikeout, Federalism, RFRA, Standing, and a Stealth Court," 33 *Tulsa L.J.* 77, 87, 88 (1997). For an incisive analysis of judicial activism see Henry, supra note 18, at 39–44; see also Sullivan, supra note 36.

51. Prof. Bernard Schwartz, more than anyone, has received access to unpublished opinions, drafts and other internal correspondence which provide particularly revealing insights into the Rehnquist Court. See Schwartz, *Decisions: How the Supreme Court Decides Cases* (1996). But there are many others. See, e.g., "The Court Diary of William O. Douglas," *J. Sup. Ct. History* (1995). A comprehensive bibliography of such revelations appears in Schwartz and Thomson, "Inside the Rehnquist Court, a Sanctum Sanctorum," 66 *Miss. L.J.* 177 (1996). See also Lazarus, supra note 48. Lazarus, a former law clerk to Justice Blackmun, has been accused, particularly by Judge Alex Kozinski, of violating the law clerk's obligation of confidentiality. But Lazarus essentially relies on the Marshall papers and other documents accessible to scholars. Kozinski's comments seem mean-spirited and off base.

52. In this article, the brevity of which compels an impressionistic view, I have not attempted to analyze the complexities of the philosophies of Justices, such as Justices Breyer, Ginsburg, and Souter, whose philosophies are still evolving. See, e.g., the insightful article by Jeffery Rosen, in which he presents Justice Ginsburg as the most restrained Justice on the Court, although her decision in the VMI case could certainly lead to a different conclusion. Rosen, infra note 108. Professor Schwartz has written perceptively of the Justices in the middle who often did not have a defined juristic *weltanschaung,* at times tilting in one direction, at times in the other. Schwartz, "The Burger Court in Action," in *The Burger Court,* supra note 2, at 261; see Sullivan, supra note 36.

53. Simon, supra note 35 at 308.

54. Compare Bates v. Arizona, 433 U.S. 350 (1977), with Florida Bar v. Went For It, Inc., 515 U.S. 618 (1995).

55. Swidler & Berlin v. United States, 524 U.S. 399 (1998).

56. Phillips v. Washington Legal Found., 524 U.S.156 (1998).

57. The Chief Justice's penchant for elevating the Takings Clause to a far reaching and exalted position in constitutional jurisprudence lacks a sound foundation in any doctrine of original intent or historical interpretation. See Schwartz, "Takings Clause, Poor Relations No More," 47 *Okla. L. Rev.* 417 (1994). For an "odd man out" view of the Takings Clause, see Epstein, "The Takings Jurisprudence of the Warren Court," in The *Warren Court*, supra note 29, at 159.

58. Clinton v. Jones, 519 U.S. 925 (1996).

59. Oral argument in *Florida Bar v. Went For It*, 515 U.S. 618 (1995).

60. As reported by Nina Totenberg of National Public Radio, during the oral argument on the line-item veto case, Justice Scalia remarked that he could not find anyone harmed by the line-item veto, and the Chief Justice responded, "There are probably a lot of people who are, I just don't want [them] to spend all their money paying it to lawyers."

61. Mauro, *American Lawyer, Section: Courtside* 10 (Jan. 23, 1995), quoting from oral argument in the Florida Bar v. Went For It case, 515 U.S. 618 (1995).

62. Post, "Judicial Management and Judicial Disinterest: The Achievements and Perils of Chief Justice William Howard Taft," 1 *J. Sup. Ct. History* 50, 69 (1998).

63. Id.

64. See generally Shestack, supra note 2.

65. Id.

66. Id.

67. I refer to my conversations with federal judges active in the Federal Judicial Center.

68. *Remarks of Chief Justice William H. Rehnquist, D.C. Circuit Judicial Conference Session on Long Range Planning* (June 10, 1993).

69. See, e.g., *The Chief Justice's Year End Reports on The Federal Judiciary for the Years 1992–1998; Remarks of the Chief Justice, National Conference of the Federal Judges Association* 3 (May 13, 1997).

70. Greenhouse, "A Window on the Court, Justices Take An Assertive Role to Reduce Habeas Corpus Petitions by State Inmates," N.Y. *Times*, May 6, 1992, at A1, A20. Initially, Rehnquist attempted to curtail habeas corpus by urging Congress to do so. When this did not materialize to the extent he wished, he turned to judicial means to do so. See also Smith and Jones, supra note 36.

71. Greenhouse, "Judges Challenge Rehnquist's Rule on the Death Penalty: An Extraordinary Move," N.Y. *Times*, Oct. 6, 1989, at A1. In February 1991, Chief Justice Rehnquist shuffled the Justices' circuit responsibilities and chose Justice Scalia as the Circuit Justice to oversee the Fifth Circuit—the circuit with the nation's largest number of death-row cases. Justice Scalia announced immediately that he would not grant extensions for filing deadlines, even for prisoners who were forced to represent themselves because they lacked professional assistance in seeking Supreme Court review. Greenhouse, "Scalia Tightens Ruling on Death Penalty Appeals," N.Y. Times, Feb. 22, 1991, at B16.

72. *Federal Judiciary Year-End Rep.* (1996).

73. *Federal Judiciary Year-End Rep.* (1997).

74. As President of the ABA, I met several times with Senator Orrin Hatch, chairman of the Senate Judiciary Committee, to urge prompt hearings on judicial nominees. Resolutions of the ABA Board of Governors and articles and speeches by ABA spokespersons did likewise.

75. See, e.g., *1996 Year-End Report on the Federal Judiciary*. "This disparity between the salaries of the judicial and legal professions cannot continue independently without compro-

mising the morale of the federal judiciary and eventually its quality" (p. 3); *Remarks of the Chief Justice, National Conference of the Federal Judges Association* (May 13, 1997). During my term as president of the ABA, I marshaled a grass-roots lobby to increase judicial salaries and to delink them from congressional salaries. The most we could achieve was a cost-of-living increase in judicial salaries.

76. See, e.g., Marcotte, "Rehnquist: Cut Jurisdiction," 75 *A.B.A. J.* 27 (1989); Rehnquist, "Seen in a Glass Darkly: The Future of the Federal Courts, *American University Commencement Speech* (April 9, 1996); 35 (2) *ABA, Wash. Letter,* 3 (1999).

77. See, e.g., *Federal Judiciary Year-End Rep.* (1994–97). On occasion, the Chief Justice has spoken forcefully and effectively on independence of the judiciary. See, e.g., Editorial, "An Alert From the Chief Justice," *N.Y. Times,* April 11, 1996, at A 24.

78. See, e.g., White, *The American Judicial Tradition Profiles of Leading American Judges* 428–31 (expanded ed. 1988); Garrow, supra note 6.

79. In 1986, Rehnquist had volunteered that a one-third decline in the Court's annual caseload from 150 to 90 would be unseemly, but by the tenth anniversary of his statement, the Court had reduced its annual workload by more than half, from 150 to 75. An average of about ninety cases a year is popular with the Justices. See Garrow, supra note 6. Lawyers who petition the Court for certiorari are less approving, as many important issues never get heard. See Rehnquist, "The Changing Role of the Supreme Court," 14 *Fla. St. U.L. Rev.* 1 (1986). (At that time, he stated that review of 150 cases was not enough to address "the numerous important statutory and constitutional questions. . . .")

80. Kennedy, "Law and Belief," *Address to American Bar Association, San Francisco, CA* (Aug. 1997).

81. Justice Thomas, for example, is often lavish in his praise of the civility of his colleagues. Yet, some of his opinions have been quite acerbic toward other Justices. In an implausible speech before a restauranteurs group, he said, "There is no effort whatsoever to horse trade. We rarely know how someone will vote before they come to conference. I have yet to hear an unkind word spoken between Justices." *USA Today,* Sept. 15, 1998, at 5A.

82. 517 U.S. 620 (1996).

83. Id. at 639 ("our constitutional jurisprudence has achieved terminal silliness"); id. at 645 ("The Court's portrayal . . . is so false as to be comical"; and "It is also nothing short of preposterous . . . ").

84. 492 U.S. 490 (1989). See also Garrow, supra note 6.

85. Garrow, supra note 6, at 69.

86. United States v. Virginia, 518 U.S. 515, 594 (1996) ("Any lawyer who gave that advice to the Commonwealth ought to have been either disbarred or committed.").

87. Biskupic, "The Distant Voices of Justice Remarks are Reminders of High Court's 9 Separate Personalities," *Dallas Morning News,* May 3, 1998, at A 26.

88. Przybyszewski, "The Dilemma of Judicial Biography or Who Cares Who Is the Great Appellate Judge? Gerald Gunther or Learned Hand," 21 *Law & Soc. Inquiry* 135,144 (1996).

89. Breyer, *Address to American Bar Association House of Delegates, Chicago, IL* (Aug. 8, 1988).

90. Id.

91. The nonjudicial writings of the Justices can have a profound influence on the legal profession. Oliver Wendell Holmes's *Common Law,* Benjamin N. Cardozo's *Nature of the Judicial Process,* and Felix Frankfurter's many articles on statutory interpretation and legal process are prime examples. See, e.g., Frankfurter, *Some Reflections on the Reading of Statues* (1947); Frankfurter, *The Public and Its Government* (1930). To be sure, few Justices have that jurisprudential depth, but other Justices, such as Hughes, Black, Brennan, and

Goldberg, have also been able to give direction to the bar, stimulate initiatives, and inspire the profession. See, e.g., Hughes, *The Supreme Court of the United States: Its Foundation, Methods, and Achievements, and Interpretation* (1928); Black, *A Constitutional Faith* (1968); Brennan, *Why Have a Bill of Rights?* H.L.A. Hart Lecture, University College, Oxford, England (May 26, 1989); Goldberg, *The Defenses of Freedom: The Public Papers of Arthur J. Goldberg* (Daniel Patrick Moynihan ed., 1966).

92. Brennan, in particular, has written profoundly on constitutional issues and professional topics. Brennan, supra note 91;. Brennan, "The Worldwide Influence of the U.S. Constitution as a Charter of Human Rights," *Address at Columbia Law School Bicentennial Celebration* (Nov. 20, 1997). See generally, the essays in *Reason and Passion* (Rosenkranz and Schwartz ed., 1997).

93. See Shestack, supra note 2.

94. See, e.g., "Thomas Jefferson and His Contemporaries," *Remarks at the University of Virginia* (April 12, 1993) (impeachment); "The Future of the Federal Courts," *Remarks at American University* (April 9, 1996); "Civil Liberty and the Civil War," *Edward & Marion Gauer Lecture* (Sept. 10, 1996); "Civil Liberty and the Civil War," *Remarks at University of Indiana* (Oct. 26, 1996); "The American Constitutional Experience, *Remarks at Third Circuit Judicial Conference* (April 2, 1996); *Remarks at the Columbia University School of Law Commencement* (May 25, 1981); *Remarks at the Volpariso University School of Law Commencement* (May 21, 1991); *Remarks at the George Mason University Commencement* (May 22, 1993).

95. Rehnquist, *All the Laws But One: Civil Liberties in War Time* (1998).

96. In 1997, Chief Justice Rehnquist applied four thick golden stripes to the upper part of each sleeve of his robe. The Court's press officer said that "The Chief Justice designed the robe himself," after viewing a performance of Gilbert and Sullivan's *Iolanthe*, in which the Lord Chancellor wore a similar robe. Reske, "Showing His Stripes," 81 A.B.A. *J.* 35 (1995). The Chief Justice was later quoted in the press defending his robe by saying that the British Lord Chancellor's robe is similarly decorated. Professor Schwartz has wryly noted that the Gilbert and Sullivan touch here is that the robe of the Lord Chancellor is not similar. Schwartz, "Symposium," 31 *Tulsa L.J.* 521 (1996).

97. *Remarks of the Chief Justice at the Catholic University School of Law Commencement* (May 25, 1996); *Remarks at Valpariso University School of Law Commencement*, supra note 94.

98. *Remarks at closing session* of *Just Solutions: A Public Forum on the Justice System* (May 3, 1994); *Remarks at The Warner Theatre* (Oct. 21, 1993). One of the Chief Justice's more probing speeches was the Kastemeier Lecture Reprise at the Fourth Circuit Judicial Conference (June 2, 1993). See also *Seen in a Glass Darkly: The Future of the Federal Courts*, University of Wisconsin, Madison, WI (Sept. 15, 1992).

99. Cornell School of Law, *The United States Supreme Court* (last modified March 30, 1999) <http://supct.law.cornell.edu/supct/Justices/Stevens.bio.html>.

100. Speech at Opening Assembly of the American Bar Association, Orlando, FL (Aug. 3, 1996). Justice Stevens's official biographical data lists only twenty-eight citations to his writings and addresses. *Almanac of the Federal Judiciary, The Supreme Court* (1998).

101. Savage, "First Woman on Supreme Court Carves out Influential Niche Among Justices," 83 A.B.A. *J.* 98 (Aug. 1997).

102. These were Oliver Wendell Holmes, Charles Evans Hughes, Tom C. Clark, Felix Frankfurter, Lewis E. Powell, Warren E. Burger, Thurgood Marshall and William J. Brennan, Jr.

103. Justice O'Connor usually attends annual two- to three-day meetings of the CEELI volunteers, as she did in Krakow, Poland, in 1997 and Bucharest, Romania, in 1998.

104. O'Connor, "The History of the Suffrage Movement," *Address on the 75th Anniversary of Women's Right to Vote, Phoenix, Arizona* (Sept. 23, 1995).

105. O'Connor, "Vital Values," *Address to Women in Democracy Conference, Vienna, Austria* (July 11, 1997).

106. O'Connor, "Religious Freedom: America's Quest for Principles," *Howard Trienen lecture at Northwestern University Law School, Chicago, IL* (March 4, 1997).

107. O'Connor, "The Life of the Law: Principles of Logic and Experience from the United States, *Address at University of Wisconsin, Madison, WI* (Oct. 20, 1995).

108. O'Connor, *Address to the ABA Standing Committee on Law and National Security, Washington, D.C.* (Nov. 1998).

109. Epstein, "The Heat Seeking Justice," *Phila. Inquirer* (Magazine,) Oct. 5, 1997, at 25; see also Rosen, "Original Sin," *New Republic*, May 5, 1997, at 26; Kunen, "One Angry Man," *Time*, July 8, 1997; Elsasser, "No Contest: Top Court's Top Fighter Is Scalia," *Chi. Trib.*, May 27, 1997; Rosen, "Ruth Bader Ginsburg and the Clinton Era Court," *N. Y. Times* (Magazine), Oct. 5, 1997, at 60.

110. Garrow, supra note 6, at 68 (quoting Judge Kozinski).

111. The only issue I have heard Justice Scalia state was not "germane" was the ABA's endorsement (about a decade ago) of a resolution that government should not interfere with a woman's choice regarding abortion.

112. "A Justice Among Us," *Vanderbilt Mag.*, 1997, at 2.

113. Anthony Kennedy, "Law and Belief," *Address to the American Bar Association, San Francisco* (Aug. 2, 1997).

114. Pollack, "A U.S. District Court Judge in Philadelphia Says Civility Matters for Lawyers (and that includes Judges), Both as Professionals and as Citizens," 84 *A.B.A.J.* 66 (Aug. 1998).

115. *Remarks delivered in Philadelphia*, PA (Dec. 4, 1998); Pollack supra note 114.

116. Stein, "The Asian Law Initiatives Council Coordinates Programs and Activities That Foster the Establishment of the Rule of Law in China and Other Asian Countries," 85 *A.B.A.J.* 86 (Feb. 1999).

117. Sloviter, "Reflections as We Approach the Millennium," 70 *Temp. L. Rev.* 1081-82 (1997).

118. "As He Turns 90 Brennan Criticizes Death Penalty," *Wash. Post*, April 28, 1996, at A 7.

119. McGrory, "So Long, Pal," *Wash. Post*, July 31, 1997, at A 2.

120. Carmody, "The TV Column," *Wash. Post*, March 11, 1994, at G 4.

121. Walker, "Black Lawyers Not Likely to Warm to Thomas; Speech Today Is Expected to Renew Civil Rights Debate," *Boston Globe*, July 29, 1998, at A 3.

122. In a July 31, 1998 editorial, *The New York Times* observed: "Clarence Thomas unloaded on his critics the other day, twisting the case against him just as he did seven years ago when the Senate was considering his nomination to the Supreme Court. Then he complained he was the target of a 'high-tech lynching.' This week he charged critics with vilifying him because he is a black who does not hold his liberal views. . . . What Justice Thomas seems unable to appreciate is that the issue is not his race, but the content of his ideas." *N.Y. Times*, July 31, 1998, at A 20. See also Higginbotham, Jr., "An Open Letter to Justice Clarence Thomas From a Federal Judicial Colleague," 140 *U. Pa. L. Rev.* 1005 (1992).

123. Rosen, "Ruth Bader Ginsburg and the Clinton Era Court," *N.Y. Times* (Magazine), Oct. 5, 1997, at 60, 62.

124. See, e.g., Ginsburg, "Remarks for American Law Institute Annual Dinner: May 19, 1994," 38 *St. Louis U. L.J.* 881 (1994), her witty and altogether delightful address to the American Law Institute on May 19, 1994, about the Court's processes; see also *Remarks for White*

House Ceremony (Aug. 10, 1993); *Remarks at Celebration 40, Harvard Law School* (Oct. 2, 1993); *Address for Georgetown University Law Center* (April 28, 1995); *Remarks for American Jewish Committee Dinner, Washington, DC* (May 4, 1995); *An Overview of Court Review for Constitutionality in the United States, Louisiana State University* (Oct. 24, 1996).

125. *Atlanta J. & Const.*, July 13, 1994, at A 20.

126. Breyer, supra note 89.

127. Savage, "Out of the Extraordinary," 81 *A.B.A.J.* 42, 44 (March 1995).

128. Breyer, "Judicial Review: A Practicing Judge's Perspective," *H.L.A. Hart Memorial Lecture, University College, Oxford* (May 7, 1998).

129. *Address at the Annual Meeting of the American Association for the Advancement of Science, Philadelphia, PA* (Feb. 16, 1998); see also Breyer, "The Interdependence of Science and Law," 82 *Judicature* 24 (1998).

130. Breyer, *Speech to the Accent on Architecture Awards Gala* (Jan. 30, 1996).

131. Breyer, "Three Supreme Court Justices and the Zionist Ideal," *Address to Conference of Presidents of Major American Jewish Organizations* (Nov. 13, 1997).

132. Breyer, *Diritto Communitario Europe, E. Diritto Nazinale* (Milano–Dott. A. Giuffre ed., 1997).

133. Breyer, "The Media and Its Relations with the Supreme Court," *delivered at meeting of the Organization of the Supreme Courts of America, Panama* (Jan. 29, 1998).

134. Breyer, "Crimes Against Humanity: Nuremberg 1946," *Keynote address for the 1996 Days of Remembrance, Capitol Rotunda, Washington, DC* (April 16, 1996); see also Breyer, "Crimes Against Humanity: Nuremberg," 1946, 71 *N.Y.U. L. Rev.* 1161 (1996).

135. "In Memoriam: Louis L. Jaffe," 116 *Harv. L. Rev.* 1203 (1997); In Memoriam: Philip E. Areeda," 104 *Harv. L. Rev.* 889 (1996); *Donald F. Turner, Antitrust Bull.* 725 Winter 1996.

136. See Rehnquist, supra note 7 at 655.

137. Id.

11

THE CONSTITUTIONAL JURISPRUDENCE
OF THE REHNQUIST COURT

ERWIN CHEMERINSKY

Is There a Constitutional Jurisprudence of the Rehnquist Court?

I was honored in 1997 when Bernard Schwartz called to ask me to present a paper on the constitutional jurisprudence of the Rehnquist Court. I have so admired Professor Schwartz's work and tremendously looked forward to meeting him at this symposium. In our telephone conversation, my immediate response to the topic was to ask him if he thought that there was a constitutional jurisprudence of the Rehnquist Court. He chuckled and said that he'd be interested in what I had to say about that.

It is tempting to say that there is no constitutional jurisprudence to the Rehnquist Court's decisions. Indeed, almost a decade ago, I wrote that "[t]he Rehnquist Court lacks a theory for how the Constitution should be interpreted, and instead approaches judicial review by an oft-stated desire to avoid judicial value imposition. Thus, the Court's jurisprudence is largely defined negatively, by what it wants to avoid."[1]

The Rehnquist Court is, and has been throughout its existence, an ideologically divided Court which often fails to produce majority opinions. The practical reality, at least since 1991 when Clarence Thomas joined the Court, is that results usually depend on whether the conservative bloc of Rehnquist, Scalia, and Thomas can get the votes of O'Connor and Kennedy. Frequently they do and many cases have been decided by five to four margins with that group in the majority. For example, the affirmative action cases and the federalism rulings in the 1990s—undoubtedly among the most important decisions of the Rehnquist Court—have had Rehnquist, O'Connor, Scalia, Kennedy, and Thomas in the majority, with Stevens, Souter, Breyer, and Ginsburg dissenting.[2] But this description of the internal political reality of the Rehnquist Court does not reveal its constitutional jurisprudence.

It is tempting to say that the jurisprudence of the Rehnquist Court is simply Reagan conservatism. Six of the nine Justices on the Court were appointed by Presidents Reagan or Bush. In many areas, such as affirmative action and criminal procedure and capital punishment, the Court has been everything a conservative Republican could have hoped for. Yet, in other areas, the Court undoubtedly has disappointed conservatives.

In its early years, it found that flag burning is constitutionally protected speech, with Justices Scalia and Kennedy providing two of the votes for the majority in the five to four decisions.[3] The Rehnquist Court, to the chagrin of the political right, has not overturned *Roe v. Wade*[4] or *Lemon v. Kurtzman*[5] or *Miranda v. Arizona*.[6] The conservative desire to revitalize economic liberties has barely happened; some greater protections have been provided under the Takings Clause,[7] but the Court has refused to use either the Contracts Clause or substantive due process to protect economic rights.[8]

In its initial years, the Court was staunchly majoritarian. In the 1988–89 Term—perhaps the first real Term of the Rehnquist Court because it was Justice Kennedy's initial full Term on the Court—the Court rarely declared a government action to be unconstitutional. For example, in the forty-seven nonunanimous constitutional cases that Term, Chief Justice Rehnquist voted against the government only twice.[9] In more recent years, the Court has been less majoritarian. A year ago, for instance, the Supreme Court declared unconstitutional several major federal statutes including the Religious Freedom Restoration Act,[10] the Communications Decency Act of 1996,[11] and the Brady Bill.[12]

Is there a jurisprudence, a philosophy of law, that unifies this? Indeed, before even considering whether the Court as a whole as a constitutional jurisprudence, do the individual Justices have what can be fairly described as their own philosophy of law? Undoubtedly, Justice Scalia has such a philosophy and has articulated it in both his opinions and in scholarly writings.[13] And Justice Thomas seems to have a philosophy too: agree with Scalia.[14] But is it possible to identify the constitutional jurisprudence of Justice O'Connor or Stevens or Ginsburg?

The initial step in determining whether there is a constitutional jurisprudence for the Rehnquist Court is to see if there is any pattern to its decision making. Are its results largely random, simply a product of who can put together a coalition of five in a given case? In the second section of this chapter, I suggest that there are patterns that can be used to describe a large percentage of the Rehnquist Court's constitutional cases. My focus in this part of the chapter is descriptive in identifying the pattern, not normative in evaluating it.

In the third section, I consider whether there is a constitutional jurisprudence that underlies the pattern. I suggest that the Rehnquist Court strongly emphasizes history in its decision making. Although not invariably, often decisions are justified, at least in large part, by reference to history. Moreover, the Rehnquist Court's approach to history is different from its predecessors. Previously, the Court focused on statements from the Constitutional Convention or from the *Federalist Papers* as the primary evidence of the framers' intent.[15] But the Rehnquist Court's analysis quite often centers on historical practices at the time of the ratification of a constitutional provision as evidence of meaning.

In the fourth section, I criticize this approach to constitutional interpretation. It rests on numerous unjustified, and I believe unjustifiable, assumptions: that history should control contemporary constitutional analysis; that there were uniform practices at the timing of the framing, and that the framers and ratifiers wanted to constitutionalize the practices of their time.

Finally, in the conclusion, I briefly return to the question whether there is a constitutional jurisprudence of the Rehnquist Court and conclude that there is, although not one evident in every decision. It is a jurisprudence animated by conservative political values and that uses history selectively to justify its conclusions.

Is There a Pattern to Rehnquist Court Constitutional Rulings?

The first step in identifying a jurisprudence of the Rehnquist Court is to see whether there is any pattern to its rulings. I would suggest that there is a pattern and that the vast majority of its decisions, though certainly not all, can be accounted for in five propositions.

1. *In conflicts between the federal government and state governments, state governments prevail.*[16] The most dramatic area of change in the law during the Rehnquist Court has been in the protection of federalism. Indeed, the Court has shown little deference to Congress in matters of federalism and has aggressively protected states from perceived federal encroachment. The Court has accomplished this in three ways.

First, the Court has narrowly construed the scope of Congress's powers. For the first time in sixty years, in *United States v. Lopez,*[17] the Supreme Court declared a federal law unconstitutional as exceeding the scope of Congress's Commerce Clause authority. By a five to four margin, the Supreme Court declared unconstitutional the Gun-Free School Zones Act of 1990, which made it a federal crime to have a gun within 1,000 feet of a school.[18] In *City of Boerne v. Flores,*[19] the Court narrowly circumscribed the scope of Congress's authority to legislate under section five of the Fourteenth Amendment. The Court ruled that Congress may not expand the scope of rights or create additional rights but, rather, only may provide remedies for rights recognized by the judiciary.

Second, the Court has used the Tenth Amendment to limit Congress's powers. The Burger Court briefly flirted with this in *National League of Cities v. Usery*[20] but ultimately abandoned it in Garcia v. *San Antonio Metropolitan Transit Authority.*[21] In *Garcia,* the Court concluded that the protection of state sovereignty is left to Congress and that the judiciary should not use the Tenth Amendment to invalidate federal statutes. However, in *New York v. United States*[22] and in *Printz v. United States,*[23] the Supreme Court revived the Tenth Amendment as a limit on Congress and concluded that federal laws are unconstitutional if they compel states to enact statutes or regulations or to administer federal programs.

Finally, the Court has expanded states immunity to suit in federal court. In *Seminole Tribe v. Florida,* the Court limited the ability of Congress to authorize suits against states in federal court.[24] The Court ruled that Congress may permit litigation against state governments in federal courts only when acting under section five of the Fourteenth Amendment; Congress may not do so when acting under its Commerce Clause power or any other Constitutional authority.

In each of these cases, a federal statute was declared unconstitutional based on federalism considerations. A cornerstone of the Rehnquist Court's approach to constitutional law has been the protection of states from perceived federal intrusions.[25]

2. *Conservative moral judgments are upheld; government actions combatting sin—sex, drugs, and gambling—are upheld.* A striking but often overlooked pattern for the Rehnquist Court has been its consistency in deferring to government efforts to combat what often has been regarded as sinful behavior: nonmarital sex, drugs, and gambling. In this way, the Court's decisions have reflected and embodied conservative morality.

First, some of the Rehnquist Court's most troubling decisions have been in deferring to government regulation of sexual activity.[26] For example, in *Bennis v. Michigan*,[27] the Court upheld confiscating a car that had been used in picking up a prostitute, even though there also was an innocent owner of the automobile. John Bennis was arrested for having sex with a prostitute in his automobile. Bennis was convicted of gross indecency. In addition, a Michigan court ordered the car forfeited as a public nuisance because it had been used in committing the crime. The automobile, however, was jointly owned with Bennis's wife, Tina Bennis. She argued that due process was violated by the state's failure to accord her an innocent owner defense to the seizure.

In a five to four decision, with Chief Justice Rehnquist writing the majority opinion, the Court ruled in favor of the state and rejected this due process claim. The Court said that the forfeiture action was permissible because "[t]he State here sought to deter illegal activity that contributes to neighborhood deterioration and unsafe streets. The Bennis automobile, it is conceded, facilitated and was used in criminal activity."[28] The car, of course, was completely incidental to the sexual act; it could have occurred anywhere. Yet, the Court sided with the government, even over the innocent wife's protestation.

Another case reflecting the Court's conservative morality toward matters of sex is *Alexander v. United States*.[29] The Court held that the seizure and destruction of books, magazines, and films from a person convicted of an obscenity law violation did not constitute a prior restraint. Ferris Alexander, an owner of more than a dozen bookstores and theaters dealing in sexually explicit material, was convicted of selling seven items (four magazines and three videotapes) that were deemed to be obscene. He was sentenced to six years in prison and fined $100,000. In addition, pursuant to the federal RICO statute, the court ordered that the contents of all of his stores be seized.[30] The books and magazines were literally burned by the government; the videotapes were crushed. Some $9 million in merchandise was destroyed, even though only seven items had been found to be obscene.

The Court, in a five to four decision, upheld this action as constitutional and ruled that it did not constitute a prior restraint. Chief Justice Rehnquist, writing for the majority, said that the government may seize the assets of businesses convicted of violating RICO and it is irrelevant if those assets are in the form of books and videos that are protected by the First Amendment. The Court's decision, allowing $9 million worth of books, magazines, and films to be destroyed without any finding that they were obscene or unprotected by the First Amendment is deeply troubling and reflects its conservative morality.

Not every case involving sex has produced a victory for the government.[31] Yet, decisions such as *Bennis* and *Alexander* are notable and can be most easily explained by the Court's underlying view toward the activity involved.

Second, many commentators have noted that the Rehnquist Court has essentially carved a drugs exception to the Fourth Amendment. In case after case, the Court has upheld government enforcement efforts against drugs ranging from drug testing[32] to drug couriers profiles[33] to searches with low-flying airplanes.[34] Indeed, in criminal cases involving drugs, it is difficult to think of cases in which the government has lost before the Rehnquist Court.

Finally, as to gambling, although the Rehnquist Court often has been protective of commercial speech,[35] in *United States v. Edge Broadcasting Co.*, the Court upheld a federal law that prohibited lottery advertising by radio stations located in States that did not operate lotteries.[36] A radio station in southern Virginia wished to broadcast advertisements for the North Carolina lottery. Evidence demonstrated that more than 92 percent of the broadcast station's audience resided in North Carolina, where lotteries were legal. However, the federal law prohibited the radio station from broadcasting such advertisements because it was located in Virginia, which did not have a lottery. The Court upheld the law based on the government's substantial interest in discouraging gambling by limiting advertisements for it.

All these cases reflect the Court's accepting the government's justifications of combatting behavior that traditionally would be regarded as "victimless crimes." In each decision, the Court reflected traditional conservative moral sensibilities.

3. *No new fundamental rights have been recognized; existing fundamental rights are often substantially narrowed.* During the eleven-year history of the Rehnquist Court, not one additional fundamental right has been recognized. The Court's decisions rejecting the claim of a right to physician-assisted suicide are typical and reveal why it will be virtually impossible to persuade the Rehnquist Court to recognize new fundamental rights. In *Washington v. Glucksberg*, the Court rejected the claim that the Washington law prohibiting assisted suicide violated a fundamental right protected under the Due Process Clause.[37] Chief Justice Rehnquist's opinion for the Court began by observing that a right is protected as fundamental under the due process clause only when supported by history or tradition. Rehnquist then stated that "for over 700 years, the Anglo-American common-law tradition has punished or otherwise disapproved of both suicide and attempting suicide."[38] Rehnquist noted that "[i]n almost every State—indeed, in almost every western democracy—it is a crime to assist suicide."[39]

Because the Court determined that "the asserted 'right' to assistance in committing suicide is not a fundamental liberty interest protected by the due process clause,"[40] the Washington law was to be upheld as long as it meet a rational basis test. The Court found that the law reasonably served many legitimate interests. The Court found, for example, that the state has important interests in the preservation of life, in protecting the integrity and ethics of the medical profession, in protecting vulnerable groups, and in stopping the path to voluntary and even involuntary euthanasia.

Similarly, in *Vacco v. Quill*,[41] the Supreme Court held that laws prohibiting physician-assisted suicide do not violate the Equal Protection Clause. Chief Justice

Rehnquist, again writing for the majority, initially noted that the prohibition of assisted suicide neither discriminated against a suspect class, such as against a racial minority, nor violated a fundamental right, because *Washington v. Glucksberg* had expressly repudiated that contention. Under equal protection analysis this means that the law was to be upheld so long as it met a rational basis test.

The rejection of a right to physician-assisted suicide is reflective of the Rehnquist Court's unwillingness to recognize additional fundamental rights. The methodology—claiming that a right will be found only if there is a clear tradition of protecting such a liberty—makes it extremely unlikely that any additional fundamental rights will be recognized. The focus on history and tradition, described in more detail in the third section of this chapter and criticized in the fourth section, virtually by definition negates the ability to safeguard additional rights; the absence of protection for the right evidences its nonexistence.

Moreover, the Supreme Court has substantially narrowed the scope of some previously recognized rights. This has been so both with regard to enumerated and unenumerated rights. For example, in 1990, in *Employment Division v. Smith*,[42] the law of the Free Exercise Clause changed dramatically. The Court held that the Free Exercise Clause cannot be used to challenge a neutral law of general applicability. In other words, no matter how much a law burdens religious practices, it is constitutional under *Smith* as long as it does not single out religious behavior for punishment and was not motivated by a desire to interfere with religion.

For example, in *Smith*, the Court said that a law prohibiting consumption of peyote, a hallucinogenic substance did not violate the Free Exercise Clause even though such use was required by some Native American religions. The Court explained that the state law prohibiting consumption of peyote applied to everyone in the state and did not punish conduct solely because it was religiously motivated. Justice Scalia, writing for the majority, declared "that the right of free exercise does not relieve an individual of the obligation to comply with a 'valid and neutral law of general applicability of the ground that the law proscribes (or prescribes) conduct that his religion prescribes (or proscribes).'"[43] The vast majority of free exercise challenges are to neutral laws of general applicability that burden religion; all are virtually certain to fail after *Smith*.[44]

Finally, an important example of the narrowing of existing nonenumerated rights is *Michael H. v. Gerald D.*[45] Although prior decisions expressly recognized parental rights as fundamental even for nonmarried fathers,[46] the Supreme Court ruled that a state may create an irrebuttable presumption that a married woman's husband is the father of her child even though it negates all of the biological father's rights.

Michael H. involved a married woman who conceived a child as a result of an affair. The biological father was regularly involved in the child's life and sought a court order granting visitation rights. California law, however, created a presumption that a married woman's husband is the father of her child if they were cohabitating and if the husband is not impotent or sterile. The California law allowed this presumption to be rebutted only within two years after the child's birth and only if the husband or wife filed a motion in court. The California court relied on this statute to deny the biological father of all parental rights, including visitation.

The Supreme Court, in a five to four decision, held that this was constitutional. The Court said that the biological father did not have a liberty interest in a relationship with his child because there was no tradition of protecting father's rights when the mother is married to someone else. Justice Scalia, writing for the plurality, remarked: "What counts is whether the States in fact award substantive parental rights to the natural father of a child conceived within, and born into, an extant marital union that wishes to embrace the child. We are not aware of a single case, old or new, that has done so. This is not the stuff of which fundamental rights qualifying as liberty interests are made."[47]

Justice Scalia, writing at this point just for himself and Chief Justice Rehnquist,[48] said that the Supreme Court should protect rights under the Due Process Clause only if there is a tradition, stated at the most specific level of abstraction, for safeguarding the liberty.[49] Scalia's point was that the general tradition of protecting unmarried father's rights was irrelevant because there was not a specific tradition of protecting unmarried fathers when the child was conceived as a result of an adulterous relationship. Scalia wrote: "The need, if arbitrary decisionmaking is to be avoided, [is] to adopt the most specific tradition as the point of reference. . . . Although assuredly having the virtue (if it be that) of leaving judges free to decide as they think best when the unanticipated occurs, a rule of law that binds neither by text nor by any particular, identifiable tradition is no rule of law at all."[50]

This approach ensures that virtually no nontextual rights will be protected by the Court. Again, the absence of legislative protection of a right becomes virtually unrefutable evidence of its nonexistence. I regard these cases—*Washington v. Glucksberg, Employment Division v. Smith, Michael H. v. Gerald D.*—as among the most important rulings of the Rehnquist Court; they clearly reflect its views toward judicial protection of individual rights.

To be sure, in some areas, the Rehnquist Court has not fulfilled the conservative's hope for overruling earlier decisions recognizing individual rights. For instance, in *Planned Parenthood v. Casey*,[51] there only were four votes to overrule *Roe v. Wade*. Yet, even here, the Rehnquist Court has cut back on the scope of the right, for example, by holding that strict scrutiny no longer is to be used in evaluating government regulations of abortions prior to viability.

4. No new suspect classifications have been recognized; affirmative action programs to benefit minorities have been invalidated. The Rehnquist Court has not approved the use of intermediate or strict scrutiny for any additional type of discrimination. Before the Rehnquist Court began, it was clearly established that strict scrutiny is to be used for discrimination based on race, national origin, and alienage, and intermediate scrutiny is applied to discrimination against nonmarital children and based on gender.[52] No additional type of discrimination has been recognized as worthy of heightened scrutiny. For example, in *Heller v. Doe*,[53] the Court found that discrimination based on mental disability should receive only rational basis review. In *Romer v. Evans*,[54] the Court used the rational basis test to invalidate a state initiative that repealed laws protecting gays and lesbians from discrimination and that precluded the enactment of future antidiscrimination laws.

Perhaps the most notable feature of the Rehnquist Court's equal protection decisions has been its almost unflagging hostility to all forms of affirmative action. In

Richmond v. J.A. Croson Company,[55] the Supreme Court expressly held that strict scrutiny should be used in evaluating state and local affirmative action programs. The Court invalidated a Richmond, Virginia plan to set aside 30 percent of public works monies for minority-owned businesses.[56] Five Justices—O'Connor, Rehnquist, White, Kennedy, and Scalia—wrote or joined in opinions declaring that strict scrutiny was the appropriate test in evaluating such affirmative action plans.[57]

Although a year later, in *Metro Broadcasting, Inc. v. Federal Communications Commission*[58] the Supreme Court held that congressionally approved affirmative action programs only need to meet intermediate scrutiny, this was expressly overruled in *Adarand Constructors Co. v. Pena.*[59] Between 1990, when *Metro Broadcasting* was decided, and 1995, when *Adarand* was before the Court, four of the Justices in the *Metrobroadcasting* majority, but none of the Justices in the dissent, resigned. In *Adarand*, the four dissenters from *Metro Broadcasting* were joined by Justice Thomas to create a majority to overrule *Metro Broadcasting.*[60] The Court thus concluded that "federal racial classifications, like those of a State, must serve a compelling governmental interest, and must be narrowly tailored to further that interest." [61]

Justice O'Connor, writing for the plurality in *Adarand*, said that although the Court was adopting strict scrutiny as the appropriate test for all affirmative action, it wanted to "dispel the notion that strict scrutiny is strict in theory, but fatal in fact."[62] O'Connor said that "[w]hen race-based action is necessary to further a compelling interest, such action is within constitutional constraints if it satisfies the 'narrow tailoring' test this Court has set out in previous cases."[63]

However, although Justice O'Connor says that strict scrutiny for affirmative action need not be fatal in fact, she never has voted in favor of a race-based affirmative action program. Indeed, the other major area in which the Court has considered affirmative action has been in the area of voting. In a series of decisions, the Court has held that the government cannot draw election districts based on race to help elect racial minorities.[64]

5. *Criminal defendants virtually always lose in cases involving criminal procedure and habeas corpus.* The area in which the Rehnquist Court has most satisfied conservative expectations is in the areas of criminal procedure and habeas corpus. Although the Court did not overrule major precedents such as *Miranda v. Arizona* or abolish the exclusionary rule, it repeatedly has cut back on Fourth and Fifth Amendment rights. Likewise, though the Court did not eliminate the exclusioanry rule, it did expand the good faith exception to it.[65]

For example, as mentioned earlier, the Court essentially has carved a drugs exception to the Fourth Amendment. This is especially true in cases involving cars and drugs. A particularly notable case is *Whren v. United States,*[66] which makes it virtually impossible to challenge a police stop as pretextual. *Whren* involved a traffic stop made by plainclothes police officers who were prohibited from making routine traffic stops by their department's regulations. Nonetheless, the Court held that this was not an unconstitutional pretextual stop in violation of the Fourth Amendment's prohibition against unreasonable searches and seizures as long as there was sufficient probable cause to justify it. Police officers can virtually always find something to justify stopping a person.

In *Maryland v. Wilson,*[67] the Court held that when police officer makes a lawful traffic stop, the officer's automatic right to order the driver to exit the vehicle extends to the passenger. And in *Ohio v. Robinette,*[68] the Court ruled that the Fourth Amendment does not require police officers to inform motorists, lawfully stopped for traffic violations, that legal detention has concluded before any subsequent interrogation or search will be found to be consensual. Together these cases give the police broad authority to stop any car, search all of its occupants, and question them almost indefinitely.

Even more significant has been the Rehnquist Court's restrictions on habeas corpus. Although perhaps now overshadowed by the even more dramatic limitations imposed by the Antiterrorism and Effective Death Penalty Act,[69] the Rehnquist Court has substantially narrowed the availability of habeas corpus relief, especially in capital cases.[70] For example, in *McCleskey v. Zant,*[71] the Court held that successive habeas corpus petitions could not be brought unless the inmate could show "cause" for not presenting the issue in the first petition and "prejudice" to not having the successive petition heard. *Teague v. Lane*[72] is one of the Supreme Court's most important habeas corpus decisions in decades in that it substantially limited the ability of federal courts to hear constitutional claims raised in habeas corpus petitions. In *Teague*, the Supreme Court ruled that when a habeas petition asks a federal court to create a new rule recognizing a constitutional right, the court may not decide the matter unless it is a right that would be applied retroactively. The Court declared that "[r]etroactivity is properly treated as a threshold question."[73]

Until *Teague*, the Supreme Court considered habeas corpus petitions alleging constitutional violations, even when they asked the Court to recognize a new constitutional right that would not be applied retroactively to other cases. When the Court articulated a new right it benefitted the habeas petitioner and future criminal defendants. The Court subsequently would decide, in another case, whether it was to be applied retroactively to others. But in *Teague*, the Supreme Court ruled that retroactivity must be determined first; federal courts may not hear habeas petitions asking the Court to recognize new rights unless such rights would be retroactively applied in all cases.

The Court broadly defined what is a "new" right, thus limiting the constitutional claims that can be presented to a federal court on habeas corpus. The Court said that a "case announces a new rule when it breaks new ground or imposes a new obligation on the States or Federal government. . . . [A] case announces new rule if the result was not *dictated* by precedent existing at the time the defendant's conviction became final."[74] *Teague* has been repeatedly applied to preclude habeas petitions from being heard.[75]

Is There a Methodology to the Rehnquist Court's Constitutional Rulings?

The question thus becomes whether underlying this pattern is what might be regarded as a constitutional jurisprudence. Although a philosophy of constitutional decision making might take many forms, one key aspect is its view as to how the

Constitution should be interpreted. Over the past several decades, and certainly throughout the history of the Rehnquist Court, there has been a heated debate among scholars as to the proper method of constitutional interpretation. Over the last two decades, the debate frequently has been characterized as one between originalism, sometimes synonymously called interpretivism, and nonoriginalism, sometimes termed "noninterpretivism." Originalism is the view that "judges deciding constitutional issues should confine themselves to enforcing norms that are stated or clearly implicit in the written Constitution."[76] In contrast, nonoriginalism is the "contrary view that courts should go beyond that set of references and enforce norms that cannot be discovered within the four corners of the document."[77]

Originalists believe that the Court should find a right to exist in the Constitution only if it is expressly stated in the text or was clearly intended by its framers. If the Constitution is silent, originalists say it is for the legislature, unconstrained by the courts, to decide the law. Nonoriginalists think that it is permissible for the Court to interpret the Constitution to protect rights that are not expressly stated or clearly intended. Originalists believe that the Constitution should evolve solely by amendment; nonoriginalists believe that the Constitution's meaning can evolve by amendment and by interpretation.

There have been few, if any, pronouncements from the Rehnquist Court as to which of these philosophies it is following. This is not because such articulation of overall interpretive philosophy are unusual in Supreme Court decision making. It is possible to find many such declarations, both supportive of originalism and of nonoriginalism, in prior Court decisions. For example, in *South Carolina v. United States*, in 1905, the Court stated: "The Constitution is a written instrument. As such its meaning does not alter. That which it meant when adopted, it means now."[78] But there are equally strong statements from the Court rejecting an originalist approach. In *Home Building and Loan Association v. Blaisdell*, in 1934, the Court declared:

> It is no answer to say that this public need was not apprehended a century ago, or to insist that what the provision of the Constitution meant to the vision of that day it must mean to the vision of our time. If by the statement that what the Constitution meant at the time of its adoption it means today, it is intended to say that the great clauses of the Constitution must be confined to the interpretation which the framers, with the conditions and outlook of their time, would have placed upon them, the statement carries its own refutation. It was to guard against such a arrow conception that Chief Justice John Marshall uttered the memorable warning—"We must never forget that it is a constitution we are expounding."[79]

However, although the Rehnquist Court has not made such general pronouncements of interpretive philosophy, in practice it has placed a great emphasis on history. In decisions involving virtually every aspect of constitutional law, the Court has stressed history to justify its conclusions. In fact, the Rehnquist Court has subtly shifted the basis for originalist analysis. Previously, the key question was what the framers' intended as to the meaning of a specific provision. For instance, in *Immigration and Naturalization Service v. Chadha*,[80] decided by the Burger Court, the Supreme Court declared unconstitutional the legislative veto and relied exclusively on statements from the *Federalist Papers* and the text of the Constitution to justify its conclusions.

In contrast, however, the Rehnquist Court consistently has emphasized the contemporary practice at the time the constitutional provision was approved. In other words, the Rehnquist Court has focused not on historical intent as evidenced by the statements of the framers but instead on historical meaning as evidenced by the practices at the time the Constitution was ratified.[81]

This can be illustrated with examples of decisions from literally every part of the Constitution. For example, in its federalism decisions, the Court frequently invoked historical practices to support its conclusion. The most recent federalism decision is *Printz v. United States*,[82] which declared unconstitutional portions of the Brady Handgun Prevention Act.[83] The Court held that forcing state and local law enforcement personnel to conduct background checks before issuing permits for firearms violates the Tenth Amendment.

Justice Scalia, writing for the majority, said that "[b]ecause there is no constitutional text speaking to this precise question, the answer . . . must be sought in historical understanding and practice, in the structure of the Constitution, and in the jurisprudence of the Court."[84] Justice Scalia began by reviewing the experience in early American history and found that there was no support for requiring states to participate in a federal regulatory scheme. As to history, Justice Scalia said that Congress, in the initial years of American history, did not compel state activity and since "early Congresses avoided use of this highly attractive power, we would have reason to believe that the power was thought not to exist."[85]

As Justice Souter points out in dissent, there is a strong argument that Justice Scalia is incorrect in terms of the framers' intent.[86] Strong statements exist from Madison and Hamilton that Congress could call upon states to execute federal laws. Yet, for the Court's majority, historical practice early in American history, is better evidence of the Constitution's meaning than any statements from the framers. Indeed, it is striking that the Court finds constitutional meaning from the absence of a contemporaneous practice.

In First Amendment decisions, too, historical practices often have been crucial in the Justices' analysis. In the Supreme Court's recent decision of *Rosenberger v. Rector and Visitors of the University of Virginia*, which concerned whether a public university could deny student activity funds to a religious group, both Justice Thomas in a concurring opinion and Justice Souter dissenting focused at length on James Madison's views of religious freedom.[87] The key question for both Justices was what the opposition to the Virginia tax, protested in James Madison's 1785 *Memorial and Remonstrance*, meant.

In *McIntyre v. Ohio Elections Commission*,[88] the Court declared unconstitutional a law that prohibited the distribution of anonymous campaign literature. In an opinion concurring in the judgment, Justice Thomas relies exclusively on the historical practices at the time the First Amendment was adopted and concludes that "the Framers understood the First Amendment to protect an author's right to express his thoughts on political candidates or issues in an anonymous fashion."[89] Justice Thomas expressly declared that the meaning of the Constitution is unchanging and stated: "We should seek the original understanding when we interpret the Speech and Press Clauses, just as we do when we read the Religion Clauses of the First Amendment. When the Framers did not discuss the precise question at issue, we have turned to what history reveals was the contemporaneous understanding of the guarantees."[90]

Admittedly, in these cases historical practice was used more in concurring and dissenting opinions than in the majority opinions. But in many other cases, it was the majority opinion that relied on contemporary practices to justify its conclusion. For example, an issue recently arose before the Supreme Court as to whether the Fourth Amendment requires that police officers "knock and announce" before searching a residence.[91] Justice Thomas, writing for the Court, decided the issue by considering the law as of 1791 when the Fourth Amendment was adopted and concluded that knock and announce is generally required because it was part of the law at that time. Justice Thomas's opinion said, however, that "knock and announce" was not then an absolute requirement, so it is not one now. Because exigent circumstances were recognized as an exception in the law of 1791, there are similar exceptions under the Fourth Amendment in the 1990s.

The area in which emphasis on contemporary practices has been most evident is in the Court's due process analysis. For example, in the due process cases discussed in the second section of this chapter, the Court consistently stressed historical practices. In *Bennis v. Michigan*, which upheld the forfeiture of the automobile, Chief Juistice Rehnquist, writing for the Court, stated that "a long and unbroken line of cases holds that an owner's interest in property may be forfeited by reason of the use to which the property is put even though the owner did not know that it was to be put to such use."[92] Rehnquist stressed the permissibility of such forfeitures under admiralty law in the eighteenth and early nineteenth centuries.

In *Michael H. v. Gerald D.*, Justice Scalia stated that the existence of a "liberty interest [must] be rooted in history and tradition."[93] Justice Scalia then defended the constitutionality of an irrebuttable presumption of legitimacy by citing as authority H. Nicholas's 1836 work, *Adulterine Bastardy*, which cited Bracton's 1659 book, and quoting from Blackstone's 1826 treatise.[94]

In countless other cases, involving many different constitutional provisions, the Court has similarly stressed contemporaneous practices as the basis for constitutional analysis. In *Solorio v. United States*, the Court considered the authority of the military to try an individual in a court martial proceeding for non–service-related activity.[95] The Court looked to the American Articles of War of 1776 and concluded that "[t]he authority to try soldiers for civilian crimes may be found in the much-disputed 'general article' of the 1776 Articles of War, which allowed court martial jurisdiction over "all crimes not capital."[96] The Court then considered the history of court-martial jurisdiction in the years immediately following the adoption of the Constitution, focusing on the provisions of a law adopted by Congress in 1800.[97]

In *Harmelin v. Michigan*,[98] the Supreme Court upheld a mandatory sentence of life imprisonment without the possibility of parole for possession of more than 650 grams of cocaine. In rejecting the claim that the mandatory sentence constituted cruel and unusual punishment in violation of the Eighth Amendment, the Court began with a discussion of punishments imposed by the infamous Lord Jeffreys of the King's Bench during the Stuart reign of James II.[99] After considering permissible punishments in seventeenth-century England, the Court focused on acceptable sanctions in nineteenth-century America. Largely on the basis of this historical common-law analysis, the Court upheld the harsh sentence.

Countless other examples could be given of cases in which the Court's opinion focuses on contemporaneous practices at the time of a constitutional provision's adoption. I am not making the claim that the Rehnquist Court always uses such an approach; it clearly does not. Rather, the point is that the Rehnquist Court frequently takes an originalist approach and its form of originalism places emphasis on practices as evidence of constitutional meaning. The historical approach to constitutional decision making is an important aspect of the constitutional jurisprudence of the Rehnquist Court.

Should Original Meanings Evidenced by Contemporaneous Practices Matter?

Thus far, this chapter has tried to be descriptive rather than normative. In this section, I want to critique the Rehnquist Court's increased reliance on historical and especially on contemporaneous practices as a basis for constitutional decision making. This approach to constitutional law is based on unjustfied, and unjustifiable, assumptions.

"Law Office History": The Inevitable Manipulation of History to Justify Conclusions

First, the search for original meaning in contemporaneous practices assumes a unanimity, or near unanimity, about what was occurring at the time of the ratification of the Consitution. As to most issues, this unanimity rarely was present. The result is that the Court simply looks back and finds some practices to support the conclusions it wants to reach. More than a quarter of a century later, Alfred Kelly complained of what he called "law office" history practiced by the Supreme Court.[100] Practices often varied. The Court picks and chooses from its reading of history and selects those practices that confirm the conclusion that it wants for each. The Court purports that history is the basis for the discovery of its conclusion, when in reality history seems to be no more than a part of the justification for conclusions reached on other grounds.

A powerful example of this is a Supreme Court decision from the Burger Court: *Stump v. Sparkman* [101] The issue before the Supreme Court was whether a judge has absolute immunity, when sued pursuant to 42 U.S.C. § 1983, for imposing involuntary sterilization on a teenager without any semblance of due process. The Supreme Court based its holding of absolute immunity largely on its view that judges historically had absolute immunity at common law in 1871 when section 1983 was adopted. Yet, a closer look at history reveals that judges had absolute immunity in only thirteen of thirty-seven states that existed in 1871.[102]

The same questionable reading of history is often present in First Amendment cases. *In Heffron v. International Society of Krishna Consciousness, Inc.,*[103] the Supreme Court upheld a Minnesota State Fair Rule that prohibited inidividuals from soliciting funds or distributing literature while walking through the fairgrounds. The Court concluded that state fairs should not be regarded as traditional public fora. Yet, historical research shows that government fairs have long been a primary place for the gathering of people and the dissemination of information.[104] The Court purportedly based its reading on history, yet choose the historical practices that supported its conclusion and ignored the others.

Another example from the First Amendment concerns a relatively little discussed provision: the clause that protects the right to petition Congress for redress of grievances. In *McDonald v. Smith,*[105] the Supreme Court relied almost exclusively on historical analysis as the basis for rejecting constitutional protection. Yet, as Eric Schnapper has persuasively demonstrated, had the Court accurately described and followed history, the decision would have been different.[106] McDonald involved letters written by Robert McDonald to President-Elect Ronald Reagan, Edwin Meese, the Federal Bureau of Investigation, and four members of Congress opposing the nomination of David Smith for the position of United States Attorney for North Carolina. Smith brought a defamation suit against McDonald for the content of the letters. McDondald defended by claiming a privilege based on the petition clause. The Supreme Court ruled in favor of Smith, concluding that there was no historical basis for McDonald's contention that the framers understood the right to petition to include a privilege against suits for defamation.[107] The Court's analysis was based almost exclusively on historical analysis and old precedents.

In his article aptly subtitled "Bad Historiography Makes Worse Law," Professor Schnapper shows that at English common-law statements in petitions were deemed absolutely privileged. Professor Schnapper's historical research shows that the petition clause owes its origin to the *Seven Bishops Case* in 1689, which was the immediate cause of the petition clause in the 1689 Bill of Rights. The *Seven Bishops Case* involved prosecution of the Archbishop of Canterbury and six other bishops for seditious libel based on the content of a petition presented to King James. The response to that case led to the conclusion that there should be an absolute privilege for the content of petitions to the government. Yet, the Court never discussed this history in deciding *McDonald v. Smith*, even though its decision rested on historical analysis.

Professor Neil M. Richards has carefully analyzed the Rehnquist Court's use of history.[108] He describes how in case after case the Court manipulates the historical record to justify its conclusion. This seems virtually inevitable to the Court's use of history. None of the Justices are trained historians. They are looking at history out of its context to support a particular conclusion. They tend to use history when it offers that support and ignore it when it does not. For example, legal historian, Professor Stephen Siegel has powerfully documented that the historical practices around the time of the ratification of the Fourteenth Amendment strongly support the constitutionality of affirmative action.[109] Yet for all their purported devotion to history as the guide for original meaning, Justices Scalia and Thomas never mention this history because it does not support their vehement opposition to affirmative action.

Questionable Relevance of Contemporaneous Practices in Determining Constitutional Meaning

Even assuming that a particular practice was universal at the time the constitutional provision was drafted and ratified, that still does not establish that the Constitution was meant to enshrine that behavior. The search for original meaning in contemporaneous practices assumes that the Constitution sought to codify those particular behaviors. Yet, there is no basis for this assumption. It certainly is possible that the framers might have wanted to embody a specific practice in the Constitution, but it also is possible that the framers wanted the constitutional provision to disapprove the practice or that the framers simply did not think one way or another about the specific practice when they adopted the particular constitutional provision.

Consider the example mentioned earlier of the Supreme Court's requiring that police knock and announce before searching dwellings.[110] It is conceivable that those drafting the Fourth Amendment had this common-law rule in mind and wanted to include it in the Constitution. It also is plausible that they thought that the exceptions were too broad and that by enacting the Fourth Amendment they wanted to disapprove the ongoing practice. And it also is possible that the framers and ratifiers of the Fourth Amendment were not thinking about "knock and announce" at all. The existence of a practice tells nothing by itself as to its relationship to a constitutional provision.

Nor are practices soon after the enactment of the provision necessarily useful in determining its meaning. It certainly is possible that subsequent practice reflects the framers' understanding of what was Constitutionally permissible under the new provision. But it also is possible that the framers meant the Amendment to outlaw the practice, but the political realities were that in governing they saw no alternative but to engage in the forbidden behavior. There is a fundamental difference between constituting a government and governing. The choices made in creating a government may not necessarily be reflected in governing. The Alien and Sedition Act of 1798 (1 Stat. 576) might be indicative that the framers of the First Amendment, many of whom were still in Congress, meant to allow punishment of seditious libel. But it also might mean that those with political power and an incentive to use it acted differently than when they were creating the government.

It seems even more dubious to rely on the absence of a practice in the first Congresses to establish a constitutional limit. In *Printz v. United States*,[111] the Court stressed the absence of congressional compulsion of states in the early Congresses as evidence of the meaning of the Tenth Amendment and the scope of Congress' powers. There are countless reasons why the federal government did not require state action then, including that they did not think of the possibility, or they thought that their goals could best be achieved by direct federal action, or they sought to establish the federal government's own authority to act, or political pressures at the time prevented specific mandates. To infer rejection of congressional power from inaction is to assume the truth of one explanation to the exclusion of all others. The absence of a particular practice at specific time does not mean that those then in power thought it unconstitutional. There are many explanations for why a type of law was not used at a given moment.

Generally, the presence or absence of a practice does not have any necessary relationship to a constitutional provision adopted at a particular time. The Rehnquist Court's use of contemporaneous practices assumes a meaning that simply cannot be assumed or accepted.

Should Original Meanings Control Modern Constitutional Interpretation: The Undesirability of Limiting Constitutional Meaning to Historical Practices

Third, and most important, the Rehnquist Court assumes that original meaning should control constitutional interpretation. Even if history were clear and even if it could be shown that historical practices reflect the original meaning, the question still arises as to whether the original meaning should be dispositive in modern constitutional interpretation. History, at most, can provide descriptions of practices and perhaps intentions; such descriptions do not determine the normative meaning of the Constitution. There must be a separate normative theory as to why original meanings should control contemporary decision making.

There are many reasons why it is preferable to follow a nonoriginalist approach and eschew reliance on the original meaning in constitutional decision making. First, it is not desirable to have the modern world governed by the practices of a vastly different time more than 200 years ago. First, a commitment to following contemporaneous historical practices would lead to abhorrent conclusions. Justice Brennan explained this when he stated: "[D]uring colonial times, pillorying, branding, and cropping and nailing of the ears were practiced in this country. Thus, if we were to turn blindly to history for answers to troubling constitutional questions, we would have to conclude that these practices would withstand challenge under the cruel and unusual clause of the eighth amendment."[112]

Second and closely related, it is desirable to have the Constitution evolve by interpretation and not only by amendment. The cumbersome amendment process, requiring approval by two-thirds of both Houses of Congress and three-fourths of the states, makes it likely that few amendments will be added to the Constitution. Just seventeen amendments have been added in two centuries. The claim is that nonoriginalist review is essential so that the Constitution does not remain virtually static, so that it can evolve to meet the needs of a society that is advancing technologically and morally.

Nonoriginalists argue, for example, that equal protection in the last half of the twentieth century must mean that government-mandated racial segregation is unacceptable; yet, there is strong evidence that the framers of the Fourteenth Amendment approved this practice.[113] The drafters of the Equal Protection Clause did not intend to protect women from discrimination, and in the nineteenth century discrimination against women was endemic,[114] but it is widely accepted that the clause should apply to gender discrimination. Indeed, the argument is made that under originalism it would be unconstitutional to elect a woman as President or Vice President because the Constitution refers to these officeholders with the word "he," and the framers clearly intended that they be male.[115]

Third, there is compelling evidence that nonoriginalism is the preferable method of interpretation because it is the approach intended by the framers. In other words, the claim is that following originalism requires that originalism be abandoned because the framers did not intend this method of interpretation. Prof. H. Jefferson Powell stated: "It is commonly assumed that the 'interpretive intention' of the Constitution's framers was that the Constitution would be construed in accordance with what future interpreters could gather of the framers' own purposes, expectations, and intentions. Inquiry shows that assumption to be incorrect. Of the numerous hermeneutical options that were available in the framers' day . . . none corresponds to the modern notion of intentionalism."[116] In other words, the framers probably did not intend that their intent would govern later interpretations of the Constitution.

The key response to these arguments is that originalism and the search for original meaning is necessary as a constraint on the Court. The Rehnquist Court has stressed its desire to avoid the appearance that its decisions are based on the personal values of the Justices and thus seeks to ground its rulings on external sources.[117] The Court has expressly defended history on the ground that it provides an objective basis for decisions as an alternative to impermissible value imposition by the Court.

For instance, in *Stanford v. Kentucky*,[118] the Court upheld the imposition of capital punishment on an individual for a crime committed at sixteen or seventeen years of age as permissible under the Eighth Amendment. While rejecting the proportionality analysis established by precedent, the Court applied its own historical analysis, stating that to adopt the proportionality analysis would be improperly to follow "our personal preferences" and "to replace judges of the law with committee of philosopher kings."[119] Justice Scalia, writing for the plurality in *Michael H. v. Gerald D.*, warned that failing to follow tradition, stated at the most specific level of abstraction, would make constitutional law "'the predilections of those who happen to be members of the Court.'"[120]

Yet, the reality is that the use of historical practices to determine constitutional meaning fails to provide the desired constraint. Historians long have taught that history is a matter of interpretation.[121] The Court's presentation of history as an objective basis for decisions really has subjective choices masquerading as objective rulings.

There is a need to decide which practices matter, especially when there were differences in behavior or where the context has vastly changed over 200 years. There also is a need to decide the level of abstraction for stating a particular right. Deciding the level of abstraction necessarily requires a value choice by the Justices.[122]

Thus, the search for original meaning provides little constraint on the Court's decision making. Rather, it yields a constitutional jurisprudence that falsely assumes an ascertainable original meaning that can be determined from historical practices and that wrongly assumes that it should control modern constitutional decision making.

Conclusion

All constitutional law is about value choices. The Supreme Court must decide which values are so important as to be worthy of constitutional protection. There is no value-neutral manner for the Court to complete this task. The Rehnquist Court's emphasis on original meaning is itself a value choice. Moreover, as described earlier, the patterns of Rehnquist Court decisions reveal its value choices. These value choices, looked at cumulatively, are the constitutional jurisprudence of the Rehnquist Court.

Notes

I want to thank Catherine Fisk for many very helpful conversations about this topic and David Wang for his excellent research assistance.

1. Chemerinsky, "Foreword: The Vanishing Constitution," 103 *Harv. L. Rev.* 43, 46 (1989).

2. See, e.g., Printz v. United States, 521 U.S. 898 (1997) (Brady Bill violates Tenth Amendment); Adarand Constructors, Inc. v. Pena, 515 U.S. 200 (1995) (federal affirmative action program violates equal protection); Shaw v. Reno, 509 U.S. 630 (1993) (use of race in drawing election districts to benefit minorities must meet strict scrutiny); United States v. Lopez, 514 U.S. 549 (1995) (Gun Free School Zone Act unconstitutional as exceeding the scope of Congress's Commerce Clause authority).

3. United States v. Eichman, 486 U.S. 310 (1990); Texas v. Johnson, 491 US. 397 (1989).

4. 410 U.S. 113 (1973).

5. 403 U.S. 602 (1971).

6. 384 U.S. 436 (1966).

7. See, e.g., Eastern Enter. v. Appel, 524 U.S. 498 (1998) (plurality opinion) (creation of retroactive liability is taking); Lucas v. South Carolina Coastal Council, 505 U.S. 1003 (1992) (regulatory taking exists when there is the preclusion of almost all economically viable use of property regardless of government's justification).

8. See, e.g., General Motors v. Romein, 502 U.S. 181 (1992) (Contracts Clause not used to invalidate state law).

9. Chemerinsky, supra note 1, at 57.

10. City of Boerne v. Flores, 521 U.S. 507 (1997).

11. Reno v. ACLU, 521 U.S. 844 (1997).

12. Printz v. United States, 521 U.S. 702 (1997).

13. See, e.g., Michael H. v. Gerald D., 491 U.S. 110 (1989); Scalia, *A Matter of Interpretation: Federal Courts and the Law* 38 (1997); Scalia, "Originalism: The Lesser Evil," 57 *U. Cin. L. Rev.* 841 (1989).

14. Justices Thomas and Scalia agree in over 90 percent of the cases, the highest agreement rate among Justices on the current Court. See, e.g., "IV. The Statistics," 111 *Harv. L. Rev.* 431 (1997).

15. See, e.g., INS v. Chadha, 462 U.S. 919 (1983).

16. Prof. David Shapiro identified this as a characteristic of Justice Rehnquist's jurisprudence early in his tenure on the Court. See Shapiro, "Justice Rehnquist: A Preliminary View," 90 *Harv. L. Rev.* 292 (1976). It was not until the 1990s, however, that a majority of the Court accepted this view.

17. 514 U.S. 549 (1995).

18. 18 U.S.C. § 922(q)(1)(a), 921(a)(25).

19. 521 U.S. 507 (1997).

20. 426 U.S. 833 (1976).

21. 469 U.S 528 (1985).

22. 550 U.S. 144 (1982).

23. 521 U.S. 898 (1997).

24. 517 U.S. 44 (1996).

25. This trend was continued by three decisions in June 1999: Alden v. Maine, 527 U.S. 706 (1999) (provision of Florida Statutes Annotated apparently authorizing private actions against states in state courts without their consent is unconstitutional); College Sav. Bank v. Florida Prepaid Postsecondary Educ. Expense Bd., 527 U.S. 666 (1999); and Florida Prepaid Postsecondary Educ. Expense Bd. v. College Sav. Bank, 527 U.S. 627 (1999) (alleged violation of Lanham Act and a patent infringement suit, respectively; Florida's defense of sovereign immunity applied, but not absolute. For additional background, see Chemerinsky, "Bulletproof States?," 85 *A.B.A.J.* 32 (April 1999).

26. Bowers v. Hardwick, 478 U.S. 186 (1986), which upheld the government's ability to punish private, consensual homosexual activity, was decided in the last Term of the Burger Court.

27. 516 U.S. 442 (1996).

28. Id. at 453.

29. 509 U.S. 544 (1993).

30. RICO refers to the Racketeer Influenced and Corrupt Organization Act, 18 U.S.C. § 1963.

31. See, e.g., Reno v. ACLU, 521 U.S. 844 (1997) (declaring unconstitutional the Communications Decency Act of 1996); Sable Communications v. FCC, 492 U.S. 115 (1989) (declaring unconstitutional the dial-a-porn law's prohibition of indecent commercial phone calls).

32. See, e.g., Vernonia Sch. Dist. v. Acton, 513 U.S. 1145 (1993); Von Raab v. National Treasury Employees Union, 482 U.S. 912 (1987). But see Chandler v. Miller, 519 U.S. 1111 (1983).

33. United States v. Sokolow, 490 U.S. 1 (1989).

34. Riley v. United States, 459 U.S. 1111 (1983).

35. See, e.g., City of Cincinatti v. Discovery Network, Inc., 507 U.S.410 (1993); Edenfield v. Fane, 507 U.S. 761 (1993).

36. United States v. Edge Broadcasting Co., 509 U.S. 418 (1993).

37. Washington v. Glucksberg, 521 U.S. 702 (1997).

38. Id. at 711.

39. Id.

40. Id. at 728.

41. 521 U.S. 793 (1997).

42. 494 U.S. 872 (1990).

43. Id. at 879 (citation omitted).

44. Congress enacted the Religious Freedom Restoration Act to overturn *Smith*, but this was declared unconstitutional in City of Boerne v. Flores, 521 U.S. 507 (1997).

45. 491 U.S. 110 (1989).

46. See, e.g., Stanley v. Illinois, 405 U.S. 645 (1972).

47. Michael H., 491 U.S. at 127.

48. For a fascinating account of how Justice Scalia added this footnote to the decision and how other Justices rejected it, see Lazarus, *Closed Chambers* 388–91(1998).

49. Michael H., 491 U.S. at 127 n.6.

50. Id. at 127 n. 6. Justice Scalia also followed this approach in Reno v. Flores, 507 U.S. 292 (1993), which upheld the Immigration and Naturalization Service's regulations concerning detention of children. A child who did not have a parent, close relative, or guardian in the United States would remain in federal custody. The Court rejected the argument that the government had to provide care in a manner that was narrowly tailored to promote the child's best interests. The Court said that "[t]he best interests of the child is . . . not an absolute and exclusive constitutional criterion for the government's exercise of the custodial responsibility that it undertakes, which must be reconciled with many other responsibilities. Thus, child-care institutions operated by the state in exercise of its *parens patriae* authority . . . are not constitutionally required to be funded at a level to provide the *best* schooling or the *best* health care available." Id. at 304 (emphasis in original). Justice Scalia rejected the claim that children have a right to a private custodian rather than the government and stated: "The mere novelty of such a claim is reason enough to doubt that substantive due process sustains it; the alleged right certainly cannot be considered 'so rooted in the traditions and conscience of our people' as to be ranked as fundamental." Id.

51. 505 U.S. 833 (1992).

52. Schwartz, A *History of the Supreme Court* 326–27 (1993).

53. 509 U.S. 312 (1993).

54. 517 U.S. 200 (1996). It can be argued that although the Court used the language of rational basis review, it actually was applying heightened scrutiny. However, Justice Kennedy's majority opinion expressly applied rational basis review and pointed to the lack of any legitimate purpose for excluding the ability of a particular group to use the political process in the manner available to all others.

55. 488 U.S. 469 (1989).

56. The permissibility of set-asides as an affirmative action technique is discussed infra note 64.

57. In addition to Justice O'Connor's opinion, which was joined by Chief Justice Rehnquist and Justice White, using strict scrutiny, Justice Scalia, 488 U.S. at 520, and Justice Kennedy, 488 U.S. at 518, wrote concurring opinions using strict scrutiny.

58. 497 U.S. 547 (1990).

59. 515 U.S. 200 (1995).

60. Id. at 227.

61. Id. at 235.

62. Id. at 237 (citations omitted).

63. Id. at 237.

64. See Shaw v. Reno, 509 U.S. 630 (1993) (holding that strict scrutiny should be applied when race is used in drawing election districts to increase the likelihood that minorities would be elected. This was later reaffirmed in Miller v. Johnson, 515 U.S. 900 (1995); Shaw v. Hunt, 517 U.S. 899 (1996); and Bush v. Vera, 517 U.S. 592 (1996).

65. Arizona v. Evans, 514 U.S. 1 (1995) (the good-faith exception to the exclusionary rule applies if a warrant had been quashed prior to the search due to a judicial computer error and the police were unaware of this at the time of the search.)

66. 517 U.S. 806 (1996).

67. 519 U.S. 408 (1997).

68. 519 U.S. 33 (1996).

69. Pub. L. No. 104-132 (April 24, 1996).

70. For a thorough summary of the Rehnquist Court's attitude toward and handling of capital cases, *see* Lazarus, supra note 48, at 134–35, 139–41, 143–44, 145–47, 150, 491–92, 501–502, 508, 510.

71. 499 U.S. 467 (1991).

72. 489 U.S. 288 (1989). For a discussion of the impact of *Teague*, see Arkin, "The Prisoner's Dilemma: Life in the Lower Federal Courts After *Teague v. Lane*" 69 N.C. L. Rev. 371 (1991); Berger, "Justice Delayed or Justice Denied: A Comment on Recent Proposals to Reform Death Penalty Habeas Corpus," 90 *Colum. L. Rev.* 1665 (1990); Dow, "*Teague* and Death: The Impact of Current Retroactivity Doctrine on Criminal Defendants," 19 *Hastings Constit. L.Q.* 23 (1991); Friedman, "Habeas and Hubris," 45 *Vand. L. Rev.* 797 (1992); Hoffman, "Retroactivity and the Great Writ: How Congress Should Respond to *Teague v. Lane*," 1990 *B.Y.U. L. Rev.* 183; Hutton, "Retroactivity in the States: The Impact of *Teague v. Lane* on State Postconviction Remedies," 44 *Ala. L. Rev.* 421 (1993).

73. 489 U.S. at 300.

74. Id. at 301.

75. See, e.g., Butler v. McKellar, 494 U.S. 407 (1990); Saffle v. Parks, 494 U.S. 484 (1990); Sawyer v. Smith, 497 U.S. 227 (1990); Gray v. Netherland, 518 U.S. 152 (1996).

76. Ely, *Democracy and Distrust* 1 (1980).

77. Id.

78. 199 U.S. 437, 448 (1905).

79. 290 U.S. 398, 442–43 (1934).

80. 462 U.S. 919 (1983).

81. In his scholarly writings, Justice Scalia has expressly drawn this distinction and defended original meaning as the appropriate basis for constitutional decision-making. See Scalia, *A Matter of Interpretation: Federal Courts and the Law* (1997). The distinction is discussed in detail in Greenberg and Litman, "The Meaning of Original Meaning," 86 *Geo. L.J.* 569 (1997).

82. 521 U.S. 898 (1997).

83. 18 U.S.C. § 922.

84. Printz, 521 U.S. at 905.

85. Id. at 905.

86. Id. at 971 (Souter, J., dissenting).

87. 515 U.S. 819, 854–58 (1995) (Thomas, J., concurring); id. at 863–99 (Souter, J., dissenting). James Madison issued his famous *Remonstrance* in arguing against a Virginia decision renew a tax to support the church. This is reviewed in detail in Everson v. Board of Educ., 330 U.S. 1, 12, 31–34 (1947) (Rutledge, J., dissenting).

88. 514 U.S. 334 (1995).

89. Id. at 370 (Thomas, J., concurring in the judgment).

90. Id. at 359.

91. Wilson v. Arkansas, 514 U.S. 92 (1995).

92. 516 U.S. 442, 446 (1996).

93. 491 U.S. at 123.

94. Id. at 124.

95. Solorio v. United States, 483 U.S. 435 (1987).

96. Id. at 444–45.

97. Id. at 446 n. 11.

98. 501 U.S. 957 (1991).

99. Id. at 966–70.

100. Kelly, "Clio and the Court: An Illicit Love Affair," 1965 *Sup. Ct. Rev.* 119.

101. 435 U.S. 349 (1980).

102. Note, "Liability of Judicial Officers Under Section 1983," 79 *Yale L.J.* 322, 326–27 (1969); see also Block, "Stump v. Sparkman and the History of Judicial Immunity," 1980 *Duke L.J.* 879, 899.

103. 452 U.S. 640, 657 (1980).

104. Brief for the American Civil Liberties Union, the Minnesota Civil Liberties Union, and the National Council of Churches, *Amici Curiae* at 18–19.

105. 472 U.S. 479 (1985).

106. Schnapper, "'Libelous' Petitions for Redess of Grievances: Bad Historiography Makes Worse Law," 74 *Iowa L. Rev.* 303 (1989).

107. 472 U.S. at 482–83.

108. Richards, "Clio and the Court: A Reassessment of the Supreme Court's Uses of History," 13 *J. L. & Pol'y* 809 (1997).

109. Siegel, "The Federal Government's Power to Enact Color-Conscious Laws: An Originalist Inquiry," 92 *Nw. U. L. Rev.* 477 (1998).

110. Wilson v. Arkansas, 514 U.S. 927 (1995).

111. 521 U.S. 898 (1997).

112. Brennan, Jr., "Constitutional Adjudication and the Death Penalty: A View From the Court," 100 *Harv. L. Rev.* 313, 327 (1986).

113. The same Congress that ratified the Fourteenth Amendment also approved the segregation of the District of Columbia public schools. See Dworkin, *Law's Empire* 360 (1986). This legislation was later declared unconstitutional in Bolling v. Sharpe, 347 U.S. 497 (1954). But see McConnell, "Originalism and the Desegregation Decisions," 81 *Va. L. Rev.* 947 (1995) (arguing that the framers of the Fourteenth Amendment did intend to desegregate public schools).

114. See, e.g., The Slaughter-House Cases, 83 U.S. (16 Wall.) 36, 81 (1872) (stating that the Equal Protection Clause was meant only to protect racial minorities and never would be extended beyond this).

115. Saphire, "Judicial Review in the Name of the Constitution," 8 *U. Dayton L. Rev.* 745, 796–97 (1983).

116. Powell, "The Original Understanding of Original Intent," 98 *Harv. L. Rev.* 885, 948 (1985).

117. Chemerinsky, supra note 1, at 96.

118. 482 U.S. 361 (1989).

119. Id. at 379 (plurality opinion).

120. 481 U.S. at 121 (plurality opinion).

121. See, e.g., Collingwood, *The Idea of History* 218–19 (1946).

122. Brest, "The Fundamental Rights Controversy: The Essential Contradictions of Normative Constitutional Scholarship," 90 *Yale L.J.* 1063, 1091–92 (1981) ("The fact is that all adjudication requires making choices among the levels of generality on which to articulate principles, and all such choices are inherently non-neutral.").

12

THE REHNQUIST COURT AND
STATE CONSTITUTIONAL LAW

MARIE L. GARIBALDI

On September 26, 1986, William Rehnquist was sworn in as Chief Justice of the United States Supreme Court. At that time the renaissance in state constitutional law was at its peak and the Supreme Court had decided *Michigan v. Long*.[1] My task today is to discuss how the Rehnquist Court affected state constitutional law. As background, I discuss some general principles concerning state constitutional law prior to the *Long* decision. Then, I examine the response of the Rehnquist Court and state courts to the plain-statement requirement of *Long*,[2] focusing specifically on the vexing problem of how a state court determines that its constitution provides greater protection of individual rights than are afforded under similar or identical federal constitutional provisions. Finally, I hope to demonstrate that the "criteria approach" used by the Supreme Court of New Jersey[3] best balances the dual concerns of a state court, which are (1) to prevent its state constitution from becoming a mere shadow of the federal Constitution, and (2) to ensure that its state constitution does not unduly expand its citizens' rights so that they bear only a slight resemblance to the protections found under parallel provisions in the federal Constitution.[4]

Background of *Michigan v. Long*

State Constitutional Law Prior to *Michigan v. Long*

The renaissance in state constitutional law, the "new judicial federalism,"[5] was first recognized in Justice Brennan's oft-quoted statement:

> State constitutions, too, are a font of individual liberties, their protections often extending beyond those required by the Supreme Court's interpretation of federal law. The legal revolution which has brought federal law to the fore must not be allowed to inhibit the independent protective force of state law—for without it, the full realization of our liberties cannot be guaranteed.[6]

Later, Justice Brennan wrote:

> Our states are not mere provinces of an all powerful central government. They are political units with hard-core constitutional status and with plenary governmental responsibility for much that goes on within their borders . . . . [T]he composite work of the courts of the fifty states probably has greater significance in measuring how well America attains the ideal of equal justice for all. . . . We should remind ourselves that it is these state court decisions which finally determine the overwhelming aggregate of all legal controversies in this nation.[7]

The emphasis on state constitutions is a return to the earliest days of our country. Before the adoption of the federal Constitution, citizens relied on their state constitutions to protect their rights.[8] Indeed, many state constitutions provided the model for the federal Bill of Rights.[9] In the 1960s, under the Warren Court, the pendulum swung in the other direction and the federal Constitution replaced state constitutions as the primary source of protection of individual rights.[10] At that time, the federal Constitution ascended to center stage and state constitutions faded into the background.[11] From 1969 to 1986, the Burger Court, however, retreated from some of the more liberal holdings of the Warren Court, and state courts began to turn to their state constitutions as a means to provide their citizens with greater rights than they were receiving under the federal Constitution.[12]

The Long Requirements

"[A]s a historical matter, state constitutions exist and function independently of the federal Constitution."[13] All states have their own constitutions. Many of those constitutions are long, detailed documents containing a number of provisions that are only applicable to that state and for which no similar or identical federal constitutional provisions exist.[14] In interpreting those provisions, it is undisputed that state law governs.[15]

Several provisions exist, however, in state constitutions that are comparable or analogous to provisions contained in the federal Constitution.[16] Traditionally, in those cases, the Supreme Court has declined to review "judgments of state courts that rest on adequate and independent state grounds."[17] Yet, the Supreme Court has acknowledged that "cases in which the record is ambiguous but presents reasonable grounds to believe that the judgment may rest on decision of a federal question," present vexing problems to the Court.[18] Whether a state court decision plainly sets forth an "adequate and independent" state ground has often been difficult to determine.[19] That issue "typically arises where a state court opinion discusses both state and federal constitutional grounds for a decision without making clear whether the court meant to expand the state guarantee beyond what it believed to be the federal standard."[20]

Before *Michigan v. Long*,[21] "it was safe to assume that any lack of clarity as to the basis of a state court judgment would be resolved in favor of the state court as the final arbiter, and against further review."[22] If the state court opinion cited both grounds, the United States Supreme Court would apply one of the following three approaches: (1) "if the ground of decision was at all unclear . . . dismiss the case," (2) remand the case to the state court to "obtain clarification about the nature of a state court decision," or (3) examine state law to determine whether the state court had applied federal law "to guide its application of state law or to provide the actual basis for [its] decision."[23]

Finding all those approaches unsatisfactory, in 1983, the Supreme Court in *Long* replaced those approaches with a presumption in favor of Supreme Court review.[24] That presumption arises when (1) "a state court decision fairly appears to rest primarily on federal law, or to be interwoven with the federal law," and (2) "the adequacy and independence of any possible state law ground is not clear from the face of the opinion."[25] In such cases, the Court will assume "that the state court decided the case the way it did because it believed that federal law required it to do so."[26] However, the *Long* Court declared that if the state court indicates "clearly and expressly" by "a plain statement in its judgment or opinion that the federal cases are being used only for the purpose of guidance, and do not themselves compel the result . . . reached," then federal review of the case is not permitted.[27] The Supreme Court believed that requiring state courts to make a plain statement would "provide state judges with a clearer opportunity to develop state jurisprudence unimpeded by federal interference, and yet [would] preserve the integrity of federal law."[28]

Critics were divided on whether the Court in *Long* was attempting to prevent state courts from exceeding federal courts in the protection of fundamental rights or merely holding "state courts directly accountable for their decisions, thereby preventing them from hiding beneath the robes of the Supreme Court."[29] Probably the best summation of *Michigan v. Long* is Professor Tribe's statement that *Long* "advances interests which lie at the root of our federal system" and "also protects the autonomy of state law."[30] Regardless of the reasons for the Supreme Court's decision in Long, Associate Justice Pollock of the New Jersey Supreme Court noted that it "created an opening for state courts to strengthen their position in the federalist system."[31] Requiring state courts to set forth plainly the "adequate and independent" state grounds that form the basis of their decisions forces those courts to look beyond the federal law and rely on their own state jurisprudence.

The Rehnquist Court's Adherence to *Long*

During the Rehnquist term, there have been numerous Supreme Court cases in which the Supreme Court has affirmed its adherence to the Long doctrine.[32] Some of those cases simply relied on boilerplate paragraphs from *Long*. For example, in *Illinois v. Rodriguez*,[33] the Court stated:

> When a state-court decision is clearly based on state law that is both adequate and independent, we will not review the decision. *Michigan v. Long*, 463 U.S. 1032, 1041 (1983). But when "a state court decision fairly appears to rest primarily on federal law, or to be interwoven with the federal law," we require that it contain a " 'plain statement' that [it] rests upon adequate and independent state grounds," id., at 1040, 1042; otherwise, "we will accept as the most reasonable explanation that the state court decided the case the way it did because it believed that federal law required it to do so." Id., at 1041. Here, the Appellate Court's opinion contains no "plain statement" that its decision rests on state law. The opinion does not rely on (or even mention) any specific provision of the Illinois Constitution, nor even

the Illinois Constitution generally. Even the Illinois cases cited by the opinion rely upon no constitutional provisions other than the Fourth and Fourteenth Amendments of the United States Constitution. We conclude that the Appellate Court of Illinois rested its decision on federal law.[34]

In *Pennsylvania v. Muniz*,[35] the Court held that the decision of the Pennsylvania Supreme Court did not "rest on an independent and adequate state ground," because the state court had interpreted the challenged Pennsylvania Constitution's provision as offering a protection identical to that provided in the Federal Constitution.[36] Similarly, in *Maryland v. Garrison*,[37] the Court held that because Maryland's Court of Appeals relied not only on Article 26 of the Maryland Declaration of Rights but also on the Fourth Amendment of the federal Constitution and federal cases, the Supreme Court had jurisdiction.[38]

In three recent cases, the Rehnquist Court again reaffirmed its adherence to the *Long* doctrine.[39] In *Arizona v. Evans*,[40] an opinion written by Chief Justice Rehnquist, the police stopped the defendant for a traffic violation and a subsequent check with the patrol car's computer revealed an outstanding arrest warrant.[41] While placing the defendant under arrest, the police officer noticed a marijuana cigarette in respondent's hand and found a small bag of marijuana in the car.[42] When the police later discovered that the warrant for respondent's arrest had been quashed, respondent moved to suppress the marijuana as the fruit of an unlawful arrest.[43]

In *Evans*, the Court found that the decision of the Supreme Court of Arizona to suppress the evidence "was based squarely upon its interpretation of federal law. Nor did it offer a plain statement that its references to federal law were 'being used only for the purpose of guidance, and d[id] not themselves compel the result that [it] reached.' "[44] Therefore, applying federal constitutional law, the Supreme Court determined that the exclusionary rule did not require suppression of evidence seized during an unlawful arrest resulting from a clerical error of either a court employee or a sheriff's office employee.[45]

In reaching its decision in *Evans*, the Supreme Court emphasized its commitment to *Long*, stating that "[w]e believe that *Michigan v. Long* properly serves its purpose and should not be disturbed."[46] Under that decision, the Court noted, "state courts are absolutely free to interpret state constitutional provisions to accord greater protection to individual rights than do similar provisions of the United States Constitution."[47] The Rehnquist Court further reiterated its belief that the "the plain statement" rule will ensure "that state courts will not be the final arbiters of important issues under the federal constitution; and that [the United States Supreme Court] will not encroach on the constitutional jurisdiction of the states."[48]

Similarly, in *Pennsylvania v. Labron*,[49] a 1996 case, the Court held that the opinion of the Supreme Court of Pennsylvania did not rest on an adequate and independent state ground, but was "interwoven with the federal law."[50] The Supreme Court reached that conclusion because in some of the Pennsylvania state court cases, the Supreme Court of Pennsylvania relied on an analysis of federal cases.[51] In his dissent, joined by Justice Ginsburg, however, Justice Stevens opined that the Court's decision "not only extend[ed] *Michigan v. Long* beyond its original scope, but stands its rationale on its head. . . . [E]very indication is that the rule adopted [by Pennsylvania] . . . rests primarily on state law. Nor are these holdings 'interwoven' with federal law."[52] Justice Stevens went onto explain that "[b]ecause the state-law ground supporting these judgments is so much clearer than has been true on most prior occasions, these decisions exacerbate [the unfortunate] effects [of the *Long* decision] to a nearly intolerable degree."[53]

In another 1996 opinion written by Chief Justice Rehnquist, over the dissent of Justice Stevens and the concurrence of Justice Ginsburg, the Court in Ohio v. Robinette [54] once more affirmed its commitment to *Long*.[55] The Supreme Court framed the issue in that case to be whether "[t]he Fourth Amendment . . . require[s] that a lawfully seized defendant be advised that he is 'free to go' before his consent to search will be recognized as voluntary."[56] The Court held that it did not.[57]

The Court in *Robinette* found that the state court's opinion "clearly relie[d] on federal law. . . . Indeed, the only cases it discusses or even cites are federal cases, except for one state case which itself applies the Federal Constitution."[58] The Court found that "when the [Ohio] syllabus, as here, speaks only in general terms of 'the federal and Ohio Constitutions,' it is permissible for us to turn to the body of the opinion to discern the grounds for decision."[59] The Court again refused to depart from *Michigan v. Long* and reaffirmed the *Long* presumption.[60]

The Court's finding that many cases, as evidenced by the foregoing, were based primarily on federal grounds seems to conflict with Chief Justice Rehnquist's previous statement at his confirmation hearing, as follows:

> I do not think the [United States Supreme] Court is necessarily the final arbiter of the law of the land. It is the final arbiter of the U.S. Constitution and of the meaning of Federal statutes and treaties. But we still live in a somewhat pluralistic society where the States' highest courts are the final arbiters of the meaning of their State constitutions.[61]

The Court's application of *Long*, however, has led it to hold that a substantial number of state cases do not support the conclusion that they were decided on independent and adequate state grounds.[62] Indeed, in the five years before *Long*, "the Supreme Court reviewed 50 percent of the cases raising state grounds arguments."[63] In the five years after *Long*, "the Court reviewed 86.7 percent of the cases arguing independent nonfederal grounds."[64] These percentages suggest that the "justifications offered by the Court for preserving the adequate and independent state grounds doctrine," namely the "[r]eluctance to render advisory opinions and respect for state court decisions . . . are not being realized under the post-*Long* era."[65]

Response of Courts to the *Long* Requirements

Nevertheless, because of the *Long* decision, state courts have had to determine whether their state constitutions offer greater protection of individual rights than those offered under similar or identical provisions of the federal Constitution. One commentator noted,:"

In the past several decades, during which judicial federalism came of age, state courts adopted a variety of methodologies in approaching litigants' arguments that they should be accorded more rights under the state constitution than were currently (or were likely to be) recognized under the Federal Constitution.[66]

Some state courts have followed well-established federal precedent when interpreting a similar or identical state constitutional issue; indeed, some courts have followed in "lockstep," with the Supreme Court's interpretation of the federal Constitution.[67] Others have given federal constitutional law some deference but have used state constitutional law "as a supplementary or interstitial source of rights," justifying their departure from federal holdings.[68] Still others have adopted "the primacy approach," in which courts conduct a completely independent analysis of their state constitutions without giving United States Supreme Court decisions any more weight than is given to other state court decisions.[69] In light of these various practices employed by the courts, "[s]cholars continue to catalog the different sequential approaches to state and federal constitutional analysis. . . ."[70]

As Justice Souter observed while serving on the Supreme Court of New Hampshire, in the field of state constitutional law, state courts are often faced with difficult choices.[71] Justice Souter stated: "If we place too much reliance on federal precedent we will render the State rules a mere row of shadows; if we place too little, we will render State practice incoherent."[72]

Although New Jersey, the home of Justice Brennan, has always been a strong advocate of the new judicial federalism, the Supreme Court of New Jersey has chosen the "criteria" approach, under which we apply certain criteria to both the federal and state constitutions to determine whether we will rely on federal constitutional law rather than state constitutional law.[73] There appears to be a growing trend among state courts to adopt the "criteria approach."[74]

In *State v. Hunt*, Justice Handler, a member of my court, in a concurring opinion, set forth the judicial principles that a New Jersey court should consider in determining whether our state constitution affords its citizens greater protections than found under parallel provisions in the federal Constitution.[75] In *Hunt*, Justice Handler acknowledged that it is essential that a "considerable measure of cooperation must exist in a truly effective federalist system. Both federal and state courts share the goal of working for the good of the people to ensure order and freedom under what is publicly perceived as a single system of law."[76] Justice Handler recognized the danger of erosion or dilution of constitutional doctrine if "state courts [turn] uncritically to their state constitutions for convenient solutions to problems not readily or obviously found elsewhere."[77]

Justice Handler then identified seven standards or criteria that our state courts should consider in determining whether to invoke the New Jersey Constitution.[78] First, a state court must examine the textual language of the two constitutional provisions.[79] That examination is relevant for two reasons: (1) distinctive provisions of the state constitution may recognize rights not identified in the United States Constitution, and (2) "the phrasing of a particular provision in our [constitution] may be so significantly different from the language used" in the federal Constitution as to suggest an independent interpretation under the state constitution.[80] Second, the court should examine the legislative history of the state constitution to determine whether its drafters had a different intention in formulating the state constitution than the founding fathers had in drafting the federal Constitution.[81]

Third the court should examine preexisting state law, which may "suggest distinctive state constitutional rights."[82] Under the fourth criteria, a court should examine the structural differences between the federal and state constitutions to see whether they "also provide a basis for rejecting the constraints of federal doctrine at the state level."[83] For example, the federal Constitution grants enumerated powers while our state constitution "serves only to limit the sovereign power [that] inheres directly [to] the people."[84] Therefore, "the explicit affirmation of fundamental rights in [the New Jersey] Constitution can be seen as a guarantee of those rights and not as a restriction upon them."[85] The fifth criteria requires the court to determine whether the contested issue concerns a matter of particular state interest or local concern.[86] Closely aligned to the fifth criteria is the sixth: whether the "state's history and traditions" call for an "independent application of [the state] constitution."[87] Finally, the court should examine the public attitude of the state's citizenry to ascertain if general opinion may provide grounds to broaden state constitutional rights.[88]

The criteria are illustrative and not exhaustive; "[t]hey share a common thread—that distinctive and identifiable attributes of a state government, its laws and its people justify recourse to the state constitution as an independent source for recognizing and protecting individual rights."[89] The Supreme Court of New Jersey adopted the *Hunt* criteria in *State v. Williams*.[90] Although *Hunt* and *Williams* were decided before *Long*, we continue to adhere to those principles.

Some commentators,[91] and indeed, Justice Pashman, in a separate concurrence in *Hunt*,[92] believe that the "criteria approach" establishes a presumption in favor of the federal Constitution:

> [By using that approach], a state court is compelled to focus on the Supreme Court's decision, and to explain, in terms of the identified criteria, why it is not following the Supreme Court precedent. It is a relational, or comparative approach, which analyzes the relationship between, or comparison of, federal and state constitutional law. The stated criteria form a checklist of hurdles or prerequisites for the applicability of a state's highest law. A truly independent state constitutional interpretation "that will stand the test of detached criticism" is, under this approach, not enough.[93]

Interestingly, Justice Handler, the author of the *Hunt* criteria, criticized the Supreme Court of New Jersey in a capital-murder case for attempting "to clone the federal constitution to determine and define critical capital-murder issues and rights."[94] He asserted that "the random selection of constitutional protections, sometimes federal, sometimes state," has resulted in inconsistent approaches in capital-murder cases.[95] Another member of my court, Justice Pollock, in *State v. Lund*,[96] also chided the court for relying solely on federal constitutional law and failing to address state constitutional issues.[97]

As expected from such generalized criteria, even if my court agreed that the criteria were to be considered, the Supreme Court of New Jersey rarely has been unanimous about whether such guidelines have established an adequate and independent basis on which to ground a judgment. An examination of *State v. Hempele*[98] best illustrates the court's dilemma in determining whether the criteria approach should be used, and if used, how it should be applied.

Despite the United States Supreme Court opinion in *California v. Greenwood*,[99] in which the Court refused to extend Fourth Amendment protection to curbside garbage left out for collection, both New Jersey[100] and the state of Washington,[101] which also favors the criteria approach, have provided constitutional protection to an individual's garbage. In *Hempele*, a majority of the Supreme Court of New Jersey reasoned that the United States Supreme Court may be reluctant to impose Fourth Amendment protection that would bind every state.[102] That consideration, combined with New Jersey's efficient search warrant process, led the majority to extend state constitutional protection to an individual's curbside garbage.[103]

The decision, however, was not unanimous. Justice O'Hern, in his dissenting opinion, eloquently described his reluctance to interpret the provisions of the New Jersey Constitution as more protective than identically worded federal constitutional provisions. He listed two reasons: (1) a deep respect for the federal Constitution and the Supreme Court of the United States, and (2) "a pragmatic concern that the reservoirs of the [New Jersey Constitution] may be drained by overconsumption."[104]

Justice O'Hern wrote:

> For me, it is not enough to say that because we disagree with a majority opinion of the Supreme Court, we should invoke our State Constitution to achieve a contrary result. It sounds plausible, but one of the unanticipated consequences of that supposedly benign doctrine of state-constitutional rights is an inevitable shadowing of the moral authority of the United States Supreme Court. Throughout our history, we have maintained a resolute trust in that Court as the guardian of our liberties.[105]

Justice O'Hern believed that relying on state constitutional doctrine when an issue touches on the national identity may undermine respect for the Supreme Court. He observed that with regard to garbage, a citizen in Trenton ought not to have greater rights than a citizen across the Delaware River in Morrisville, Pennsylvania.[106] At a more pragmatic level, Justice O'Hern also "expressed concern about the expansion of rights based solely on state constitutional grounds because of the ease with which state constitutions may be amended."[107] Indeed, one of the major differences between state constitutions and the federal Constitution is the facility with which state constitutions can be and are amended.[108]

I also dissented in *Hempele*.[109] I disagreed with the majority's claim that because of certain factors unique to New Jersey, federal constitutional law should not apply. Applying the *Hunt* criteria, I concluded that there were no independent state-constitutional grounds to justify our divergence from federal law in this area. As I explained:

> The textual language, phrasing, and structures of the Fourth Amendment and article I, paragraph 7 are virtually identical. There is no state statute on this issue and hence no legislative history that would support interpreting the provision independently of federal law . . . Nor do I find that discarded garbage is a matter of par-

ticular state interest that affords an appropriate basis for resolving this issue on independent state grounds. New Jersey garbage is not unique, nor is there any reason to suppose that New Jersey citizens have a greater expectation of privacy in their trash than do citizens of most other states.[110]

I found that no public policy justified such a departure from federal law, and I believed that "federal law better comports with the reasonable expectation of privacy that most New Jersey citizens have for their discarded garbage placed on the street for collection."[111] I found it impossible to discern a unique New Jersey state attitude about garbage.

In my dissent, I also expressed concern that the majority's opinion would perplex the public. I observed the following:

> A citizen becomes confused when he or she finds that under virtually identical constitutional provisions, it is permissible for a federal agent, but not a New Jersey law-enforcement officer, to search his or her garbage. Such distinctions between federal and state constitutions are difficult for a citizen to fathom. In my view, garbage does not change its constitutional dimensions based on who searches the garbage in a particular location. Different treatment of such an ordinary commodity appears illogical to the public and hence breeds a fundamental distrust of the legal system that develops such distinctions.[112]

I recognize that, in some areas, state traditions may sustain a broader interpretive context. For example, the free-speech provisions of the New Jersey Constitution have long been interpreted as having a more expansive sweep than the comparable provisions of the United States Constitution.[113] We have also, in certain instances, found that article 1, paragraph 7, of the New Jersey Constitution affords greater protection against unreasonable seaches and seizures than does the Fourth Amendment of the federal Constitution. For instance, we have held that a vehicular search incident to an arrest for a traffic offense is unreasonable under the New Jersey Constitution.[114] We have also refused to adopt the good-faith exception under our state constitution.[115] We have held that the New Jersey Constitution protects privacy interests in telephone toll billing records,[116] and that our state constitution has more liberal criteria for standing to challenge the validity of a search than those under the federal Constitution.[117] We have even imposed a heavier burden on the State in showing the validity of a noncustodial consent to search under our state constitution than that required under the federal Constitution.[118]

Despite those rulings, however, we recently held that two warrantless, suspicionless searches were lawful under both the federal and state constitutions.[119] In each case, we declined to fashion our own analytical state constitutional framework but, instead, relied on the Supreme Court's analysis for considering the protections afforded by the Fourth Amendment. In *New Jersey Transit*, we applied the Fourth Amendment special-needs balancing test to determine the lawfulness of suspicionless searches of public employees and held that random drug testing of transit police officers was not unreasonable under the New Jersey Constitution.[120] In *New Jersey ex rel J.G.*, we again relied on the special-needs analysis and held that the statutes providing for the testing of charged or convicted sex offenders for acquired immune deficiency syndrome (AIDS) or infection with human immunodeficiency virus (HIV) did not violate the Fourth Amendment or our state constitution.[121]

New Jersey's New Judicial Federalism

Based on those recent decisions, some commentators have suggested that the New Jersey Supreme Court's commitment to new judicial federalism is waning.[122] I do not think so.

Today, there is much disagreement among the experts about the status of state constitutional law. Some have concluded that the new judicial federalism has failed because of its lack of doctrinal consistency in state court opinions.[123] Another scholar champions state constitutionalism as "a process of giving voice to the state court's understanding of the values and principles of the national community."[124] At least one commentator argues that the new judicial federalism has led to a "tidal wave of state court opinions that diverge from the standards established under the federal Constitution."[125] Nevertheless, he recognizes that the new federalism is alive and well and will continue.[126]

For various reasons, the new judicial federalism still meets with resistance.[127] As observed by Justice Pollock, that conclusion is supported by the findings of Professor Esler, who estimates that state supreme courts based their decisions primarily on state grounds in only 22 percent of their cases.[128] In addition, in 98 percent of the decisions based on state law, the state supreme courts deferred to precedents of the United States Supreme Court.[129] According to Professor Esler, only eight states consistently use state law, basing at least half of their decisions on state law grounds: Alaska, Arkansas, Florida, New Jersey, New York, South Dakota, Tennessee, and Texas.[130]

Several reasons have been cited to explain why interest in state constitutional jurisprudence appears to have diminished. The Rehnquist Court's emphasis on federalism has shifted the focus of legal scholars from the "new judicial federalism" that started in the late 1970s and flourished in the 1980s to the traditional garden-variety federalism. Moreover, many state judges and attorneys, trained primarily to consider the federal Constitution as the fundamental protector of individual rights, are reluctant to rely on state constitutional law. Federal law and jurisprudence is much more developed than state law. Indeed, many state constitutions do not have much history, and records of the constitutional conventions may be difficult to find or are nonexistent.[131] Senior Justice Ellen Peters of the Supreme Court of Connecticut has suggested that the lack of history and state law jurisprudence also results from the fact that even though most legal business is done in state courts (approximately 95 percent), and state courts determine the totality of rights of most litigants, most law reviews and law professors still discuss only federal law.[132]

Furthermore, because it is perceived that the new judicial federalism arose primarily from an attempt to give criminal defendants greater rights under state constitutions than they were receiving under the federal Constitution, a backlash developed among the legislators and voters. That backlash presented a practical problem for some judges, particularly those who had to run for election or retention.[133] To avoid negative repercussions, some state judges may have preferred to place blame for an unpopular decision on the United States Supreme Court. For instance, in 1982, the voters of both California and Florida amended their respective state constitutions to ensure that the state judiciaries did not exclude evidence that was admissible under federal law.[134] On June 8, 1982, the California electorate adopted Proposition 8, which amended article I, section 28(d) of the California Constitution to read, "relevant evidence shall not be excluded in any criminal proceeding."[135] In Florida, voters adopted a constitutional amendment requiring the Florida courts to construe state law "in conformity with the Fourth Amendment to the United States Constitution, as interpreted by the United States Supreme Court."[136]

In New Jersey, the legislature and voters also have expressed their disapproval of some of the state supreme court's decisions that expanded protection for criminal defendants. For example, the Supreme Court of New Jersey held that the New Jersey Constitution prohibited the imposition of a death sentence when a defendant had been convicted of causing only serious bodily injury resulting in death, as opposed to purposely or knowingly causing death.[137] Several years later, the voters approved a constitutional amendment explicitly permitting imposition of the death penalty "on a person convicted of purposely or knowingly causing death or purposely or knowingly causing serious bodily injury resulting in death."[138] Similarly, the New Jersey legislature enacted a statute limiting the state supreme court's proportionality review in death penalty cases "to a comparison of similar cases in which a sentence of death has been imposed" rather than to all cases in which the death penalty could have been imposed.[139]

As Justice Pollock, a member of our court, has written:

> Even if the [Supreme Court] is perceived as infallible only because it is final, the perception of infallibility, or something close to it, survives. As a practical matter, a state court that reaches a decision on a state ground contrary to a decision of the United States Supreme Court on a parallel federal ground must justify its decision to the legal community and to the public. In an era of constant public concern about crime, a state court's justification for granting enhanced protection to the rights of criminal defendants better be persuasive.[140]

One of the strongest arguments against the new judicial federalism is that "[a] national culture and a national media support a national political life. In all of these ways—from defense to art—modernity works against federalism."[141] As noted by Paul Kahn:

> Although some states may have been founded to secure a place for difference from existing political communities, most states were founded not in order to be different, but to realize for their own communities the ideals that are the common heritage of the nation. Whatever the differences in historical origins, those differences are less and less relevant to today's communities.[142]

However, some commentators reason that rather than fragmenting, "[t]his [new] federalism can make of us a better national community."[143] They believe that by freeing "state courts to place themselves in the tradition of American constitutionalism . . . then the meaning of American citizenship is enriched. . . . It is especially enriched because fifty different courts will talk with each other, as well as with the federal courts[.]"[144] Ultimately, how you view the new judicial federalism will depend on your views of the "federalist system, the role of state courts in a constitutional democracy, and the relative roles of law and order and fundamental rights at the close of the twentieth century."[145]

Conclusion

It is clear today that the assertion that a state constitution provides greater protection than the federal Constitution is no longer novel. In my Court, when we base our decision on the New Jersey Constitution, we state clearly the "adequate and independent" state grounds that form the basis for that opinion. Nonetheless, there will continue to be cases in which state courts will be faced with having to determine whether its constitution provides greater protection of individual rights than afforded under the federal Constitution. In making that determination, state courts will still be presented with the vexing problem of how to prevent state constitutions from becoming "a mere row of shadows" of the federal Constitution and from gleaning such little guidance from federal law as to make state law "incoherent."[146]

I believe that New Jersey's "criteria approach" best solves that problem. By providing criteria that must be considered in every case, the New Jersey Supreme Court has furnished consistency, at least in method, if not in analysis. I am concerned about the extent to which fifty independent state court systems can substitute for the federal courts in the protection of fundamental rights [147] and for the "common ideal of American constitutionalism."[148] I agree with Justice O'Hern that "[t]he great moral disasters of the twentieth century . . . all occurred in societies in which there was no genuine rule of law, no appeal of last resort, no guarantee of liberties."[149] I also agree that, "[b]ecause the United States Supreme Court enjoys a profound residue of trust, it occupies the position of the final arbiter, the as yet unassailable guardian of our rights and liberties."[150]

I recognize that "state constitutional law plays a vital role in the federalist system."[151] Nonetheless, to me, the New Jersey criteria approach, which gives slight deference to the United States Constitution, best achieves the appropriate balance for determining whether a state constitution provides greater protection of individual rights than a similar federal constitutional provision. Requiring a state court to explain its departure from the interpretation of an identically worded federal constitutional provision focuses the court's attention on reconciling seemingly analogous provisions of state and federal constitutions. Unless the state court can show from an examination of the textual language of the two constitutional provisions, the legislative history of the state constitution, or the state's history and tradition that the matter is of particular state interest or concern, it should not expand federal constitutional rights under an identical state constitutional provision. Those cases in which there is a discernible reason to interpret identical federal and state provisions differently will be limited.

Applying the criteria approach will not diminish the importance of state constitutions or state courts. As observed by Chief Judge Judith Kaye of the New York Court of Appeals, "[o]verwhelmingly, our nation's legal disputes are centered in the state courts, which handle more than ninety-seven percent of the litigation."[152] Entire "categories of cases affecting the day-to-day circumstances, indeed survival, of our citizens are largely[,] if not exclusively adjudicated in the state courts."[153] State courts determine in large part "how well this nation attains its ideal of equal justice."[154] In doing that work, the state courts will rely not only on their state constitutions but on that "golden and sacred rule of reason," the common law.[155] "As the courts both literally and figuratively closest to the people, it is beyond question that state courts [will] continue to play a vital role in shaping the lives of our citizenry"[156] and that state constitutional law will continue to play a vital role in the federalist system.

Notes

1. 463 U.S. 1032 (1983).

2. See id. at 1041.

3. See State v. Hunt (Merrel), 450 A.2d 952, 965–67 (N.J. 1982) (Handler, J., concurring) (hereinafter M. Hunt).

4. See Williams, "In the Glare of the Supreme Court: Continuing Methodology and Legitimacy Problems in Independent State Constitutional Rights Adjudication," 72 *Notre Dame L. Rev.* 1015, 1063–64 (1997).

5. Id. at 1015.

6. Brennan, Jr., "State Constitutions and the Protections of Individual Rights," 90 Harv. L. Rev. 489, 491 (1977).

7. Brennan, Jr., "State Supreme Court Judge Versus United States Supreme Court Justice: A Change in Function and Perspective, 19 *U. Fla. L. Rev.* 225, 227, 236 (1966) (explaining different roles in constitutional interpretative theory and practice).

8. See Kaye, "Dual Constitutionalism in Practice and Principle," 61 *St. John's L. Rev.* 399, 400–01 (1987).

9. See id. at 400.

10. See Howard, "The Renaissance of State Constitutional Law," 1 *Emerging Issues In St. Consti. L.* 1, 6 (1988).

11. See id.

12. See id. at 7.

13. Kaye, supra note 8, at 403.

14. See Williams, "In the Supreme Court's Shadow: Legitimacy of State Rejection of Supreme Court Reasoning and Result," 35 *S.C. L. Rev.* 353, 355 (1984).

15. See id.

16. Compare N.J. Const. art. I, § 7 with U.S. Const. amend. IV (both dealing with unreasonable searches and seizures).

17. Herb v. Pitcairn, 324 U.S. 117, 125 (1945).

18. Id. at 126.

19. Kaye, supra note 8, at 407.

20. Tribe, *American Constitutional Law* § 3-24, at 164 (2d ed. 1988).

21. 463 U.S. 1032 (1983).

22. Kaye, supra note 8, at 407.

23. See Long, 463 U.S. at 1038–39.

24. See id. at 1040–41.

25. See id.

26. Id. at 1041.

27. Id.

28. Id.

29. Pollock, "The Court and State Contstitutional Law, Remarks on the Burger Court at the University of Tulsa," in *The Burger Court: Counter Revolution or Confirmation?* 244, 245 (Bernard Schwartz ed., 1998). See, e.g., Gormley, "Ten Adventures in State Constitutional Law," 1 *Emerging Issues in St. Const. L.* 29, 37 (1988) (suggesting that the United States Supreme Court's decision in *Long* was an attempt to expand Supreme Court review "over potentially unpalatable state constitutional decisions"); Esler, "State Supreme Court Commitment to State Law," 78 *Judicature* 25, 30 (1994).

30. Tribe, supra note 20, at 165.

31. Pollock, supra note 29, at 245–46.

32. For a complete list of cases in which the Supreme Court has repeatedly followed *Michigan v. Long*, see Arizona v. Evans, 514 U.S. 1, 7–8 n. 2 (1995); Wright et al., 16B *Federal Practice and Procedure* § 4032, at 444 n. 14 (2d ed. 1996).

33. 497 U.S. 177 (1990).

34. Id. at 182.

35. 496 U.S. 582 (1990).

36. See id. at 588 n.4.

37. 480 U.S. 79 (1987).

38. See id. at 83–84 (1987).

39. See, e.g., Arizona v. Evans, 514 U.S. 1 (1995); Pennsylvania v. Labron, 518 U.S. 938 (1996); Ohio v. Robinette, 519 U.S. 33 (1996).

40. 514 U.S. 1 (1995).

41. See id. at 4.

42. See id.

43. See id.

44. Id. at 10 (quoting *Long*, 463 U.S. at 1041) (citation omitted).

45. See id. at 16.

46. 514 U.S. at 8 (1995).

47. Id.

48. Id. at 9 (quoting Minnesota v. National Tea Co., 309 U.S. 551, 557 (1940)).

49. 518 U.S. 938 (1996).

50. See id. at 941 (quoting Long, 463 U.S. at 1040–41).

51. See id.

52. Id. at 947 (Stevens, J., dissenting).

53. Id. at 950 (Stevens, J., dissenting) (citation omitted).

54. 519 U.S. 33 (1996).

55. See id. at 33.

56. Id. at 33-34.

57. See id.

58. Id. at 37.

59. Id.

60. See id at 33–35.

61. Kauger, "Reflections on Federalism: Protections Afforded by State Constitutions," 27 *Gonz. L. Rev.* 1, 2 (quoting *Nomination of Justice William Hubbs Rehnquist: Hearings Before the Senate Committee on the Judiciary*, 99th Cong., 2d Sess. 141 (1986)).

62. See Wright, supra note 32, § 4032, at 444.

63. Williams, "Constitutional Law: Premature Federal Adjudication Through the Plain Statement Rule," 8 *U. Fla. J.L. & Pub. Pol'y* 129, 138 n. 64 (1996).

64. See id.

65. See id. at 135.

66. Williams, supra note 4, at 1018; see also Diehm, "New Federalism and Constitutional Criminal Procedure: Are We Repeating the Mistakes of the Past?," 55 *Md. L. Rev.* 223, 259 (1996).

67. See Maltz, "The Political Dynamic of the 'New Judicial Federalism,'" 2 *Emerging Issues in St. Const. L.* 233, 233–34 (1989).

68. See Williams, supra note 4, at 1019.

69. See also id. at 366.

70. Id. at 1018.

71. See id. at 1063.

72. Id. (quoting State v. Bradberry, 522 A.2d 1380, 1389 (N.H. 1986) (Souter, J., concurring specially)).

73. See id. at 1021–22; see also State v. Hunt, 450 A.2d 952 (N.J. 1982) (Handler, J., concurring).

74. See Williams, supra note 4, at 1025.

75. See *M. Hunt*, 450 A.2d at 965–67.

76. Id. at 964.

77. Id. at 963, 965–67.

78. Id. at 965–67.

79. See id. at 965.

80. Id.

81. See id. at 965.

82. Id.

83. Id. at 965–66.

84. Id. at 966.

85. Id.

86. See id.

87. Id. at 966.

88. See id.

89. Id. at 967.

90. State v. Williams, 459 A.2d 641, 650 (N.J. 1983).

91. See Williams, supra note 14, at 386–89.

92. See *M. Hunt*, 450 A.2d at 960 & n.1 (Pashman, J., concurring).

93. Williams, supra note 4, at 1023 (quoting Howard, "State Courts and Constitutional Rights in the Day of the Burger Court," 62 *Va. L. Rev.* 873, 934 (1976)).

94. State v. Hunt (James), 558 A.2d 1259, 1292 (N.J.) (Handler, J., dissenting), *reconsideration denied*, 564 A.2d 873 (N.J. 1989) (hereinafter J. Hunt).

95. Id.

96. 573 A.2d 1376 (N.J. 1990) (Pollock, J., concurring).

97. See generally id. at 1385–87.

98. 576 A.2d 793 (N.J. 1990).

99. 486 U.S. 35 (1988).

100. See *Hempele* 576 A.2d at 813.

101. See State v. Boland, 800 P.2d 1112, 1115–18 (Wash. 1990).

102. See *Hempele*, 576 A.2d at 800-01.

103. See id. at 814.

104. O'Hern, *Remarks at the Occasion of the Harvard Law School Conference on the Honorable William J. Brennan, Jr.*, 10 (March 14, 1998).

105. *Hempele*, 576 A.2d at 815 (O'Hern, J., concurring in part and dissenting in part).

106. See id. at 816 (O'Hern, J., concurring in part and dissenting in part); cf. Right to Choose v. Byrne, 450 A.2d 925, 950–51 (N.J. 1982) (O'Hern, J., dissenting) (regarding public

funding of abortions, citizen of New Jersey should not enjoy greater equal protection rights than other citizens of this nation).

107. O'Hern, supra note 104, at 10.

108. See, e.g., Kaye, supra note 8, at 408–09.

109. *Hempele*, 576 A.2d at 816 (Garibaldi, J., dissenting).

110. Id. at 817–18 (Garibaldi, J., dissenting).

111. Id. at 816-17 (Garibaldi, J., dissenting).

112. Id. at 817 (Garibaldi, J., dissenting).

113. See, e.g., New Jersey Coalition Against the War in the Middle East v. J.M.B. Realty Corp., 650 A.2d 757, 770–71 (N.J. 1994), *cert. denied*, 516 U.S. 812 (1995); State v. Schmid, 423 A.2d 615, 626–28 (N.J. 1980), *appeal dismissed*, 455 U.S. 100 (1982).

114. See State v. Pierce, 642 A.2d 947, 960 (N.J. 1994).

115. See State v. Novembrino, 519 A.2d 820, 856–57 (N.J. 1987).

116. See *Hunt*, 450 A.2d at, 956–57.

117. See State v. Alston, 440 A.2d 1311, 1318–19 (N.J. 1981).

118. See State v. Johnson, 346 A.2d 66, 67–68 (N.J. 1975).

119. See New Jersey Transit PBA Local 304 v. New Jersey Transit Corp., 701 A.2d 1243 (N.J. 1997) (hereinafter *New Jersey Transit*); New Jersey ex rel. J.G., 701 A.2d 1260 (N.J. 1997).

120. See *New Jersey Transit*, 701 A.2d at 1255–60.

121. See 701 A.2d at 1266–75.

122. See, e.g., Snider and Winokur, "In First Cases, Poritz Shows No Liberal Bent," *N.J.L.J.*, Sept. 29, 1997, at 1.

123. See, e.g., Pollock, supra note 29, at 254; Diehm, supra note 66, at 238. See also Gardner, "The Failed Discourse of State Constitutionalism," 90 *Mich L. Rev.* 761 (1992) (contending that state constitutional law has failed to produce coherent body of law).

124. Kahn, "Interpretation and Authority in State Constitutions," 106 *Harv. L. Rev.* 1147, 1168 (1993).

125. Diehm, supra note 66, at 238.

126. See id. at 260.

127. See Grodin, "The New Judicial Federalism: A New Generation Symposium Issue," 30 *Val. U.L. Rev.* 601, 608 (1996); Diehm, supra note 66, at 260.

128. See Pollock, supra note 29, at 252 (citing Esler, supra note 29 at 28–29).

129. See id.

130. See id. at n. 95.

131. See id. at 253 (discussing Esler, supra note 29, at 28–31).

132. Honorable Ellen Peters, Senior Justice of the Connecticut Supreme Court, *Remarks at the Fourth New York University Justice William J. Brennan, Jr. Lecture on State Courts and Social Justice* (Feb. 11, 1998).

133. See Pollock, supra note 29, at 252.

134. See Cal. Const. art. I, § 28(d) (amended 1982); Fla. Const. art. I, § 12 (amended 1982).

135. Cal. Const. art I, § 28(d) (amended 1982). For a review of some of the reasons the voters adopted Proposition 8 and for a review of the California courts' subsequent treatment of the amendment, see Trask, II and Searight, "Proposition 8 and the Exclusionary Rule: Towards a New Balance of Defendant and Victim Rights," 23 *Pac. L.J.* 1101 (1992).

136. Fla. Const. art. I, § 12 (amended 1982). For an excellent historical analysis of Florida constitutional law, see Hawkins, "Florida Constitutional Law: A Ten-Year Retrospective on the State Bill of Rights," 14 *Nova L. Rev.* 693 (1990).

137. See State v. Gerald, 549 A.2d 792, 807 (N.J. 1988).

138. See N.J. Const. art. I, ¶ 12 (amended 1992).

139. N.J. Stat. Ann. § 2C:11-3(e) (West Supp. 1998).

140. Pollock, supra note 29, at 251–52.

141. Kahn, supra note 124, at 1150.

142. Id. at 1166.

143. Id. at 1168.

144. Id.

145. Pollock, supra note 29, at 251.

146. Williams, supra note 4, at 1063.

147. See Diehm, supra note 66, at 244–45.

148. Kahn, supra note 124, at 1166.

149. State v. Hempele, 576 A.2d 793, 815–16 (N.J. 1990) (O'Hern, J., concurring in part and dissenting in part).

150. O'Hern, supra note 104, at 8.

151. Pollock, supra note 29, at 255.

152. Kaye, "State Courts at the Dawn of a New Century: Common Law Courts Reading Statutes and Constitutions," 70 *N.Y.U. L. Rev.* 1, 3 (1995).

153. Id. at 4.

154. Id. at 5.

155. Id. (quoting Mullet, *Fundamental Law and the American Revolution, 1760–1776*, 46 (1966)).

156. Id.

13

THE IMPORTANCE OF DIALOGUE
Globalization, the Rehnquist Court, and Human Rights

CLAIRE L'HEUREUX-DUBÉ

Introduction

There are two aspects of any review of the Rehnquist Court from a global perspective: the Court's impact on courts in other parts of the world and on international law and the impact of others courts and international law on its decisions.

For most of the twentieth century, the human rights provisions of the United States Constitution, primarily found in the first ten Amendments [the "Bill of Rights"] and the Fourteenth Amendment, served as models for similar provisions in the laws and governing documents of other nations and in international agreements and covenants. The highest courts of nation-states and international courts and tribunals looked to the decisions of Supreme Court of the United States as most persuasive when it came time to apply and interpret their own governing constitutions.

Just over ten years ago, shortly after William Rehnquist became Chief Justice of the United States Supreme Court, leading British barrister Anthony Lester, Q.C. (now Lord Lester of Herne Hill) wrote:

> [T]he Bill of Rights is more than an historical inspiration for the creation of charters and institutions dedicated to the protection of liberty. Currently, there is a vigorous overseas trade in the Bill of Rights, in international and constitutional litigation involving norms derived from American constitutional law. When life or liberty is at stake, the landmark judgments of the Supreme Court of the United States, giving fresh meaning to the principles of the Bill of Rights, are studied with as much attention in New Delhi or Strasbourg as they are in Washington, D.C., or the State of Washington, or Springfield, Illinois.[1]

In recent years, globalization in the process of judging and lawyering and growing international links and influences have affected judicial decisions, particularly at the level of top appellate courts throughout the world. And as courts look *all* over the world for sources of authority, the process of international influence has changed from *reception* to *dialogue*. Judges no longer simply *receive* the cases of other jurisdictions, particularly the United States, and then apply them or modify them for their own jurisdiction. Rather, cross-pollination and dialogue between ju-risdictions is increasingly occurring.

There is, unfortunately, one large exception to this general worldwide trend. The United States Supreme Court seems to operate almost totally in a legal isola-tion booth. The failure of the Justices of the Rehnquist Court to take part in the in-ternational dialogue among the courts of the world is contributing to a growing iso-lation and diminished influence. This failure is a loss for American jurisprudence, and for the development of human rights around the world.[2]

This chapter looks at the development of global law, particularly in the area of human rights, and the historic impact of United States Supreme Court jurispru-dence on the courts of other nation-states. It will then look at why and how that im-pact has declined during the period of the Rehnquist Court.

Historical Role of the United States Supreme Court on Foreign Courts

As most of today's nation-states started out as colonies, their law was dependent on "reception" of other courts decision, usually from their mother country.[3] For exam-ple, the common law was as declared by the House of Lords and the Privy Council, in Britain, and their cases were applied by colonial courts throughout the world.[4] Even as the formal bonds of colonialism were loosened, and adherence to these de-cisions was no longer necessary, the influence of British jurisprudence on former colonies's courts remained strong.

However, with this loosening, the prominence of American jurisprudence grew throughout the world.[5] This is particularly true in the field of constitutional-ism and human rights. The very concept of judicial review of legislation in accor-dance with guaranteed rights originated in the United States Supreme Court, in the classic case of *Marbury v. Madison*.[6]

As one of the pioneer rights documents, and the first to be interpreted and given meaning by the judiciary, the United States Bill of Rights had a long history that made it natural for other countries to look to its text and interpretation when drafting and interpreting their own constitutions and human rights protections. This process took into account not only the textual wording of American provisions but also interpretations of them by the American courts.[7]

In Canada, for example, immediately after the passage of the 1982 *Canadian Charter of Rights and Freedoms*[8] scholars compared and contrasted its language with that of the United States Bill of Rights for indications of how the *Charter* should be interpreted, focusing on both the similarities and the differences in the two documents.[9]

Our courts, particularly the Supreme Court of Canada, have followed the lead of scholars. Though other international sources are cited, especially judgments of the European Court and Commission of Human Rights, American jurisprudence on the Bill of Rights was most prominent, particularly in the early years.

Our court has used this jurisprudence in a number of ways. First, the Supreme Court of Canada often cited United States precedent in setting forth principles of interpretation for the *Charter*.[10] Second, judicial interpretations of specific rights in the United States Bill of Rights have been considered in determining the equivalent interpretations of Canadian rights. American jurisprudence on rights such as freedom of religion, due process guarantees, and free speech are some examples.[11]

Third, we have considered American solutions to particular problems before ruling on the same issues. This has given us the advantage of wisdom in areas including the constitutionality of restrictions on abortion, hate speech, and publication of court proceedings,[12] to name just a few.

Fourth, the rights guaranteed under Canada's *Charter* may be infringed by the government if the law is "demonstrably justified in a free and democratic society."[13] Our courts have held that one factor in making this determination is examination of experience and practice in other free and democratic societies.[14] As a neighboring country, with values similar in some ways to our own, the statutes and jurisprudence of the United States have played a prominent role in this comparison of foreign approaches. Of course, the fact that we look to the United States does not mean that we always or even usually followed the United States approach.[15]

In fact, because the focus of this chapter is on the impact of the Rehnquist Court, it is important to note that current references to United States Supreme Court precedent are seldom from recent holdings. Rather, we rely on cases from the 1950s, 1960s, 1970s, and early 1980s—from the Warren and Burger Courts. During these years, particularly those of the Warren Court, the United States Supreme Court engaged in a redefinition, expansion and modernization of Bill of Rights interpretation. Cases such as *Miranda* v. *Arizona* [16] and *Brown* v. *Board of Education*[17] have had a large impact on the spirit and development of human rights protections worldwide.[18]

The strength of these judgments comes not only from the fact that the Court was interpreting a Constitution that had been in place for over a century. They also attempted to make the principles of their constitution relevant for modern times.[19]

Globalization and the Broader International Judicial Dialogue

There were other reasons, of course, for the strong influence of countries such as the United States and Britain. Until recently, only certain countries' law reports were widely available in many places. Legal literature also focused on the largest and most important jurisdictions. Judges and litigants, naturally, looked to places with the most easily accessible materials.

Another especially influential factor is the importance of education. Judges, lawyers, and academics who go abroad for parts of their education usually attend universities overseas and, until recently, increasing numbers went for their postgraduate work in the United States. When time came to look for solutions to similar problems, they naturally turned for inspiration and comparison to those jurisdictions whose ideas are familiar to them.[20]

Current trends, however, show how dramatically this picture is changing.[21] Rather than a one-way transmission, the development of human rights jurisprudence, in particular, is increasingly becoming a dialogue. Judges look to a *broad* spectrum of sources in the law of human rights when deciding how to interpret their constitutions and deal with new problems. To a greater and greater extent, they are *mutually* reading and discussing each others' jurisprudence.[22]

There are a number of reasons for this cross-fertilization. First, perhaps more than ever, the same issues are facing many courts throughout the world. Issues such as assisted suicide, abortion, hate speech, gay and lesbian rights, environmental protection, privacy, and the nature of democracy are being placed before judges in different jurisdictions at approximately the same time. As social debates and discussions around the world become more and more similar, so, of course, do the equivalent legal debates.[23]

A second factor leading to globalization is in the field of human rights and the nature of those rights and their guarantees. Since World War II, there has been a global emphasis on human rights, which led to the passage of the Universal Declaration of Human Rights and the signing of International Covenants on Civil and Political Rights and on Economic, Social, and Cultural Rights. These have been reflected in regional human rights treaties and in human rights guarantees in national constitutions.[24] Because the legal protection of human rights is new to many countries, there is sometimes little or no domestic jurisprudence to consult in giving them meaning, and judgments from elsewhere are particularly useful and necessary. International treaties and foreign decisions interpreting these provisions are often used as a "springboard" to begin development of human rights jurisprudence, and to fill in gaps when no precedent exists.[25]

Links to international law help form a kind of "common denominator" of understanding for judges interpreting national or regional human rights documents. National human rights guarantees are inspired by or linked to internationally guaranteed rights, and jurists around the world are increasingly trained in international human rights law.

A third factor leading to the growing internationalization of the judiciary is the advancement of communication technology.[26] Decisions of courts worldwide are diffused electronically, while numerous Internet sites consolidate access to banks of case law, statutes, and other materials from various jurisdictions. These developments make it much easier to consult comparative constitutional sources in argument and in judgments.

A fourth contributor to the increasing internationalization of the judicial world is the growing personal contact between members of the judiciary from different countries. Judges often discuss common problems at international judges' conferences, by e-mail and over the telephone. I know that the friendships I have developed with judges from countries such as the United States, Zimbabwe, South Africa, and Israel, to name just a few, have enabled me to discuss and correspond with them about decisions of our court and theirs, and about issues that cross national boundaries.

Recounting the increasing globalization of the law means also noting the pitfalls. First, foreign reasoning should not be imported without sufficient consideration of the context in which it is being applied.

As Justice Breyer noted in his dissenting judgment in *Printz v. United States*,[27] after referring to the constitutions of several other countries:

Of course, we are interpreting our own Constitution, not those of other nations, and there may be relevant political and structural differences between their systems and our own. But their experience may nonetheless cast an empirical light on the consequences of different solutions to a common legal problem.[28]

And perhaps most important, it is necessary to remember that this should be a process of *dialogue*. We should not be global jurists only when constitutions are new and then turn inward once jurisprudential principles have been developed. Interaction must continue long after the rights themselves are articulated and tests for interpretation have been developed. Jurists in all countries must be careful to ensure that we do not slip into the familiar pattern of defining themselves as countries that *give* or *receive* law. Nation-states such as the United States and Canada which have had a long history of being cited by the courts in other nations must be willing to listen to arguments citing precedents from other nations.

The Rehnquist Court in the Era of Globalization

In general, the Rehnquist Court is less influential internationally than its predecessors. I suggest several reasons for this decline in influence, some of which are within the Court's control and others which are beyond its power to change.

The Difficulty of Assessing Impact

First, it is appropriate to note the difficulty of coming to conclusions about the impact of a given court on others. Though an examination of the number of citations to the judgments of a certain court may generate impressive statistics, these statistics only give a partial picture of a court's "impact." A large number of citations, for example, may reflect great influence, or may simply show a number of authorities all standing for the same proposition. Similarly, a judgment of a foreign court may influence the deciding judge, or instead may be simply another authority used to buttress a conclusion already reached. Citations to the judgments of a foreign court may be passing references, or may reflect extensive consideration of that court's approach. Finally, decisions of other courts may be considered or applied in a very narrow area of the law, or may instead influence an approach to interpretation or to an area of law in general.

Indeed, courts (especially the U.S. Supreme Court under different Chief Justices) are often defined by their general approach to constitutional decision making. Commentators often embark on a search for the defining mood or tenor of a court's approach, and there is frequent debate over the direction in which a court is heading. The tenor or general approach of a court can also have an impact internationally, and indeed, this is in many ways what is most important in terms of impact.

The Warren Court's two decisions in *Brown v. Board of Education*[29] are cited in judgments ranging from a decision about the expulsion of a student from school in Trinidad and Tobago for wearing a *hijab*[30] to a judgment in New Zealand applying a treaty on Maori fishing rights,[31] not only because the cases are directly applicable, but because they stand for a principle and an approach to constitutional interpretation taken by the court that rendered it. Though this spirit incontestably has an impact, it is hard to capture or measure.

In addition, the fact that decisions often build on each other makes it hard to assess "impact." For example, a citation from the Rehnquist Court may show that court's influence, or it may show the impact of a long line of precedents that are confirmed or developed by that decision. In addition, the impact of a given court may not be seen right away. During the period in which the Warren Court was sitting, references to United States cases by the Canadian Supreme Court were fewer than in any other period in Canadian history.[32] However, the influence of the Warren Court on Canada's *Charter* jurisprudence is incontestably very strong and is reflected by stronger, more dramatic statistics in subsequent years.

In addition, the impact of a court always takes some time to be felt, because it may be several years before other courts have the opportunity to consider the jurisprudence and apply it as appropriate cases arise. Therefore, an assessment of the impact of the Rehnquist Court during its term, just twelve years after it began sitting, is necessarily preliminary and may be different over time.

"Impact," in short, is impossible to completely assess in a scientific way and its measure will necessarily be based on general impressions formed by talking to judges and reading judgments from around the world. As one judge, working in one country, I cannot give a complete picture of the impact of the Rehnquist Court in jurisdictions throughout the world and how this has changed relative to other U.S. Supreme Courts in history. What I can do, however, is add to any data that are available my impressions and observations, formed while being a judge in Canada, reading judgments from courts in different jurisdictions, and talking and meeting with judges from around the world. These observations, I hope, can be combined with those of others to form a more comprehensive picture of the place of the Rehnquist Court on the international judicial scene.

A Declining Impact

Despite these cautions, there is a general perception that the Rehnquist Court's impact has declined relative to that of its predecessors. First, this is borne out by statistical analysis, at least of the situation in Canada. An informal analysis of Canadian Supreme Court decisions since 1986 revealed that the Rehnquist Court was cited in fewer than one-half as many cases as the Warren Court, and in just under one-third the number of Burger Court cases.

There is an even greater disparity if one compares the number of Rehnquist Court decisions cited by the Canadian court to the number of its predecessors' cases cited; Burger Court cases, in particular, vastly outnumber cases from the Rehnquist Court.

Though I have not compiled statistics, a similar trend is easily discernible through reading judgments from other countries. When the U.S. Supreme Court is cited, it is usually Warren or Burger Court decisions, and sometimes older ones. The Rehnquist Court is much less frequently cited. A couple of examples will suffice, beginning with the Indian Supreme Court decision in *Rajagopal and Another v. State of Tamil Nadu.*[33]

Central to the *Rajagopal* case were issues of balancing freedom of expression and of privacy, and the court relied heavily on American jurisprudence. The court devoted several pages to the cases of *New York Times Co. v. Sullivan*,[34] *Cox Broadcasting Corp. v. Cohn*,[35] *Griswold v. Connecticut*,[36] and *Roe v. Wade*,[37] all classic Warren and Burger Court cases. It included extensive descriptions of the facts and holdings, and provided lengthy citations from several of these cases. The only reference to Rehnquist Court jurisprudence, however, was a one sentence comment that "[t]hough [*Roe v. Wade*] received a few knocks in the recent decision in *Planned Parenthood v. Casey* (1992), the central holding of this decision has been left untouched—indeed affirmed."[38] This decision illustrates the trend of focusing on Warren and Burger Court decisions, and giving less attention to Rehnquist Court judgments modifying or explaining those decisions. The contrast between the strong focus on the reasoning of the older decisions and the passing reference to the Rehnquist Court decision is striking.

Another example is the opinion of Justice Ackermann of the Constitutional Court of South Africa in *Ferreira v. Levin NO*.[39] The case dealt with the right to liberty and freedom from self-incrimination. The court examined the protections of the Fifth Amendment and referred to the judgments in *Miranda, Feldman v. United States*,[40] *Hoffman v. United States*,[41] *United States v. James*,[42] *Ullmann v. United States*,[43] *Bolling v. Sharpe*,[44] *Board of Regents v. Roth*,[45] and *Meyer v. Nebraska*,[46] quoting from several of them. Again, though the court cited a wide variety of Fifth Amendment decisions from various eras of constitutional jurisprudence, no Rehnquist Court decisions were considered. The *Ferreira* decision also illustrates the declining prominence of American constitutional jurisprudence in general, because American cases were much less prominent in this opinion than those of Canadian, German, and British Courts, as well as the European Court of Human Rights. This is true of other cases as well. Thus, though the Rehnquist Court's impact has declined internationally, so has the influence of the United States Supreme Court in general.

Therefore, though the Rehnquist Court's jurisprudence is regularly consulted and considered and the "overseas trade"[47] in the Bill of Rights is far from being at an end, numbers and general perceptions suggest a decline relative to previous courts. This, of course, is not scientifically demonstrable, at least not at this stage and not without more in-depth research.

Reasons for the Decline

As noted earlier, the Rehnquist Court has not relied on the decisions of the highest courts of other nation-states and international courts. In fact, the Court has seldom even made reference to those tribunals. Moreover, it has isolated itself from the globalization trend of law, lawyering, and judging. These actions, of course, have led to a reciprocal reluctance by the courts in other nations to rely on American case law.

In addition, the changing nature of Supreme Court jurisprudence under the Rehnquist Court has accelerated the decline. Before I analyze these factors, it must be pointed out that there could have been a decline in influence of the United

States Supreme Court, even without any ideological changes, because of the structural dissimilarity between the U.S. Constitution and those written more recently.

Most twentieth-century constitutions, which are drafted in language that has its sources in European and international human rights conventions, are more detailed and frequently expressly permit limitations of the enumerated rights, either within the rights themselves or as a general limitation provision. These make it less likely that American jurisprudence will be cited as directly applicable to the interpretation of the human rights provisions of another country.

For example, more recent constitutions contain "justification provisions," where rights, unlike those in the United States Constitution are not absolute, and courts are called on to determine whether laws that infringe them are justifiable. The language of many justification provisions is similar. The European Convention on Human Rights, for example, contains justification clauses, which note usually that limitations on the rights must be "prescribed by law and justified in a democratic society."[48] The Canadian *Charter* states that the rights and freedoms guaranteed in it are guaranteed "subject only to such reasonable limits prescribed by law as can be demonstrably justified in a free and democratic society."[49] Justification provisions that are similar in language and intent exist in South Africa,[50] Israel,[51] Namibia,[52] and New Zealand.[53]

In addition to these general differences, constitutions in other nation-states are different in structure and language than that of the United States, and courts, not surprisingly, look to countries in which constitutions are similar in structure and language to their own. For example, in *Kauesa v. Minister of Home Affairs*,[54] Justice O'Linn of the Namibian High Court emphasized the importance of the distinction in that country's constitution between fundamental rights and fundamental freedoms and suggested that Indian jurisprudence was of the greatest use in interpreting that document because of the strong similarities in structure and language between the two documents.

Similarly, in *S.v. Zuma*,[55] Kentridge A.J. of the Constitutional Court of South Africa held that section 11(d) of the Canadian *Charter* "bears a close relationship to section 25(3)(a) and (c) of [the South African] Constitution. In both Canada and South Africa the presumption of innocence is derived from the centuries-old principle of English law . . . Accordingly, I consider that we may appropriately apply the principles worked out by the Canadian Supreme Court. . . ."[56] Other courts have also emphasized that similarities in definitions of rights make the jurisprudence of certain countries, on certain questions of interpretation, particularly worthwhile.

That is not to say that when there are differences in the language or structure of a constitution, the jurisprudence from these countries is useless or unhelpful. On the contrary, comparing the human rights provisions of another country with one's own, articulating the differences, and using them to analyze why the jurisprudence of that country should or should not be followed is particularly useful. For example, in *Kauesa*,[57] though Justice O'Linn had already noted that Indian law was most useful, he went on to consider the jurisprudence of several other countries, examining whether their approaches were appropriate in Namibia.

Because it remains useful to consider other nations' jurisprudence even when constitutional provisions are different, to fully explain the decline in influence of the Rehnquist Court, other factors, mostly jurisprudential and ideological, must also be considered.

American Debate Over the Intent of the Framers

A second factor contributing, in my view, to the decline in the influence of the Rehnquist Court is the frequently expressed belief of many of its members that the Court's interpretations of the Constitution should be based on originalism—a search for the intent of those who drafted a given provision.[58] Indeed, much constitutional debate in the United States is focused on the question of whether an originalist or evolving approach should be taken to constitutional interpretation.[59]

Of course, if an American constitutional decision is focused on the intent of those who passed a given provision in the late eighteenth century, this is unhelpful to those who are interpreting constitutions or human rights provisions drafted in the latter half of the twentieth century—a different time and in a different context.

Second, and perhaps more important, there is generally less debate elsewhere over whether the intent of the framers of a constitution is what should govern its interpretation. Originalism, an extremely controversial question in the United States, is usually simply not the focus, or even a topic, of debate elsewhere. Not that there are not heated differences of opinion about "judicial activism" or whether judging can be merely the interpretation of words on a page,[60] but this debate is for the most part not as focused on textualism and originalism as that in the United States.

Though the legitimacy of judicial review is certainly controversial, and there are many different views of the appropriate role of a judge, the worldwide debate does not usually occur within the same terms as it does in the United States. In Canada, there are few judges or commentators who would dispute the notion that the rights and other provisions in our Constitution should be interpreted "as a living tree capable of growth and expansion within its natural limits,"[61] in the words of Lord Sankey in a 1930 Privy Council case from Canada about whether the term "persons" in our Constitution included women.[62]

Examples of just how different the dialogue on constitutional interpretation often is from the American approach are two judgments of the Australian High Court rendered in 1992.[63] In these decisions, the High Court determined that the Australian Constitution, which does not contain any enumerated rights guarantees, nevertheless contained an implied freedom of political communication and discussion, and this meant that laws that interfered with that freedom could be overturned by the High Court. Justice Brennan, in a manner similar to that of other members of the Court, reasoned that "once it is recognized that a representative democracy is constitutionally prescribed, the freedom of discussion which is essential to sustain it is as firmly entrenched in the Constitution as the system of government which the Constitution expressly ordains."[64]

In a subsequent case, discussing the "implied" rights found in the constitution, Justice Deane noted that there was no evidence that the framers of the Australian Constitution intended to preclude the implication of constitutional rights by the absence of the inclusion of a bill of rights.[65] But, he held as follows:

[E]ven if it could be established that it was the unexpressed intention of the framers of the Constitution that the failure to follow the United States model should preclude or impede the implication of constitutional rights, their intention in that regard would be simply irrelevant to the construction of provisions whose legitimacy lay in their acceptance by the people. Moreover, to construe the Constitution on the basis that the dead hands of those who framed it reached from their graves to negate or constrict the natural implications of its express provisions or fundamental doctrines would deprive what was intended to be a living instrument of its vitality and adaptability to serve succeeding generations.[66]

Because elsewhere it is generally accepted, as Justice Deane argues, that a judge's role is to determine the appropriate current meaning of the words of a Constitution, contemporary American constitutional debates often do not "speak to" judges and lawyers elsewhere, and the judgments at the centre of those debates may be less useful for us.

This also suggests why judgments of the Warren and Burger Courts, written at a time at which the dominant American approach was arguably closer to our current approach (although the Court admittedly moved away from it during the Burger Court years) may be more attractive and influential outside the United States.

A SMALLER CASELOAD, FEWER "GROUNDBREAKING" DECISIONS, AND A FOCUS ON FEDERALISM   The diminished influence of the United States Supreme Court may also be partially explained by changes in its caseload, the nature of the decisions it has reached, and the topics on which decisions are being made. It has been generally noted that the Rehnquist Court's docket has shrunk since the early 1990s. Justice Souter, in a recent interview, attributed the drop to the fact that fewer controversial issues came out of legislation from recent presidential administrations, that the basic standards on criminal justice had been determined in the 1960s, 1970s, and 1980s, and there was generally a lower level of division between federal courts than in the past.[67]

In terms of international impact, the shrinking caseload necessarily means fewer decisions on which to rely, and therefore would naturally contribute to a declined impact.

Justice Souter's explanations for the decreased caseload also help explain the reasons for the decreased influence. At a time at which a larger percentage of the Supreme Court's work consists of clarifying or modifying the details of previous precedents, it is understandable that this jurisprudence is less influential than the broad changes in approach to constitutional rights that characterized the Warren Court and some of the decisions of the Burger Court.

In addition, an important part of the Rehnquist Court's work has been in the area of American federalism.[68] Many of the important and influential cases that will likely constitute an important part of the Rehnquist Court's legacy, as, for example, the decision on the Brady gun legislation,[69] focused on the principles of American federalism. Decisions on federalism, which are necessarily focused on the particularities of the United States Constitution, are less likely to be influential elsewhere in the world than those on principles that are more universal and have application in different jurisdictions. Though the Rehnquist Court's federalism jurisprudence is an important part of its work, it is the part of American constitutional law likely to make the smallest impression elsewhere.

DIFFERING CONSTITUTIONAL PHILOSOPHIES Another factor which I believe makes the United States more isolated from other countries in the field of human rights is a fundamental difference between the approach and goals of the Bill of Rights and those of many other constitutional documents. In my view, the Bill of Rights and its current interpretation are focused on individual civil liberties, while the *Charter* [70] and other twentieth-century human rights instruments are more concentrated on balancing the rights of individuals and those of society and on recognizing the importance of group identity and group values.

Let me give several examples. The first section in the South African Bill of Rights states that it "is a cornerstone of democracy in South Africa. It enshrines the rights of all people in our country and affirms the democratic values of human dignity, equality and freedom."[71] It also says that "[t]he state must respect, protect, promote and fulfil the rights in the Bill of Rights."[72] The South African Bill includes, among others, rights to citizenship, fair labor practices, the protection of the environment, housing, health care, education, language, and culture, all rights that are fundamentally different from those in the United States Bill of Rights. As Justice Ruth Bader Ginsburg has noted:

> Modern human rights declarations in national and international documents do not follow the United States Bill of Rights' spare, government-hands-off style. Not only do contemporary declarations contain affirmative statements of civil and political rights; they also contain economic and social guarantees, for example, the right to obtain employment, to receive health care and free public education, even—more grandly—the state's assurance of the conditions necessary to the development of the individual and the family. . . . Our courts, through judicial review, are accustomed to telling government what it may not do; they are not, by tradition or staffing, well-equipped to map out elaborate programs detailing what the government must do.[73]

It is also notable that some of the areas that are particularly controversial among the members of the Rehnquist Court, and on which its most important decisions have been made, are less contentious in other countries because of these different attitudes and because of express provisions in their constitutions. For example, the Rehnquist Court's decisions on the validity of racially based restructuring of electoral districts emphasize the majority view on the Court that the Equal Protection Clause mandates laws that are color-blind.[74] In the words of Justice Kennedy, writing the opinion of the Court in *Miller v. Johnson*, the "central mandate" of the equal protection clause is "racial neutrality in governmental decision making."[75] He emphasized that this required strict scrutiny of any racial or ethnic distinctions "regardless of 'the race of those burdened or benefited by a particular classification.'"[76]

However, these principles are inapplicable in many other parts of the world, because these debates are settled elsewhere by the language of human rights provisions. For example, the New Zealand Bill of Rights Act 1990[77] states that "measures taken in good faith for the purpose of assisting or advancing persons or groups of persons disadvantaged because of colour, race, ethnic or national origins, sex, marital status, or religious or ethical belief do not constitute discrimination."[78]

In Canada, we have a similar provision.[79] But more important, Canadian jurisprudence has emphasized that for our Court, equality "entails the promotion of a society in which all are secure in the knowledge that they are recognized at law as human beings equally deserving of concern, respect and consideration. It has a large remedial component."[80]

Similar approaches to equality have been taken in other parts of the world as well. Because of these differences in approach, which also affect our Court's approach to many other issues such as hate speech, pornography, and the rights of the accused, United States jurisprudence often has less influene on us than that of those countries in which the basic approach is closer to ours in terms of defining the appropriate balance between the rights of individuals and of society. Therefore, the combination of the facts that the Rehnquist Court has put out fewer groundbreaking decisions that define major areas of the law and many of the decisions that do so are in areas in which the terms of the debate are different helps explain the Court's diminished impact.

FAILURE TO TAKE PART IN INTERNATIONAL DIALOGUE   Finally, I want to mention again the factor that I think is playing one of the most important roles in the Rehnquist Court's diminished influence, one entirely within the control of the Justices. In my opinion, the failure of the United States Supreme Court to take part in the international dialogue among the courts of the world, particularly on human rights issues, is contributing to a growing isolation and diminished influence.[81] The United States Supreme Court has failed to look with any regularity outside the borders of the United States for sources of inspiration. In my view this tendency to look inward may well make the judgments of United States courts increasingly less relevant internationally.

An examination of the Rehnquist Court's jurisprudence shows how infrequent references are to the decisions of other courts. For example, on human rights issues, the Court has referred to Canadian Supreme Court judgments only twice — once noting that our Court, like other courts around the world, also had dealt with the question of assisted suicide,[82] and once referring to a prominent judgment of our Court on the issue of abortion.[83] Several decisions have cited the Supreme Court of Canada's judgments in matters which have an obvious international component: issues of private international law[84] and the interpretation of the Warsaw Convention.[85] Finally, one other case noted the Canadian position on exemplary damages.[86] Other than these, there are no other citations to Canadian cases. In addition, none of these citations was accompanied by any analysis of the details of the judgment or the reasoning in the Supreme Court of Canada.

References to other jurisdictions, including Britain, are similarly scarce, and American judgments almost never consider the reasoning of other courts. Of particular note is the fact that the United States Supreme Court has never referred to any decisions of the European Court or Commission of Human Rights. In short, the United States Supreme Court is not a participant in the international dialogue about human rights and other issues mentioned earlier. Indeed, use of international material by the U.S. Supreme Court is so rare that Justice Breyer's references to foreign constitutions in *Printz* attracted newspaper comment.[87] As noted by constitutional law scholar Mark Tushnet, "[t]he Supreme Court has almost never treated constitutional experience anywhere else as relevant."[88]

Why might the United States Supreme Court's failure to consider the judgments of other courts lead to its diminished impact elsewhere? In my view, the most useful judgments for courts looking to comparative sources are those that use comparative materials themselves and situate their judgments in the context of international debates and discussions. Decisions which look only inward, which see only the situation in the place where they are rendered, have less relevance to those outside that jurisdiction than do decisions which take account of international debates and discussions. American decisions that fail to articulate the similarities with and differences from other countries' legal systems are less useful than decisions that consider their jurisdiction's place in the judicial world and consider that place relative to other countries'.

I want to be clear that I am not advocating that the United States Supreme Court should change its constitutional interpretations to accord with decisions anywhere else in the world. Nor am I suggesting that the doctrines and approaches particular to American constitutional law that I discussed earlier should be abandoned. However, I do believe that considering and comparing judgments from various jurisdictions makes for stronger, more considered decisions, even if the result is the same.[89] Foreign comparison broadens the perspectives for decision making and leads to consideration of the solutions of others who have considered the problem in a world facing increasingly similar issues.

I want to conclude, therefore, by pointing to several examples of cases in which recent Rehnquist Court judgments could have considered judgments of other appellate courts from around the world.[90] In *Miller v. Albright*,[91] for example, the Court was asked to decide on the constitutionality of a statute that imposed more stringent requirements for U.S. citizenship on children born out of wedlock to American fathers and foreign mothers than on those born to American mothers and foreign fathers. The previous year, our Court had decided a case on the constitutionality of a statute denying citizenship to children of Canadian mothers but not to children of Canadian fathers.[92] Though the issues were somewhat different, because the Canadian statute denied citizenship based on the nationality of the mother rather than the father surely some of the opinions written by the U.S. Supreme Court Justices on both sides of the issue might have been strengthened by referring to the unanimous judgment of Canada's Supreme Court on the question of gender-based citizenship distinctions.[93]

Similarly, in *Glucksberg*,[94] the assisted-suicide decision, the Court could have done much more than simply note that assisted suicide is a crime in most other Western democracies in a reference to the Canadian case of *Rodriguez*. Instead, it might have considered the reasoning of the four opinions by the Canadian Supreme Court Justices. The Canadian Court divided on the constitutionality of allowing a crime, splitting five to four, with considerable convincing and careful reasoning on both sides. The U.S. Court also might have considered the judgment of the Supreme Court of India in *Gian Kaur (Smt) v. State of Punjab*,[95] which unanimously upheld the constitutionality of the criminalization of assisted suicide after having considered U.S., British, and Canadian decisions.[96] Surely a closer examination of the reasoning of those who had considered this issue before would have contributed to the strength of the decision in *Glucksberg*.

Finally, in another of the most important decisions of the Rehnquist Court's Term, the Court considered, in *R.A.V. v. City of St. Paul, Minnesota*,[97] the constitutionality of the St. Paul Bias-Motivated Crime Ordinance.[98] A consideration of the Canadian cases which have dealt with the constitutionality of hate speech, and the strongly reasoned opinions on both sides of the issue, surely would have helped both the majority and minority decisions place the issue in an international context.[99] The United States Supreme Court could also have considered various decisions written by United Nations and European human rights decision-making bodies.[100]

Conclusion

Judging at the turn of the millennium is undergoing fundamental changes. Among these is the fact that consideration of foreign decisions is becoming standard practice for more and more courts throughout the world. What has been called by Professor Tushnet "the globalization of constitutional law"[101] is a fundamental reality of decision making. No longer is it appropriate to speak of the impact or influence of certain courts on other countries but, rather, of the place of all courts in the global dialogue on human rights and other common legal questions.

So far, the Rehnquist Court has not often taken part in this dialogue. It is to be hoped, however, that the United States Supreme Court will begin to consider, in more depth, the opinions of other High Courts around the world. In doing so, perhaps the Court will benefit from the work of others, as those around the world have learned and continue to learn so much from the United States. If we continue to learn from each other, we as judges, lawyers, and scholars will contribute in the best possible way not only to the advancement of human rights but to the pursuit of justice itself, wherever we are.

Notes

I would like to thank my law clerk, David Wright, for his exceptional contribution to the preparation of this chapter. I would also like to thank my former law clerk, Stéphane Perrault, for his research and suggestions.

1. Lester, "The Overseas Trade in the American Bill of Rights," 88 *Colum. L. Rev.* 537, 541 (1988).

2. See id. at 561.

3. See Glenn, "The Use of Comparative Law by Common Law Courts in Canada," in Contemporary Law [*Droit Contemporain*] 85 (Canadian Comp. Law Ass'n & Québec Soc'y of Comp. Law eds., 1994) (discussing the use of foreign decisions by Canadian common law courts).

4. See Hogg, *Constitutional Law of Canada* 30–31 (3d ed. 1992).

5. See e.g. La Forest, "The Use of American Precedents in Canadian Courts," 46 *Me. L. Rev.* 211, 212–13 (1994).

6. 5 U.S. (1 Cranch) 137 (1803).

7. See Rapaczynski, "Bibliographical Essay: The Influence of U.S. Constitutionalism Abroad," in *Constitutionalism and Rights: The Influence of the American Constitution Abroad* 405 (Louis Henken & Albert J. Rosenthal eds., 1990) (hereinafter *Constitutionalism and Rights*) (discussing the influence of the U.S. Constitution on drafters and interpreters of other constitutions); Brennan, Jr., "The Worldwide Influence of the United States Constitution as a Charter of Human Rights," 15 *Nova L. Rev.* 1 (1991); Lester, supra note 1; see also *American Constitutionalism Abroad* (George Athan Billias ed., 1990); *Constitutionalism and Rights*, supra; *Constitutionalism in Asia: Asian Views of the American Influence* (Lawrence Ward Beer ed., 1979) (hereinafter *Constitutionalism in Asia*); Garro et al., "The Influence Abroad of the United States Constitution on Judicial Review and a Bill of Rights," 2 *Temp. Int'l and Comp. L.J.* 59 (1987–88).

8. Can. Const. (Constitution Act, 1982) pt. I (Canadian Charter of Rights and Freedoms) (hereinafter referred to as charter).

9. See, e.g., Bender, "The Canadian Charter of Rights and Freedoms and the United States Bill of Rights: A Comparison," 28 *McGill L.J.* 811 (1983); Hogg, supra note 4; Tarnopolsky, "The New Canadian Charter of Rights and Freedoms as Compared and Contrasted with the American Bill of Rights," 5 *Hum. Rts. Q.* 227 (1983).

10. See Manfredi, "The Canadian Supreme Court and American Judicial Review: United States Constitutional Jurisprudence and the Canadian Charter of Rights and Freedoms," 40 *Am. J. Comp. L.* 213, 214–18 (1992); see also Hunter v. Southam, [1984] 2 S.C.R. 145 at 156 (Can.).

11. See, e.g., R. v. Big M Drug Mart, [1985] 1 S.C.R. 295 (Can.); Ford v. Québec, [1988] 2 S.C.R. 712 (Can.); R. v. Oakes, [1986] 1 S.C.R. 103 (Can.).

12. See R. v. Morgentaler, [1988] 1 S.C.R. 30 (Can.) (abortion); R. v. Keegstra, [1990] 3 S.C.R. 697 (Can.) (hate speech); Edmonton Journal v. Alberta (A.G.), [1989] 3 S.C.R. 1326 (Can.) (publication of court proceedings).

13. *Charter*, supra note 8, § 1.

14. See, e.g., Lavigne v. Ontario Pub. Serv. Employees' Union, [1991] 2 S.C.R. 211, 298 (Can.).

15. See, e.g., R. v. Keegstra, [1990] 3 S.C.R. 697 (Can.) (hate speech); Lavigne v. Ontario Pub. Serv. Employee's Union, [1991], 2 S.C.R. 211 (Can.) (mandatory contributions to unions).

16. 384 U.S. 436 (1966).

17. 347 U.S. 483 (1954).

18. However, it is important to note that one area in which the Warren Court was not forward looking or expansive was that of women's rights. See Hoyt v. Florida, 368 U.S. 57 (1961).

19. See Sorabjee, "Equality in the United States and India," in *Constitutionalism and Rights*, supra note 7, at 94, 114–15 (discussing the importance of the Warren and Burger Courts in India.).

20. For example, Israeli Supreme Court Justice Shimon Agranat, who was educated in the United States, made extensive use of American principles in several of his judgments. See Lahav, "American Influence on Israel's Jurisprudence of Free Speech," 9 *Hastings Const. L.Q.* 21 (1981); see also Jacobsohn, *Apple of Gold: Constitutionalism in Israel and the United States* (1993) (noting particularly chapter 5).

In Canada, too, educational backgrounds have clearly contributed to the influence of certain jurisdictions on our law. Supreme Court Justices who were educated in the United States have referred to the United States with more frequency than others. Bushnell, "The Use of American Cases," 35 *U.N.B.L.J.* 157, 169 (1986). More and more Canadian postgraduate education in law was done in the united States and not Great Britain. "The lessons from American constitutional experience were then taught in the Canadian law schools." McWhinney, "The Constitutional Patriation Project, 1980–82," 32 *Am. J. Comp. L.* 241, 262 (1984).

21. See, e.g., Ackerman, "The Rise of World Constitutionalism," 83 *Va. L. Rev.* 771 (1997).

22. See, e.g., McGinty v. State of Western Australia, [1996] 1 L.R.C. 599 (Austl.); R. v. Van der Peet, [1996] 2 S.C.R. 507 (Can.); Lee Miu Ling & Another v. Attorney General, [1995] 4 L.R.C. 288 (C.A.) (H.K.); State v. Van den Berg, [1995] 2 L.R.C. 619 (Namib.); Martin v. Tauranga Dist. Ct., [1995] 2 L.R.C. 788 (C.A.) (N.Z.); Pub. Prosecutor v. Manogaran s/o R Ramu, [1997] 2 L.R.C. 288 (C.A.) (Sing.); DuPlessis v. Dekler, [1997] (1) L.R.C. 280 (S. Afr.); Sookermany v. Dir. of Pub. Prosecutions, [1996] 2 L.R.C. 292 (Trin. & Tobago); M'Membe & Another v. The People, [1996] 2 L.R.C. 280 (Zambia); Re Chikweche, [1995] 2 L.R.C. 93 (Zimb.).

23. A good example of how parallel changes in social thinking can lead to more "international" solutions is jurisprudence on Aboriginal law, which has been particularly prominent and controversial in recent years in Canada, Australia, and New Zealand. Within the past several decades, Aboriginal peoples in these countries have been demanding judicial recognition of their ownership of lands and other Aboriginal rights. Courts have become more responsive to these claims than they were in the past. In developing doctrines to modernize and recognize Aboriginal land claims, they have referred extensively to the solutions developing elsewhere. The fact that this development of the law is occurring in parallel in different jurisdictions is a result of changing social attitudes to Aboriginal peoples worldwide; the recognition that previous legal doctrines were unfair and improper is being reflected across borders and continents. Though legal solutions have not been identical, I believe that they would not have been so similar had the dialogue not taken place.

24. As noted earlier, the United States stands out for the fact that its Bill of Rights predates this explosion of international human rights. But more recently, there are numerous genealogical "links" between national human rights guarantees and international rights documents. For example, the drafters of the Canadian *Charter* drew extensively on international human rights treaties. See Bayefsky, "International Human Rights Law in Canadian Courts," in *Enforcing International Human Rights in Domestic Courts* 295, 310 (Benedetto Conforti and Francesco Francioni eds., 1997); Claydon, "International Human Rights Law and the Interpretation of the Canadian Charter of Rights and Freedoms," 4 *Sup. Ct. L.R.* 287 (1982). Later South African and Israeli drafters looked both to those treaties and to the *Charter* among their sources. See, e.g., Dodek, "The Charter . . . In the Holy Land?," 8:1 *Constit. Forum* 5 (1996); Weinrib, "The Canadian Charter as a Model for Israel's Basic Laws," 4:3 *Constit. Forum* 85 (1993). These links are reflected in the similar language, organization, and principles of many human rights guarantees. Because the drafters of human rights protections have drawn on earlier documents, it only makes sense for judges to make use of the expertise and experience of interpreters of similar documents.

25. It is not surprising that reference to foreign jurisprudence is made most frequently when human rights protections are new, as in Canada in the 1980s and early 1990s and in New Zealand, Israel, and South Africa today. For example, the drafters of the Canadian Charter drew extensively on international human rights treaties, while later South African and Israeli drafters looked both to those treaties and to the Charter among their sources. These links are reflected in the similar language, organization, and principles of many

human rights guarantees. See, e.g., Bayefsky, supra note 24, at 310; Claydon, supra note 24; Dodek, supra note 24; Weinrib, supra note 24.

26. See Abrahamson and Fisher, "All the World's a Courtroom: Judging in the New Millennium," 26 *Hofstra L. Rev.* 273, 291 (1997).

27. 521 U.S. 898 (1997).

28. Id. at 975 (citation omitted).

29. 347 U.S. 483 (1954) (Brown I); Brown v. Board of Educ., 349 U.S. 294 (1955) (Brown II).

30. Summayyah Mohammed v. Moraine & Another, [1996] 3 L.R.C. 475 at 493 (Trin. & Tobago).

31. Te Rananga o Muriwhenua Inc. v. Attorney-General, [1990] 2 N.Z.L.R. 641, 656 (C.A.).

32. See Bushnell, supra note 20.

33. [1995] 3 L.R.C. 566 (India).

34. 376 U.S. 254 (1967).

35. 420 U.S. 469 (1975).

36. 381 U.S. 479 (1965).

37. 410 U.S. 113 (1973).

38. Rajagopal & Another v. State of Tamil Nadu, [1995] 3 L.R.C. 566, 577.

39. 1996 (1) SA 984 (CC) (S. Afr.).

40. 322 U.S. 487 (1944).

41. 341 U.S. 479 (1950).

42. 60 F. 257 (1894).

43. 350 U.S. 422 (1955).

44. 347 U.S. 497 (1954).

45. 408 U.S. 564 (1972).

46. 262 U.S. 390 (1923).

47. See Lester, "The Overseas Trade in the American Bill of Rights," 88 *Colum. L. Rev.* 537 (1988).

48. European Convention for the Protection of Human Rights and Fundamental Freedoms, Nov. 4, 1950, arts. 8(2), 9(2), 10(2), 11(2), 213 U.N.T.S. 221, 230–32.

49. Charter, supra note 8, § 1.

50. See S. Afr. Const. § 36(1):

(1) The rights in the Bill of Rights may be limited only in terms of law of general application to the extent that the limitation is reasonable and justifiable in an open and democratic society based on human dignity, equality and freedom, taking into account all relevant factors, including—(a) the nature of the right; (b) the importance of the purpose of the limitation; (c) the nature and extent of the limitation; (d) the relation between the limitation and its purpose; and (e) less restrictive means to achieve the purpose.

Id.

51. See *Basic Law: Human Dignity and Liberty*, 1992 § 8 (Isr.). "There shall be no violation of rights under this Basic Law except by a Law fitting the values of the State of Israel, designed for a proper purpose, and to an extent no greater than required. . . ." § 1a. "The purpose of this Basic Law is to protect human dignity and liberty, in order to anchor in a Basic Law the values of the State of Israel as a Jewish and democratic state." Id.

52. See Namib. Const., art. 21(2):

[Fundamental freedoms in this constitution] shall be exercised subject to the law of Namibia, in so far as such law imposes reasonable restrictions on the exercise of the rights and freedoms conferred by the said paragraph, which are necessary in a democratic society and are required in the interests of the sovereignty and integrity of Namibia, national security, public order, decency or morality, or in relation to contempt of court, defamation or incitement to an offence.

Id.

53. Bill of Rights Act, 1990 § 5 (N.Z.). "Subject to section 4 of this Bill of Rights, the rights and freedoms contained in this Bill of Rights may be subject only to such reasonable limits as can be demonstrably justified in a free and democratic society." Id.

54. [1994] 2 L.R.C. 263 (Namib.).

55. 1995 (2) SA 642 (CC).

56. Id. at * 48.

57. [1994] 2 L.R.C. 263 (Namib.).

58. See, e.g., Rehnquist, "The Notion of a Living Constitution," in *Judges on Judging: Views From the Bench* 141 (D.M. O'Brien, ed., 1997); Scalia, "Originalism: The Lesser Evil," in *Judges on Judging: Views From the Bench* 187 (D.M. O'Brien, ed., 1997); Scalia, A *Matter of Interpretation: Federal Courts and the Law* (1997).

59. See, e.g., Malitz, *Rethinking Constitutional Law: Originalism, Interventionism, and the Politics of Judicial Review* (1994); Smith, *The Constitution and the Pride of Reason* (1998).

60. For the debate in Australia, see Kirby, "Judicial Activism," *U.W. Austl. L. Rev.* 1 (1997); Mason, "The Judge as Law-maker," 3 *James Cook U.L. Rev.* 1 (1996) (Austl.); "Tensions in Law-making Examined in Canberra," *Australian Lawyer*, Feb. 1995, at 16. In Canada, for examples of the contours of the recent debate, see Bakan, *Just Words: Constitutional Rights and Social Wrongs* (1997) (Can.); Black and Vriend, "Rights, and Democracy," 7 *Constit. Forum* 126 (1996); Hogg and Bushell, "The Charter Dialogue Between Courts and Legislators," 35 *Osgoode Hall L.J.* 75 (1997) (Can.); Morton and. Knopff, "Permanence and Change in a Written Constitution: The 'Living Tree' Doctrine and the Charter of Rights," 1 *Sup. Ct. L. Rev.* 533 (1990) (Can.); Morton, "Canada's Judge Bork: Has The Counter-Revolution Begun?," 7 *Constit. Forum* 121 (1996) (Can.).

61. Edwards v. A-G Canada, [1930] A.C. 114 at 136 (Can.).

62. Lord Sankey decided that women were "persons," even if the intention of the drafters of the Constitution was that the term did not include female persons See id.

63. See Nationwide News Pty. Ltd. v. Wills, [1992] 177 C.L.R. 1 (Austl.); Australian Capital Television Pty. Ltd. v. The Commonwealth, [1992] 177 C.L.R. 107 (Austl.).

64. Nationwide News, [1992] 177 C.L.R. at 48 (Austl.). As an aside it is worth noting that among the most prominent sources on which the Court relied were a number of Canadian decisions that predated the passage of the *Charter*. See Switzman v. Elbling, [1957] S.C.R. 285 (Can.); Reference re Alberta Statutes, [1938] S.C.R. 100 (Can.); Saumur v. Québec (Attorney-General), [1953] 4 D.L.R. 641 (Can.).

65. *See* Theophanous v. Herald & Weekly Times Ltd., [1994] 124 A.L.R. 1, 49 (Austl.).

66. Id. at 51.

67. Garrow, "The Rehnquist Reins," *N.Y. Times*, Oct. 6, 1996, sec. 4, at 4.

68. See, e.g., Schwartz, "Federalism, Administrative Law, and the Rehnquist Court in Action," 32 *Tulsa L.J.* 477 (1997).

69. See Printz v. United States, 521 U. S. 898 (1997).

70. Charter, supra note 8.

71. S. Afr. Const. ch. II, § 7(1).

72. S. Afr. Const. ch. II, § 7(2).

73. Ginsburg, "An Overview of Court Review for Constitutionality in the United States," 57 *La. L. Rev.* 1019, 1025–26 (1997).

74. See, e.g., Bush v. Vera, 517 U.S. 952 (1996); Shaw v. Hunt, 517 U.S. 899 (1996); Miller v. Johnson, 515 U.S. 900 (1995); Shaw v. Reno, 509 U.S. 630 (1993).

75. Miller v. Johnson, 515 U.S. at 904.

76. Id. (quoting Richmond v. J.A. Croson Co., 488 U.S. 469, 494 (1989)).

77. Bill of Rights Act, 1990 (N.Z.).

78. Bill of Rights Act § 19(2).

79. Charter, supra note 8, § 15(2).

80. Andrews v. Law Soc'y of British Columbia, [1989] 1 S.C.R. 143 (Can.).

81. See generally Ackerman, supra note 21; Abrahamson and Fisher, supra note 26 (noting the reluctance of American courts to consider foreign law).

82. See Washington v. Glucksberg, 117 S. Ct. 2258, 2263 (1997) (Rehnquist, C.J., delivering the opinion of the Court) (citing Rodriguez v. British Columbia (Attorney-General), [1993] 107 D.L.R. (4th) 342, 404 (Can.)).

83. See Planned Parenthood v. Casey, 505 U.S. 833, 945 (1992) (Rehnquist, C.J., dissenting) (citing R. v. Morgentaler [1988] 1 S.C.R. 30 (Can.)).

84. See American Dredging Co. v. Miller, 510 U.S. 443, 466 (1994) (Kennedy, J., dissenting) (citing cases from Canada, England, France and Scotland); Sun Oil Co. v. Wortman, 486 U.S. 717, 741 n.3 (1988) (Brennan, J., concurring) (citing cases from Canada and South Africa).

85. See Chan v. Korean Air Lines, 490 U.S. 122, 135 (1988) (Scalia, J., delivering the Opinion of the Court) (citing Ludecke v. Canadian Pac. Airlines Ltd., [1979] 98 D.L.R. (3d) 52 (Can.)).

86. See Browning-Ferris Indust. v. Kelco Disposal Inc., 492 U.S. 257, 273 n. 18 (1988) (Blackmun, J., delivering the Opinion of the Court) (citing various cases from England, as well as Canadian and Australian decisions to show they have not followed the English approach to the issue).

87. See Greenhouse, "Appealing to the Law's Brooding Spirit," N.Y. *Times*, July 6, 1997, at 4.

88. Id.

89. See Abrahamson and Fisher, supra note 26.

90. See id. at 288–91 (noting other examples of Rehnquist Court opinions referring to cases from other countries).

91. 523 U.S. 420 (1998).

92. Benner v. Canada (Secretary of State), [1997] 1 S.C.R. 358 (Can.).

93. It is notable that four members of the U.S. Court decided the case on issues other than the statute's constitutionality. See *Miller*, 523 U.S. at 1442 (O'Connor, J., concurring) (reasoning, joined by Kennedy, J., that the petitioner did not have standing); id. at 1446 (Scalia, J., concurring) (reasoning, joined by Thomas, J., that the Court did not have the power to give the relief requested even if the constitutional claim were valid).

94. Washington v. Glucksberg, 521 U.S. 702 (1997).

95. [1996] 2 L.R.C. 264 (India).

96. See id.

97. 505 U.S. 377 (1992).

98. St. Paul, Minn., Legis. Code § 292.02.

99. See R. v. Zundel, [1992] 2 S.C.R. 731 (Can.); R. v. Keegstra, [1990] 3 S.C.R. 697 (Can.).

100. See *Keegstra*, 3 S.C.R. at 753 (citing these decisions).

101. Greenhouse, supra note 87, at 4.

14

LIBERALISM, THE CONSTITUTION, AND THE SUPREME COURT

ROBERT H. HENRY

ARTHUR G. LEFRANCOIS

Introduction

This chapter began as a paper we were invited to present at the Rehnquist Court symposium at the University of Tulsa. Bernard Schwartz, of course, was the symposium's organizer. He was open to a number of areas of inquiry and we looked forward to a long conversation with him. Most tragically, that conversation was cut short. However, Professor Schwartz's legacy is so rich that in reengaging some of his scholarship, in recalling his presentations, and in reliving conversations with him, we have been able to have a new and—we hope—productive dialogue with him nevertheless. His observations shape this review, and appropriately so, at a time that scholars and others are reconsidering the last three decades' radical critiques of an older, mainstream liberalism.[1]

This chapter focuses on three concerns of Professor Schwartz that relate to the Constitution and to the Court as an institution: originalism, cost-benefit analysis, and the "Junior Supreme Court." The first of these represents textual–interpretive concerns, the second an analytic–doctrinal issue, and the last a problem of institutional structure. Uniting them is a vision of the Court as an institution responsible for making the Constitution speak in new ways to new problems.

Originalism

To demonstrate the fallacies of naive originalism, commentators such as Professor Schwartz can point to the Coinage Clause of our Constitution,[2] which grants Congress the power "To coin Money, [and] regulate the Value thereof. . . ." Unlike so many other clauses, goes this well-worn story the understanding of the framers as to the exact meaning of this clause was crystal clear. Not so clear was whether they intended their intention to control, and if so, for how long. "Coin" did not mean "print," and specie—good, hard, metallic money—was what everyone had in mind, especially after the experience with paper money during the revolutionary period. Disaster nearly resulted when, after the rise of paper currency in the Civil War era, the Court put in its two bits worth by trying to enforce the constitutional norm.[3] When the Court—after President Grant put two new Justices in place—finally ruled in favor of paper money as legal tender, the tragicomedy was over.[4]

At least in this situation, "original intention had been tried and ultimately found wanting, even though this was one case where the framers' intent was as clear as it could possibly be."[5] This is a consistent theme uttered by many opponents of originalism: The Constitution, in Frankfurter's words, is not to be read as "an insurance clause in small type, but a scheme of government . . . intended for the undefined and unlimited future."[6]

Moreover, how would original intentions or understandings be determined? As has often been observed, Madison's notes, remarkable though they were, were taken when he was actively engaged in the debate and are, along with what little he said about his "Bill of Rights," an incomplete guide. Further, whose intention is to govern? Were all framers "intentionally equal," or was what Madison said more important than the words of, say, Representative Samuel Livermore?[7] What about the intentions of the state ratifying conventions? What if some of the founders intended to have no (specific) intention,[8] or meant simply to state the touchstones with generality, recalling, as Jefferson wrote to John W. Eppes, "The earth belongs to the living, not to the dead."?[9]

Critics of originalism fear that a focus on the framers and the text, and nothing more, cannot do justice to the hard work of the law. Consider the Fourth Amendment protection against unreasonable search and seizure and the long line of cases,[10] including cases decided by the Rehnquist Court, that maintains a preference for search warrants.

There are good reasons to believe that the Fourth Amendment was written for little reason other than to check the increasingly oppressive power of warrants. The amendment as initially drafted did not contain a warrant clause meaningfully independent of the reasonableness clause,[11] the latter of which has featured prominently in cases from *Terry v. Ohio*[12] forward.

It is not clear that the language of the Fourth Amendment was ever consciously passed by the house.[13] Certainly, there was no specific intention[14] to prefer warrants over warrantless searches.[15] The proposed amendment was tailored to curb the excesses of the general warrant and simply stated limits on warrants—that the right of the people to be free from unreasonable searches and seizures should not be violated by warrants issued without probable cause and without particularly describing what (or whom) their bearers sought to search for or seize. The idea was as follows: Warrants are dangerous to liberty; let us subject them to constitutional regulation. But the current and relatively long-standing official preference for them likely makes good constitutional sense, because the kinds of warrants required by the amendment are in no meaningful sense general.

Similarly, in construing rules regarding the use of deadly force by police officers in apprehending fleeing felons, there are real issues relating to what the framers might have thought. The common-law rule seems to have allowed deadly force to apprehend fleeing felons. The Supreme Court, in *Tennessee v. Garner*,[16] determined that the common law at the time of the framing of the Fourth Amendment needed to be examined with a bit more care. At issue in *Garner* was whether a deadly-force seizure was reasonable under the Fourth Amendment. The Court concluded that at the time of the framing, the rule regarding deadly force made good sense, because felonies were somewhat limited in number, were punishable by death, and were generally quite dangerous, and because guns were significantly less capable of effectuating death at a distance.

Put simply, felons were presumptively quite dangerous, and using deadly force to apprehend them generally meant one was engaged in something approximating hand-to-hand combat. Unsurprisingly, the Court determined that in today's world, where guns are effective at great distances, and where there is often a less than clear danger line between felonies and misdemeanors, the literal application of the common-law rule did not do justice to the values that lay behind it. Thus, the Court required more than the mere fact of a felon in flight to justify, under the Fourth Amendment, the killing of the suspect. Essentially, it required probable cause that the suspect posed a threat of serious physical harm or death.[17]

This is the sort of "taking account of circumstance" that Professor Schwartz and other critics of originalism encourage us to do. Courts, in such cases, should be able to take account of very real changes in circumstances in order to do justice to the principles and values that gave rise to written constitutional commandments. To some, this view is challenged by, for example, the new "forceful voice" of Justice Clarence Thomas on originalism and historicism.

Justice Thomas's concurrence in *Lopez*[18] demonstrates that the framers did not intend that the Commerce Clause carry its current "broad meaning." But the Commerce Clause *needs* to say something different, the contrary argument goes, to a postindustrial society than to "a small parochial, largely agricultural society."[19]

> [The framers] could not even have dimly foreseen the type of post-industrial society we have come to be, with the new means of production, transportation, and the fantastic communications revolution that have been developed. Perhaps Justice Thomas is right on intent at the time the Constitution was drafted. But that is largely beside the point. The Court is not interpreting the Constitution in 1789; it is interpreting it to meet the needs of today's society. If Justice Thomas and those who join with him on the "original intent" interpretation of the Constitution were to prevail, we would have a very different instrument and one which could not be adapted to the "ever-changing conditions of national . . . life."[20]

At least in the warrant cases and in *Garner*, the fundamental charter is respected exactly by tipping its original meaning on its head. It is by this means, oddly, that the design of the framers is likely preserved. Perhaps expansive readings of the Commerce Clause are similarly justifiable.

But this, of course, is merely to describe another kind of originalism. The Fourth Amendment cases, for instance, might be described as cases in which constitutional design is respected through accommodating changed circumstances—tangible facts in the world. George III is not issuing general warrants; the number and nature of felonies have grown like weeds; guns can do incalculable havoc in almost no time at almost any distance. So we interpret the constitutional text accordingly. What *about* the text?

Justice Scalia argues that a good textualist is neither a literalist nor a nihilist.[21]

And he rejects a theory of drafters' intention.[22] This kind of textualism can be seen in a number of Scalia opinions, including his dissent in *Holloway v. United States*.[23] There, Justice Scalia, construing statutory language regarding carjacking "with the intent to cause death or serious bodily harm," rejects the views that such a mental state can be made out upon a showing of conditional intent and that the purpose of the statute should be divined in order to permit the conditional reading of intent.

Justice Scalia's theory of intent (as an element of crime) is here influenced by "customary English usage,"[24] a legal dictionary's definition,[25] an absence of "term-of-art" status of the word ("intent") at issue,[26] and plausible (not actual) congressional purpose.[27] "[T]he actual intent of the draftsmen is irrelevant," he reminds us, because "we are governed by what Congress enacted."[28] Only Justice Scalia and Justice Thomas dissented from the opinion affirming the conviction for the federal crime of carjacking.

Justice Scalia's opinion in *Holloway* is not unlike his approach in *Smith v. United States*,[29] where he rejected the majority's theory that trading a gun for cocaine triggered a punishment enhancement aimed at those who "use[d] . . . a firearm" "during and in relation to" drug trafficking. In searching for the fair meaning of "uses a gun," Justice Scalia consulted context,[30] dictionary meanings,[31] ordinary use,[32] and the *United States Sentencing Commission Guidelines Manual*,[33] and noted the absence of any "artful" definition of the term ("uses").[34] Only Justices Stevens and Souter joined the dissent.

But this textualism is not limited to matters of statutory construction. He also rejects drafter's intention as an interpretive strategy directed to the Constitution.[35] Instead, he seeks original meaning. One sees this early on, for example, in *Arizona v. Hicks*,[36] where Justice Scalia, for the Court, finds that moving an object in plain view "'even a few inches'" constitutes a search[37] because "[a] search is a search."[38] Justices Powell and O'Connor, and Chief Justice Rehnquist dissented, citing, among other concerns, "the tangible and severe damage [the search is a search approach] inflicts on legitimate and effective law enforcement."[39]

In *Maryland v. Craig*,[40] Scalia reacts against a construction of the Confrontation Clause that allowed an alleged victim of child sexual abuse to testify outside the presence of the defendant, noting the Court's "subordination of explicit constitutional text to currently favored public policy."[41] The Court, he says, "abstracts from the right to its purposes, and then eliminates the right."[42]

Scalia's take is simply that "For good or bad, the Sixth Amendment requires confrontation," and, therefore, the majority "has applied 'interest-balancing' analysis where the text of the Constitution simply does not permit it."[43] Justices Brennan, Marshall, and Stevens joined the dissent.

If one were looking for a normative or political disposition that predicted, say, pro-government outcomes at least in criminal cases, one would have better luck locating such a disposition—although perhaps not a theory—in a Justice other than Scalia.[44]

But the kind of interpretive theory presented by Justice Scalia is quite different from that presented by Professor Schwartz. Schwartz and other "liberal constructionists" would give judges latitude to reinterpret clear text that stands against clear history by not merely taking into account neutral but relevant factual changes but by taking into account, and acting on, changes in public sentiment and in public feeling, attitudes, mores, and morals as well. Insofar, they move beyond the kind of originalism sometimes suggested by Schwartz[45] and made express by Justice Scalia.

Brown v. Board of Education[46] represents for older liberal critics the impossibility of even sophisticated forms of originalism. This was not a case about guns or felonies or the king's surrogates breaking and entering. For Earl Warren, *Brown* was a case that presented a moral question, segregation on grounds of alleged racial inferiority.[47] Chief Justice Warren, during the December conference on the case, "'proceeded immediately and very calmly and graciously, to the ultimate values involved—the ultimate constitutional values, the ultimate human values.' "[48]

It is this sort of nonoriginalism that Bernard Schwartz, among others, clung to like a religion. The country's vision of equality, the promise of the postwar amendments, the invidiousness of state- and law-sanctioned racial animus—all this and more conspired to necessitate a theory of law and judging that mixed respect for precedent and tradition with a willingness to fight for a morally decent vision of ordered life under democratic principles, as long as those principles were sufficiently capacious to accommodate, if need be, an active federal judiciary. This was a mainstream liberalism whose constitutional world view coincided with its politics.

What about originalism and the present and future Rehnquist Court? Justice Scalia, who ought to know about these things, has been quoted as saying that "Justice Thomas and I are the only two originalists on the Court and probably within the Beltway. . . ."[49] Chief Justice Rehnquist might disagree with this, and so too might Judge Bork, who, at least in 1990, argued that "no Justice renounces the power to override democratic majorities when the Constitution is silent."[50] As Judge Posner has written,

> The idea of the Constitution as a binding contract is an incomplete theory of political legitimacy, not an erroneous one. A contract induces reliance that can make a strong claim for protection; it also frees people from having continually to reexamine and revise the terms of their relationship. These values are independent of whether the original contracting parties are still alive. But a long-term contract is bound eventually to require, if not formal modification (which in the case of the Constitution can be accomplished only through the amendment process), then flexible interpretation, to cope effectively with altered circumstances. Modification and interpretation are reciprocal; the more difficult it is to modify the instrument formally, the more exigent is flexible interpretation. . . .
>
> A theory of constitutional interpretation that ignores consequences is no more satisfactory than one that ignores the political importance of building a bridge between the contemporary judge's pronouncement and some authoritative document from the past.[51]

It is worth noting that Justice Scalia's originalism, too, makes room for changed circumstances. Indeed, he is at pains to demonstrate that his interpretive theory is neither "wooden" nor "unimaginative,"[52] although he does react against models of interpretation that celebrate a "morphing"[53] or "evolutionist"[54] Constitution. Justice Scalia's theory is sufficiently roomy to take account of new circumstances (e.g., technological advancements in the context of the First Amendment),[55] but it is also sufficiently delimited so as to exclude new values.[56]

For Justice Scalia, the choice is between "original meaning" and "current meaning."[57] For Scalia, advocates of the latter argue not only for a flexible Constitution that adapts to changed circumstances through consideration of what meanings it can reasonably be said to bear. They press also for a *Constitution* that changes,[58] an idea that to him is incoherent. He rejects a "living" model that suggests that values, like circumstances, change and evolve, or at least that such changes are of constitutional moment. There is instead a permanence of moral principles,[59] meant to privilege the framers' moral values—or at least those enshrined in the Constitution.[60]

It is *because* majoritarian perceptions of values might change (might, for example, "rot,"[61] as well as evolve) that the "purpose of a constitution" is "antievolutionary,"[62] is "to prevent change"[63] (i.e., to *secure* rights). What Justice Scalia wants to know from nonoriginalists such as Schwartz is the authoritative *source* of a newly imagined right, rule, or principle, and the limits, if any, on any interpretive theory that creates—or recognizes—them.

There *is* something freewheeling about nonoriginalist interpretive theories. Adherents of a framers' intent theory can point to such intentions (however difficult they may be to conceive or to show) as a limiting principle. Proponents of original meaning can point to text and either its semantic or expectational meaning[64] as historically determined. Some notion of stability is achieved by claiming that, for example, original meaning means that constitutional rules and principles are those imposed by the framers. It is just this stability that liberal critics deplore.

Fearing permanent fluidity, originalists react against interpretive theories that extol the virtues of flexibility and the vices of certainty. If it is "values,"[65] or changing "necessities,"[66] or "insights and perspectives"[67] that animate constitutional interpretation, originalists fear that there will be, at bottom, no principled brake on such Constitution-doing at all. As Professor Tribe has said, "I leave myself exposed, of course, to the charge that I have no genuine 'theory' of my own (at least no global, unified theory that can be reduced to a sound bite) defining precisely how the task of textual interpretation *should* proceed."[68]

The problem with originalism, or at least with its "intention" variants, say critics such as Professor Schwartz, is amply demonstrated by its inability to justify the *Brown v. Board* result.[69] As importantly, for such critics the "delusive simplicity" of the concept of original intention always has appeal (scholarly opinion notwithstanding), and its use could mean, at least metaphorically, a return to "Jim Crow, the rack and the pillory, and no paper money."[70] The living Constitution, the argument goes, deserves better. The argument—like so many—is unabashedly normative and riddled with antinomies, its constitutional attractions largely a function of its political charms.

Cost-Benefit Analysis

Another significant weapon in the Rehnquist Court's arsenal is cost-benefit analysis. Critics such as Professor Schwartz fear that it "can have a narcotic effect, creating as it does an illusion of mathematical precision."[71] Cost-benefit analysis could "be used to justify virtually any outcome," and "reduces our rights to the level of the counting house."[72] And it will, in cases analyzing putative rights, "tend to a weighing of the balance on the cost side of the scale."[73]

Cost-benefit analysis finds an earlier incarnation in Jeremy Bentham's utilitarianism. Bentham rejected any theory of natural law or natural rights[74] in favor of a view that demands that law and morals focus on what will lead to the greatest good for the greatest number.[75] A problem, even for those otherwise disposed to accept such a measure of right and wrong, is that weighing pains and pleasures, especially across populations, is a quite difficult thing to do. Enter law and economics.

This school is thought by its liberal critics to seek to establish a more doable moral and legal calculus by focusing on what people spend limited resources on, on the economic assumption that "'people are [always] rational maximizers of their satisfaction.'"[76] Because transfers of wealth are readily measurable, and generally voluntary, they tell us more precisely what we value, and how much we value it.

Now enter cost-benefit analysis. Like utilitarianism and law and economics, cost-benefit analysis focuses on (putatively measurable) consequences.[77] But however attractive its appearance of quantification, liberal critics fear it as a tool of a conservative judiciary.

There are three central criticisms of utilitarianism. The first is, as we have mentioned, is the problem of measurement. It seems that one can press for nearly any outcome on utilitarian grounds. Whose pains and pleasures count? Which ones? How much? Over how long a term? What about degrees of intensity? How do we compare utilities across populations, given subjective preferences? Is there a common measure by which to compare utilities when we have different, even competing, value schemes?[78]

The second problem with utilitarianism is its very consequentialism. Deontology, by way of contrast, is a kind of ethical theory that looks to something other than consequences as the measure of right and wrong. Kant, for example, looked to the motive behind conduct, not to its consequences.[79] Liberal critics worry about the manipulability and evanescence of rights under consequentialist treatments. Professor Schwartz, for example, challenged Judge Posner's approach, delineated in the *Van Harken* case:[80] "In the Posner approach, an affirmative answer to the question of whether a procedural right has been violated is not enough. Instead, CBA [cost-benefit analysis] must be applied to determine whether the right itself is guaranteed in the particular proceeding. If the CBA balance tilts against the right in the given case, the government will be upheld even though it has violated the right concerned."[81]

Schwartz and other critics are just not ready to concede that it makes sense to determine the existence of a right by examining its costs and benefits. In fact, he seems unwilling to concede that such a balancing *could* extinguish a right. Justice Blackmun, dissenting in a Rehnquist Court habeas corpus case, argued that a right should not be too vulnerable to being lost because of an inquiry into the consequences of its being *exercised*.[82] This is an example of the second criticism of utilitarianism—it removes all argument for rights (and wrongs) except those based on consequences. It deabsolutizes the moral world in a fashion that makes rights vulnerable to consequentialist critiques.

And this leads to the last of the relevant criticisms of utilitarianism. Not only can moral and legal rights be lost in the calculus of pains and pleasures, but such rights are *likely* to lose in a contest with the interests of the government, the society, the many.[83] The claim is that rights, as litigated, are typically sought to be exercised by individuals, and often (in criminal cases, for example, or constitutional cases) as against the government. It is tempting to take a large view of the government's pains and pleasures and a small view of the individual's (even where the individual is seen as a stand-in for individuals). Put differently, the individual is likely to fare poorly where her pains and pleasures are balanced against those of all others.[84]

All three criticisms focus on the manipulability of the exercise: (1) pain and pleasure calculations are too malleable for precise reckoning, (2) rights are too easily trumped by calculations of utility, and (3) the individual is likely to lose a contest in which rights are balanced against social concerns. Cost-benefit analysis is vulnerable to the same complaints. Where liberal critics may see ossification in originalism, they often see chaotic (and conservative) subjectivity in cost-benefit analysis. Moreover, as Justice Scalia has indicated, cost-benefit analysis can be seen as inconsistent with a stricter interpretation of the Constitution.[85]

In *Moran v. Burbine*,[86] an early Rehnquist Court cost-benefit case, the issue was whether police were obligated to inform a suspect they were interrogating that an attorney was trying to contact him regarding his arrest. The Court decided that the police had no such obligation, in part because the "minimal benefit [to protection of the Fifth Amendment right to silence] . . . would come at a substantial cost to society's legitimate and substantial interest in securing admissions of guilt"[87] since so informing such suspects "might have convinced respondent not to speak at all."[88]

Dissenting, Justice Stevens (joined by Brennan and Marshall) argued that the Court's cost-benefit analysis, if accurate, militates against the "right to a warning about counsel itself."[89] This is the kind of consequentialism that made critics, especially liberal critics, nervous.

In *United States v. Leon*,[90] a case decided just before the beginning of the Rehnquist Court, but which has been used by that Court as an analytic standard, the Supreme Court held that evidence obtained in good-faith, reasonable reliance on an invalid search warrant is admissible at trial. In reaching this conclusion, the Court, in an opinion by Justice White, determined that it made sense to consider the costs and benefits of the exclusionary rule. The issue of the underlying Fourth Amendment right was one thing, the possible exclusionary consequences quite another. Indeed, this latter (for some, remedial) question "must be resolved by weighing the costs and benefits of preventing the use in the prosecution's case in chief of inherently trustworthy tangible evidence obtained in reliance on a search warrant . . . found to be defective."[91]

This is a typical cost-benefit case. The Court examines alleged costs and benefits without the aid of dollar signs. Social costs include impeding the search for truth, some guilty defendants going free, and disrespect for law.[92] In the end, these costs carried the day. In a dissenting opinion, Justice Brennan (joined by Justice

Marshall) lamented what he called the Court's "determined strangulation of the [exclusionary] rule."[93]

> [T]he language of deterrence and of cost/benefit analysis, if used indiscriminately, can have a narcotic effect. It creates an illusion of technical precision and in-eluctability. It suggests that not only constitutional principle but also empirical data support the majority's result. When the Court's analysis is examined carefully, however, it is clear that we have not been treated to an honest assessment of the merits of the exclusionary rule, but have instead been drawn into a curious world where the "costs" of excluding illegally obtained evidence loom to exaggerated heights and where the "benefits" of such exclusion are made to disappear with a mere wave of the hand.[94]

This was the "seductive call of expediency" that Brennan decried.[95]

Justice Brennan claimed further that the costs associated with the rule were ac-tually costs imposed by the Fourth Amendment itself, on the simple theory that if it had been complied with—in *Leon* or any other case in which an illegal search un-covered evidence—there would be clear evidentiary consequences (some relevant evidence would not have been discovered and so would not be introduced at trial).[96] Moreover, Brennan argued, "[T]he entire enterprise of attempting to assess the benefits and costs of the exclusionary rule in various contexts is a virtually im-possible task for the judiciary to perform honestly or accurately."[97] "The Court," Brennan continued, "mistakenly weighs the aggregated costs of exclusion in *all* cases, irrespective of the circumstances that led to exclusion . . . against the po-tential benefits associated with only those cases in which evidence is excluded be-cause police reasonably but mistakenly believe that their conduct does not violate the Fourth Amendment."[98]

Judge (then Professor) Easterbrook praised the turn taken by the Court's exclu-sionary rule jurisprudence. "Exclusionary rule cases, once addressed in terms of 'ju-dicial integrity' or the moral standing of the police, are today treated as occasions for the assessment of the marginal deterrent effects of excluding particular cate-gories of evidence."[99]

Perhaps this was the sort of objective standard constitutional law scholars had so long been seeking.[100] Professor Laurence Tribe, responding to Professor Easter-brook, argued that the Court's cost-benefit jurisprudence was "pseudoempirical" and that it could not do justice to the constitutional command of exclusion that the Court had announced in *Weeks v. United States*[101] because such jurisprudence "can assimilate only marginal utilities and cannot allow for the introduction of an awkwardly irreducible procedural principle into its analysis."[102]

Professor Robert Weisberg locates in Justice Brennan's attacks on exclusionary rule cost-benefit analysis a reflection of the "occasional liberal attack on the entire phenomenon of cost-benefit analysis as false economics."[103] But Weisberg also claims that "the usual liberal rebuttal has been to accept the calculus, and then to question the conservatives' data or arithmetic."[104] In so doing, "the liberals demon-strate that they are relatively defenseless against the conservative strategy of estab-lishing instrumental and empirical arguments as the relevant terms of debate."[105]

Consider the difficulties of attacking the cost-benefit approach, now adopted by the Rehnquist Court. Why should "empirical arguments" *not* frame the relevant terms of the debate? Who can argue that costs and benefits, that consequences, should not play an important, if not dispositive role, in even constitutional adjudication?[106] Do we ignore the world and drop to some odd default of formalism?[107] Isn't Professor Erwin Chemerinsky driven a bit by consequences when he observes that the Rehnquist Court, in the 1988 term, "made normative judgments in permitting the execution of juveniles and the mentally retarded, in allowing more state regulation of abortion, and in limiting affirmative action"?[108] And if we are going to attend to—to care about—the consequences of legal rules, principles, and standards, shouldn't we try to maximize good consequences and minimize bad consequences? Surely, we shouldn't do the reverse!

This is the "seductive call of expediency," the "narcotic effect" of cost-benefit analysis that Professor Schwartz sought to oppose. It is, again, the problem of norms and rights being vulnerable to a utilitarian calculus. In constitutional norms, he saw something more abiding, more permanent, than the vicissitudes of a subjective "pseudoempiricism." At least if those norms were values with which he was comfortable.

Justice Scalia said, more than a decade ago, that conservatives "'must decide whether they really believe . . . that the courts are doing too much, or whether they are actually nursing only the less principled grievance that the courts have not been doing what they want.'"[109] We might ask the same question about opponents of cost-benefit jurisprudence. Is it the utilitarian, consequences–trumping-rights problem that bothers liberal critics?[110] Is it, that is, the principle of cost-benefit analysis to which they object, or is it instead the current use to which such analysis is put? Do they object to the counting of the consequences, or do they object to the consequences of the counting?

Professor Chemerinsky, in his early piece on the Rehnquist Court quoted earlier, seeks to make the point that "constitutional law, now and always, is about values. The critics' task is to expose and identify the value choices that the Court is making, and to explain why the Court's rulings are undesirable. Inevitably, much of what looks like a difference in approach is really a disagreement over substantive goals." Professor Chemerinsky goes on: "Scholarship should reveal and debate the Court's value choices. . . . Ultimately, the decisions must be defended or criticized for the value choices the Court made. There is nothing else."[111]

The problem Professor Chemerinsky had with, at least, the early Rehnquist Court was that while it had, for him, no substantive constitutional theory, it subscribed to an institutional theory by which its role was to be value neutral. The result was deference to governmental decisions, a default to majoritarianism. The irony he saw was the construction of values in constitutional law that sprang from an apparent commitment to value neutrality. (The irony Justice Scalia sees in "evolutionary" constitutional interpretation is also its ultimate appeal to majoritarian norms.)[112]

What liberal critics—such as Chemerinsky, Tribe, and Schwartz—are reaching for is a conscious normativity that is not exhausted by empiricism, however nonpseudo it may be. They want to discuss consequences against the backdrop of norms, and not the other way around. They want a set of values to frame the discussion of consequences, and not the reverse. They do not want the entire field of value occupied by lists of costs and benefits. As a technical matter, the difference between norms as context and norms as factors might be seen in issues such as standards of review, presumptions, or remedies for rights violations. But it might also feature in more substantive discussions of the contours and scope of certain rights themselves. Schwartz and Tribe seem to think this is the case as to procedural rights, for example. Each is concerned that cost-benefit jurisprudence, at least as currently practiced, can not do justice to such rights. Once again, a political vision harmonizes otherwise discordant claims regarding interest balancing, instrumentalism, and absolutism in constitutional theory.

The Junior Supreme Court

Professor Bernard Schwartz revered no institution more than the Supreme Court. As a loving teacher, he graded the Courts and the Justices. He was struck, therefore, by the criticisms of his "insider work," such as *Super Chief*,[113] criticism suggesting that such work might have significant—and unfortunate—consequences for the Court. He had written about the effects of leaks and the publication of *The Brethren*[114] on Chief Justice Burger and the Court generally.[115] Suddenly, he faced criticisms from Erwin Griswold and Anthony Lewis, among others, that his insider work could have a chilling effect on the Court's deliberative process.[116]

Schwartz claimed that public interest justified—even demanded—that the Court's veil of secrecy be lifted, if just a bit.[117] He invoked the public's right to know, and argued that the Court requires public support and that such support requires information.[118] But he also claimed the status of a mere reporter, and disavowed that his project was intended to provide public support, even if this was a likely consequence, as it turned out, of his reporting.[119] Demonstrating again his affection for the institution, he said that no other institution of government would have fared so well under similar scrutiny.[120]

But there was one group of "insiders" who Schwartz feared—the clerks of the "Junior Supreme Court." These foot soldiers polluted the selection of cases for review, through the use of a cert. pool,[121] potentially corrupted the law through ideological zeal,[122] and usurped the opinion-writing function from the Justices.[123] Their existence was the "one great defect in the Supreme Court's operation that, if not corrected, threatens to weaken both the effectiveness of our high tribunal and the public confidence on which the Court ultimately depends."[124]

The certiorari or "cert" pool point relates to the practice, since 1972, of having individual clerks assigned to evaluate the petitions.[125] This practice has flourished during the Rehnquist Court. By 1991, only Justice Stevens did not participate in the pool.[126] The problem is that clerks, not Justices, screen the petitions. Defenders argue that the dramatic increase in the number of cases filed necessitated delegation and screening.[127] Critics reject the view that the workload justifies this change and cringe at the notion of fresh law school graduates deciding which issues of the day will get a Supreme Court hearing.[128] Defenders respond that the only realistic alternative would be another tier between the courts of appeals and the Supreme Court.[129] The potential abdication of judicial responsibility to decide what to decide is accentuated by the fact that there is no effective "independent review" of the pool.[130]

There are really two issues here. First is the concern that Justices are not even seeing cases, because of the ideological screening of their clerks. Second is the fear, fed by anecdotal evidence, that a law clerk can actually determine the decision of a Justice when a case is selected for review.[131] The implications of this delegation are of concern to liberals and conservatives alike. For example, Professor Schwartz complained:

> Law clerks could play a crucial role in elevating New Right jurisprudence to the level of accepted doctrine. Followers of the Posner economic approach have proliferated among the nation's law teachers. The many students who have been taught à la Posner leave the classroom as Posner disciples, eager to translate what they have learned into the law of the land. Those who become law clerks, fresh from exposure to New Right doctrine, have the opportunity to do so at the outset of their legal careers. For every academic critic of his work, a professor such as Richard Epstein has hundreds of avid acolytes, ready to mold the law in the Epstein model.
>
> Thus New Right jurisprudence matters both because of its direct influence on law students and its consequent indirect influence on the judges themselves. At any rate, it is a mistake to assume that the views of most of the New Right theorists are so extreme that they will fall into obscurity of their own accord. On the contrary, valid or not, the jurisprudence of the "academic scribblers" such as Professors Posner and Epstein has begun to affect the way jurists think about law and even the way in which the courts decide cases. Their influence will only grow as increasing numbers of law clerks, and ultimately judges, issue from the classrooms of New Right academics.[132]

A similar concern is raised—from another perspective—by Professor Robert Bork.

> Ideas, or at least attitudes, developed in the law schools do influence courts. . . . Professors steeped in the revisionist liberal culture of the law schools may themselves become judges. . . . Many students become judicial clerks for a year or two after law school and carry the attitudes of the revisionist academic culture directly to federal judges. . . . The relationship between law school faculties and the federal judiciary is closer than many people realize.[133]

This is not a new issue. Over forty years ago, William Rehnquist, just after his clerkship under Justice Robert Jackson, was concerned about liberal clerks whose views included "extreme solicitude for the claims of Communists and other criminal defendants . . . in short, the political philosophy now espoused by the Court under Chief Justice Earl Warren."[134] We might do well to call to mind what Anthony Lewis wrote of an earlier era.

> Some of today's right-wing critics of the Supreme Court have picked on the law clerks as a convenient target, attributing to them Svengali-like powers over the justices. The truth is less interesting. Law clerks assist in research and may write drafts of material for the justice. They also perform the function of keeping him in touch with current trends of legal scholarship, especially the often critical views of the law schools about the Supreme Court. That is an important role in a Court which could so easily get isolated in its ivory tower. But the law clerks do not judge. They

can only suggest. As a practical matter, a young man who is there only briefly is unlikely to make any significant change in the actual votes cast on cases by a judge
who has been considering these problems for years.[135]

In politically based allegations of undue law clerk influence, clerks become an
easy proxy for influential academics. The problem is not that judges are being corrupted by twenty-something clerks, for surely they are not. Instead, judges are being
influenced—if at all—by new generations of academics.

Conclusion

Bernard Schwartz was one of the last denizens of an earlier era in which academics
such as he and Alexander Bickel had privileged access to Justices Black and Douglas,
Harlan and Frankfurter, Brennan and Warren. Perhaps this is why, if law is a "magic
mirror" in which we see reflections of "not only our own lives, but the lives of all [who]
have been,"[136] Professor Schwartz, taken though he may have been with history, was
more taken with the reflections of the present and with projections of the future. At all
events, his criticism of the Rehnquist Court was animated in equal parts by his own
constitutional vision and his respect for the institution he studied so passionately.

The divide between his constitutional aspirations and the Rehnquist Court's
constitutional actualities is great. It is a divide that has existed in every era of the development of the United States. "Conservatism makes no poetry, breathes no
prayer, has no invention; it is all memory. Reform has no gratitude, no prudence,
no husbandry," observed Emerson.[137]

Schwartz was a humanist, an optimist, a sort of constitutional visionary plead-
ing if not for a future that does not yet exist, then at least for a present that must be
liberated from the past. The constitutional world he envisioned was one of uncertainty and flux, discovery and growth. It was a world bottomed, essentially, on optimism, on hope, on faith in the direction of human progress. In his constitutional
theology, values evolved, they did not decay.

About conservative certainty in the past, he would likely agree with Voltaire
that "doubt is not a pleasant condition, but certainty is absurd."[138] And yet, as for
his own faith in the constitutionalism of present necessities, he would likely invoke
an aphorism of Charles Sanders Peirce he once used to describe the Warren Court.
"Let us not pretend to doubt in philosophy what we do not doubt in our hearts."[139]

Notes

The authors thank Alfred L. Brophy for his thoughtful comments on an earlier version of this
chapter.

1. Attacking critical theories of all varieties, Professor Schwartz agreed with those strains
of critical feminist and critical race theory that respected the role of rights. See Schwartz,
Main Currents in American Legal Thought 616 (1993). Compare Kennedy, "Legal Education
as Training for Hierarchy," in *The Politics of Law: A Progressive Critique* 54, 62 (David Kairys
ed., 1993) ("Rights discourse is internally inconsistent, vacuous, or circular. Legal thought
can generate equally plausible rights justifications for almost any result. Moreover, the discourse of rights imposes constraints on those who use it that make it difficult for it to function

effectively as a tool of radical transformation. Rights are by their nature 'formal,' meaning that they secure to individuals legal protection for as well as from arbitrariness—to speak of rights is precisely *not* to speak of justice between social classes, races, or sexes. . . . Because it is incoherent and manipulable, traditionally individualist, and willfully blind to the realities of *substantive* inequality, rights discourse is a trap.") with Rhode, "Feminist Critical Theories," 42 *Stan L. Rev.* 617, 634–35 (1990) ("[C]ritical feminism has . . . emphasized certain empowering dimensions of rights strategies. . . . [T]he rubric of autonomy and equality have made enormous practical differences in the lives of subordinate groups. Undermining the conceptual foundations of rights like privacy . . . involves considerable risks.") and Crenshaw, "Race, Reform and Retrenchment: Transformation and Legitimation in Anti-Discrimination Law," 101 *Harv. L. Rev.* 1331, 1357–58 (1988) ("The most troubling aspect of the Critical program, therefore, is that 'trashing' rights consciousness may have the unintended consequence of disempowering the racially oppressed while leaving white supremacy basically untouched.").

2. U.S. Const. art. I, § 8, cl. 5.

3. See Schwartz, *The New Right and the Constitution: Turning Back the Legal Clock* 10–14 (1990) (discussing Hepburn v. Griswold, 75 U.S. (8 Wall.) 603 (1870), overruled by Legal Tender Cases, 79 U.S. (12 Wall.) 457 (1871)).

4. One scholar has observed that the appointment of Justices Strong and Bradley was "[t]he only arguably successful Court packing." Friedman, "Attacks on Judges: Why They Fail," 81 *Judicature* 150, 154 (1998).

5. Schwartz, *New Right and the Constitution*, supra note 3, at 14. See generally. Dam, "The *Legal Tender Cases*," 1981 *Sup. Ct. Rev.* 367, 389 (noting the difficulty of plausibly denying that the framers intended to prohibit paper money as legal tender).

6. Schwartz, *A Book of Legal Lists* 5 (1997). Professor Schwartz, in the closing of his book, *New Right and the Constitution*, supra note 3, at 264–65 (1990) articulated the position of early opponents of originalism:

> A basic document, drawn up in an age of knee-breeches and three-cornered hats, can serve the needs of an entirely different day only because our judges have recognized the truth of Marshall's celebrated reminder that it is a *constitution* they are expounding—an instrument that could hardly have been intended to endure through the ages if its provisions were fixed as irrevocably as the laws of the Medes and Persians. The constantly evolving nature of constitutional doctrine has alone enabled our system to make the transition from the eighteenth to the twentieth century.

Schwartz's mentor, Judge and Dean Arthur T. Vanderbilt, had taught of the common law's usefulness in "its inherent capacity" to "adapt[] itself gradually and piecemeal to meeting the demonstrated needs of the times." Fox v. Snow, 76 A. 2d 877, 878 (N.J. 1950) (Vanderbilt, C.J., dissenting), quoted in Schwartz, *Main Currents*, supra note 1, at 495. As Oliver Wendell Holmes asserted in his *Common Law*, "The life of the law has not been logic: it has been experience," and the law finds its philosophy in "considerations of what is expedient for the community concerned." Schwartz, *Main Currents*, supra note 1, at 394 (footnotes omitted) (quoting Oliver Wendell Holmes, Jr., *The Common Law* 1, 35 (1881)).

7. See Schwartz, *New Right and the Constitution*, supra note 3, at 9.

8. See generally Powell, "The Original Understanding of Original Intent," 98 *Harv. L. Rev.* 885 (1985) (claiming framers did not envision original intention as appropriate interpretive theory); Berger, "'Original Intention' in Historical Perspective," 54 *Geo. Wash. L. Rev.* 296, 336 (1986) (accusing Powell of "persistent disregard of evidence that stares him in the face" regarding original intention theory); Lofgren, "The Original Understanding of Origi-

nal Intent?," 5 *Const. Commentary* 77 (1988) (distinguishing original understandings of framers' intention and ratifiers' intention and suggesting that the latter was not foreclosed by the original understanding); Clinton, "Original Understanding, Legal Realism, and Interpretation of 'This Constitution,'" 72 *Iowa L. Rev.* 1177, 1186–87 (1987) (claiming historical evidence on original understanding of originalism more mixed than Powell allows, but conceding that "intentionalism" was not the "predominant interpretive strategy"); Baade, " 'Original Intent' in Historical Perspective: Some Critical Glosses," 69 *Tex. L. Rev.* 1001, 1024 (1991) (characterizing original understanding as "not a very significant tool of constitutional hermeneutics" in the eighteenth century); Rakove, "The Original Intention of Original Understanding," 13 *Const. Commentary* 159, 161–66 (1996) (concluding that framers and ratifiers did not think evidence of their understandings would be helpful in ascertaining Constitution's meaning); Boyce, "Originalism and the Fourteenth Amendment," 33 *Wake Forest L. Rev.* 909, 956–57 & nn. 212–19 (1998) (claiming Powell's "central insight has not been effectively rebutted" and discussing the works cited above).

9. *Thomas Jefferson: Writings* 1280 (Merrill D. Peterson ed., Library of America, 1984) (letter to John Wayles Eppes, June 24, 1813). But see Sloan, " 'The Earth Belongs in Usufruct to the Living,'" in *Jeffersonian Legacies* 281, 303 (Peter S. Onuf ed., 1993) ("Whatever else the principle may have meant to Jefferson, it was decidedly not an invocation of the 'living constitution'—though the New Deal tried hard to make it appear so.").

10. See, e.g., Ornelas v. United States, 517 U.S. 690, 699 (1996); Massachusetts v. Sheppard, 468 U.S. 981, 988 n. 5 (1984); United States v. Leon, 468 U.S. 897, 913–14 (1984); Illinois v. Gates, 462 U.S. 213, 236 (1983) Johnson v. United States, 333 U.S. 10, 14 (1948). See generally LeFrancois, "The October 1995 Supreme Court Term: Selected Criminal Cases," 21 *Okla. City U. L. Rev.* 423, 434 (1996) (suggesting reason for and discussing doctrinal incentives regarding the warrant preference); id. at 442–43 (discussing incentives for warrant preference).

11. See LeFrancois, "On Exorcising the Exclusionary Demons: An Essay on Rhetoric, Principle, and the Exclusionary Rule," 53 *U. Cin. L. Rev.* 49, 78 n. 132 (1984).

12. 392 U.S. 1 (1968).

13. See LeFrancois, "On Exorcising the Exclusionary Demons," supra note 11, at 78 n. 132 (1984). See also Lasson, *The History and Development of the Fourth Amendment to the United States Constitution* 101 (1937). Compare Maclin, "The Central Meaning of the Fourth Amendment," 35 *Wm. & Mary L. Rev.* 197, 209 (1993) (characterizing as "undisputed" Fourth Amendment history that suggests the text of the amendment was not of great moment to framers or ratifiers) *with* Amar, *The Constitution and Criminal Procedure: First Principles* 185 n. 64 (1997) (characterizing as a "triply troubling" "canard" the view that the text of the Fourth Amendment was not the product of careful deliberation and noting Maclin's contrary treatment).

14. See generally White, "The Fourth Amendment as a Way of Talking About People: A Study of *Robinson* and *Matlock*," 1974 *Sup. Ct. Rev.* 165, 172–73 & n. 14 (discussing relationship between warrant and reasonableness clauses and absence of specific intention of framers).

15. "The Fourth Amendment's text hardly seems to invite the use of warrants ('no Warrants shall issue, but upon . . .') and its historical context was one of fear of general warrants." LeFrancois, "The October 1995 Supreme Court Term," supra note 10, at 442 n. 103. Dissenting in a Burger Court Fourth Amendment case, Justice Rehnquist observed, "There is significant historical evidence that we have over the years misread the history of the Fourth Amendment in connection with searches, elevating the warrant requirement over the necessity for probable cause in a way which the Framers of that Amendment did not intend." Payton v. New York, 445 U.S. 573, 621 (1980) (Rehnquist, J., dissenting).

16. 471 U.S. 1 (1985).

17. Id. at 11.

18. United States v. Lopez, 514 U.S. 549, 584–602 (1995) (Thomas, J., concurring).

19. Schwartz, "Term Limits, Commerce, and the Rehnquist Const," 31 *Tulsa L.J.* 521, 530 (1996).

20. Id. at 530 (omission in original) (quoting Justice Brennan, quoted in Schwartz, *Main Currents*, supra note 1, at 639).

21. See Scalia, *A Matter of Interpretation: Federal Courts and the Law* 24 (1997).

22. Id. at 38.

23. 119 S. Ct. 966, 972 (1999) (Scalia, J., dissenting).

24. Id. at 972–73.

25. Id. at 973.

26. Id. at 973–74.

27. Id. at 975-76 & n. 2.

28. Id. at 975 n. 2.

29. 508 U.S. 223, 241 (1993) (Scalia, J., dissenting).

30. Id.

31. Id. at 242.

32. Id. at 242–43.

33. Id. at 243.

34. Id. at 244–45.

35. See Scalia, *A Matter of Interpretation*, supra note 21, at 38.

36. 480 U.S. 321 (1987).

37. Id. at 325 (quoting Powell, J., dissenting, 480 U.S. 321, 333).

38. Id.

39. Id. at 339 (O'Connor, J., dissenting).

40. 497 U.S. 836 (1990).

41. Id. at 861 (Scalia, J., dissenting).

42. Id. at 862.

43. Id. at 870.

44. Although it is not true that Chief Justice Rehnquist, for example, *never* comes down on the side of the criminal defendant, he does not join Scalia the textualist in cases in which Justice Scalia finds constitutional commands that require pro-defendant holdings. In an interesting case in which Chief Justice Rehnquist wrote the majority opinion vacating the judgments and remanding the case to the court of appeals for de novo review of a district court's probable cause and reasonable suspicion determinations, the Chief Justice also provided a sort of recipe whereby the court of appeals can come to the same conclusions as did the district court (that probable cause and reasonable suspicion existed). Chief Justice Rehnquist, in so doing, notes that a reviewing court should review factual findings only for clear error and should "give due weight to inferences drawn from those facts by resident judges and local law enforcement officers." Ornelas v. United States, 517 U.S. 690, 699 (1996). Dissenting, Justice Scalia notes that "in de novo review, the 'weight due' to a trial court's finding is zero." Id. at 705 (Scalia, J., dissenting). Though the issue was the proper standard of review for a mixed question of law and fact—and not a constitutional command—Justice Scalia's concern was triggered not simply by what he took to be a misallocation of appellate resources but by the internal inconsistency of the opinion that brought this result about. See id.

45. See supra text accompanying notes 19–20.

46. 347 U.S. 483 (1954).

47. See Schwartz, *A Book of Legal Lists*, supra note 6, at 51; Schwartz, *A History of the Supreme Court* 293 (1993).

48. Schwartz, *History of the Supreme Court*, supra note 47, at 292–93 (quoting Abe Fortas).

49. "Scalia Answers Critics of Originalism," *Blackacre*, April 22, 1997, at 2.

50. Bork, *The Tempting of America: The Political Seduction of the Law* 240 (1990).

51. Posner, *Overcoming Law* 244–45 (1995).

52. Scalia, *A Matter of Interpretation*, supra note 21, at 23.

53. Id. at 47.

54. Id. at 46.

55. See id. at 45, 140.

56. "'[M]oral principles,' most of us think, are permanent. The Americans of 1791 . . . were embedding in the Bill of Rights *their* moral values." Id. at 146.

57. Id. at 38.

58. See id. at 45–46.

59. See id. at 146.

60. See id.

61. Id. at 41. Nonoriginalists might point to "rotten history" as a reason to embrace a vision of a constitution whose organic nature allows it to grow. This is the sort of attack launched by Schwartz on the constitutional jurisprudence of "historical tradition." Schwartz, "'Brennan vs. Rehnquist'—Mirror Images in Constitutional Construction," 19 *Okla. City U. L. Rev.* 213, 243–50 (1994).

62. Scalia, *A Matter of Interpretation*, supra note 21, at 44.

63. Id. at 40.

64. Prof. Ronald Dworkin distinguishes between "semantic intention" (what drafters intended to say) and "expectation intention" (what drafters envisioned as the consequence of saying what they said). See Dworkin, "Comment," in Scalia, *A Matter of Interpretation*, supra note 21, at 116–18.

65. See Chemerinsky, "The Vanishing Constitution," 103 *Harv. L. Rev.* 43, 104 (1989).

66. See Schwartz, *Main Currents*, supra note 1, at 394.

67. See Tribe, "Comment," in Scalia, *A Matter of Interpretation*, supra note 21, at 73.

68. Id. at 72–73. Compare Posner, *The Problems of Jurisprudence* 299 (1990): "Maybe there is no formula, no methodology" that we might use for "distinguishing sound interpretations from unsound ones."

69. See Schwartz, *New Right and the Constitution*, supra note 3, at 22. Judge Posner says the opinion "cannot be shown to be correct as a matter of legal interpretation" and that "its correctness is political rather than epistemic, pragmatic rather than apodictic." Posner, *Problems of Jurisprudence*, supra note 68, at 302. He finds this not uncommonly true of legal decisions. Id.

70. Schwartz, *New Right and the Constitution*, supra note 3, at 35.

71. Schwartz, "Administrative Law and the Dismal Science: Cost-Benefit Analysis and Traffic Adjudications," *Adlaw Bull.*, Feb 18, 1997, at 3. See also Schwartz, *New Right and the Constitution*, supra note 3, at 179.

72. Schwartz, "Administrative Law and the Dismal Science," supra note 71, at 3. See also Schwartz, *New Right and the Constitution*, supra note 3, at 179.

73. Schwartz, "Administrative Law and the Dismal Science," supra note 71, at 3. See also Schwartz, *New Right and the Constitution*, supra note 3, at 181.

74. See Bentham, "Anarchical Fallacies," in *Human Rights* 28, 32 (A. Melden ed., 1970).

75. See Bentham, *An Introduction to the Principles of Morals and Legislation* 38–41 (J.L. Burns and H.L.A. Hart eds., 1970).

76. Bix, *Jurisprudence: Theory and Context* 162 (1996) (brackets in original).

77. See, e.g., Van Harken v. Chicago, 103 F.3d 1346, 1351–52 (7th Cir. 1997) (estimating that requiring Chicago police who gave parking tickets to testify at hearings would cost 134,000 police hours annually and would save innocent drivers an average of $1.38 and observing that "the use of cost-benefit analysis to determine due process is not to every constitutional scholar's or judge's taste, but it is the analysis prescribed by the Supreme Court and followed by the lower courts including our own.") (discussed in Schwartz, "Administrative Law and the Dismal Science," supra note 71, at 1–2).

78. There is a rich literature on the problem of incommensurables. See, e.g., Epstein, "Are Values Incommensurable, or Is Utility the Ruler of the World?," 1995 *Utah L. Rev.* 683; Radin, "Compensation and Commensurability," 43 *Duke L.J.* 56 (1993); Smith, "Incommensurability and Alterity in Contemporary Jurisprudence," 45 *Buff. L. Rev.* 503 (1997); Schauer, "Commensurability and Its Constitutional Consequences," 45 *Hastings L. J.* 785 (1994); Sunstein, "Incommensurability and Valuation in Law," 92 *Mich. L. Rev.* 779 (1994).

79. There are arguments that Kant's categorical imperative actually rests on utilitarian grounds. Prof. Richard Epstein makes a more general point that there is a "deep convergence" between deontology and consequentialism. See Epstein, "The Utilitarian Foundations of Natural Law," 12 *Harv. J.L. & Pub. Pol'y* 713, 716 (1989). In part, this is because "natural law thinkers had a very acute and sound sense of the basic rights that any utilitarian would want to adopt in his society." Id. at 718.

80. Van Harken v. Chicago, 103 F.3d 1346, 1351–52 (7th Cir. 1997).

81. Schwartz, "Administrative Law and the Dismal Science," supra note 71, at 3. See also Schwartz, *New Right and the Constitution*, supra note 3, at 178.

82. "The Court's habeas jurisprudence now routinely, and without evident reflection, subordinates fundamental constitutional rights to mere utilitarian interests. Such unreflective cost-benefit analysis is inconsistent with the very idea of rights." Coleman v. Thompson, 501 U.S. 722, 764-65 (1991) (Blackmun, J., dissenting) (citation omitted).

83. See Maryland v. Craig, 497 U.S. 836, 861 (1990) (Scalia, J., dissenting) ("Because the text of the Sixth Amendment is clear, and because the Constitution is meant to protect against, rather than conform to, current 'widespread belief,' I respectfully dissent.").

84. Schwartz, "Administrative Law and the Dismal Science," supra note 71, at 3. See also Schwartz, *New Right and the Constitution*, supra note 3, at 181.

85. Justice Scalia, on the basis of textualism, rejected the Court's reading of the Confrontation Clause that allowed a victim-witness to testify outside the presence of the defendant. "We are not free to conduct a cost-benefit analysis of clear and explicit constitutional guarantees, and then to adjust their meaning to comport with our findings." Maryland v. Craig, 497 U.S. 836, 870 (1990) (Scalia, J., dissenting). See supra text accompanying notes 40–43.

86. 475 U.S. 412 (1986).

87. Id. at 427.

88. Id.

89. Id. at 459 (Stevens, J., dissenting).

90. 468 U.S. 897 (1984).

91. Id. at 906–07.

92. See id. at 907–08.

93. Id. at 928–29 (Brennan, J., dissenting).

94. Id. at 929. Compare id. with text accompanying supra note 71 (quoting Schwartz).

95. Leon, 468 U.S. at 930 (Brennan, J., dissenting).

96. See id. at 941.

97. Id. at 942.

98. Id. at 951 (1984) (Brennan, J., dissenting) (citations omitted).

99. Easterbrook, "The Court and the Economic System," 98 *Harv. L. Rev.* 4, 59 n. 157 (1984).

100. See Chemerinsky, "The Vanishing Constitution," supra note 65, at 46 (noting scholarly quest for "objective constitutional principles").

101. 232 U.S. 383 (1914).

102. Tribe, "Constitutional Calculus: Equal Justice or Economic Efficiency?," 98 *Harv. L. Rev.* 592, 608 (1985). Professor Tribe also decried the Court's "disregard for the constitutive dimension of its judicial role." He thought the exclusionary rule cost-benefit cases implicitly trumpeted as benefits things that we—the people—had heretofore seen as costs (such as positively sanctioning governmental lawbreaking, or deceiving the public about the costs of abiding by the Fourth Amendment). Id. at 610.

103. Weisberg, "Criminal Procedure Doctrine: Some Versions of the Skeptical," 76 *J. Crim. L. & Criminology* 832, 837 (1985).

104. Id.

105. Id.

106. "[T]here is no longer a useful sense in which law is interpretive. This is true of statutory and constitutional law as well as common law. Interpretation butters no parsnips; it is at best a reminder that there is a text in the picture. . . . The essence of interpretive decision making is considering the consequences of alternative decisions. There are no 'logically' correct interpretations; interpretation is not a logical process." Posner, *The Problems of Jurisprudence*, supra note 68, at 460.

107. But see Scalia, *A Matter of Interpretation*, supra note 21, at 25 ("Of all the criticisms leveled against textualism, the most mindless is that it is "formalistic.' The answer to that is, *of course it's formalistic!* The rule of law is *about* form.").

108. Chemerinsky, "The Vanishing Constitution," supra note 65, at 104.

109. Stengel, "Warm Spirits, Cold Logic," *Time*, June 30, 1986, at 30.

110. "[T]he first question to be proposed by a rational being is, not what is profitable, but what is Right." Channing, *Slavery* 1 (1835). See generally Brophy, "Humanity, Utility, and Logic in Southern Legal Thought: Harriet Beecher Stowe's Vision in *Dred: A Tale of the Great Dismal Swamp*," 78 *B.U. L. Rev.* 1113 (1998) (discussing utilitarian calculations in antebellum legal thought).

111. Chemerinsky, "The Vanishing Constitution," supra note 65, at 104. Compare Schwartz, *The Ascent of Pragmatism: The Burger Court in Action* 6 (1990): "[Chief Justice Burger's] votes were based upon his own scale of values, which were different from those that had motivated members of the Warren Court. When he considered a fundamental value to be at stake, Burger could be as stubborn as his predecessor. 'Someone,' he insisted to a law clerk, 'must draw the line in favor of basic values and, even if the vote is eight-to-one, I will do it.'"

112. "If the courts are free to write the Constitution anew, they will, by God, write it the way the majority wants; the appointment and confirmation process will see to that. This, of course, is the end of the Bill of Rights. . . ." Scalia, *A Matter of Interpretation*, supra note 21, at 47. See also id. at 149: "The glorious days of the Warren Court, when the *judges* knew that the Constitution means whatever it ought to, but the *people* had not yet caught on to the new game (and selected their judges accordingly), are gone forever. Those were the days in which genuinely *unpopular* new minority rights could be created—notably, rights of criminal defendants and prisoners. That era of public naiveté is past, and for individual rights disfavored by the majority I think there are hard times ahead." Compare Schwartz, "Brennan vs. Rehnquist," supra note 61, at 241: "It is the very purpose of a Constitution—and particularly of the Bill of Rights—to declare certain values transcendent, beyond the reach of temporary political majorities. The majoritarian process cannot be expected to rectify claims of minority right that arise as a response to the outcomes of that very majoritarian process."

113. Schwartz, *Super Chief, Earl Warren and His Supreme Court* (1983).

114. Woodward and Armstrong, *The Brethren: Inside the Supreme Court* (1979).

115. See Schwartz, *Ascent of Pragmatism*, supra note 111, at 5–6.

116. See Schwartz, *Decision: How the Supreme Court Decides Cases* x (1996).

117. See id. at x–xi.

118. See id. at xi–xii.

119. See id. at xii.

120. See id.

121. See Schwartz, *Decision: How the Supreme Court Decides Cases*, supra note 116, at 50–51, 258; Schwartz, *History of the Supreme Court*, supra note 47, at 370–71. Schwartz, *Ascent of Pragmatism*, supra note 111, at 36–37.

122. See Schwartz, *New Right and the Constitution, supra* note 3, at 263–64.

123. See Schwartz, *Decision: How the Supreme Court Decides Cases*, supra note 116, at 48-55, 259–62; Schwartz, *History of the Supreme Court*, supra note 47, at 371–72; Schwartz, *New Right and the Constitution*, supra note 3, at 262–63; Schwartz, *Ascent of Pragmatism*, supra note 111, at 37–39.

124. Schwartz, *Decision: How the Supreme Court Decides Cases*, supra note 116, at 257.

125. In 1972, Justice Powell suggested combining the efforts of the clerks to better manage the increasing number of certiorari petitions. The pool divides the petitions among the clerks of the participating Justices. The clerks circulate to the Justices memos that summarize the petitions and make disposition recommendations. See Schwartz, *History of the Supreme Court*, supra note 116, at 370–71; Rehnquist, *The Supreme Court: How It Was, How It Is* 263–66 (1987).

126. See Schwartz, *Decision: How the Supreme Court Decides Cases*, supra note 116, at 258.

127. In 1953, there were 1,463 cases on the Court's docket. By 1969 that number had grown to 4,202, and by 1994 to over 8,000. See O'Brien, "Join-3 Votes, the Rule of Four, the Cert. Pool, and the Supreme Court's Shrinking Plenary Docket," 13 *J. L. & Pol'y.* 779 (1997). Schwartz cites "sheer volume" as the reason for the existence of the pool and the Justices' reliance on the recommendations of the clerks. See Schwartz, *Decision: How the Supreme Court Decides Cases*, supra note 116, at 258; Schwartz, *History of the Supreme Court*, supra note 47, at 371.

128. See Schwartz, *Decision: How the Supreme Court Decides Cases*, supra note 116, at 261. "For [Justices incapable of explaining their decisions] the law clerk system is a godsend; but for the law it is a disaster, since it will inevitably lead to a dilution not only in the quality but also in the reputation of the Court." Id.

129. The Freund Committee, appointed by Chief Justice Burger, recommended in 1972 a national screening court. Earl Warren saw the proposal as a threat to the integrity of the Court and the proposal died, due in some measure to his opposition. See Schwartz, *Decision: How the Supreme Court Decides Cases*, supra note 116, at 258–59.

130. See Schwartz, *Decision: How the Supreme Court Decides Cases*, supra note 116, at 258.

131. See Lazarus, *Closed Chambers* 314–15 (1998) (attributing alleged switch in Justice Kennedy's position on a case to "a crucial midterm changeover in his clerk coterie and the machinations of the cabal that followed," and describing in breathless detail the maneuvering of the most influential member of the coterie, Paul Cappucio, a former Scalia clerk referred to by Ken Starr as "Justice Cappucio" and by "cabal" members as "the Don").

132. Schwartz, *New Right and the Constitution*, supra note 3, at 263-64.

133. Bork, *The Tempting of America: The Political Seduction of the Law* 135–36 (1990).

134. Rehnquist, "Who Writes Decisions of the Supreme Court?," *U.S. News & World*

Report, Dec. 13, 1957, at 74, 75. Rehnquist dismissed the idea of the clerks as "legal Rasputin[s]" who exert meaningful influence in decided cases. See id. He did claim, however, that the clerks unconsciously slant certiorari materials according to their personal views. See id.

135. Lewis, *Gideon's Trumpet* 32 (1964).

136. Holmes, Jr., *The Speeches of Oliver Wendell Holmes* 17 (1891).

137. Emerson, "The Conservative," in 1 *Emerson's Works* 279, 282 (1883).

138. Voltaire, Letter to Frederick the Great, April 6, 1767 (quoted in *Dictionary of Quotable Definitions* 153 (Eugene E. Brusell ed., 1970)).

139. See Schwartz, *Main Currents*, supra note 1, at 547 (paraphrasing Charles Sanders Peirce, "Some Consequences of Four Incapacities," in *Writings of Charles S. Peirce* 211, 212 (Edward C. Moore et al. eds., 1984).

15

WILLIAM H. REHNQUIST IN
THE MIRROR OF JUSTICES

DAVID J. GARROW

I

Once again it was a great honor to be back here at the University of Tulsa College of Law for the Rehnquist Conference. Cumulatively perhaps it is the nicest honor of all to have been invited to be part of all three of these sequential Supreme Court symposia, beginning with the Warren Court conference in 1994 and then followed by the Burger Court conference in 1996.[1] The other participants in this symposia have perhaps said somewhat less than one might expect about both William H. Rehnquist as an individual jurist and about the eight Justices with whom he currently serves. Thus my remarks here are going to focus both on William H. Rehnquist's individual judicial voice since 1972 and on William Rehnquist's service as Chief Justice since 1986.

When I was invited, Professor Schwartz asked me to use this talk to speak evaluatively about how William H. Rehnquist compares to the previous Chief Justices of this century. The first thing for us to remember when considering William H. Rehnquist's now twenty-six years of service on the United States Supreme Court is that back in 1952–53 the Chief Justice spent eighteen months at the Court as a law clerk to Justice Robert H. Jackson.[2] As some of you who are familiar with the historical literature on the Court at that time will certainly remember, there are a number of case memos which the future Chief Justice prepared for Justice Jackson in 1952–53 which survive in Justice Jackson's papers.[3] The best known and most controversial of these memos, of course, is one which appears to articulate Rehnquist's opposition to the Court's forthcoming decision in *Brown v. Board of Education*.[4]

But there are also other forty-five-year-old memos in the Jackson papers which give voice to future Chief Justice Rehnquist's views on issues such as federalism and federal habeas corpus. When one looks at the judicial track record that Justice Rehnquist has accumulated over these last twenty-six years, those long-forgotten, early 1950s memos concerning relatively little-remembered cases such as *Brown v. Allen*[5] and *Stein v. New York*[6] give us the richest possible context for appreciating the extent to which William H. Rehnquist has had remarkably consistent legal views not only since his own elevation to the Court in 1972 but indeed ever since he first served there as a clerk in 1952–53.

As many scholars full well appreciate, during his first fourteen years on the Burger Court, Justice Rehnquist oftentimes served as a conservative "Lone Ranger" voice of dissent,[7] particularly in cases involving federal habeas.[8] Nowadays it often seems to be forgotten that even at the time of his promotion to Chief Justice in 1986, Justice Rehnquist remained a fairly controversial jurisprudential presence. In 1971 the Senate's confirmation vote on Justice Rehnquist was sixty-eight votes in the affirmative and twenty-six in the negative,[9] but all the more strikingly, when the vote for confirmation as Chief Justice took place in the summer of 1986, only sixty-five Senators voted yes and thirty-three voted no—thirty-three votes cast against someone who already had served on the Court for more than fourteen years.[10]

That extent of political opposition to William Rehnquist's presence on the Supreme Court stemmed in significant part from the controversy over whether the Jackson memorandum concerning *Brown v. Board of Education* did indeed indicate that Rehnquist had at that time opposed ending racially segregated public schooling. However, that significant degree of senatorial apprehension about Rehnquist stood in remarkably stark contrast to the strongly unanimous respect and support which Justice Rehnquist enjoyed—both in 1986 and in the years that have followed—within the Court's own conference and indeed throughout the entire Court building.[11] Many students of the Court who are well familiar with the literature on the Burger Court already appreciate just how much personal dislike, and how many doubts about his professional competence, other justices had come to have regarding Warren Burger.[12] Thus when William H. Rehnquist was nominated by President Reagan to succeed Burger as Chief Justice, there was tremendous enthusiasm for Rehnquist's selection among his colleagues and perhaps most notably or most surprisingly on the part of Justices William J. Brennan and Thurgood Marshall in particular.[13]

II

Especially in 1986 and perhaps also to an unfortunate extent even today, many casual observers of the Court fail to appreciate not only the personal popularity but also the doctrinal and jurisprudential success that William Rehnquist has managed to attain during his years as a Justice. Two cases which date from the Burger Court era illuminate the way in which Rehnquist as Chief Justice has enjoyed judicial success to a degree that was all but unimaginable in the years preceding his promotion. Both *Fry v. United States*,[14] a commerce power case, and *Coleman v. Balkcom*,[15] involving a federal habeas question, featured solo dissents by then-Justice Rehnquist[16] which exemplified the so-called Lone Ranger period of Rehnquist's jurisprudence. *Balkcom* will be discussed again later in this chapter, but it is important to appreciate that once Justice Rehnquist became Chief Justice in 1986, the "Lone Ranger" moniker became a thing of the past and three significant new patterns began to emerge.

The first pattern, as commentators discussed quite extensively in the late 1980s, was the surprising degree to which Chief Justice Rehnquist appeared to be moderating the tone and demeanor of his written opinions.[17] An early and highly visible example involved some of the First Amendment questions that Burt Neuborne impressively addresses in chapter 2 (this volume). The second important pattern, and one which should not be overshadowed or forgotten in light of the first, concerned the intensity with which Chief Justice Rehnquist continued to pursue the devolutionary federalism agenda to which he had remained consistently loyal ever since 1952 and 1953.[18] Most notable of all was the sustained energy with which Chief Justice Rehnquist continued to pursue his long-standing commitment to an almost revolutionary degree of change or reform concerning capital habeas cases.[19] Third, and this has perhaps received too little comment or attention in the presentations included in this volume, personnel changes on the Court from 1986 up through the present have brought about a dramatic transformation of the Rehnquist Court's internal world, and I want to take some time to underscore this point in particular.

When Rehnquist became Chief Justice, Warren Burger's seat was of course filled by Antonin Scalia, and as a number of people have noted the past few days, there was a widespread expectation that Scalia would become an extremely influential presence on the Rehnquist Court, perhaps succeeding to the "Lone Ranger" role that the new Chief Justice himself had previously played. But far more important is the fact that the Court through 1990–91, and in one instance even until 1994, continued to have Thurgood Marshall, William Brennan, and Harry Blackmun among its members.

I think it is incumbent upon us to draw some very clear distinctions between what on the one hand might be called the early Rehnquist Court, which one might say stretched from 1986 through June 1992, and the late or mature Rehnquist Court, which has existed from 1992—and even more so since 1994—to the present. Too often, people put forward characterizations of what in reality was the "early" Rehnquist Court, emphasizing the intensity of conflict, division, and fragmentation that was highly visible in the late 1980s and early 1990s, as also applying to the "later" Rehnquist Court of the last half dozen or so terms.[20] This is misleadingly simplistic and in some instances almost wholly erroneous, and students of the Court need to correct this misimpression whenever it innocently or not so innocently is put forward.

III

In his last "on the record interview" more than thirteen years ago, in 1985, then-Justice Rehnquist expressed ambivalence about whether a Court should ever have a sense of mission or missions.[21] He also at that time volunteered very straightforwardly, and quite accurately, that the Burger Court was a Court without any sense of mission.[22] However, William Rehnquist as Chief Justice has certainly had one, and perhaps arguably two, explicit missions, notwithstanding the degree to which he has forsaken his previous "Lone Ranger" role. The first of those concerns is that devolutionary federalism agenda that reaches all the way back to Rehnquist's clerkship with Justice Jackson and particularly to *Brown v. Allen* and *Stein v. New York*.[23] In a number of instances, particularly in 1989–90, Rehnquist's pursuit of his federal habeas corpus reform agenda was a pursuit that he undertook with such intensity that he manifested some "bull in the China shop" qualities during his unsuccessful effort to win the endorsement of the Judicial Conference of the United States for his position.[24]

Rehnquist's commitment to federal habeas reform was not only the most pronounced element of his early agenda as Chief Justice but also eventually turned out to be far and away the greatest and most important victory that he has achieved as Chief Justice. That victory was initially signaled and affirmed in the 1991 case of *McClesky v. Zant*,[25] and it was then further ratified by Congress and by President Clinton with the passage and signing of the Anti-Terrorism and Effective Death Penalty Act of 1996.[26] What the *McClesky* victory in 1991 and the 1996 passage of the death penalty statute both ratified was not only precisely the position that then-Justice Rehnquist had advocated in his solo opinion in *Coleman v. Balkcom* in 1981 but also precisely the position that the young William Rehnquist had advocated in his 1953 clerkship memos to Justice Jackson.

Similarly, but in a much more widely known context, the other primary portion of the Chief Justice's very successful sense of mission with regard to federalism can be seen in decisions such as *United States v. Lopez*,[27] striking down the Gun Free School Zones Act as an unconstitutional abuse of Congress's commerce power, *Printz v. United States*,[28] voiding a major provision of the congressionally approved Brady Handgun Violence Prevention Act, and, perhaps most important of all, the Eleventh Amendment case of *Seminole Tribe of Florida v. Florida*.[29] All in all, the degree to which Chief Justice Rehnquist has brought about a dramatic revolution in the Supreme Court's basic jurisprudence concerning federalism has to be acknowledged as far and away his most important substantive legacy.

If Chief Justice Rehnquist and at least a narrow majority of the Rehnquist Court have more than just one single sense of mission, then their second consciously held mission involves what was articulated so impressively by Judge Wilkinson of the Fourth Circuit in chapter 4 (this volume) where he addresses the topic of the Rehnquist Court and race. Perhaps less on account of the Chief Justice than because of Justice Kennedy and to some significant extent Justice O'Connor, the Rehnquist Court has without a doubt extensively altered American law concerning race in the direction of what can accurately be termed a nondiscrimination principle. *Adarand Constructors v. Pen*[30] is, of course, the leading and best known case in this area, and there is no need for me to repeat or recapitulate what can be found in chapter 4. However, there can be no denying that from the vantage point of the Chief Justice himself, the changes that have taken place since *City of Richmond v. J.A. Croson Co.*[31] in 1989 and *Metro Broadcasting v. Federal Communications Commission*[32] would be among the most important victorious elements of the Rehnquist Court's legacy.

IV

Several years ago, Prof. Erwin Chemerinsky published an article in the *Creighton Law Review* titled "Is the Rehnquist Court Really That Conservative?"[33] Now with a bit of poetic excess and with the purpose of being intentionally provocative, one can argue quite credibly that notwithstanding how dramatically transformative the

Rehnquist Court's federalism revolution has been with regard both to criminal cases and more broadly with regard to state sovereignty or autonomy, on a number of notable occasions the Rehnquist Court has actually rendered decisions that are actually quite surprisingly liberal.

If, for example, one looks at what are arguably the five best known and most widely remembered decisions of the Rehnquist Court, there is no escaping the fact that the same moniker that scholars have already applied to the Burger Court—"the counter-revolution that wasn't"[34]—can likewise also be applied to the Rehnquist Court as well. First was *Texas v. Johnson*,[35] the flag-burning case which was decided, as Burt Neuborne emphasizes in chapter 2, five to four in favor of free expression. Second was *Lee v. Weisman*,[36] in 1992, also a five to four decision concerning religious observance in a public school context. Third, of course, was *Planned Parenthood of Southeastern Pennsylvania v. Casey*,[37] also in 1992, involving abortion and the Court's dramatic reaffirmation of the constitutional core of *Roe v. Wade*.[38] Fourth, and perhaps most surprising of all, in 1996 was *Romer v. Evans*,[39] the gay rights ruling which struck down a homophobic Colorado state constitutional amendment.

In all four of those historic cases Chief Justice Rehnquist himself ended up on the losing side. In the fifth, *United States v. Virginia*,[40] the Virginia Military Institute gender discrimination case, Chief Justice Rehnquist concurred with the majority in what many people might rightly view as the most striking example of the sometimes notably moderate votes he on occasion has been casting ever since his two surprising 1988 votes in the cases of *Hustler Magazine v. Falwell*[41] and *Pennell v. City of San Jose*.[42]

In light of the "time lag" that often seems to leave at least some people still looking at the Rehnquist Court through a lens that dates from 1989 or 1990, it is important both for the sake of argument and for the sake of understanding to stress the degree to which this Court has handed down important decisions that are neither reactionary nor even conservative.

If, for example, one looks in a First Amendment context, both *O'Hare Truck Service v. City of Northlake*[43] and *Reno v. American Civil Liberties Union*[44] are additional recent decisions of a nonconservative and arguably "progressive" nature that readily come to mind. Similarly, one can likewise note the quite striking degree of consensus the Court manifested during October Term 1997 with regard to a quartet of sexual harassment cases.[45] Thus everyone should be on notice that the Rehnquist Court in a very significant number of important instances has not been any sort of counter-revolutionary or conservatively activist court.

There are several explanations or partial explanations for why this aspect of the Rehnquist Court's record usually receives significantly less attention than it merits. Some of these are probably quite well appreciated by most serious observers of the Court, and ergo require only brief notation. First, as at least one or two other contributors to this volume have noted, one can quite respectably argue that the present-day Supreme Court ought to be spoken of as the Kennedy Court rather than the Rehnquist Court. This of course echoes the contentions that we similarly should speak of the Powell Court rather than the Burger Court and the Brennan Court rather than Warren Court.

As a result, Justices Scalia and Thomas and, to some extent, the Chief Justice have been fundamentally constrained in what they have been able to pursue because of the balance wheel roll that Justice Kennedy—and to a somewhat lesser degree Justice O'Connor—has consistently played. When one combines the relative moderation of Justices Kennedy and O'Connor with the even more constraining influence of Justice David H. Souter, the impact of those three Justices has gone a long way toward explaining why the Rehnquist Court since 1991 has been measurably more moderate than the earlier Rehnquist Court of 1986 through 1991.

Interestingly enough, this Court in its last few terms has manifested dramatically less fragmentation and division than the Rehnquist Court of a decade ago. Over the past five terms a cumulative average of fully 45 percent of the cases that have reached full plenary decision have come down unanimously. Most important, and perhaps most tellingly of all, the Justices' actual voting patterns in nonunanimous cases has also, in a significant number of instances, contradicted the simple "pigeon-holing" of factional alliances that many of us have employed in recent years when we have repeatedly spoken of a tripartite four–two–three division among the justices featuring Stevens, Souter, Ginsburg, and Breyer on one wing, Justices Kennedy and O'Connor as the duo in the middle, and the conservative trio of Scalia, Thomas, and Rehnquist on the other wing. But when one looks carefully at the voting patterns for the last few terms, particularly this most recent term, that categorization scheme proves inaccurate more often than we might assume, for what we have instead witnessed, which is of tremendous importance, is that the Chief Justice is actually now more often aligned with Justices Kennedy and O'Connor in the middle and relatively less attached to Justices Scalia and Thomas than our inherited wisdom leads us to presume.

During the 1997–98 term, when the Court issued plenary decisions in ninety-one cases, Justice Kennedy was in dissent only five times. Tied for second with regard to the fewest dissents were Justice O'Connor and the Chief Justice, each with ten. Hence what we are seeing here is not simply the control of divided cases by Justice O'Connor and even more often Justice Kennedy but also, especially during the three most recent terms, even if we fail to recognize it, is a dramatic decline in the intensity or heartfeltness of division within the Court. There are two crucial elements to this. First, the evidence suggests that the Chief Justice is no longer anywhere near as invested in some issues as was he was eight or ten years ago.

Look for example at such recent Rehnquist opinions as his dissent in *Lindh v. Murphy*,[46] concerning retroactivity with regard to noncapital habeas corpus, and the majority opinions that he wrote this past May in *Stewart v. Martinez-Villareal*[47] involving capital habeas and in *Bousley v. United States*[48] involving collateral relief. These are not "sexy" or well-known decisions that have received front-page news coverage, but these opinions may well reflect both how Chief Justice Rehnquist rightly believes that he now has won almost all of his federal habeas corpus reform agenda *and*, indirectly, how he also is no longer as intensely invested in some of the more dramatic questions that come before the Court, such as abortion, gay rights, or flag burning, as he was in the years before he was named Chief Justice in 1986.

A second reason this decline in the Court's intensity of division has occurred is that in all honesty Justice Scalia has become increasingly irrelevant to debate and discussion within the Court. All of us who regularly read the Court's opinions may remember many of the rhetorical hand grenades that Justice Scalia has lobbed at his colleagues. His name calling with regard to Justice O'Connor in *Webster v. Reproductive Health Services*[49] in 1989 may be the most infamous or the most widely remembered, but the aspersions that Justice Scalia cast upon the Chief Justice in his highly splenetic dissent in the Virginia Military Institute case, *United States v. Virginia*,[50] are probably even more remarkable. Many students of the Court can also no doubt recall some phrases from Justice Scalia's equally energized dissent in *Romer v. Evans*,[51] the Colorado gay rights case, as well as some of his comments in his 1994 dissent in the well-known establishment case of *Kiryas Joel*.[52]

All in all, there is now good reason to believe that even Justice Scalia himself realizes that he has lost such significant influence within the Court—and lost it in a way that he is not going to be able to recompense or repair—that he is thus relatively freer to give vent to angry emotions in a way that he otherwise would not if he were still truly seeking to persuade his colleagues of the attractiveness of his interpretive stances.[53]

V

In conclusion, let me underscore several points about how we should understand the evolution of this Court over the past twelve years. First, if we look at William H. Rehnquist within a longer term comparative context encompassing the last seventy or eighty years, much to many people's surprise perhaps the most inescapable historical conclusion of all is that Chief Justice Rehnquist is someone who in the longer run of history will be evaluated as having been a very good Chief Justice of the United States. In part, that very positive evaluation is a result of how very negative an evaluation his immediate predecessor, Warren Burger, is inevitably and appropriately going to receive.

Now one can argue quite seriously about whether Earl Warren's historical reputation is perhaps somewhat better than is truly merited, but second only to Warren, Rehnquist will probably go down in history as one of the two best Chief Justices of this century, or at least run neck and neck for second and third with Charles Evans Hughes. Warren Burger, Fred M. Vinson, Harlan Fiske Stone, and even William Howard Taft inescapably rank well below Rehnquist, and there is no doubt that both within the Supreme Court itself as well as within the parameters of the larger role of Chief Justice of the United States that William Rehnquist has been extremely successful Chief Justice. It again bears repeating that today's Court, just as has also been true of the Court ever since 1986, is a generally friendly and pleasant place where even those justices who disagree most often with Rehnquist on the merits of hard-fought cases nonetheless—such as Thurgood Marshall and William J. Brennan, Jr., before them—speak most positively about the Chief Justice.

Many observers now believe that the Rehnquist Court probably has just three more years to run and that this present Chief Justiceship will most likely come to an end in the summer of 2001, especially if come that time the United States is in the first year of the second Bush administration. There are, of course, reasons to doubt that William H. Rehnquist will necessarily retire at the first politically appropriate opportunity, even though he will be seventy-seven years old by the end of October Term 2000. But this is a Court which, barring unexpected medical events, is no doubt going to remain intact until June 2001.

However, today's Rehnquist Court is a Court which almost unanimously, with perhaps only the exception of Justices Scalia and Thomas, wants to have and believes that it should have a smaller role in American life than the Court traditionally has played throughout almost all of this century. This is perhaps the single most important reason why during the past five or so terms we have been seen less division and more unanimity within this Court. It is important to appreciate that not only is this relatively happy and relatively unified Court, especially in comparison to other Courts of the last seventy years, but it also is a Court that is actively implementing its belief that the federal judiciary is not supposed to have as large presence in American life as has been the case for the past half century. This belief is shared even by some if not all of the Rehnquist Court's relative liberals—and certainly by Justices Souter and Ginsburg—so once again it is incumbent upon us to realize and acknowledge that there are far fewer truly fundamental disagreements inside the Rehnquist Court than the day-to-day news coverage of newly decided cases leads almost all of us to believe. Irrespective of whether the Rehnquist Court comes to an end in 2001 or only in some subsequent year, its most important historical legacy—just like the long-term individual judicial legacy of William H. Rehnquist—will be remembered as the championing of a measurably smaller role for the Supreme Court itself in life in the United States.

Notes

1. See Garrow, "What the Warren Court Has Meant to America," in *The Warren Court: A Retrospective* 390–97 (Bernard Schwartz ed., 1996); Garrow, "Liberty and Sexuality," in *The Burger Court: Counter-Revolution or Confirmation?* 83–92 (Bernard Schwartz, ed., 1998).

2. See Rehnquist, *The Supreme Court: How It Was, How It Is* 17–98 (1987).

3. See Brenner, "The Memos of Supreme Court Law Clerk William Rehnquist: Conservative Tracts, or Mirrors of His Justice's Mind?," 76 *Judicature* 77–81 (Aug.–Sept. 1992).

4. 347 U.S. 483 (1954).

5. 344 U.S. 443 (1953).

6. 346 U.S. 156 (1953).

7. On the origin and subsequent repeated usage of the "Lone Ranger" nickname, see Jenkins, "The Partisan: A Talk With Justice Rehnquist," *N.Y. Times* (Magazine), March 3, 1985, pp, 28, 34; Savage, "14 Years on Court; Rehnquist's Conservatism Remains Firm," *L.A. Times*, June 18, 1986, at 1; Saperstein and Lardner, Jr., "Rehnquist: Nixon's Long Shot for a 'Law and Order' Court; On the Bench, a Confirmed Lone Ranger," *Wash. Post*, July 7, 1986, at A1; Elsasser, "Order in the Court: Once the Words of Dissent, Chief Justice's Views Now Predominate," *Chi. Trib.*, July 9, 1989, at P1.

8. For early evaluations of Rehnquist's judicial service, see Shapiro, "Mr. Justice Rehnquist: A Preliminary View," 90 *Har. L. Rev.* 393–57 (Dec. 1976); Denvir, "Justice Rehnquist and Constitutional Interpretation," 34 *Hastings L.J.* 1011–53 (May–July 1983); Riggs and Proffitt, "The Judicial Philosophy of Justice Rehnquist," 16 *Akron L. Rev.* 555–604 (Spring 1983); and especially Powell, "The Compleat Jeffersonian: Justice Rehnquist and Federalism," 91 *Yale L. J.* 1317–70 (June 1982).

9. See *N. Y. Times*, Dec. 11, 1971, at 1.

10. See Greenhouse, "Senate, 65 to 33, Votes to Confirm Rehnquist as 16th Chief Justice," *N.Y. Times*, Sept. 18, 1986, at. A1.

11. See Garrow, "The Rehnquist Years," *N.Y. Times* (Magazine), Oct. 6, 1996, at 65, 67.

12. See Woodward and Armstrong, *The Brethren: Inside the Supreme Court* (1979); Schwartz, *The Ascent of Pragmatism: The Burger Court in Action* 1–39 (1990).

13. See Garrow, "The Rehnquist Years," supra note 11, at 67.

14 . 421 U.S. 542 (1975).

15. 451 U.S. 949 (1981).

16. See Fry, 421 U.S. at 549, Coleman, 451 U.S. at 956.

17. See Taylor Jr., "A Pair of Rehnquist Opinions Set Legal Experts Buzzing," *N.Y. Times*, Feb. 28, 1988, at. IV-1; Kamen, "Rehnquist, Moving to Center, Gains More Control of Court," *Wash. Post*, July 3, 1988, at. A4.

18. See especially Powell, supra note 8.

19. See Garrow, "The Rehnquist Years," supra note 11.

20. See, e.g., Lazarus, *Closed Chambers* 8, 262 (1998). See also Garrow, "Dissenting Opinion," *N.Y. Times* (Book Review), April 19, 1998, at. 26; Garrow, "'The Lowest Form of Animal Life?': Supreme Court Clerks and Supreme Court History," 84 *Cornell L. Rev.* 855, 876 (March 1999).

21. See Jenkins, supra note 7, at 35.

22. Id.

23. See Greenhouse, "Of Rehnquist's Mission, And Patience to Match," *N.Y. Times*, May 1, 1991, at. A18. See also Savage, "Rehnquist Wins Confession Battle," *L.A. Times*, March 30, 1991, at A2.

24. See Greenhouse, "Judicial Panel Urges Limit on Appeals by Death Row Inmates," *N.Y. Times*, Sept. 22, 1989, at. B20; Greenhouse, "Judges Challenge Rehnquist's Role on Death Penalty," *N.Y. Times*, Oct. 6, 1989, at. A1; Greenhouse, "Rehnquist Renews Request to Senate," *N.Y. Times*, Oct. 13,1989, at. A21; Greenhouse, "Vote is a Rebuff for Chief Justice," *N.Y. Times*, March 15, 1990, at A16; Greenhouse, "Rehnquist Urges Curb on Appeals of Death Penalty," *N. Y. Times*, May 16, 1990, at. A1.

25. 499 U.S. 467 (1991).

26. See Mitchell, "Clinton Signs Measure on Terrorism and Death Penalty Appeals," *N.Y. Times*, April 25, 1996, at A18.

27. 514 U.S. 549 (1995).

28. 521 U.S. 898 (1997).

29. 517 U.S. 44 (1996).

30. 515 U.S. 200 (1995).

31. 488 U.S. 469 (1989).

32. 497 U.S. 547 (1990).

33. See Chemerinsky, "Is the Rehnquist Court Really That Conservative? An Analysis of the 1991–92 Term," 26 *Creighton L. Rev.* 987–1003 (June 1993).

34. See *The Burger Court: The Counter-Revolution That Wasn't* (Vincent Blasi ed. 1983).

35. 491 U.S. 397 (1989).

36. 505 U.S. 577 (1992).

37. 505 U.S. 833 (1992).

38. 410 U.S. 113 (1973).

39. 517 U.S. 620 (1996).

40. 518 U.S. 515 (1996).

41. 485 U.S. 46 (1988).

42. 485 U.S. 1 (1988).

43. 518 U.S. 712 (1996).

44. 521 U.S. 844 (1997).

45. See Oncale v. Sundowner Offshore Serv., 523 U.S. 75 (1998); Gebser v. Lago Vista Independent Sch. Dist., 524 U.S. 274 (1998); Burlington Indust. v. Ellerth, 524 U.S. 742 (1998); Faragher v. City of Boca Raton, 524 U.S. 775 (1998).

46. 521 U.S. 320 (1997).

47. 523 U.S. 637 (1998).

48. 523 U.S. 614 (1998).

49. 492 U.S. 490 (1989).

50. 518 U.S. 515 (1996).

51. 517 U.S. 620 (1996).

52. Board of Educ. of Kiryas Joel Sch. Dist. v. Grumet, 512 U.S. 687 (1994).

53. See Garrow, "One Angry Man—Antonin's Scalia's Decade," *N.Y. Times* (Magazine), Oct. 6, 1996, at 68–69.